P I M L I C O

69

CENTURIES OF D..

Peter James graduated in ancient history and archaeology at Birmingham University and is now engaged in postgraduate research at University College, London. He is the editor of the periodical *Studies in Ancient Chronology*, and has contributed articles to *New Scientist* and *Current Archaeology*.

I. J. Thorpe graduated at Reading University and received his PhD on prehistoric Britain from London University. He is currently directing fieldwork projects in Cumbria and Denmark, and has published papers on prehistoric astronomy, burial practices and chronology.

Nikos Kokkinos graduated at the Institute of Archaeology, London, and is now Dorothea Gray Senior Scholar at St Hugh's College, Oxford. He was a contributor to *Chronological Studies for Jack Finegan* (1989) and is the author of *The Enigma of Jesus the Galilean* (in Greek, 1980) and *Antonia Augusta* (forthcoming).

Robert Morkot graduated in ancient history and Egyptology at University College, London. He is the G. A. Wainwright Research Fellow in Near Eastern Archaeology at Oxford University and is currently preparing the excavation reports of Sesibi (Egypt Exploration Society) and Faras (Oxford University).

John Frankish, Aegean archaeologist, graduated at Liverpool University before taking up research studies at University College, London, and the British School at Athens. Between 1987 and 1989 he received a scholarship from the Greek government for fieldwork in Crete.

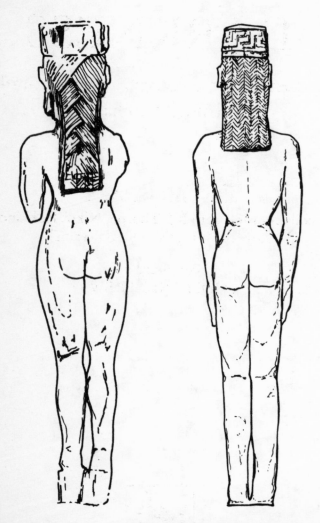

Ivory figurines from 12th-century Megiddo, Palestine (left), and 8th-century Athens (right). Despite the four-century gap they clearly belong to the same artistic tradition.

CENTURIES
OF
DARKNESS

A challenge to the conventional chronology
of Old World archaeology

PETER JAMES
in collaboration with I. J. Thorpe, Nikos Kokkinos,
Robert Morkot and John Frankish

Foreword by
COLIN RENFREW

PIMLICO

To our parents

PIMLICO

20 Vauxhall Bridge Road, London SW1V 2SA

London Melbourne Sydney Auckland Johannesburg
and agencies throughout the world

First published by Jonathan Cape 1991
Pimlico edition 1992

© Peter James, I. J. Thorpe, Nikos Kokkinos,
Robert Morkot and John Frankish 1991
Maps © Richard Baker and Malcolm Porter

Printed and bound in Great Britain by
Mackays of Chatham PLC, Chatham, Kent

ISBN 0-7126-5518-2

Contents

Illustrations

PLATES

FIGURES

TABLES

MAPS

Acknowledgments

For reading early drafts or supplying information, feedback, encouragement and discussion at various stages of the work, many friends and colleagues must be thanked, although of course they accept no blame for the views expressed in this book: Dr Jacqueline Balensi, Dr John Bimson, Dr Rupert Chapman, Dr Victor Clube, Aidan Dodson, Catherine Dyer, Dr Anthony Frendo, Geoffrey Gammon, Leslie Gardner, Vronwy Hankey, David Hawkins, Lorna Heaslip, Allison Hewitt, Dr Stephen Instone, Carl Olof Jonsson, Dr Vassos Karageorghis, Dr Timothy Kendall, Kyriakos Lambrianides, Mark Lowery, Alison Mansbridge, Dr Phil Mason, Bob Porter, Professor Fergus Millar, Brian Moore, Peter Parr, Sandra Parker, Dr Andy Rayes, Professor Colin Renfrew, Sue Rollin, Eddie Schorr, Professor Anthony Snodgrass.

Our profound thanks also to Patricia Briggs and Rosemary Burnard for the line drawings, to Richard Baker and Malcolm Porter for the maps and to Leslie Primo for help with the reproductions, and of course to Tony Colwell, Sarah Wiesendanger, Rowan Seymour, Pascal Cariss and all at Jonathan Cape for their generous help.

While the five authors worked on the volume jointly, responsibility for the research and drafting of individual chapters fell largely as follows: 1 (Thorpe, James), 2 (Thorpe), 3 (Frankish, Thorpe, James), 4 (Kokkinos, James, Frankish), 5 (James, Kokkinos, Frankish), 6 (James), 7 (Kokkinos), 8 (James, Kokkinos), 9 (Morkot), 10 (James, Morkot), 11 (James), 12 (James), 13 (Thorpe, James, Kokkinos).

The authors gratefully acknowledge permission from the following individuals and authorities to reproduce their copyright material in our Plates: 1 – The Petrie Museum, University College London; 2 – American Schools of Oriental Research; 3 – Professor Paul Åström, Gothenberg University; 4 – Institute of Archaeology, London; 7, 8 – Alessandro Usai; 9, 10, 11, 12, 13, 14, 15, 18, 19 – Trustees of the British Museum; 16 – Musées Nationaux, Paris; 17 – Israel Antiquities Authority.

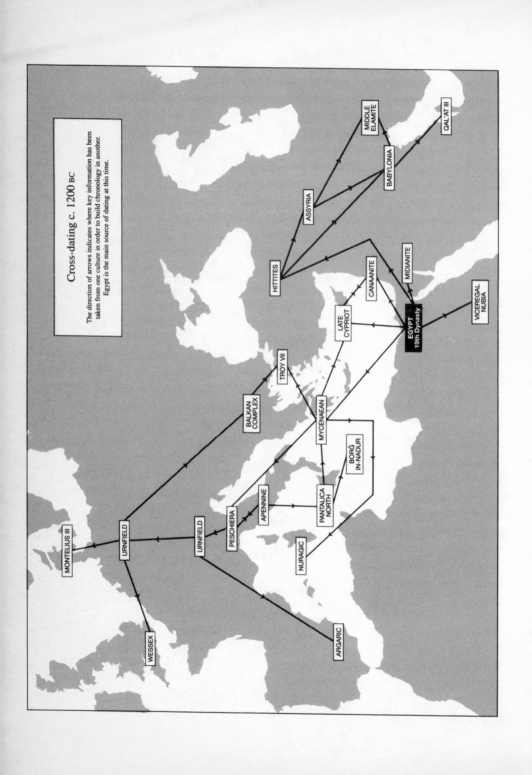

Cross-dating c. 1200 BC

The direction of arrows indicates where key information has been taken from one culture in order to build chronology in another. Egypt is the main source of dating at this time.

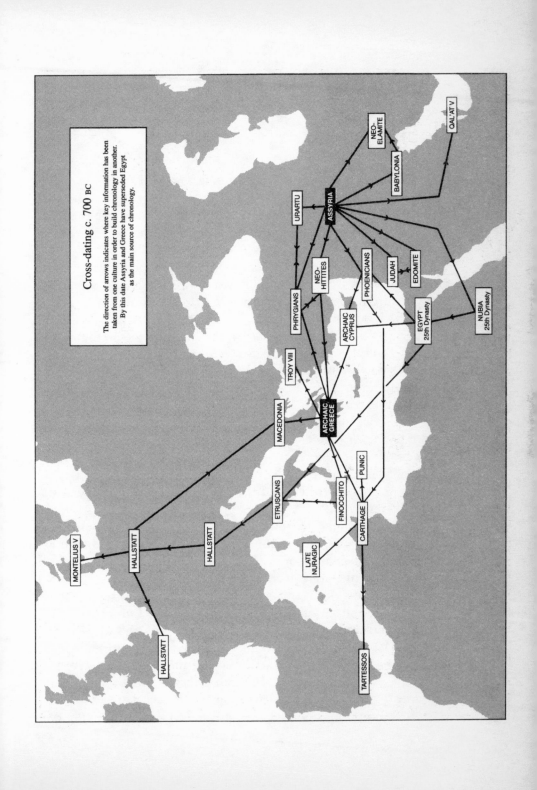

Cross-dating c. 700 BC

The direction of arrows indicates where key information has been taken from one culture in order to build chronology in another. By this date Assyria and Greece have superseded Egypt as the main source of chronology.

Foreword
by
Colin Renfrew

History needs dates. Chronology is the backbone of archaeology as well as of history. For without a time framework there can be no established sequence of events, no clear picture of what happened in the past, no knowledge of which significant development came first.

This disquieting book draws attention, in a penetrating and original way, to a crucial period in world history, and to the very shaky nature of the dating, the whole chronological framework, upon which our current interpretations rest. That period is, quite simply, the time of the emergence of the ancient world – that is to say, the classical world of ancient Greece and of Rome – following upon the decline of the great Bronze Age civilizations of the Mediterranean and the onset of the 'Dark Ages'. These civilizations – the Hittites, the Mycenaeans, Egypt in the New Kingdom – declined or collapsed. And after some centuries the new worlds of ancient Greece, of Rome, of the Etruscans and so forth, emerged. The revolutionary suggestion is made here that the existing chronologies for that crucial phase in human history are in error by several centuries, and that, in consequence, history will have to be rewritten.

Could so bold a claim possibly be right? Is so radical a change really possible? Can the accumulated scholarship of more than a century be so much in error?

Two instructive controversies of recent years show that such confusion is not unimaginable. The first was the 'Radiocarbon Revolution' – the redating of later prehistoric Europe in the Neolithic and early Bronze Age. It showed that the megalithic monuments of North-western Europe, instead of being derived from such Mediterranean achievements as the Pyramids, were in fact centuries, even millennia, earlier than these. The correction (or 'calibration') of radiocarbon dates using tree-ring dating showed that the assumptions upon which scholars had based the dating of

prehistoric Europe were, quite simply, wrong, and that dates for
Europe in the time-range 5000–1500 BC (and earlier) had to be
changed, and the textbooks rewritten.

A second major disruption is now under way. The colossal
volcanic eruption of the Aegean island of Thera had been set by
scholars, mainly using links with the established historical chronology for Ancient Egypt, between 1500 and 1450 BC. New scientific
methods, including radiocarbon dating, suggest that it should be set
as much as 150 years earlier. This will have a major impact on many
aspects of Mediterranean archaeology.

But could a chronological upset on so major a scale also be
contemplated for the very much more recent time-period considered here, within the time-range 1100–700 BC? Is it not the case
that the chronology for a phase significantly closer to our time, and
to that of the scholarly historians of Greece and of Rome, is much
better established?

The authors of this book show conclusively that it is not! They
indicate that the Egyptian chronology for the time-period in question – the so-called 'Third Intermediate Period' – is altogether
shaky. They show that there are problems also with the historical
chronology of the Near East. And the sad fact is that the historical
chronology for the rest of the Mediterranean, until well after
700 BC, rests upon these. It is already widely known that the
chronology for early Italy, during the Iron Age period, down to and
including the foundation of Rome, is a complete shambles. Swedish
scholars debate with Italian scholars over dates which may differ by
as much as two centuries.

I have myself (influenced by the canny scepticism of Professor
Robert Cook) been deeply aware that the calendar dates for ancient
Greece in the time-range 1000–600 BC are based on a very odd line
of reasoning. Greek pottery in this period is dated by finds of such
pottery made in Italy (in the Greek colonies in the west), and is
based on the 'foundation dates' for these colonies given by such
respected historians as Thucydides. But no one has ever explained
to me why we should pin our faith on dates given by Thucydides
for events some centuries before his own time. Nor has it been
shown that the Greek pottery found on these sites was not imported
(by trade) long before the colonies were officially founded there.

The authors here suggest that many of these dates should be made
later. I suspect the opposite, and am more impressed by their

destructive reasoning – that the existing chronologies are unreliable – than by their alternative proposals. To my mind there is only one solution: scientific dating, based on the two methods currently available. The first of these is dendrochronology: tree-ring dating. I predict that we shall fully understand the chronology of ancient Egypt in the centuries after 1000 BC only when a proper tree-ring chronology has been worked out for the abundant wood samples available in Egypt. The second method is 'wiggle matching', where sequences of radiocarbon dates from a single site are studied statistically, drawing on our increasingly detailed knowledge of the radiocarbon time-scale. But both of these are projects for the future. Without them we shall have no reliable chronology for Geometric Greece, for the Phoenicians, for Italy in the Iron Age, for early Rome.

The first step, however, is to recognize the depths of our ignorance. To realize how the existing 'chronologies' in different parts of the Mediterranean are bolstered up by circular arguments, where specialists in one area believe that those in other areas must know what they are talking about, and blindly use dating systems which are no better than their own.

The authors of this book do a great service by the very breadth of the survey which they undertake. By considering the whole of the Mediterranean, from Iberia to the Levant, from Egypt to Cyprus and Greece, and indeed by looking north from Italy into Central Europe, they are able to show the frailty of the links by which the whole ramshackle chronological structure is held together. I feel that their critical analysis is right, and that a chronological revolution is on its way. Whether their proposed solution is the correct one we shall know only when tree-ring dates and radiocarbon sequences based on 'wiggle matching' become more widely available. But their central claim is just: these have been and remain 'Centuries of Darkness'. Perhaps now we can begin to see the light at the end of the tunnel.

Professor of Archaeology
Cambridge University
August 1990

Preface

A superbly fashioned hand-axe or a solid gold Egyptian funerary mask may work as a picturesque museum-piece, but by itself can actually tell us very little about the past. Unless we know more – exactly where it was discovered at an archaeological site and what it was found with – it will remain a curio without a context. Date, of course, is a crucial aspect of context. One of the first things anyone wants to know about an ancient find is simply: how old is it?

Despite this, dates in archaeology and history seem to have acquired a bad name, perhaps not surprisingly, given the generations of school children forced to digest tedious lists of events with no apparent logic in their order other than their chronological sequence. Trainee archaeologists and ancient historians, too, have to learn basic sets of dates and, having absorbed the information, put it to the back of their minds. From then on it can be taken for granted, and chronology, for those eager to press on with the deeper study of ancient societies, is all too often treated as a necessary evil. Unfortunately there are also some scholars who, like poor history teachers, become totally preoccupied with the minutiae of dating and miss the point of the exercise. These prompted the great Sir Mortimer Wheeler to write: 'we have . . . been preparing time-tables; let us now have some trains'.

The problem with Wheeler's impatient demand is that timetables in themselves are not enough; they have to be accurate before the trains can start running, otherwise you'll miss the connections between them. In archaeological terms, the cultural interactions of the ancient world remain a complete jumble unless we have a reliable time-scale.

When the authors of this book met at the London Institute of Archaeology in 1985, we discovered a mutual scepticism of the claimed accuracy for the timetables of Old World archaeology. Above all, we became increasingly convinced that something was seriously wrong with the conventional picture of a centuries-long Dark Age descending over a vast area at the end of the Late Bronze Age c. 1200 BC. With a background of research in many different but related fields (specifically prehistoric Britain, Minoan Crete,

Mycenaean Greece, biblical archaeology and Pharaonic Nubia), we pooled our resources and began an in-depth investigation of the archaeological chronology of the entire ancient Mediterranean and Near East. Everything we found confirmed our suspicion that the original spanner in the works was the Egyptian time-scale, and that the 'centuries of darkness' inserted into the histories of so many areas between 1200 and 700 BC were largely illusory.

Initial questions and conclusions were then circulated in the form of a discussion paper, published in *Studies in Ancient Chronology*, volume 1.* The responses we received from scholars in fields ranging from Egyptology to astronomy were immensely encouraging, and the expansion of the project towards an eventual book followed naturally.

We were now also confident that we had fingered a genuine solution to the widespread problems. In the meantime a steady stream of new papers was spontaneously appearing in the archaeological literature, in which the framework of ancient Mediterranean chronology was beginning to be laid bare. The feeling is now in the air that it is time to return to basics and re-examine fundamental assumptions. To mention only two examples: in 1987, a special international conference was held at Gothenburg in Sweden under the title of *High, Middle or Low?* with the aim of resolving the long-standing uncertainties in the Middle Bronze Age chronology of the Near East and Aegean; the second concerns the latest issue of the *Bulletin of the American Schools of Oriental Research* (Spring 1990), which was entirely devoted to a debate on a major question of biblical archaeology – which levels of the ancient cities of Palestine belong to the time of King Solomon, Israel's most famous monarch? Neither of these prestigious ventures came to a definite conclusion.

But how can there still be such a degree of uncertainty? After all, scientific methods of dating, such as the radiocarbon technique, which should have resolved the problems, have now been available for a generation. Despite this, take-up of the new methods has been surprisingly slow; all too often a dozen or so radiocarbon dates are included in an archaeological site report merely as scientific window dressing. This attitude is clearly reflected in a regrettably

---

*A series of occasional publications, available c/o Institute of Archaeology, University College London, 31–4 Gordon Square, London WC1H 0PY.

common practice: when a radiocarbon date agrees with the expectations of the excavator it appears in the main text of the site report; if it is slightly discrepant it is relegated to a footnote; if it seriously conflicts it is left out altogether.

Lack of understanding of the method by many archaeologists has led to the submission of large numbers of samples of little or no value in dating the contexts from which they come. There have also been problems caused by inconsistent treatment of samples by different laboratories. As the senior radiocarbon scientist Professor Ingrid Olsson frankly concluded at the Gothenburg conference: 'Honestly, I would say that I feel that most of the dates from the actual Bronze Age are dubious. The manner in which they have been made . . . forces me to be critical.'

Where there have been enough good-quality radiocarbon dates available, for example in tracing the spread of agriculture across Europe, the technique has been of immense value. In the Near East and Aegean, however, the lack of systematic sampling means that radiocarbon is still too blunt a tool to resolve the perennial controversies of Bronze to Iron Age chronology. (Relevant radiocarbon dates are generally discussed here in the notes to individual areas). It needs to be stressed that the youngest dates from a given context or cultural phase are really the most significant. Old, residual material can always be present to supply misleading dates for a context; the younger dates will more accurately reflect the time when the deposit was formed and when most of its assemblage was made. Simply averaging the results for a phase or context, as is often done, will obviously produce a false impression of antiquity. On the other hand, we are able to note for many areas an increasing number of radiocarbon dates which, though currently treated as 'anomalous', are consistent with our theory; but they fail to be decisive because of the general problems affecting the method and its application. Sadly, for the later part of the period under review in this book, radiocarbon may never be able to provide meaningful answers (see Appendix I).

New scientific work in progress holds out interesting prospects for absolute chronology. Recently, attempts have been made to date the volcanic explosion which devastated the Minoan colony on the Aegean island of Thera (towards the beginning of the Late Bronze Age) by tracing climatic effects in the tree-ring records from California and Northern Europe and peaks of acidity in ice cores from Greenland. The difficulty with this is that it is impossible to be sure whether such effects always originate from volcanic eruptions, and, if so, which volcano was responsible. As volcanologist David Pyle (1989, 90) wrote concerning the Thera eruption:

> Direct radiocarbon dating has so far yielded a large scatter of dates that can, at present, be interpreted according to one's prejudice. Indirect methods (acidity peaks, tree rings) are beguiling, being potentially more precise but at the same time highly ambiguous, and should only be treated with the utmost caution.

The outcome for the absolute dating of Minoan civilization thus remains uncertain. More definite results may come from the on-going development of a tree-ring sequence for ancient Anatolia (Turkey) and Greece. When complete, the Anatolian dendrochronology will provide a more precise calibration for Near Eastern radiocarbon dates. Further, if it can be firmly linked with local Bronze Age archaeology, we will also have an invaluable control on historical chronology, including that of Egypt itself, because of the close connections which existed between the Hittite kings and the pharaohs.

In the meantime, radiocarbon dating is still of little help in providing answers to the conundrum of Dark Age chronology. In practice, we have to fall back on traditional methods, primarily pottery dating. Being virtually indestructible, pottery is found in vast quantities on ancient sites, and constitutes the bread-and-butter of archaeologists. Basic typological sequences for the development of ceramic styles are well established (though the pigeonholing into minute phases by some experts can be excessive). Pottery thus enables the strata of a given site to be easily dated within a local sequence. Discoveries of imported pottery allow links to be made between the chronologies of different cultures, while finds of key styles of pottery in those areas with written records allow the whole framework to be attached to historical dates.

Ancient history has often been compared to a mosaic, a patchwork built up from tiny scraps of evidence. A jigsaw puzzle is a much better metaphor, especially when dealing with chronology. For well-known periods (such as the time of the Roman Empire) the edge pieces of the puzzle, representing the dating framework, can be set down with confidence. But before about the 7th century BC the task is different. The edges of the puzzle, in this case the chronologies of ancient Egypt and Mesopotamia, are not as certain as they are usually thought to be. The major argument of this book is that the dates conventionally attributed to ancient Egyptian history are inflated by as much as two and a half centuries. Imagine, then, trying to complete a jigsaw where the sides are far too long. Frustratingly, many pieces will appear to fit into two places in the puzzle, while many 'ghost pieces' will be needed to fill the space that is unaccounted for.

This is precisely the dilemma into which so many archaeologists have been forced, dating and redating artefacts backwards and forwards across the span of the Dark Age, in attempting to fit their evidence into a framework defined by Egyptian chronology. Stretching the sides of the time puzzle by raising the dates further would only make the problems more acute. The only remedy, as our investigation shows, would seem to be to shorten the sides and compress the overall scheme.

The idea of a radical shift in the chronology of this period is not entirely new. At the turn of the century the classical scholar Cecil Torr and Egyptologist Jens Lieblein stood firm against the newly established 'high' Egyptian chronology, but their arguments for a lower dating fell on stony ground. The next challenge to the status quo came in the 1950s from Immanuel Velikovsky, the wayward polymath whose work outraged scientists in many fields other than ancient history. His model for a 'revised chronology', based on a new series of links between Egyptian and Israelite history, proved to be disastrously extreme. Involving a reduction of Egyptian dates by a full eight centuries at one point, it produced a rash of new problems far more severe than those it hoped to solve. Sadly, while he pointed the way to a solution by challenging Egyptian chronology, Velikovsky understood little of archaeology and nothing of stratigraphy.

Rocking the boat, of course, has never been popular in any field of study. Torr went against the grain of contemporary trends, while Velikovsky was too much of an outsider. But the major problem with the attempts of these writers was that they were working as individuals, and realistically could never have tackled the vast range of material from the many disciplines embroiled in the argument. Since their time, academic inertia and the convenience of following long established teachings has discouraged any serious challenge to the accepted chronology. Further, modern archaeologists are not immune to the fascination with the sheer antiquity of their finds in their search for the origins of any given development.

What has been conspicuously lacking is a workable alternative to the conventional chronology. This volume provides the outlines of a comprehensive model, covering every major region from the Western Mediterranean to Iran. Clearly, a colossal amount of work lies ahead in building new detailed chronologies for individual areas. What is here is only a beginning, but one which is long overdue. As James Mellaart wrote in 1979:

> Conventional chronologies have served us long enough and not too well as an interim tool. Most tools need sharpening over the years and finally replacement.

'The time is out of joint . . .'

William Shakespeare
Hamlet, I.v.189

CHAPTER I

The Evolution of Old World Chronology

In July 1953 Richard Atkinson, director of excavations at Stonehenge, was photographing a 17th-century graffito on one of the massive sarsen stones when he noticed the faintly carved 'outline of a hilted dagger, point downwards'. In Atkinson's opinion, this fortuitous discovery gave 'the first direct evidence of the date of the erection of the sarsen stones at Stonehenge'.

Despite the fascination it has long held for antiquarians and archaeologists, the unique monument of Stonehenge has always been difficult to date. The complexity of its many phases, using bluestones brought to Salisbury Plain from Wales as well as local sarsens, meant that only broad estimates of its age could be made. Identifying his dagger as a 16th-century BC specimen from the historically dated Mycenaean civilization of Greece, Atkinson argued that since no actual examples of this kind of dagger 'are known from Britain, or indeed from N.W. Europe, it is reasonable to suppose that this carving was executed at Stonehenge within the lifetime of someone who was personally familiar with this type of weapon in its homeland; in other words, not later, say, than 1470 B.C.'[1]

This precise date was welcomed by British prehistorians. Already they had deduced that the final arrangement of Stonehenge was built for the Bronze Age chieftains of the Wessex Culture, whose rich burials in barrows, dotting the landscape around the monument, had attracted excavators since the earliest days of archaeology. As well as local pottery and bronzework, these aristocratic graves contained amber and faience jewellery, goldwork and bone carvings – exotic and unusual items thought to be proof of trade between Britain and the early Mycenaean world.[2] Atkinson was inspired to speculate further, transforming his new link between Wessex and the Aegean into a connection with profound repercussions. For him the dagger provided evidence that 'the architect of the monument was himself a Mycenaean'. Although it was pointed out that the techniques used at Stonehenge were not found in Mycenaean architecture, Atkinson still felt it was 'surely more fitting to see them as the product of the relatively sophisticated civilization of Mycenae, rather than of the essentially barbarous, even if commercially successful, aristocracy of our native Wessex Culture'.[3]

A second dagger carving was found later in 1953. By 1956, Atkinson had developed an extraordinary model in which 'the architect' of Stonehenge was commissioned by 'some far-voyaging Mycenaean prince' who, having carved a kingdom in Wessex, was buried near Avebury 'in the quiet darkness of a sarsen vault beneath the mountainous pile of Silbury Hill', the largest artificial mound in Europe.[4]

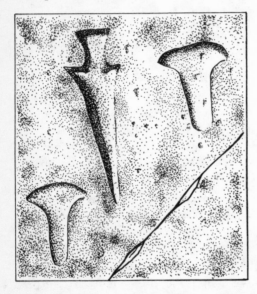

FIG. 1:1 The controversial Stonehenge dagger, flanked by carvings of two Early Bronze Age axes (after Atkinson 1978).

We now know that, far from being a decisive breakthrough, Atkinson's discovery actually led him to make an error in archaeological dating with drastic consequences – one which seriously distorted our understanding of Stonehenge for many years. Radiocarbon dating (see Appendix 1) has shown the magnitude of his error and it is now accepted that the Stonehenge sarsen circle was set up around 2000 BC.[5] The discrepancy is even greater for Silbury Hill, where later excavations by Atkinson failed to discover any burials but did lead to radiocarbon dates which place its construction before 2700 BC – a thousand years too early for any Mycenaean prince, let alone his imaginary builder of Stonehenge.[6]

In any case, Atkinson's comparison between Mycenaean daggers and the carvings at Stonehenge hardly warrants its description as a Mycenaean monument. Anthony Harding, author of the standard work on *The Mycenaeans and Europe*, is far more realistic:

> . . . it seems extraordinary that weathered carvings of such ambiguity should be compared with a rather rare type thousands of kilometres away . . . All in all, the eye of faith is needed to detect any genuine similarity to Mycenaean daggers.[7]

Finally, even *if* an accurate identification of the style, origin (and therefore date) of the Stonehenge daggers were possible, we would still be little the wiser. It could only tell us that the stone circle already existed before the carvings. The gap in time between the two could be vast. The point, ironically enough, is driven home by the very inscription of the 17th century AD which led Atkinson to photograph the stone in the first place. Adding graffiti to existing monuments is a time-honoured practice, something which he unfortunately forgot in his excitement at finding a 'Mycenaean link' with Stonehenge.

Chronology – the backbone of history

The Atkinson case underlines just how important it is to be sure of the relative order of past events. Without this knowledge, jumping to conclusions about major developments such as the building of Stonehenge is obviously a dangerous exercise.

Until recently it was generally believed that copper was first smelted and worked into tools by the 'high civilizations' of Egypt and Sumer (in modern Iraq) around 3500 BC – although, strangely enough, neither area contains any copper. By contrast, it was thought that those parts of Europe with rich ore deposits only later developed the technology to exploit them. Even the Balkan copper industry, the earliest in Europe, was thought to have been stimulated by Near Eastern prospectors. This was widely held to be 'a striking exemplification' of the innovating nature of Egyptian and Sumerian culture.[8] As it happens, the theory of a Near Eastern origin has been swept away on a tide of radiocarbon dates which establish beyond doubt that copper-working had started in the Balkans by 4500 BC. The new dating enables a more logical pattern to emerge in which metallurgy spread from regions with the required raw materials to areas relying on outside supplies.[9]

Thus relative dating, at its most simple, is about whether A happened before B, or B before A. In archaeology, however, many problems are not as clear-cut as the example of copper-working. It is often far from easy to tie down specific events in the past and place them in a unified sequence. A classic instance involves the comparisons which have naturally been made between early Hebrew poetry and Egyptian literature. As Egyptologist Donald Redford, amongst others, has recognized, there is a close parallel between a psalm traditionally ascribed to King David of the 10th century BC and a hymn written in the reign of Pharaoh Akhenaten, conventionally dated to the 14th century BC:

> Psalm 104 in the Hebrew Psalter bears a striking resemblance to the Hymn of the Sun-Disc which was carved in . . . the necropolis at Akhetaten. A comparison of the two texts reveals that Psalm 104 was clearly inspired by the Hymn to the Sun-Disc.[10]

The gap in time between the two has baffled many scholars. Further, the quasi-monotheistic ideas which can be read into Akhenaten's hymn have given rise to numerous theories regarding his possible relationship with a much earlier figure in Hebrew history, Moses the law-giver. Sigmund Freud, the founder of psychoanalysis, was fascinated by the personalities of these two great figures, and wrote a book proposing that they were contemporaries[11] – a theory which was acceptable to early 20th-century archaeologists, but is now, rightly or wrongly, out of favour. A connection clearly exists between ancient Egyptian and Hebrew poetry, but, until we are absolutely certain of the relative order of Akhenaten, Moses and David and the religious developments surrounding them, to say anything more must remain mere speculation.

While these problems demonstrate the value of relative chronology, absolute dating is just as important. This alone makes it possible to track the rate of technological, social, religious and other cultural developments. As Sir Mortimer Wheeler observed, 'Without an absolute chronology . . . the fluctuating tempo of human achievement cannot be estimated.'[12]

The present chronology for the ancient world has succeeded in giving a broad sequence which allows the interplay between different cultures to be understood. Nevertheless, certain stages are plagued by inexplicable anomalies. The most notorious of these points is the 'Dark Age' which descended on the Old World after the fall of Bronze Age civilization. It forms the focus of a vast range of long-standing, and as yet unresolved, historical puzzles.

Why, for instance, would the 8th-century Greeks have borrowed an alphabet from Phoenicia that was 300 years out of date? How could the Cypriots and the Babylonians have left virtually no evidence of writing for 300 years, after which they continued to use basically the same scripts?

Why do bronzes made in Cyprus during the 12th century BC frequently occur elsewhere in 9th-century or later deposits? How is it that the objects of Egyptian pharaohs from the 10th to 9th centuries are always found abroad in contexts 100–200 years later? What caused the gap in the apparently continuous tradition of Eastern Mediterranean ivory-working between 1175 and 850 BC? Why indeed have the Iron Age levels of Israel produced nothing reflecting the 'Golden Age' of King Solomon?

The questions do not end there. Did the Phoenician colonization of the West occur in the 12th or the 8th century BC? How is it that archaeologists cannot agree on a date for the earliest remains at Rome, traditionally founded around 750 BC? Where are the archaeological remains of the native Sicilians who were expelled by Greek colonists in the 8th century BC?

Even more intractable puzzles surround how the Hittite kings and civilization of Syria could have sprung from ancestors who vanished without trace nearly three centuries earlier. And what really happened to the people of Nubia, who supposedly vanished only to return with the same material culture 250 years later? Did the Trojans and Elamites also disappear and reappear in their homelands over the same period? Where is the archaeological evidence for the arrival of the Israelites in Palestine?

Within the presently accepted scheme these problems appear to be insoluble. So many interlocking anomalies occur at this point in history that one begins to wonder whether, as in the case of the origins of copper-working, the root cause may really be a faulty chronology. Yet this is a period which is thought to be so well reconstructed that disagreements over dating are normally confined to matters of a decade or two at most. Any more radical change in the structure would be impossible without questioning some of the most fundamental assumptions behind the standard framework. This leads us to ask: how was the current chronology for the ancient world developed in the first place?

n and chronology

mmonplace for textbooks on the history of archaeology to begin with a joke about James Ussher, the 17th-century Archbishop of Armagh who managed to date the Creation of the World precisely to the year 4004 BC. While his results may seem bizarre by modern standards, his methods were entirely in keeping with the norms of 17th-century scholarship. Ussher had simply used the most authoritative source available to him – the Old Testament – and had reckoned up the figures given there for the history of the Hebrews back to the time of Adam.[13] Some of Ussher's contemporaries went even further. For example, Dr John Lightfoot, author of the wonderfully titled *A Few and New Observations on the Book of Genesis, the most of them certain, the rest probable, all harmless, strange and rarely heard of before* (1642), set the beginning of the world at the September Equinox. He later refined his calculation to match the start of the academic year at Cambridge (where, coincidentally, he was Vice-Chancellor), placing the Creation at precisely 9 a.m. on 23 October.

Ussher's 'verdict was widely received as final; his dates were inserted in the margins of the authorized version of the English Bible, and were soon practically regarded as equally inspired with the sacred text itself'.[14] Indeed, his calculations are still accepted by some biblical fundamentalists. The two dates of 4004 BC for the Creation and 2348 BC for the Flood, provided by Ussher and sanctified by their inclusion in the Bible, gave immovable points for any chronology. No archaeological monuments could possibly have survived the Flood; the extinct creatures known from fossil finds could be explained only by relegating them to an antediluvian era before Noah.

Early chronologists had to operate within these constraints if they were not to slide into heretical thinking. This was the insoluble problem faced by Joseph Scaliger (1540–1609), the leading Protestant scholar of his time. He was the first to make a systematic and critical study of the chronological material in the Bible together with that from the pagan classical world. Rejecting the dubious medieval compilations often relied on by rival Renaissance writers, he insisted on working only from the most ancient sources. Using these, he developed a chronology which, for the time, was both coherent and comprehensive.[15]

FIG. 1:2   Joseph Scaliger of Leiden University, Netherlands (*from Sandys, 1908*).

The authority of Scaliger's meticulous studies was generally recognized; yet the conclusions reached in his second major work, the *Thesaurus temporum* (1606), seemed impossible to reconcile with a Christian view of world history. He had recovered a Byzantine summary of the writings of Manetho, a Graeco-Egyptian priest of the 2nd century BC who had recorded a history of Egypt back to its first kings. Computing the information given by this source for the lengths of the thirty Egyptian dynasties, Scaliger set the start of the 1st Dynasty in 5285 BC. Much to his dismay, it lay 1336 years before his own date for the Creation (3949 BC). This placed Scaliger in a fearful quandary. Manetho's list was an invaluable primary source but seemed to be leading him into direct conflict with the Word of the Bible.

Scaliger's attempt to escape from this dilemma is as vague as it is unconvincing. He postulated a period of 'proleptic', i.e. anticipatory, time before the Creation – an absurd contrivance supposedly explaining how historical dynasties could have begun far earlier than the Bible seemed to allow. Scaliger's discovery of Manetho was widely acclaimed by other scholars, though not the chronological paradox it produced. Some tried to shorten Egyptian history to fit the biblical dates by simply assuming that many of the dynasties listed by Manetho reigned concurrently in different parts of Egypt. Only later did others decide that Adam, after all, had not been the first Man.[16]

By post-Renaissance times the intellectual straitjacket of the biblical chronology was already becoming uncomfortable. Scholars speculated more freely, developing schemes based on an acceptance of Manetho's dynastic chronicle. The limits on possible chronologies given by Ussher and biblical tradition were increasingly seen as irrelevant. One voice to dissent from this trend was that of Sir Isaac Newton (1642–1727). Contrary to the modern image of the man and his work, Newton actually wrote far more concerning theology, ancient history and chronology than about physics or astronomy. A devout though unorthodox Christian, he believed for religious reasons that Israel must have been the earliest kingdom in the world, existing long before the unified monarchy of Egypt. Newton accordingly argued that the Egyptians had:

> . . . anciently boasted of a very great empire under their kings . . . reaching eastward to the *Indies*, and westward to the *Atlantic Ocean*; and out of vanity have made this monarchy some thousands of years older than the world.[17]

Newton's objections had little effect, and by the 18th century a provisional Manethonian chronology had been generally accepted.[18] With the decipherment of Egyptian hieroglyphics in 1822 by the brilliant young French scholar Jean-François Champollion, the task in hand seemed to be one of simply putting flesh on an already established historical skeleton. The writings of the ancient Egyptians themselves were now accessible and nothing in them appeared to contradict the dates already derived from Manetho.

Ordering the past

The same period saw archaeology, hand in hand with geology, take its first faltering steps towards becoming a scientific discipline. Antiquarians such as Sir Richard Colt Hoare and William Cunnington made a radical break with past thinking. No longer were classical and biblical authors the sole guides to the interpretation of prehistoric times. Instead, Colt Hoare put excavated evidence first, and claimed in 1812, after digging some 300 Bronze Age barrows (including the richest Wessex Culture burials), that: 'We speak from facts not theory.'[19]

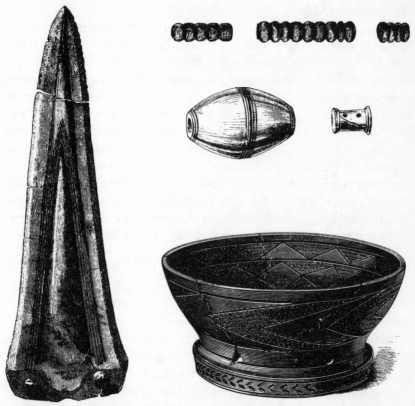

FIG. 1:3   From the barrows of the Wessex Culture – a bronze dagger, faience beads, gold ornaments, a small ceramic cup *(from Thurnam 1873)*.

Nevertheless, the influence of written authorities on their chronology was still undeniable. Lacking good reasons to challenge Ussher's figure of 2348 BC for the Deluge, Colt Hoare and Cunnington had to assign all their finds to a period after 1000 BC.[20] Without any clear concept of an archaeological sequence before the Romans, there was no real need to spread their material over a longer time, as explained by historian of science Bo Gräslund:

The early antiquarians were not able to draw correct historical conclusions because of a lack of chronological facts. Therefore, the most important task of the early archaeologists was to create, from an original chaos, a reliable chronological division of the archaeological sources.[21]

The vital breakthrough in understanding the prehistoric record was made by Christian Thomsen (1788–1865), a wealthy Danish businessman and collector, who developed the 'Three-Age System', a technological succession from Stone to Bronze to Iron. Thomsen's method was to take careful note of which types of prehistoric finds were discovered together and also of those that were never associated with each other. By this means he gradually built up a relative sequence of the use of different artefact types, working back from those found with Roman coins to the remains left by the earliest farmers. Thomsen presented his system to the archaeological world in his *Guide to Northern Archaeology*, published in Denmark in 1834 and translated into English in 1848.[22] With this new framework there was now a sensible way to order prehistoric finds. His broad chronology had found general favour across Europe by the 1860s, as a continual stream of new finds confirmed his results.

Thomsen's simple division of history into ages of Stone, Bronze and Iron is still the basis of archaeological classification throughout the world – although, of course, the various cultures around the globe went through these three stages at different times. Since Thomsen's day the sheer convenience of this terminology has often caused it to stray far from the original meaning: thus, in the Eastern Mediterranean such terms as 'Early Iron Age' were long ago adopted to describe cultural phases which are now in fact defined by their *pottery*. It should not be supposed that iron was first introduced, or even became predominant, at the beginning of the 'Iron Age'.

As early archaeologists began to arrange prehistoric cultures into a chronological sequence, it grew increasingly clear that man's past extended far beyond the cramped time-scale allowed by the biblical dates of Ussher. Shortly before the publication of Darwin's *Origin of Species* in 1859, forward-thinking scientists of both the Royal Society and the Society of Antiquaries had already accepted the idea of a great antiquity for the human race.[23] The chronology of the

Old Testament, along with its account of man's origins, fell from favour. They were replaced by the theory of evolution and its social equivalent – a notion of steady cultural progress from primitive savagery to the sophistication of Victorian Man, naturally perceived as the pinnacle of human achievement.[24]

The freedom given by removal of the shackles of biblical chronology, combined with the development of prehistory as a subject, gave a new impetus to archaeological research in the last decades of the 19th century. This coincided neatly with the Victorian collecting mania. As an 1859 article in *Leisure Hour* put it, 'there are collections of almost everything old under the sun – from old pots and pans, old metals, old stones, and old anything'.[25]

A monumental history for Egypt

The Victorian passion for collecting was increasingly channelled into sponsoring planned campaigns of archaeological fieldwork. Vast quantities of material were acquired by excavating the prehistoric cemeteries of Europe. Thomsen's sequence enabled these finds to be arranged in a relative order, but fixed points in time still remained elusive.

An answer was offered by the great Swedish scholar Oscar Montelius, who in 1885 produced a more refined typological sequence for the prehistoric cultures of Central and Northern Europe. Montelius was able to tie his European relative chronology to the Italian Iron Age sequence, which he dated by links with the known history of Greece and the Near East.[26] However, the ancient Greek historians could only help as far back as the 8th century BC. Beyond that point little could be said. A yardstick was needed against which the chronology of earlier periods of European prehistory could be measured. This had to be sought in the distant country of Egypt, where archaeology could be linked with written records stretching over thousands of years.

During the late 19th century Egyptian archaeology was undergoing a transformation from organized tomb robbing into a serious science. The man largely responsible for this momentous shift was the English archaeologist William Flinders Petrie. From his father, an engineer and devout member of the Plymouth Brethren, Petrie inherited a scientific bent which showed itself in an early passion for surveying. Both were deeply affected by the bizarre theory of their friend Charles Piazzi Smyth, who claimed that the geometry of the Great Pyramid at Giza revealed a divinely inspired system of measurement, based on an 'inch' curiously close to our own.[27]

Petrie's first expedition to Egypt, in 1880, was undertaken specifically to resurvey the pyramid, in an attempt to vindicate Piazzi Smyth. To complete the project he had to locate the original corners of the structure, and so returned to Egypt in 1881. His excavation demonstrated that the 'pyramid inch' was a myth. Petrie's interest in the eccentric ideas of Piazzi Smyth rapidly waned, to be replaced by a lifelong devotion to the past of Egypt in its own right.

After further work at Giza until 1883, Petrie went on to dig numerous other sites, including Naukratis and Daphnae in the Delta and Gurob in the Fayum. Unlike many contemporary dabblers in Egypt who merely foraged for papyri, royal inscriptions or goldwork in tombs, Petrie was equally interested in the 'nuts and bolts' of Egyptian archaeology – domestic and funerary architecture, metalwork, scarabs and, most important, pottery.

Petrie established a pottery sequence linked with written records stretching from the time of Cleopatra back to the First Dynasty. Fortunately it was the custom of the pharaohs to bespatter buildings and other monuments with their names. On a smaller scale, scarabs (small beetle-shaped amulets) bearing the royal name were frequently issued and served many functions, akin, in our own time, to postage stamps (for sealing documents), lucky charms or commemorative mugs produced to celebrate royal jubilees and other great events. Specific years of a king's reign occur on many official texts, from seals on wine delivered to the palace to records of private legal cases.

With such rich material at his disposal, it was easy for Petrie to tie his developing archaeological chronology to an absolute dating system. Manetho's list of dynasties still provided the basic framework for Egyptian history with, by Petrie's time, one vital addition. This was a theory concerning various references in Egyptian papyri to the star Sothis (known to us as Sirius). The 'ideal' ancient Egyptian year was one in which the rising of Sothis just before dawn coincided with the annual flooding of the Nile. Because the Egyptians never introduced a Leap Year, the New Year festival linked to the rising of Sothis inevitably slipped round the calendar; only after 1460 years had passed would the cycle be completed by another 'ideal' year. It therefore appeared possible to calculate where a given text fell within a 'Sothic cycle' if it mentions a rising of Sirius on a particular calendar day.[28]

Schemes for the 'Sothic dating' of Egyptian history were experimented with from the mid-17th century onwards, but all these were highly speculative.[29] The system still used today is essentially that established by the chronologist Eduard Meyer in 1904, hinging on two recently discovered Sothic references – one around 1870 BC during the 12th Dynasty and another of 1540 BC for the 18th Dynasty. In general, Egyptologists were impressed by the scientific aura which astronomy apparently lent to the Sothic theory. Different calculations produced slightly varying results, but they were close enough to convince the vast majority on the central issues. For example, the 'New Kingdom' period of the 18th to 20th Dynasties could be confidently placed between 1600 and 1100 BC.[30]

Petrie's development of a chronology for Egyptian archaeology – using Manetho's dynastic system bolstered by astronomical dates – was to prove of crucial importance for scholars investigating ancient Europe. For in the very years he began his career as an Egyptologist, spectacular discoveries were being made in the Aegean.

The 'Mask of Agamemnon'

In 1870 the wealthy businessman Heinrich Schliemann, obsessed by the romance of Troy, began his excavations at the mound of Hissarlik in north-west Turkey.[31] Most archaeologists would agree that he did discover the very city whose lengthy siege by the Greeks had inspired the epic poetry of Homer. Flushed with success he moved on to Greece, where, seeking the heroes who fought at Troy, he dug into the palaces and tombs at Mycenae and Tiryns.[32]

The Mycenaean civilization had been discovered, and, according to Schliemann and many of his contemporaries, Homer's account of the Heroic Age of the Trojan War had been dramatically confirmed. Schliemann's attempts at dating, however, were hopeless. Lifting a gold mask from a burial in the Shaft Graves at Mycenae, he convinced himself that he had found the burial of Agamemnon, the king who had commanded the Greek expedition.[33] Modern scholarship actually places the Shaft Graves several centuries before the time of the Trojan War.

FIG. 1:4   Schliemann's excavations at Troy consisted of deep soundings dug by
large gangs of workmen using picks and shovels (*from Schliemann 1884*).

With such an arbitrary approach to chronology it is no surprise that Schliemann received almost as much flak as he did acclaim in the popular and academic press. Many classicists, some barely concealing their envy, denounced his work as complete nonsense or even fraud; others claimed that he had vastly overestimated the age of his finds, which really belonged to post-Roman times, to the period of the Slavic invasions or even the Byzantine Empire. More balanced responses set aside Schliemann's most extravagant claims and welcomed his discoveries.[34]

These mixed reactions to Schliemann's work highlight the chaotic state of Aegean chronology in its early days. Yet gradually it became clear, as Schliemann and his able assistant and successor Wilhelm Dörpfeld demonstrated, that their discoveries at Troy and Mycenae lay beneath the classical and Archaic remains of known history. By 1900 Sir Arthur Evans had opened Knossos on Crete and provided further startling evidence of the heights of preclassical civilization. The Minoan culture which Evans described was contemporary with that of Mycenae, as shown, for example, by the Mycenaean pottery at Knossos.[35] The two major prehistoric Aegean societies had now been uncovered; but how much earlier they were than those of historical times was a question entirely dependent on the evidence of links with Egypt.

The great Mycenaean debate

Petrie felt he held the answer to the dilemma of the Aegean archaeologists. At Naukratis in 1885 he discovered masses of Greek pottery from the later Archaic period (6th century BC); next Tell Defenneh (Daphnae) produced earlier Greek material going back to the 7th century BC. Finally, at Gurob, he came across sherds identical to those Schliemann had excavated at Mycenae – together with Egyptian remains of the 18th to 19th Dynasties, which, according to the standard chronology, lay within the 16th to 12th centuries BC. A jubilant entry in Petrie's diary for March 1889 records having found:

> . . . one of the great prizes that we have been waiting for, the contemporary remains of the Western races in their earliest contacts with Egypt; an historical plum, verily! In quality, though not in quantity, it beats Naukratis and Defenneh. How

strange that three such places for the earliest Greek archaeology should have fallen to me, unsought for, and just in receding order.[36]

Petrie went on to find Mycenaean pottery at many other sites, always with 18th and 19th Dynasty material. In his view there was no alternative to following the Egyptian dates and placing Mycenaean civilization squarely in the 2nd millennium BC – between 1600 and 1100 BC. Petrie announced his conclusions in a seminal paper in 1890:

> . . . now the main light on the chronology of the civilizations of the Aegean comes from Egypt; and it is Egyptian sources that must be thanked by classical scholars for revealing the real standing of the antiquities of Greece.[37]

Many of the supposedly grateful classicists, however, spurned Petrie's offer of help. His Egyptian-derived dates had the extremely unwelcome result of producing an enormous void between the Mycenaean world and that of the early Greek city-states of the 8th century BC. Previously it was common practice to date the end of Mycenaean civilization as late as 800 BC, allowing continuity, or even an overlap, with the succeeding Geometric period. The cudgels were taken up on behalf of the lower dating by the classical scholar Cecil Torr, who launched a sustained attack on Petrie's claims. After four years of heated exchanges in academic journals, the Cambridge University Press invited Torr to present his case more fully. This he did in 1896 with *Memphis and Mycenae*, which begins with the dismissive words: 'A statement is current that the Mycenaean age in Greece can definitely be fixed at 1500 B.C., or thereabouts, on the strength of evidence from Egyptian sources.'[38]

Torr's attack was launched on two fronts. First he subjected Petrie's excavation reports to a barrage of nitpicking criticisms regarding the exact contexts of the Mycenaean pottery found in Egypt. More important was Torr's challenge to the consensus view of Egyptian chronology, the first since that of Sir Isaac Newton. Rejecting Sothic dating, Torr developed his own system, by using the highest regnal years known for each pharaoh and allowing greater overlaps between some of Manetho's dynasties. His new, minimum, chronology gave dates two to three centuries lower than those of Petrie, Meyer and other Egyptologists: for example, while they began the 18th Dynasty in 1580 or 1530, he started it in 1271 BC.

Thus, according to Torr, even *if* some of the claimed connections between Egypt and the Aegean were valid, there was still no need to push Mycenaean culture back as far as 1500 BC. Nor did he see anything to contradict the idea that it continued as late as the 8th century BC, blending almost imperceptibly into the civilization of Archaic and classical Greece. Torr's views attracted favourable comment from Jens Lieblein, the founding father of Swedish Egyptology. While Torr and others concentrated their fire on the gap which Petrie's synchronisms would produce in Greek history, Lieblein extended the debate to include similar problems developing in the Near East and in Egypt itself. He had compiled a substantial work containing all the genealogical information available for later Egyptian history,[39] and from this he produced conclusions remarkably similar to Torr's. The dates current for the Egyptian 18th–20th Dynasties were, he insisted, too high by some 200 years. The fault came from a misunderstanding of Manetho:

> I have never understood the obstinacy with which scholars have hung on to the regular succession of the thirty dynasties of Manetho. However many voices of incontestable authority have protested, the error still seems to be fashion in our days.[40]

He also noted that the high dates were already introducing an unnecessary 'Dark Age' into the history of the Hittites (see Chapter 6), whose remains had recently been identified in Turkey: ' . . . it is the unfortunate establishment of an erroneous Egyptian chronology which has caused the confusion and the difficulties'.[41]

Lieblein's *cri de coeur* went unheeded, along with Torr's dogged rearguard action against the advance of Petrie's high chronology for Egypt and Mycenae. Their work was eventually relegated to the status of a historical curiosity for three reasons. First, Torr was certainly wrong to deny that the Mycenaean Age was contemporary with the 18th and 19th Dynasties of Egypt, for even as the debate raged, further excavations were revealing conclusive proof that Petrie's synchronisms were sound. Second, the idea of a low chronology fell foul of the trend, current at the time, to ascribe the highest antiquity possible to Egypt and its neighbouring civilizations. The remains of the great kingdoms of Sumer, Babylonia and Assyria were steadily being recovered from the dust of Mesopotamia and assigned some extraordinarily high dates. On astronomical grounds Hammurabi, one of the earliest law-givers of Babylonia, was placed around 2100 BC (see Appendix 3 for the subsequent downdating of this king). Third, the histories of Egypt and Meso-potamia were now linked together by finds of royal correspondence (see Chapter 6), making a challenge to Egyptian chronology alone ineffectual.

The Italian connection

Scholars at the turn of the century were understandably keen to find any historical reference to the peoples of prehistoric Europe. Com-plementing Petrie's archaeological connections, it was thought that the so-called 'Sea Peoples', who launched unsuccessful sea-borne attacks on Egypt at the end of the Late Bronze Age, came from the Northern Mediterranean. The Shardana, Teresh, Shekelesh and Ekwesh mentioned in 19th Dynasty texts were frequently iden-tified (and often still are) with the early Sardinians, Etruscans, Sicilians and Achaean Greeks. George Rawlinson admitted that 'separately considered, the identifications are in almost every case doubtful', but explained in the same breath the attraction such equations held for his generation:

> . . . most minds accept the view as probably not far from the truth. They delight to think that the European nations, so far back as the thirteenth century B.C., showed signs of their inherent vigour, possessed fleets, fought naval battles and contended with the most advanced and the most powerful of then existing monarchies . . . If it is not true it ought to be.[42]

The idea of a great antiquity for European civilization, boosted by Evans's discovery of the extraordinarily high technology of the ancient Cretans, obviously had enormous appeal. By contrast, Torr and Lieblein's low dates for Mycenaean, Minoan and Hittite civi-lizations must have seemed niggardly, despite the fact that they were also trying to reduce Egyptian chronology.

A more down-to-earth approach to ancient Europe was being pursued by Montelius in Scandinavia who, together with the younger German archaeologist Paul Reinecke, laid the foundations of European prehistoric chronology. Synthesizing the evidence from different regions of Northern and Central Europe, they developed a general framework of relative chronology divided into successive phases. Scandinavian archaeologists still arrange their Bronze Age material into Montelius Periods I to VI. The division of both the Central European Bronze and Iron Ages into 'Reinecke' periods labelled A–D has also stood the test of time (see Table 1:1).

Attempting to peg their scheme to absolute dates, they were on reasonably firm ground where the Iron Age of Central Europe was concerned. This was largely due to the discovery of the rich burials at Hallstatt in a narrow pass on the northern edge of the Austrian Alps, above a massive deposit of rock salt (see Plate 5). The vital role of salt in the economy of prehistoric Europe is reflected in the cemetery of the salt-miners, which includes imports from as far afield as the Baltic and southern Italy. By 1900 over 1000 graves had been carefully dug. The starting point for their chronology came from the objects made in central Italy (Etruria). Here identical products were frequently found with Greek pottery, which could now be reasonably well dated from the 8th century BC onwards. These links set the life of the cemetery from 800 to 400 BC in round figures. Montelius and Reinecke could therefore use the Hallstatt finds to fix their relative sequence, and so absolute chronology began to make its way north of the Alps.[43]

Beyond this, further back into the Iron and then the Bronze Ages, imports of Mediterranean material dried up. Connections of a sort were found again in the European Early Bronze Age with apparent similarities between the bronzework of Central and Eastern Europe and that of the early Mycenaeans. Vague comparisons involving particular decorative motifs, especially the spiral, were also invoked. Montelius recognized the tenuous nature of this evidence but, for want of anything better, felt obliged to follow it. At this point, despite its methodical approach, the Montelius school could not escape the effects of the Petrian revolution in chronology, which had backdated the Aegean material available for comparison. The European Early Bronze Age was accordingly placed in the middle of the 2nd millennium to match the Mycenaean dates. Between these two periods of contact, providing firm synchronisms during the Middle Iron Age and far vaguer connections in the Bronze Age, lay a no-man's land.

Light from the ancient East

In 1901 Petrie summarized the achievements of Egyptian archaeology (in fact, largely his own) as follows:

> It is now twenty-one years since I began work in Egypt . . . In those days the pyramid of Khufu [Cheops] was our boundary of history . . . The situation is now completely different. The monumental history has been carried back to the very beginning of the written record, which has been entirely confirmed . . . The archaeology is better known than that of the most familiar countries: not a vase nor a bead, not an ornament or a carving, but what falls into place with known examples, and can be closely dated. The connection with Europe has been led back to the beginning of Greek records, then to Mycenaean times . . . Egypt is the sounding line for the unmeasured abyss of European history.[44]

In a strange way Petrie had underestimated the influence of his work on European prehistorians. Once the low chronologists had been swept under the carpet, the authority of Egypt and the Near East, both culturally and chronologically, became paramount. For example, Montelius accepted that 'at a time when the peoples of Europe were, so to speak, without any civilization whatsoever', the Near East had already developed flourishing cultures. Prehistoric Europe took a secondary, passive role: 'the civilization which gradually dawned on our continent was for long only a pale reflection of oriental culture'.[45]

The idea that cultural innovations had spread across a 'barbarian' Europe by a process of gradual diffusion from the 'higher civilizations' of Egypt and Mesopotamia seemed only logical at a time when world politics meant imperial politics. It also suited Christian preconceptions to believe that civilization had originated in the Near East, where the Bible naturally located man's earliest achievements.

A further, negative, reason for the continuing popularity of the Montelian view began to loom large during the early 20th century. At that time, the only other general theory of cultural development available to European prehistorians was the nationalist and racist approach of Gustaf Kossinna, founder of the Society for German Prehistory. Scholars welcomed his useful idea of an archaeological

Culture (a people sharing the same material and spiritual culture) which could be conveniently named after important sites such as Hallstatt. Although they were not averse to the general idea of racial movements promoting social change, they firmly rejected Kossinna's view that all innovations were due to the migrations of the German 'master-race'. Seeing the awful results spawned by such creeds during the late 1930s, archaeologists returned to the idea that civilization had been diffused by small groups of traders from the Near East, rather than imposed by sweeping folk movements.[46]

However, in post-war years it was increasingly realized that 'barbarian' Europe could not be seen simply as a backwater of civilization.[47] Some continued to cling to the traditional perceptions, including Atkinson, who had to invoke a wandering Mycenaean prince to explain the high level of architectural skill displayed at Stonehenge. There were also more practical reasons why it was difficult to discard diffusion. As well as being a convenient explanation for cultural change, it had long provided the only possible source of absolute dates for European prehistory as a whole: those transmitted via Italy and Greece from the respected, and apparently astronomically based, chronologies of Egypt and Mesopotamia.

Radiocarbon and the death of diffusion mania

In 1952 an entirely new dating technique was discovered which was eventually to bring about the collapse of diffusion as a universal explanation. The radiocarbon method, a scientific means of dating organic materials (see Appendix 1), provided the first independent check on the age of prehistoric cultures. Radiocarbon results, especially when calibrated by tree-ring chronologies, showed that most of the traditional dates given by diffusionist connections between the Near East and Europe could no longer hold.

The cultures of Neolithic and Early Bronze Age Europe were raised by 1000 years or more to a completely unexpected antiquity. Various developments traditionally thought to have been borrowed from the Eastern Mediterranean (such as copper-working) were now shown to have begun much earlier in Europe. The 'radiocarbon revolution' led to the dismantling of the diffusionist framework and the drawing of a chronological and cultural 'fault-line' as conceived by Colin Renfrew, between prehistoric Europe and the ancient Near East during the 3rd and early 2nd millennia

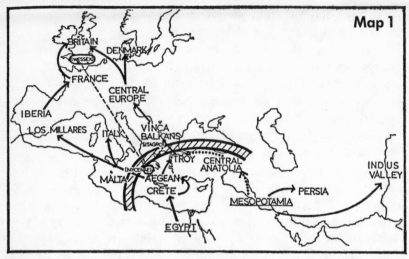

The chronological fault-line in earlier European prehistory as defined by Colin Renfrew (1973). This cut off south-east Europe, still using traditional historical dating, from the rest of the continent which was now dated by the radiocarbon method.

BC.[48] This upheaval has left an indelible mark on European prehistory. No longer are speculations that Mycenaeans built the early phases of Stonehenge permissible. The major developments in European prehistory did not depend on a simple chain of diffusion from the Near East.

On the other hand, we are not looking at a simple reversal of the picture. Nor, of course, have all the links between Europe and the Near East been broken by Renfrew's fault-line. Those during the developed Iron Age remain and are not affected by radiocarbon dating. However, the Bronze Age of Europe is a far less clear-cut matter. The accuracy of radiocarbon tests has proved good enough to show gross differences in time, as, say, the 500 years between the building of Stonehenge and the Shaft Graves of Mycenae. But the statistical uncertainty inherent in the method means that radiocarbon results are not so useful when the disputes involve smaller time-spans of a century or two.

So what impact has radiocarbon had on the dating of the Bronze to Iron Ages? Can it shed new light on the 'Dark Age' problems which bedevil the archaeology and history of so many regions at this time?

From Stonehenge to Mycenae

An unfortunate consequence of the limited accuracy of radiocarbon dating is that its impact on the Eastern Mediterranean and Near East has been, so far, only marginal. The Egyptian-based chronologies are generally believed to be fixed, and of the relatively few radiocarbon results available many conflict with the present understanding. Because of this, most archaeologists working in the area are not fully convinced by the method.

In Europe, the 6th-century connections with the Mediterranean, originally given by the Hallstatt cemetery, have become even more solid since Montelius's day, and the dates provided are now confirmed by the local 'dendrochronology' built up from tree-ring studies (see Appendix 1). For the earlier phases of the Hallstatt Culture tree-ring dating has yet to provide definite results.[49] Undisputed links with the Aegean via Italy are rarer before 600 BC, and are completely absent during the long Dark Ages of the Mediterranean world between the 12th and 8th centuries. In the absence of firmer evidence, synchronisms of extremely varying reliability have been used to create a dating scheme covering most of Europe, as shown in Table 1:1.

The traditional, non-radiocarbon, chronology for Bronze Age Central Europe has of course continued to build on the foundations laid by Montelius and Reinecke. The major development since their time has been the creation of a broad synchronism between early Urnfield Culture (Bronze D to Hallstatt A2 in Reinecke's system) and the Mycenaean world from the time before the Dark Age. Mycenaean civilization is divided into a series of 'Late Helladic' phases, based on changing pottery styles. Of these, Late Helladic IIIB (LHIIIB) is generally thought to parallel Reinecke's Bronze D and the latter is accordingly placed in the 13th century.[50] However, most of the claimed connections on which this conclusion depends are open to question. Helmets and swords of apparently Mycenaean types have been found in Europe, but the majority are chance discoveries, lacking any associations, and so of no real chronological value.[51] Even the few found with other objects do not pass without challenge. For example, the Ørskovhede sword from Denmark, frequently described as a Mycenaean weapon, was dismissed by Harding as 'plainly' of local type, and 'absolutely nothing to do with Aegean swords'.[52]

FIG. 1:5   Decorated slabs from the Bronze Age burial at Kivik in southern Sweden, excavated in 1748, believed to reflect Mycenaean influence, although some scenes are clearly Nordic, such as the horn-blowers *(from du Chaillu 1889)*.

In place of reliable direct connections between Central Europe and Mycenae, links have been forged via the rich Peschiera Culture bronzework of Italy (see Chapter 2). The European end of the equation is sound, since many Peschiera bronzes are identical to Bronze D types. However, the Mycenaean side is less clear-cut. Mycenaean material is sometimes found with Peschiera bronzes in Italy, but usually in contexts which are hard to tie into the local sequence.[53] In Greece the situation is different, as the local Mycenaean material is well-known and has a clear relative chronology. On the other hand, there are few bronzes of certain Italian manufacture in Greece.[54] Nevertheless, a number of Peschiera-style finds do have good datable associations, particularly the fibulae (brooches) found in several tombs with LHIIIB pottery.[55]

Taken together, there is enough evidence to conclude that Reinecke's Bronze D, the Peschiera complex and LHIIIB overlap to some degree. This does not mean, however, that we can simply treat Reinecke's Bronze D as the temporal equivalent of LHIIIB, as the flexibility in dating the Italian material obviously affects Central European chronology. Harding, discussing the fibulae found with LHIIIB pottery, noted that although this suggests that Bronze D started in the 13th century, 'there is no compelling reason why it should not continue considerably after 1200 B.C.'[56] Indeed, Nancy Sandars, the leading authority on prehistoric European swords, has proposed a date for Bronze D a full century lower than that generally accepted.[57]

Because of such uncertainties, some prehistorians have tried to

Table 1:1

Date (BC)	NORTHERN EUROPE	CENTRAL EUROPE		GREECE
1500				
1400	Period II	Bronze B	Tumulus Culture	LHII
		Bronze C		LHIIIA
1300				
1200	Period III	Bronze D		LHIIIB
		Hallstatt A1		LHIIIC
1100				
1000	Period IV	Hallstatt A2	Urnfield Culture	
		Hallstatt B1		DARK AGE
900				
800		Hallstatt B2		
	Period V	Hallstatt B3		Late Geometric
700				
		Hallstatt C	Hallstatt Culture	Protocorinthian
600				
	Period VI	Hallstatt D		Corinthian
500				

The generally accepted scheme for the chronology of Late Bronze to Iron Age in Northern Europe, which is divided into 100-year blocks. The numbered Periods for Northern Europe are essentially those first drawn up by Montelius. The lettered phases for Central Europe follow Reinecke's scheme, with Hallstatt A–D representing the Iron Age. The grouping of these phases into three successive Cultures emphasizes what are thought to be the points of significant social transformation within the period, such as major changes in burial practice. The European chronology is based on links with the Greek periods shown. (The 100-year divisions do not apply to the latter.)

develop a new chronology for the European Bronze Age based on radiocarbon dates, in the hope of replacing 'the rickety framework of relative chronology that has been so painstakingly built up'.[58] The few radiocarbon results initially available placed Bronze D in the 14th to 13th centuries BC, so conflicting with the traditional 13th- to 12th-century dates for the period borrowed from Greece via Italy.[59] However, more recent evidence, rather than raising the dates for Bronze D, suggests that its traditional placement may actually be too high. The radiocarbon results available for the Wessex Culture of the Stonehenge region (usually linked to the

Shaft Graves of Mycenae and Reinecke's Bronze B) give dates
between 1500 and 1200 BC.[60] A similar conclusion reached for
Montelius Period II in Denmark (equivalent to Bronze B–C) is
more significant, as it is based on large numbers of radiocarbon tests
on the outer tree-rings of oak coffins, tied in with dendrochronological analyses of the coffins and other wooden grave-goods. In
combination the two sources of evidence date Montelius II to
1500–1200 BC.[61]

The knock-on effect of these two studies might be to lower the
date for Bronze B to C (conventionally 1500–1300 BC) by at least a
century. Does that now put the Bronze Age of Europe out of step
with that in the Near East? The difficulties of establishing synchronisms between Bronze Age Europe and the Aegean mean that
these dates have no immediate impact on the Mediterranean, but
they do point to the possibility of lowering chronology there as
well. The ideal, of course, would be to assess the two chronologies
by using parallel sets of radiocarbon dates from both regions, in
order to compare like with like. Unfortunately, because of the
negative attitude of so many archaeologists working in the Eastern
Mediterranean, only a scatter of radiocarbon results are available for
this area.

The upshot is that the prehistoric cultures of South-east Europe
remain, to varying degrees, dependent for their chronology on
connections with Mycenaean civilization – itself dated by synchronisms with the accepted Egyptian chronology. Logically, one
might expect that the nearer one approaches the Mediterranean and
links with Egypt, the more precise the dates should become, so
enabling a chronology of greater accuracy and reliability to be
developed than radiocarbon can offer.

Deeper examination will reveal a very different picture, one in
which archaeological research has always been dominated by stor-
my controversies over dating. Specialists in the fields haunted by
these debates have been drawn back time and again to the unsolved
problems outlined at the beginning of this chapter. Could it be that
something went drastically wrong in the painstaking process of
developing Old World chronology? As Italy provides the main
hinge between the dating sequences of Central Europe and the
Aegean world, our investigation opens with the apparently inexplicable 'Dark Ages' of Central and Western Mediterranean
archaeology and history. A surprising answer emerges.

CHAPTER 2

To the Pillars of Heracles

Even as early as 4000 BC, in the Neolithic Age, the islands and coasts of the Mediterranean were in close contact, with obsidian (a glassy volcanic rock ideal for making stone tools) being traded hundreds of miles by sea. During the Late Bronze Age, the Mycenaeans penetrated deep into the Western Mediterranean, founding trading posts in Italy and establishing commercial links at least as far as Sardinia. After the collapse of Mycenaean civilization there was a long break. Communication between East and West was renewed when the Phoenicians of the Lebanon and then the Greeks planted colonies across the Mediterranean; both reached Spain, the former even passing beyond the 'Pillars of Heracles', which flank the present-day Straits of Gibraltar, into the Atlantic. Phoenician expansion to the west ultimately led to the creation of the Carthaginian Empire.

The dating of the different local cultures in the Western Mediterranean depends entirely on these eastern contacts, as only they provide links with apparently secure historical chronology. Between these two golden ages of prosperity – the 13th–12th centuries and 8th century BC onwards – the Western Mediterranean is thought to have sunk into a long cultural and economic recession. Strangely, this grey period has provided an arena for some highly charged academic clashes, focussing largely on the issue of how to fill this apparent gap in the history of the area. It is no coincidence that this matches the low point of civilization in the Eastern Mediterranean. But was this lengthy Dark Age so widespread because the whole Mediterranean was economically interdependent, or because the West is chronologically dependent on the East?

At both the high points of East–West trade Italy was the most important partner for Greek merchants. Before the Dark Age, the Mycenaeans fostered commercial ties with northern Italy which carried bronzes from the thriving industry in the Alpine valleys to both Greece and Crete. The typical lakeside village of Peschiera gives its name to the Middle Bronze Age culture which produced this fine metalwork. Peschiera bronzes also found their way northward across the Alps, supplying the crucial connection between

Map 2: The Central Mediterranean

1. Akragas
2. Carthage
3. Cassibile
4. Catane
5. Caulonia
6. Croton
7. Cumae
8. Dessueri
9. Finocchito
10. Frattesina
11. Gela
12. Gravisca
13. Leontini
14. Lipari
15. Megara Hyblaea
16. Motya
17. Mylae
18. Narce
19. Naxos
20. Pantalica
21. Peschiera
22. Pithekoussai
23. Rhegium
24. Rome
25. Scoglio del Tonno
26. Selinus
27. Surbo
28. Sybaris
29. Syracuse
30. Tarentum
31. Tarquinia
32. Thapsos
33. Veii
34. Vetulonia
35. Villanova
36. Vulci
37. Zancle

the Mycenaean and Central European chronologies.

To the south, in the heartland of ancient Italy, the cultural succession from *c.* 750 BC onwards becomes increasingly certain – fixed first by the Greek colonies founded at the end of the Dark Age and subsequently by the emerging local civilizations. Most important of these is that of the Etruscans in central Italy. Their anonymous beginnings lie in a culture named 'Villanovan' after a massive cemetery of cremation burials in urns near Bologna. The 7th century was the 'Orientalizing' period which saw intense eastern influence, highlighted by exotic trade goods such as a vase inscribed with the name of the Egyptian Pharaoh Bocchoris found at Tarquinia. The earliest Greek colony in Italy as a whole was Pithekoussai, dated to *c.* 750 BC, which imported Greek, Syrian, Phoenician and Egyptian goods – including a Bocchoris scarab.[1] (See Chapter 5 for an examination of the historical sources of Greek colony dates.)

FIG. 2:1   Grave-goods from the 'Bocchoris tomb' at Tarquina in Etruria. The presence of the faience vase (left) inscribed with the name of Pharaoh Bocchoris (24th Dynasty), pots influenced by Corinthian Greek wares and the Orientalizing gold plates date it to 700–675 BC *(from Randall-MacIver 1924).*

The origins of Rome

Yet even at this known end of the scale problems persist, provoking massive controversy where Rome, eventual heir to the Etruscan civilization, is concerned. Traces of wooden huts from the Iron Age on the Palatine Hill, where Romulus had supposedly lived, were discovered at the turn of the century and immediately identified as the earliest settlement at Rome. The archaeological dating of these huts, loosely synchronized with Greek pottery chronology, was for

FIG. 2:2   One of the earliest depictions of Romulus and Remus, mythical founders of Rome, being suckled by the she-wolf which raised them; from a Roman coin of *c.* 270 BC, showing Hercules on the other side (*after Crawford 1985*).

long seen as confirming the traditional foundation of 753 BC favoured by the Romans themselves (see Appendix 2). The ancient historian Howard Scullard, although acclaiming this 'remarkable coincidence' between the 'artificial calculations' of classical writers and the archaeological evidence, still treated it with some caution:

> . . . if the date of the first settlement should prove to be slightly earlier, there is always Timaeus' date of 813 to remember. Thus while few believe in a historical Romulus, the general tradition about his date makes good archaeological sense.[2]

Scullard's words show the uncertainty in the chronology of Rome some twenty years ago, when Swedish, German and Italian scholars were presenting competing dates for the earliest remains of the city. Einar Gjerstad, the leading Swedish archaeologist of his generation, had excavated a series of burials and occupation levels under the Forum. Using these discoveries as a starting point, he divided all the oldest finds from Rome into four periods. Gjerstad found associations between his later phases and 7th-century Protocorinthian Greek imports and, because the Roman pottery as a whole showed so little variation, set the start of his sequence at 800 BC.[3]

The problem with this conclusion was that it bypassed the existing chronology for the surrounding area. Going back from the

Villanovan beginnings of the Etruscans, the next benchmark was provided by Mycenaean imports which fix the end of Middle Bronze Age Apennine culture at *c.* 1200 BC. The now standard division of the Late Bronze to Early Iron Age was first defined by the Italian prehistorian Renato Peroni, and involved successive Apennine, Sub-Apennine, Proto-Villanovan and Villanovan cultures.[4] While the Sub-Apennine mostly continued earlier traditions, the Proto-Villanovan saw the introduction of cremation burials in urns, new pottery styles and different types of metal-work. All these innovations resembled Urnfield Culture practices in Central Europe. When Peroni turned to Rome he saw that Gjerstad's Forum tombs and settlement layers contained pottery derived from Sub-Apennine and Proto-Villanovan styles. Following this evidence of continuity from the Bronze Age, Peroni put the beginning of the Rome sequence in the 10th century BC. The German expert Hermann Müller-Karpe agreed with him and the battle-lines were drawn.[5]

The conflict widened when the examination of the whole Latium region by Pär Gierow, another Swedish archaeologist, produced a low chronology following Gjerstad's. On the other hand, Hugh Hencken's massive study of the entire scope of Villanovan Culture, including the Rome finds, placed its start *c.* 950 BC, in line with the high chronologists.[6] The low chronologists admitted the evidence for continuity from the Late Bronze Age shown by the Rome tombs and settlements, but according to Gierow, 'this does not prove that the tombs are early, but on the contrary, that such elements can be late'.[7] However, the debate appeared to be settled in favour of the high chronology by new evidence from the Etruscan cemetery at Veii. Here Villanovan material was found together with Greek pottery thought to belong to the early 8th century BC, making the Swedish dates for the later part of the Rome sequence too low. Combined with the Bronze Age connections at the top end this appeared to rule out the low chronology. The high dates are now standard, as is a rejection of the Swedish methodology.[8]

Alas, this happy state of affairs has recently been ruined by a re-examination of the Greek pottery at Veii, which reveals that the Swedish school's low chronology was, after all, correct for the later Rome phases. The changes concern periods of only some twenty years, but they appalled Italian archaeologists, who even wanted to adjust the Greek pottery chronology to fit their Villanovan dates.

Such a strategy was firmly rejected by John-Paul Descœdres and Rosalind Kearsley, authors of the Veii study: ' . . . this seemingly ingenious way out is nothing but a blind alley . . . In order to assign absolute dates there has been, and there still is, no other way than to link them to the historical cultures of the East.'[9]

FIG. 2:3   Villanovan hut-urn from Tarquinia in Etruria. The ashes of the dead were interred in these models of the houses of the living (*from Randall-MacIver 1924*).

The consequent realignment raises the extraordinary possibility that Gjerstad's date of 800 BC for the start of the Rome sequence may yet turn out to be right. An interim solution is to adopt the compromise suggestion of Massimo Pallottino, the leading figure in Etruscan studies, to begin it in the 9th century BC.[10]

The 'elusive centuries' of Late Bronze Age Italy

Applying Pallottino's dating beyond Rome, the earliest Villanovan material would also belong in the 9th century BC. Even then, the Sub-Apennine and Proto-Villanovan still have to fill some 300 years between the Mycenaean-linked Apennine period and the Villanovan. This central part of the span is a notorious grey area, though excavations at Narce have supported Peroni's scheme of cultural successions. There, strata containing Sub-Apennine, Proto-Villanovan and Villanovan pottery follow each other, a sequence which is now seen at several other sites.[11]

Although the relative sequence is agreed, there is a remarkable lack of consensus on the key question of the date for the Sub-Apennine to Proto-Villanovan transition (see Table 2:1). The varying interpretations of Proto-Villanovan material only compound the difficulties. Most writers use it to define an invading race. Others see its appearance as reflecting the adoption of new

Table 2:1

	Müller-Karpe 1959	Peroni 1959	Lo Porto 1963	Hencken 1968	Delpino 1979	D. Ridgway 1988
1300	Late Apennine	Late Apennine	Middle Apennine	Late Apennine	Late Apennine	Late Apennine / Sub-Apennine
1200	Proto-Villanovan	Sub-Apennine	Late Apennine	Sub-Apennine	Sub-Apennine	Proto-Villanovan
1100		Proto-Villanovan	Sub-Apennine	Proto-Villanovan	Proto-Villanovan	
1000			Proto-Villanovan			
900	Villanovan	Villanovan	Villanovan	Villanovan	Villanovan	Villanovan
800						

A comparison of the divergent chronologies for the Italian Late Bronze to Early Iron Ages. The differences in the time allocated to the Proto-Villanovan cause most of the variations.

burial customs by the already existing Apennine society. Yet a third group thinks it stayed in fashion among a backward Bronze Age population inland, out of touch with Villanovan Iron Age advances on the Etrurian coast.[12] This confusion justified Harding's criticism that, applied to metalwork, 'the term "Proto-Villanovan" is a rag-bag, containing everything that is not recognizably Peschiera/Terramara on the one hand, or Villanovan on the other'.[13]

The chronological implications of combining two of these views – that Proto-Villanovan is the funerary aspect of Apennine Culture, and that it lasted into the Iron Age in isolated inland regions – horrified David Ridgway. Reviewing the possibility in the *Cambridge Ancient History*, he noted: 'as a formula for shortening chronology, of course, a combination of these two interpretative tendencies could hardly be bettered: Sub-Apennine thus becomes the contemporary of Villanovan!'[14]

Hoping to simplify matters, many archaeologists now favour a return to the original idea of Proto-Villanovan as a new and distinct culture occupying central Italy, using cremation burials with particular pottery and metalwork types.[15] However, this apparently painless solution to the complex problem of the Sub-Apennine to Proto-Villanovan transition is ruled out by the considerable evidence for an overlap between the two. Recent surveys show that on many sites Proto-Villanovan, Sub-Apennine, and even Late Apennine finds occur with the same types of Mycenaean pottery:[16]

	LHIIIA	LHIIIB	LHIIIC
Late Apennine sites	6	8	7
Sub-Apennine sites	2	6	12
Proto-Villanovan sites	1	1	4

Were the conventional interpretation of a straightforward succession of local cultures correct, there should be relatively little overlap between their associations with different types of Mycenaean pottery. Instead, it seems as though all three lasted through the whole Late Helladic III period (conventionally 1400–1075 BC). This surprising result prompts a re-examination of two of the hypotheses already noted. Believers in Urnfield invaders bearing Proto-Villanovan culture think they were only a small minority, and that in later centuries the native Sub-Apennine population reasserted itself. Alternatively, Pallottino has suggested that in some areas Sub-Apennine and Proto-Villanovan were not separate cultures, but actually two different facets of the same society; the first being the settlements and the second the cemeteries.[17]

Both theories are ignored because of their incompatibility with the standard chronology, which is clearly set by cross-dating Apennine Culture with Mycenaean finds and Villanovan with 8th-century Geometric imports. Proto-Villanovan must bridge most of this time-span, but as John Coles and Anthony Harding note, that 'elusive century 1200–1100 BC' seems to contain almost nothing.[18] Accepting either hypothesis would overlap Proto-Villanovan with Sub-Apennine, by raising the date of many Proto-Villanovan sites. This results in leaving even less material to fill the awful void. Despite this difficulty, a version of Pallottino's theory seems perfectly viable, as it is settlements rather than burials which are missing overall.

A final mystery comes from the promontory site of Scoglio del Tonno in southern Italy, dug by Quagliati in 1899–1900 before its destruction by extensions to the modern harbour.[19] He discerned three basic strata: Stratum 3 was Early Bronze Age; Stratum 2 had well-preserved buildings and floor-levels associated with Sub-Apennine material; Stratum 1 contained Mycenaean and 8th–7th-century Protocorinthian pottery with Geometric-influenced local wares. The Mycenaean pots are of LHIIIA, B and C styles, much of which (certainly the LHIIIA) predates the Sub-Apennine in Peroni's scheme, and so ought to have been found below it rather than above.

Because this stratigraphy is hard to reconcile with current views, Quagliati's work is often put down as merely a rescue excavation and his conclusions ignored. Thus Coles and Harding claim:

> . . . of the find circumstances virtually nothing is known. The excavator, Q. Quagliati, made a valiant attempt, under rescue conditions . . . to elucidate the stratigraphical sequence, but his information is of the scantiest.[20]

A fairer assessment is given by the American archaeologist Ross Holloway, who considers that for most of the time Quagliati's team 'were carrying out a normal excavation . . . The resulting report was a remarkably detailed account with an ample series of plans and sections'.[21]

Nevertheless, Holloway argued that none of the large quantity of Mycenaean pottery recovered by the excavator was in its original position. He suggested that it came from elsewhere on the site, becoming mixed into Stratum 1 by erosion, quarrying and modern building work.[22] But although the site was badly disturbed, Quagliati did uncover the remains of oval huts in Stratum 1, showing that the disruption was not so complete as Holloway thought. Alternatively, the Swedish archaeologist Gösta Säflund tried to integrate the Mycenaean finds from Stratum 1 with the Sub-Apennine house of Stratum 2 (to make it a Mycenaean trader's residence), entirely contrary to the stratigraphy noted by the excavator. A final suggestion, that Quagliati's recording of finds was confused, is unlikely, as he wrote up the report within a year.[23]

All the ingenious hypotheses proposed to explain the problem of Scoglio del Tonno overlook one obvious possibility: to accept Quagliati's findings as they stand and instead reassess the relative date of the Sub-Apennine and Mycenaean finds. Looking more widely, the mounting evidence for overlaps between the supposedly separate phases of Late Bronze Age Italy makes it hard to sustain the view that this period lasted several hundred years.

Sicily – cemeteries without settlements?

Sicilian chronology is less confused by overlaps than the Italian, but there is still a daunting absence of material in the Late Bronze Age and Early Iron Age (1250–650 BC).

Middle Bronze Age Sicily is well known from both cemeteries and settlements of the coastal Thapsos Culture. The tombs contain burials with large numbers of Mycenaean drinking cups and a few Maltese vessels. The Thapsos settlement itself developed into an urban centre, with finds of Maltese and Cypriot pottery, but almost no Mycenaean – an interesting difference between the settlement and its cemetery.[24] The latest Mycenaean goods from tombs date the Thapsos Culture's sudden end to LHIIIB times, *c.* 1250 BC.[25] The deserted settlement was only reoccupied long afterwards. Later, around 700 BC, it was taken over by Greek colonists.

According to the accepted chronological framework, the disappearance of Thapsos sites was followed by the Pantalica Culture, lasting from *c.* 1250 until 650 BC, when Greek and Phoenician colonies had come to dominate the island. The earliest Greek

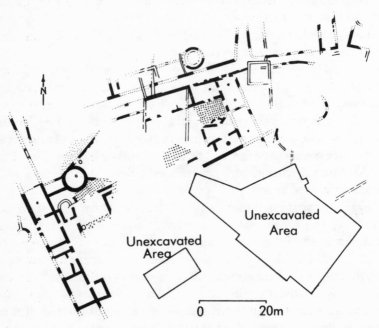

FIG. 2:4 Plan of the Middle Bronze Age settlement at Thapsos, Sicily, showing two well-planned blocks of buildings (in black) with central courtyards, and (in outline) smaller earlier houses (*after Coles & Harding 1979*).

settlement was at Naxos, traditionally dated to 734 BC, with numerous others clustering in the eastern part of Sicily by 700 BC.[26] The only Phoenician colony this early is Motya, with a few burials dated to about 720 BC by Carthaginian and Greek pottery, and a slightly later one with another Bocchoris vase.[27] Various claims are made for earlier Phoenician contacts, but none is convincing.[28]

The general belief that between these two phases of coastal settlement 'a real Dark Age set in', ended only by Greek colonization,[29] is expressed by Bernarbò Brea, the grand old man of Sicilian archaeology:

> The numerous small villages of the Thapsos culture . . . suddenly disappear. The inhabitants, abandoning the coastal plains, took refuge in the least accessible hill-country . . . with an eye only to their defensive possibilities. They settled in a few big urban centres such as those connected with the huge cemeteries of chamber-tombs at Pantalica, Cassibile, Dessueri etc. . . . Evidently life in this dark age was dominated by fear.[30]

The Pantalica Culture is always divided into four phases (named after different cemetery sites), but the lengths of the first three are much debated. The pottery of the Pantalica North period continues Thapsos styles, but new types of bronze mirrors, knives, swords and brooches appear, many showing Mycenaean influence; the find of a single LHIIIA vase at the Pantalica North cemetery suggests some overlap with the preceding Thapsos Culture.[31] The succeeding Cassibile phase has painted pottery and further new knives and brooches. The Pantalica South period shows changes in tomb types and a widespread use of iron. The final phase is the Finocchito, from 730 to 650 BC, with pottery imitating the decorated wares used by Greek colonists.[32]

The most striking fact about the Pantalica Culture overall is that, unlike its predecessor, the vast bulk of evidence for it comes from cemeteries. As Holloway remarks, the Pantalica burial grounds 'are impressive, but the settlements connected to them are strangely ephemeral or modest in scale'.[33] It is often confidently stated, as Brea does, that settlement was concentrated at a few large urban centres surrounded by thousands of burials. Yet most cemeteries have produced no associated housing. The sole candidate for urban status is the partially excavated site of Pantalica itself. Here there is a large building, the 'prince's palace', but the pottery from it belongs

exclusively to the Pantalica North period. Traces of other buildings
and an enclosing wall are visible, though the settlement remains are
still meagre.[34] Despite this, it is claimed that the population of the
site can be estimated from the tombs as 1000–2000.

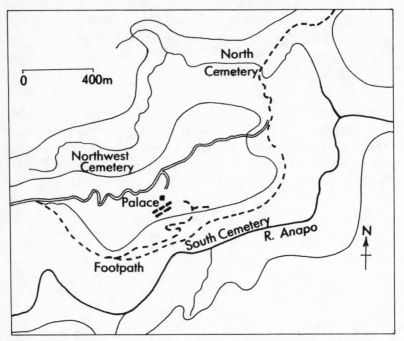

FIG. 2:5   General plan of the cemeteries and settlement at Pantalica, Sicily (*after
Trump, 1974*).

Elsewhere, substantial domestic activity is limited to the Cassa-
bile and Finocchito phases. Overall the settlement evidence is very
patchy for a culture supposedly lasting 600 years. A welcome
discovery, however, is a series of Cassibile coastal settlements in
similar locations to those occupied by the Thapsos Culture. These
new finds upset the traditional picture, drawn by Brea, of a society
devastated by warfare and deserting the coast. As Holloway realized, these settlements fall in a period 'when, according to the
"Dark Ages" theory, conditions should have been no better and
possibly worse'.[35]

While these discoveries partially alleviate the lack of occupation
evidence, at the same time they fatally undermine the standard
chronology. This places a gap of 120–320 years between the

Cassibile phase and the Greek settlement – which has to be filled by the Pantalica South period. Against this, a definite pattern is emerging from the new finds: one in which the remains of Greek towns rest directly on Cassibile settlements. It is, in theory, possible that the coast was abandoned in Pantalica North times, reoccupied in the Cassibile phase, abandoned again in the Pantalica South period, then finally resettled by the Greek colonists. However, the Greek historian Thucydides (writing in the 5th century BC) states clearly that in 733 BC the Greek colonists at Syracuse expelled its native occupants.[36] Either he was wrong, or something has removed all traces of Pantalica South activity but spared a village of Cassibile huts, many of which were burnt down.[37] Neither alternative is plausible. Instead, the very existence of Pantalica South as a distinct chronological period must now be regarded as doubtful. If it were to be scrapped, then this single step would remove at least a century from the length of the Sicilian Iron Age. How feasible is this drastic reduction? Some indication of its viability can be given by examining the sequences elsewhere in the Western Mediterranean.

Lipari and the Ausonians

Between Italy and Sicily, and having strong ties with both, lie the Aeolian islands. Major excavations on the acropolis of Lipari, the largest island, have produced an invaluable sequence.[38] Here the Middle Bronze Age, with Thapsos type pottery from Sicily, is followed by the Ausonian Culture, divided into two phases. The first reflects new influences from mainland Italy with the arrival of Sub-Apennine wares. In the destruction level of the Ausonian I settlement there are Proto-Villanovan sherds; yet surprisingly, Proto-Villanovan Culture did not take over, as the following Ausonian II is still Sub-Apennine in tradition. A real cultural mix is seen in the Ausonian II period cemetery below the acropolis – although the dead were cremated (a Proto-Villanovan practice), the grave-goods are Sub-Apennine types.[39]

Thus the Lipari excavations further confirm the overlapping of Sub-Apennine and Proto-Villanovan already seen in mainland Italy. Holloway, for example, believes that 'this and related discoveries illustrate, in a way rarely seen in archaeological contexts, the contemporary existence of two diverse groups.'[40]

The difficulties do not end here. In the final publication of the excavations at the Lipari acropolis, the Ausonian I–II transition is set at *c.* 1230 BC by the finds of Mycenaean imports.[41] This seems most unlikely, given the conventional end-date of Ausonian II around 850 BC, based on the association of Ausonian II type bronzes with Cassibile pottery in Sicily.[42] Worse still, the new evidence from Sicily clearly indicates that the Cassibile period belongs to an even later date – the combination of these two connections (the Mycenaean and Sicilian) would give Ausonian II an impossibly long span of 500 years.

Recently, the American archaeologist Hubert Allen transferred fifty years from the Cassibile period to the Pantalica South phase. His satisfied conclusion was that, with this minor adjustment, 'the last major uncertainty in the Sicilian Iron Age chronology may have been resolved'.[43] On the contrary, it seems as though the problems are only just beginning: as long as the high, Mycenaean-derived, dates for Late Bronze Age Italy are retained, it is difficult to see any sensible chronology being produced.

Malta after the temples

An equally deep recession seems to have taken place in Malta at this time. The famous Neolithic temples fell out of use before the Bronze Age, to be succeeded by the Tarxien Cemetery phase with scattered radiocarbon dates of 2500–1500 BC. After this, although Maltese prehistory can be tied to Middle Bronze Age Sicily and the Mycenaean world, there are strikingly few remains until the Carthaginian (Punic) settlement of the early 7th century BC.[44]

The Borġ in-Nadur Culture, characterized by promontory or hilltop villages defended by massive walls, fills the time between the Tarxien Cemetery period and the Carthaginian colonization.[45] The backdating of the Tarxien Cemetery phase by radiocarbon results[46] meant that Borġ in-Nadur had to start in 1500 BC to avoid creating a gap in the sequence. From his excavations at the Borġ in-Nadur promontory fort itself, David Trump divided the culture into three periods.[47] Phase 1 lacks external connections, but early Phase 2 vases are found in Thapsos Culture tombs on Sicily with LHIIIA Mycenaean ware, giving a 14th-century date. However, Borġ in-Nadur 3 pottery also reached Thapsos in the 10th to 9th-century Cassibile period settlement, and in the Mtarfa rock-cut pit, on Malta itself, is even found with 7th-century Punic finds.[48]

John Evans, who discovered many of the prehistoric remains of Malta, accepted that the Mtarfa evidence proved that Borġ in-Nadur did last until the 7th century BC. However, he saw the difficulties this raised, even with his low date (around 1300 BC) for the start of the period:

> Phase 3 would seem to have survived, if we take literally the evidence of the material . . . at Mtarfa, until the beginning of the Punic period. The total span of the culture would therefore be a period of some six hundred years or more.[49]

Thus, the pottery and metalwork of Malta appears to have remained almost unchanged for most of the Borġ in-Nadur period.[50] Even if the Mtarfa finds are misleading, those in Sicily still give a late date for Borġ in-Nadur Phase 3, and in any case nothing else exists to fill the time before the Carthaginians. The current chronology suggests a long period of inactivity in Malta, but this contrasts strangely with the evidence for overseas trade. Shortening the Late Bronze Age, as already proposed for Italy and Sicily, would certainly make more sense of Maltese prehistory.

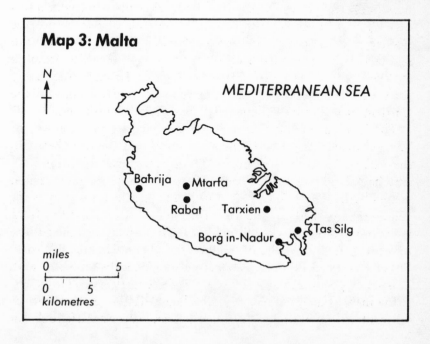

Map 3: Malta

Dating the Nuragic towers and bronzes of Sardinia

Sardinia is famous for its *nuraghi*, the great stone towers which still dominate the landscape as they did in the Bronze Age (see Plate 7). Some 7000 survive today out of over 20,000 originally. The most complex *nuraghi* have central towers and outer walls with corner towers, suggesting to some observers that garrisons of up to 200 manned the defences.[51] Around the *nuraghi* sprawling villages built up, both defended and dominated by the local chieftains in the towers.

Certain rituals of the *nuraghi*-dwellers were carried out at sacred wells. Among the cult objects consigned to their depths were bronzes. A flourishing local bronze industry developed, producing a wide range of weapons, ornaments and tools, but more notably hundreds of figurines vividly illustrating ancient Sardinian life (see Plate 8). People (wrestlers, boxers, warriors, peasants, women, children and a musician), animals, *nuraghi*, boats, and food and drink are all depicted.[52]

The art of bronze and stone sculpture in Sardinia is often thought to have been influenced or even introduced by the Phoenicians, but the earliest archaeological evidence for Phoenicians on the island falls in the late 8th century. At Tharros an abandoned Nuragic settlement was replaced by a Phoenician colony and a *tophet* (a graveyard of thousands of urns containing the cremations of small children or animals) around 725 BC. South of here was a vast cemetery first used in the early 7th century, devastated and de-spoiled by treasure-hunters in the 1850s.[53]

Unfortunately, in the period between contacts with the Eastern Mediterranean any chronology has to rely on less easily dated local materials. The relative chronology of Sardinian prehistory is large-ly based on the first modern excavation of a *nuraghe* at Su Nuraxi, Barumini.[54] Giovanni Lilliu, the excavator, used a combination of structural phases and pottery typology to construct a general Nuragic sequence.

Until recently the absolute chronology involved three stages, starting with an Archaic Nuragic period (1450–950 BC) of simple *nuraghi* and plain pottery. The Middle Nuragic (950–500 BC) fol-lowed this, with complex *nuraghi* and new, richly decorated fine wares. The Late Nuragic, from 500 to 238 BC (the date of Rome's conquest of Sardinia), had firm Carthaginian links. Working back

Map 4: Sardinia

TYRRHENIAN SEA

Santa Maria

Bosa

Monte Prama • Serri

Tharros

• Torralba

Barumini

Monte Sirai

Sulcis

Sarrok
Nora

N

miles
0   50

0   50
kilometres

MEDITERRANEAN SEA

from here, the chronology depended on vague analogies with the pottery and metalwork of Italy and Sicily, and a scatter of Sardinian finds from the latter.[55]

This picture was drastically revised by radiocarbon dating, used by Lilliu to construct a new chronology which is now standard.[56] He raised the dates of the Archaic Nuragic to 1500–1200 BC, the

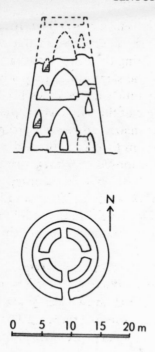

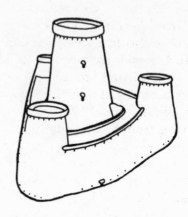

FIG. 2:6 Plan, section drawing and reconstruction of the complex *nuraghe* at Santu Antine di Torralba (*after Balmuth 1984*).

Middle Nuragic to 1200–900 and the Late Nuragic to 700–500. Lilliu's high chronology was apparently confirmed by the discovery of several hundred sherds of Mycenaean pottery (LHIIIB–C), along with local decorated fine wares, in the complex *nuraghe* at Sarrok.[57] At first glance the agreement between this Mycenaean link and radiocarbon dates suggests that all is well with Sardinian chronology. Nevertheless, only five usable radiocarbon results exist for the Archaic Nuragic, and these – despite coming from charcoal samples with their natural bias towards giving high dates (see Appendix 1)[58] – still allow the period to end around 1000 BC, two centuries later than Lilliu's estimate.

The new Sardinian chronology leaves many questions unanswered. Dating the bronze industry of Sardinia by comparison with Eastern Mediterranean examples involves some acute difficulties. The conflict is between those arguing for Late Bronze Age Cypriot or Mycenaean origins and others who favour a much later Phoenician inspiration.

The problem is encapsulated by the hoard from Santa Maria in the north of the island, which can be dated with equal ease anywhere between the 13th and the 8th century BC! The British Museum team examining this discovery concluded that it was probably collected over 200 years, favouring the 12th–11th centuries over the 11th–10th as a date.[59] At the same time, they admit there is also firm evidence suggesting much lower dates for the hoard, outside the range they allow. One of the Santa Maria pieces was a miniature bronze boat of a type manufactured in Sardinia, several examples of which are known from Etruscan 7th- and even 6th-century sites.[60] Michel Gras has proposed that they reached Etruria from Sardinia during the late 9th or early 8th century and were preserved as heirlooms until their deposition. The compilers of the British Museum report saw Gras' heirloom model as a 'desperate measure, as its author properly recognizes, but one that is rendered inevitable'.[61]

Yet Francesca Ridgway, one contributor to this study, has recently come to terms with this unsatisfactory if 'inevitable' conclusion, and now claims that 'Gras has shown convincingly how the 7th- and 6th-century contexts for some of the model boats in tombs . . . must be regarded as secondary [i.e. heirlooms],

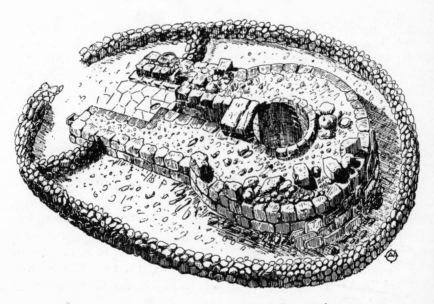

FIG. 2:7 The nuragic well at Santa Vittoria di Serri; the sacred waters were roofed over and a flight of steps led down to the well-head from a paved area (*from Taramelli 1914*).

because the production of these bronzes cannot have gone on for too long'.[62]

Gras' theory is, of course, simply his opinion of how long styles should last. One could equally well argue that all the production should lie between 800 and 600 BC. The idea that late examples must be heirlooms is a product of the chronology accepted by the British Museum team, which places these miniature boats several centuries earlier in Sardinia. David Ridgway tried to find a way out of this quandary by arguing that craftsmen from Cyprus settled in Sardinia during the 12th–10th centuries BC and thereafter continued to make bronzes in the Cypriot tradition.[63] However, they seem to have been remarkably inactive for the first two or three centuries. One can only agree with Fulvia Lo Schiavo that 'the problem is still open'.[64]

The alternative approach to filling this gap has been to try to push back the Phoenician presence in Sardinia to meet the Late Bronze Age, using the occasional finds of eastern bronzes which may predate the colonization period and the three earliest Phoenician inscriptions from the island.[65] The most important of these, the Nora Stone, is a substantial piece with eight lines of text. It is generally assigned to the 9th or 8th century BC on the basis of comparisons of the form of the letters with Phoenician inscriptions of known date, but its significance is much debated.

The three main authorities – William Albright, Frank Cross and Brian Peckham – have produced different translations of the text and thus conflicting views of its importance. Cross and Albright agree that the inscription records a Phoenician victory (according to Cross under Pygmalion, King of Tyre), and subsequent settlement at Nora. Cross believes it implies 'Phoenician colonists with military forces capable of defending them'. Albright even suggested that it was part of a public decree erected in 'a town of considerable importance'. Peckham, however, argues that the stone was set up by a defeated Phoenician army driven by storm on to the coast of Sardinia and thanking the god Pummay for their arrival on dry land: 'the fact that it is a dedicatory inscription suggests that their survival in Sardinia was a bit of luck, and does not imply that their stay was of any significant duration'.[66]

Which of these are we to believe? Archaeology strongly supports Peckham, as the earliest occupation at Nora is around 650 BC – certainly there is no possibility of Albright's 'important town'

FIG. 2:8 (Centre) A warrior of the Shardana, one of the mysterious 'Sea Peoples' (see p. 18), as depicted on Egyptian reliefs conventionally dated to the 13th and 12th centuries BC. Egyptian references to the Shardana continue until the early 11th century. (Right and left) Bronze figurines of warriors from Sardinia usually dated to the 9th–7th century BC. Sardinia was known to the Phoenicians as *Šrdn* (Shardan). While it is tempting to draw some connection between the two groups, they are presently separated by a gap of some three centuries (*from Maspero 1896*).

existing in the 8th century, let alone the 9th.[67] The absence of material for earlier 1st-millennium BC Sardinia is not filled by these few finds of doubtful significance. None of the Phoenician evidence from Sardinia requires the Iron Age to stretch back to 1000 BC, and nothing rules out the lowering of Late Bronze Age chronology suggested here.

The Kingdom of Tartessos

The southern part of the Iberian peninsula contrasts with the other areas surveyed here in showing no Mycenaean presence in the 2nd millennium BC.[68] Only much later was it affected by Phoenician colonization, while western Iberia has always looked to the Atlantic

seaboard. Late Bronze Age remains are scarce, as Glyn Daniel and
John Evans note in their survey of Mediterranean prehistory:

> . . . the last few centuries of the second millennium B.C. and the
> beginning of the first, are the most obscure in the prehistory of
> the Peninsula. From the scattered finds which exist it is extremely
> difficult to piece together an intelligible picture . . . [69]

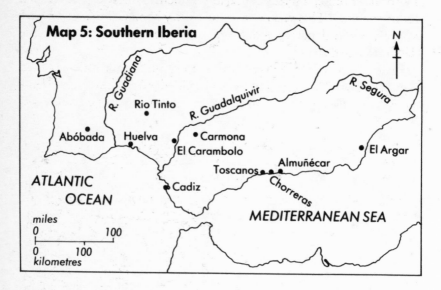

In the absence of reliable evidence, the usual view is that Early
Bronze Age material 'persisted without much change until after the
end of the 2nd millennium'.[70]

Changes in the south during the 1st millennium BC are generally
attributed to outside influences. The north-east of the peninsula was
apparently settled by Urnfield Culture groups from France between the 12th and 8th centuries,[71] but their influence reached the
south only in the 8th century BC. From 1200 BC western Iberia was
in contact with the Atlantic bronze industry of North-west Europe,
but it was not until after 900 BC that local versions of the imported
types were produced on any scale.[72] Weapons of this industry –
swords, spearheads and helmets – are depicted on Portuguese
gravestones. Later examples often show the warrior as a stick figure
surrounded by his possessions, occasionally with inscriptions in a
local alphabetic script, as yet undeciphered.

By far the most significant external influence was Phoenician colonization on the southern coast. The earliest archaeological evidence comes from Chorreras, usually dated to around 800 BC; nearby is Toscanos, settled about 750 BC, with a warehouse of *c.* 700 BC containing Phoenician storage jars and Greek Protocorinthian and Attic pottery.[73] The increasing Phoenician interest in the area stemmed from its rich mineral resources. At the famous Rio Tinto silver mines a settlement using Phoenician pottery developed about 700 BC.[74] This wealth was the reality behind the fabled riches of the powerful native Kingdom of Tartessos described by the classical Greek writers.

Earlier Phoenician contacts are often claimed, but little exists to support them. Two types of literary evidence are frequently cited – the colonization of Cadiz and biblical references to the country of

FIG. 2:9 Burial stela from Abóbada in Portugal dating to *c.* 650 BC (*after Harrison 1988*).

Tarshish. Classical historians dated the foundation of Cadiz at 1110 BC by reference to the Trojan War (see Appendix 2), but the only objects there that could possibly predate 600 BC are three religious statuettes dredged up from the sea. Moreover, the first Phoenician settlements or even stray finds in the Cadiz region are no earlier than 770 BC.[75] It is impossible to believe that a colony could have existed here for 300 years before it had any impact on the surrounding area.

According to the Bible, King Solomon of the mid-10th century BC 'had at sea a navy of Tarshish with the navy of Hiram: once in three years came the navy of Tarshish, bringing gold, and silver, ivory and apes, and peacocks' (1 Kgs 10:22). Because 'Tarshish' resembles 'Tartessos' many equate the two. However, the cargoes carried are hardly Spanish, while another biblical reference to 'Tarshish ships' describes them as being built on the Red Sea coast of Israel (2 Chr. 20:36). The whole argument is extremely flimsy,

FIG. 2:10   Phoenician ivory from Carmona, Spain. Note the warrior's Greek helmet (*after Barnett 1982*).

and indeed recent studies show that the Tarshish/Tartessos identification was first put forward in the 16th century AD by Spain to bolster its claims to world leadership against those of Portugal.[76]

Finally, there have been attempts to backdate material to bridge the gap between the supposed literary evidence and actual archaeological finds. At Carmona rich tombs were unearthed containing bronze, silver and gold vessels and ornaments, imported glass and pottery and a major group of ivory carvings. Albright, the great biblical scholar, compared the Carmona ivories to those in a cache from Megiddo in Palestine conventionally dated to the 12th century BC (but see Chapter 8). Accordingly, he placed the Spanish finds before 900 BC.[77] The Carmona cemetery belongs to the 'Orientalizing' period of Tartessian Culture, usually dated to 750–580 BC;[78] thus Albright's attempt to backdate the ivories would set the Phoenician colonization of Spain much earlier.

In the event, every authority except Albright dates the Carmona ivories to the 7th century BC. The Phoenician and Greek pottery

from other Carmona tombs is all of that time, the ivories themselves resemble 7th-century examples from Carthage and the Temple of Hera on the Greek island of Samos, and one Carmona ivory
depicts a type of Greek helmet never shown on pottery before
700 BC.[79] Altogether, there is absolutely no sound evidence from
archaeology or literary sources for Phoenicians in Iberia before
800 BC. Albright, having stated his unacceptable 10th-century placing for the Carmona ivories (without referring to any of the
contradictory evidence), tried to explain away the obvious lack of
support for his position:

> Scholars who oppose such a high dating would do well to survey
> the Spanish evidence without prejudice, noting the almost com-
> plete absence of any stratigraphical evidence, as well as the fact
> that Tartessus is presumably under the waters of the Mediterra-
> nean and that it will be difficult, if not impracticable, ever to carry
> on sufficient soundings under modern Cadiz to locate the
> Phoenician factory . . . Negative evidence is still far too in-
> adequate to justify following it against the clear-cut agreement of
> classical and biblical tradition with such archaeological indica-
> tions as we have given.[80]

Current Spanish opinion decisively rejects Albright's views, as
archaeological knowledge of Phoenician Spain has advanced enor-
mously since he wrote, and the few remaining believers in early
colonists are reduced to hoping that 'something will turn up'.

Invisible exporters – the Phoenicians in the West

The date at which the Phoenicians first reached the West has been
the subject of intense debate over the last hundred years. As in
Spain, the division is between those relying on literary traditions
and others who give priority to archaeology. In North Africa, both
Lixus, beyond the Pillars of Heracles, and Utica were supposedly
founded before 1100 BC. However, at each site the earliest finds
come from late 8th- or early 7th-century tombs.[81] A yawning gap
of 400 years therefore exists between one understanding of the
literary evidence and the archaeological remains.

While it used to be feasible to believe that 2nd-millennium
remains would eventually appear, this becomes increasingly less
likely with each new excavation. Instead, the high chronologists

now argue that although no permanent settlements occurred before
1000 BC the classical sources do demonstrate that Phoenician traders
were already active by then. The elusiveness of the trading posts
that should accompany this commercial presence is supposedly
explained by their flimsy nature, as Vincenzo Tusa argues for Sicily:

> Since they were not towns but ports of call, it is logical that
> nothing should remain on the site and hence nothing of
> archaeological interest is to be found. The kind of trade the
> Phoenicians engaged in did not call for permanent structures but
> perhaps merely a few tents at the various ports they called at to
> trade with the local population.[82]

Supporters of this theory have brought the Greek writer Herodotus, 'Father of History', into the debate. He records Punic ships
practising 'silent trade' on the west coast of Africa in his day:

> The Carthaginians also say that there is a place in Libya, and
> people living in it, beyond the Pillars of Heracles. When they, the
> Carthaginians, come there and disembark their cargo, they range
> it along the seashore and go back again to their boats and light a
> smoke signal. The natives, as soon as they see the smoke, come
> down to the shore and then deposit gold to pay for the merchan-
> dise and retreat again, away from the goods. The Carthaginians
> disembark and look; if they think that the price deposited is fair
> for the merchandise, they take it up and go home again.[83]

It is regularly inferred that the Phoenicians used similar methods in
the early 1st millennium BC.

How relevant is this passage to Phoenician activity in the Western
Mediterranean? Medieval Arab writers record dumb barter being
used to exchange gold in West Africa, but other items were traded
normally; the same may be true for the Carthaginians. It is also clear
that the cultural gap between the Phoenicians and Mediterranean
societies was far smaller than in the case Herodotus recounts. The
situations are simply not comparable. Moreover, a port of trade has
now been found on Mogador Island, off the Moroccan coast, with
Punic and Greek pottery of the 7th century BC onwards. There are
no houses, but rather a build-up of debris from intermittent visits
over many years. As Brian Warmington concludes: 'Mogador
looks precisely like the sort of bartering place described in our
sources.'[84]

There is no doubt that archaeology has now demonstrated a solid Phoenician presence in the Western Mediterranean during the late 8th century BC, but sites and even single finds earlier than this are rare and often impossible to date definitely. There is no good reason to imagine sustained Phoenician contacts with the West before the 8th century.

Major disagreements over the chronology of Phoenician activity extend even into the 8th century BC. Classical authors put the foundation of Carthage by Tyre between 846 and 746 BC (see Appendix 2). While the most reliable source, Menander of Tyre as transmitted by the Jewish historian Josephus (1st century AD), gives no precise date, he does say that the expedition left Tyre in the seventh year of King Pygmalion's reign, led by his sister Princess Elissa. Fortunately, Pygmalion can be dated to within a few years by links between the Tyrian king list and Assyrian records and the voyage to Carthage be thus placed between 805 and 799 BC.[85]

Even with this fairly low dating for the foundation there is still a significant gap of about a hundred years between history and archaeology. Several excavations have revealed houses of the late 8th century BC, but not before.[86] To fill this lacuna it is often claimed that earlier burials exist. The strongest case was presented by Pierre Cintas in his definitive work on Punic archaeology, where he assigned several tombs to the period 800–700 BC. They contain scarabs with the names of early 8th-century Pharaohs as well as pottery like that from Phoenician tombs and settlements then dated to the 10th to 9th centuries.[87] Working along similar lines, Albright compared early Carthaginian ceramics with those of 10th-century Megiddo. He found himself in some difficulty here, as the Megiddo pots date to 150 years before the traditional beginnings of Carthage, but glossed over the problem, to his own satisfaction at least:

> We must, of course, assume that this ware was brought to North Africa not later than the late tenth or the early ninth century B.C., and that it continued to be manufactured until the eighth century, some time after it had disappeared in Phoenicia. Such phenomena are exceedingly common.[88]

The key site for understanding the chronology of Punic Carthage is the Precinct of Tanit, near the port, a typical Phoenician *tophet*, containing thousands of burial urns. The earlier use of the *tophet* is divided into Tanit I and II phases, separated by a sterile clay layer. Tanit I and II pottery types are also found in tombs and so provide a general sequence for the whole city.[89] Cintas's '8th-century' burials are found with Tanit I pottery. Their true date is clearly shown by finds from the so-called Sailor's Chapel, a small shrine below the lowest level of Tanit I. Under the wall and floor of the building are two probable foundation deposits containing vessels copying Late Geometric and Early Protocorinthian styles dated to *c.* 740–710 BC.[90]

This later date for the beginning of Carthage now also has support from Phoenicia. Recent excavations at Tyre, the mother city of Carthage, produced identical pottery dated there to *c.* 750–700 BC by an inscribed Egyptian vessel (see Fig. 5:5).[91] Albright's Megiddo dates are again out of step with other areas. The general conclusion is now that no 8th-century tombs have been found at Carthage, contrary to Cintas's earlier hopes.[92]

However, a foundation date for Carthage in the late 8th century BC conflicts directly with the literary evidence. The account of Menander, via Josephus, is plausible and gives a date within tight limits, around 800 BC. An apparent gap thus remains. Attempts to explain the anomaly vary, but this example by Sabatino Moscati, the foremost expert on the Phoenicians, is typical: ' . . . a few generations would quite naturally have elapsed between the dis-embarkation of the first settlers and the production of works of art destined to survive for centuries'.[93] The Tunisian archaeologist Mohammed Fantar gives the most comprehensive list of possible factors:

> . . . the soil of the Punic capital has never been subjected to systematic, detailed and exhaustive excavations. Furthermore, the earliest signs of occupation of a given terrain are often hard to identify. Light constructions, perishable materials, the early and hesitant occupation of an area by people homesick for their native land, the destruction and reutilization of dismantled structures – these are all factors of development which tend to cover up the first signs of settlement.[94]

Wide-ranging though they are, these excuses for the lack of 8th-century remains are unconvincing. 'Works of art' or 'hesitant occupation' are not relevant. Houses of some sort, pottery production and the worship of the gods would all have started immediately, soon followed by the first burials. Moreover, Menander records that Carthage was founded by a princess, who would hardly have accepted a new life as a squatter. The inevitable conclusion has been drawn by the chronologist Molly Miller:

> The archaeological evidence from Carthage, where the earliest dateable pottery . . . is perhaps a century later than Menandros' foundation-date, gives rise to the suspicion that the Greeks may have mistranslated or misunderstood the name of the colony ascribed to the seventh year of Pygmalion . . .[95]

A solution to the problem was first proposed by Emil Forrer, who argued that Menander's *qrthdst*, or New City, was not Carthage, but Kition on Cyprus.[96] The existence of a *qrthdst* in Cyprus is proved by 7th-century Assyrian records. This Cypriot *qrthdst* having changed its name by Menander's time, he would naturally have assumed '*qrthdst*' referred to the 'Carthage in Libya' he knew. Given this, nothing remains to support a foundation of Carthage before about 720 BC.

Nor is there any reason to see Phoenicians in the West much earlier than 750 BC. Despite all attempts to the contrary, the clear gap between the Phoenicians and Greeks of the 8th century BC and the Mycenaeans of the 12th still leaves a conspicuous void in the prehistory of the Western Mediterranean. A different solution to this problem emerges quite clearly from our review: to lower the date of the Late Bronze in the Western Mediterranean. This would be favoured on both archaeological and historical grounds, but cannot be done without challenging Mycenaean chronology. Does the same conundrum arise in other areas dated by finds of Late Helladic pottery?

CHAPTER 3

Beware the Greeks Bearing Gifts

The Balkans, at the cross-roads of Europe and Asia, have witnessed some of the greatest power struggles between Old World civilizations. They were the scene of protracted conflict between Christians and Muslims in medieval times. In the 5th century BC the armies of the 'Great Kings' of Persia, Darius and Xerxes, marched westward through these lands on their way to humiliating defeats at the hands of the Greeks. Here was the Kingdom of Macedonia – homeland of Alexander the Great, the most successful general of the ancient world, who led his superbly trained troops to countless victories, first south to Greece, then on to the east as far as India. It was only his untimely death at the age of thirty-two (in 323 BC) that prevented him from adding Italy and even Carthage to his conquests.

More than 4000 years before Alexander, an advanced Balkan metalwork industry already existed. The earliest copper mine in the world, at Rudna Glava in Yugoslavia, was in production by this time.[1] The roughly contemporary cemetery of Varna in Bulgaria contained large numbers of beautiful ornaments delicately crafted from local gold. These remarkable grave-goods suggested to Colin Renfrew[2] a high level of social organization, perhaps the first culture ever to evolve beyond a village-based egalitarian community.

The Balkans became the primary source of metal for areas both to the north and the south. Early in the Late Bronze Age (usually dated c. 1400 BC) a vigorous industry producing bronze weapons and tools, as well as ornaments of gold, has left impressive evidence in the shape of massive hoards, some containing thousands of items. It was probably this mineral wealth that heightened Mycenaean interest in the region towards the end of the period.

Given their strategic position between the surrounding 'securely' dated areas of Central Europe and Greece, it should have been easy to establish an absolute chronology for the distinctive Late Bronze to Iron Age cultures of the Balkans on the basis of imported items discovered in sealed contexts. However, this has not been the case – indeed, archaeologists have yet to link together the cultural phases revealed at different sites in a single agreed sequence.

Traditionally, Balkan archaeologists have relied on general synchronisms with Mycenaean Greece for their chronologies. But
these are only rarely given by direct contacts – i.e. through the
small quantities of imported Mycenaean wares or locally made
copies. Instead, they mostly have to be provided via the Urnfield
Culture of Central Europe to the west or through Troy to the east.
Later correlations can be established by the pottery of late 7th-
century BC Greek colonists in Thrace and the Black Sea.[3]

Between these two boundaries lies a varied but coherent group of
native pottery styles called the 'Balkan Complex'. This links sites
across the area in a relative sequence but itself supplies no absolute
dates, a difficulty not relieved by occasional associated finds of
Greek Protogeometric pottery in Macedonia.[4] The Complex is
defined by a combination of sometimes exotic and occasionally
grotesque wares, with knobbed ('Buckelkeramik'), channelled,
fluted, stamped and incised decoration used on a range of shapes
including jugs, two-handled urns, bowls and cups. Across the
Balkans the dominant ware varies from site to site.[5]

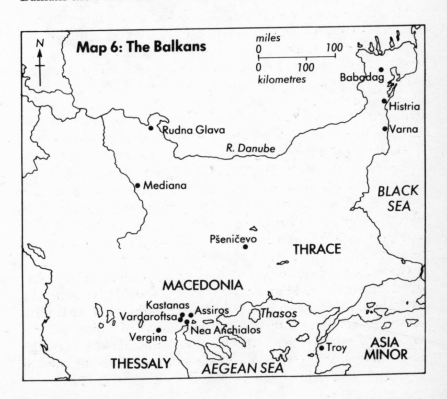

Map 6: The Balkans

FIG. 3:1 Balkan Complex
pottery: a. incised ware
from Vergina in Macedonia
(*after Andronikos 1969*);
b. channelled ware from
Vergina (*after Andronikos
1969*); c. stamped ware
from Troy (*after Garašanin
1982*); d. knobbed ware
from Troy (*from Schliemann
1881*).

In common with the 'transitional' Bronze to Iron Age cultures of
the Mediterranean (see Chapter 2), the Balkan Complex has various
links falling at both ends of its date-range which have been used to
pull the material as a whole to one chronological extreme or the
other. The consequence of looking back to Central Europe for
'fixed points' has been to place the Balkan Complex at the higher
end of this range.

The European connection

Deriving absolute dates from Central European chronology requires a tortuous series of comparisons involving material from
several sites dotted across south-east Europe. The linchpin in this
process is the extensive riverside settlement of Mediana in eastern
Yugoslavia, which stands at the boundary between Balkan and
Central European cultures. Finds from the earliest houses here

include distinctive bowls clearly influenced by the Urnfield Culture pottery of south-east Hungary.[6] The first phase at Mediana is thus tied in to the great expansion of the Urnfield Culture across Europe during the 13th–12th centuries BC (Bronze D–Hallstatt A; see Table 1:1).[7]

Mediana Phases II and III continued the pottery style of the earlier settlement with the significant addition of a new shape – the 'turban dish'. Such dishes provide a link to the lower levels at Babadag, a lakeside fortress on the fertile flood-plain near the mouth of the Danube defended by massive earthworks. The common elements of the Mediana II–III and Babadag assemblages, both of which belong to the Balkan Complex, are also seen in sites across northern Albania, Bulgaria, Macedonia and as far south-east as Troy in

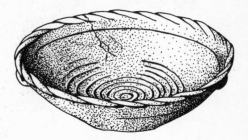

FIG. 3:2   Turban dish from Woischwitz in Czechoslovakia. Finds of such dishes at Babadag in Rumania help to tie the Balkan Complex to the Central European Hallstatt sequence (*after Childe 1929*).

Anatolia.[8] On the evidence of Mediana, this material must largely postdate the Urnfield Culture.

Attempts have been made over the years to sharpen this chronological picture by tracing later connections with Hallstatt Culture pottery and metalwork from Central Europe.[9] These synchronisms are generally far too broad to be of any real value. In any case, there are relatively few bronzes known from the 11th to 9th centuries BC. As Milutin Garašanin has said, 'Despite intensive study there are considerable gaps in our knowledge'; those finds that do exist occur almost always in hoards or as single finds rather than on stratified settlements.[10] On the other hand, certain types manufactured at this low ebb of the bronze industry, especially knives, closely resemble Mycenaean examples. However, Harding is clear that 'the late date of the Balkan pieces appears to rule out any direct connection'.[11] The next acceptable contacts are with the Hallstatt C cultures of Europe and the city-states of Archaic Greece in the 7th century BC.

The problem is that all the dates given by these correlations, impressive as the cumulative effect may seem, depend ultimately on

Greek chronology. Sandars has drawn attention to the ironically roundabout reasoning involved in using comparisons with Central European material to date the Balkan Late Bronze and Early Iron Ages:

> The chain of evidence from which these dates (however rough) are calculated has therefore to be traced back up the length of the Danube into southern Germany, over the Alps and down into Italy, and finally back to the Aegean and Egypt. This is a long detour from the mouth of the Danube, itself only a short direct voyage from Troy and the Aegean; and if ever it should be possible to find more direct methods of dating between Rumania and the eastern Mediterranean, they would stand a chance of far greater reliability.[12]

The method by which dates for the Balkan Complex are derived from Central Europe has too many inherent difficulties to make it a viable form of absolute dating. However, there are more direct means available to link the Balkans to Greek chronology. First, we can turn eastward to examine the famous site of Troy, which, as Sandars implies, ought to provide a more reliable chronological fix.

Trojans and troublesome Greek imports

The sack of Troy by the Greeks under the command of Agamemnon, King of Mycenae, has launched a thousand articles; the search for the city of Homer's *Iliad* will certainly continue to fascinate archaeologists for years to come. Schliemann correctly identified the massive mound of Hissarlik as the site of Troy, but which of the superimposed cities he found should be associated with the time of the Trojan War remains unclear. The rival candidates are currently the cities of Troy VI and VIIa. While the earlier city and its magnificent defensive walls provide a better match with Homer's account, it was apparently destroyed by an earthquake and predates the high point of Mycenaean power in the 13th century BC. The later city was burnt down but its poor remains fail to measure up to the description of the mighty city of Priam given in the *Iliad*.[13]

The dates proposed by classical writers for the destruction of Troy range from the mid-14th century to as late as 1127 BC, but none is based on solid evidence and all seem to involve a measure of

FIG. 3:3   The walls of Troy VI, superimposed by houses belonging to the settlement of Troy VII (*from Breasted 1916*).

exaggeration (see Appendix 2). Any attempt to use them to test the alternative archaeological dates for the Fall of Troy is therefore pointless.

This problem aside, the site presents other difficulties that are just as challenging. Despite numerous excavations, no strata have yet been discovered representing the period between Troy VIIb, usually linked with 12th-century Mycenaean imports (LHIIIC), and the beginning of Troy VIII, dated by Archaic Greek imports to 700 BC.[14] The classical scholar Denys Page remarked on the strange gap which results from this chronology:

> There is nothing at Troy to fill this huge lacuna. For 2000 years men had left traces of their living there; some chapters were brief and obscure, but there was never yet a chapter left wholly blank. Now at last there is silence, profound and prolonged for 400 years; we are asked, surely not in vain, to believe that Troy lay 'virtually unoccupied' for this long period of time.[15]

Yet despite the apparent lapse of several centuries, there is every indication of continuity between Troy VIIb and VIII. The excavator, Carl Blegen, could detect no sign of a break in occupation. Furthermore, the local pottery of Troy VIII was the same distinctive, lustrous grey ware used during Troy VIIb.[16] He therefore supposed that the inhabitants of Troy VIIb abandoned it for a nearby refuge, where they continued to produce this 'Grey Minyan' pottery for 400 years before returning:

> These people carried with them the tradition of making Grey Minyan pottery and maintained it down to the end of the eighth century . . . Did some of the inhabitants perhaps then return to Troy? Though there is nothing to prove this, we do know that in the seventh century BC the Trojan citadel, which had been virtually deserted for some four centuries, suddenly blossomed into life once more with occupants who were still able to make Grey Minyan pottery.[17]

Despite twenty-five years of further research in the area, no sign of Blegen's hypothetical refuge site has ever been uncovered.

The problem of the Trojan 'Dark Age' has been slightly alleviated by a subsequent downdating of the material from Troy VII. Troy VIIa was once dated only to the 13th century BC, on the basis of imported Mycenaean fine wares of the LHIIIB period, but the recent identification of imported LHIIIC sherds lowers its dating into the 12th century.[18] This has a knock-on effect: the date of Troy VIIb must be pushed down, but by how much is still uncertain. This question has even wider implications, since it is at this point in the history of Troy that Balkan Complex pottery appears.[19] Kenneth Wardle, a major figure in this debate, has cast doubt on the

FIG. 3:4   Plan of the Troy VII city (*after Blegen 1963*).

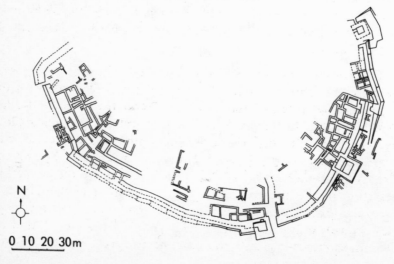

N

0 10 20 30m

identification of the very small 'LHIIIC' sherds found in the destruction layer of the latest phase of Troy VII. He also opened up the possibility that these fragments, found alongside whole vessels of Fluted and Knobbed Ware, were residual sherds from earlier periods, left lying around and then incorporated into later deposits. Therefore the Balkan Complex would be of post-Mycenaean date, an idea which is now popular,[20] and the end of Troy VIIb reduced from c. 1100 BC to some time in the 10th century BC when Knobbed Ware was still flourishing in Macedonia. Even so, we are still left with a gap in occupation of some 200–250 years.

Along with the evidence for continuity in Grey Minyan Ware between the two phases, some apparent stratigraphic anomalies suggest a radically different interpretation. The later phase of Troy VIIb contained numerous sherds, including Geometric pieces, which Blegen felt to be indistinguishable from 8th to 7th-century types common in Troy VIII. As he saw it, 'their occurrence in several areas in the stratum of Troy VIIb, below the deposits of Knobbed Ware, presents a perplexing and still unexplained problem'.[21] Furthermore, one house constructed towards the end of VIIb was still occupied in the 7th century BC. Blegen presented two possible alternatives:

> It has been argued that Troy VIIb came to its end about 1100 B.C. Generally considered, our evidence leads us to believe that a gap of 400 years exists between the end of Troy VIIb and the beginning of Troy VIII, but the possibility of a contrary view is established by the evidence of several successive floors of house 814, and also by the presence of Geometric sherds in a context of Troy VIIb.[22]

The 'contrary view' which Blegen seemed to be considering was to close the 'gap' by simply redating the end of Troy VIIb to c. 700 BC. This solution, which he shied away from, hardly seems possible within the framework of the presently accepted chronology. The same difficulty arises in respect of the schemes devised by Bernhard Hänsel and Goranka Tončeva,[23] which set the end of Troy VIIb around 800 BC in order to reduce radically the period of desertion of the site. All these would require a further drastic revision of the date of the Knobbed Ware and other Balkan Complex deposits at the end of VIIb. Unless the LHIIIC pottery found in the same stratum was also downdated, the duration of this phase would have to be stretched to a most unlikely 300–400 years, starting *c.* 1100 and ending somewhere in the 8th century BC. Simply lowering the end of Troy VIIb, without revising the whole sequence and associated chronologies, would only transform the 200 to 250-year gap into an internal problem of stratum VIIb. More likely, the problem results from a flawed absolute chronology drawn from Greece. Moreover, none of the schemes suggested so far has yet allowed us to establish any precise dating for the end of Troy VIIb, which still 'depends entirely on guesswork'.[24]

Thus, while the stratigraphy of Troy provides a partial overlap with the Balkan Complex, we are no wiser in terms of its absolute dates, beyond those traditionally offered for the LHIIIC period – that is, somewhere after 1200 BC and very likely later than 1100 BC.

Sites and stratigraphy

The extraordinarily long cultural sequence at Troy, running from Neolithic to Classical times, ensures its status as the key site in the area. However, its popularity tends to overshadow other sites of equal importance. The three settlements of Vardaroftsa, Assiros and Kastanas, together with the extensive Iron Age cemeteries on Thasos and at Vergina, are central to the debate.

The early excavations at Vardaroftsa in Macedonia were until recently thought to show that late Mycenaean material could be linked directly to the Balkan Complex.[25] At first sight its stratigraphy, with Mycenaean and Balkan Complex pottery apparently found together, seems to confirm the claimed Trojan connection between the two. Unfortunately, the rough and ready methods employed at the time of its excavation in the 1920s mean that the evidence from Vardaroftsa cannot be taken at face value.[26]

Just to the north, modern excavations at Assiros and Kastanas have provided a more reliable dating of the Balkan Complex relative to LHIIIC. At Assiros the successive Late Bronze Age settlements on the mound can be fixed by Mycenaean imports. The quantity of building remains suggested to Wardle, the excavator, that something like a century has to be allowed between Phase 6, the last Bronze Age occupation, which produced local LHIIIC imitations, and the first substantial Iron Age level, Phase 2, dated to 950–900 BC. The Balkan assemblage, which begins to appear only in Phase 2, is thus separated from the Mycenaean material by three intervening strata. The discovery of two local Protogeometric vessels in the destruction debris of Phase 2 is used to set the end of this level at 900 BC.[27] At the nearby mound of Kastanas the Balkan ceramic group even appears to postdate the earliest Protogeometric on the site. After two levels in which LHIIIC imitations were found, there was a destruction layer with late LHIIIC and Early Protogeometric pottery; the following strata contained the familiar Balkan Complex assemblage, which reached a peak in later levels when Knobbed Ware like that from Troy was adopted.[28]

On the basis of these two sites Wardle has dated the beginning of the Macedonian Iron Age to c. 1050–1000 BC and the Balkan Complex to the 10th century BC.[29] In his scheme the Complex falls not only subsequent to the last phases of Mycenaean culture, but also ceases to occupy the transition between the Bronze and Iron Ages. Instead it becomes a wholly Iron Age phenomenon.

Anthony Snodgrass has considered the length of the Balkan Complex in the light of the Vardaroftsa evidence. He proposed that local imitations of Mycenaean wares continued in the region as late as 900 BC, when the influence of Protogeometric forms began to be felt. His date of 900 BC for this changeover was obtained by a guesstimate allowing a time-lag of fifty years for Attic (Athenian) Geometric styles to reach the far north (see Chapter 5 for an account of the general background to the Attic dates). He observed that, following this, 'the Protogeometric style is succeeded not by a Geometric school but by a period of extreme obscurity in which datable Greek imports are notably rare until 600 B.C.'[30] The scarcity of Greek finds after 850 BC means that a date for the end of the Balkan Complex has not yet been established.

Even lower dates for the Balkan Complex might be suggested by the cemetery of Vergina near Assiros, later the necropolis of the great kings of Macedonia, where it appears together with locally made pottery echoing post-Mycenaean Greek styles.[31] These finds, plus comparisons with the Protogeometric of nearby Thessaly, led Snodgrass to date the Greek-influenced ware at Vergina to c. 900–750 BC at the earliest. On this basis he remarked:

The early Iron Age period of use of the Vergina cemetery must have lasted . . . three centuries at the very least. Yet over this period it shows a quite astonishing consistency in metalwork.[32]

Indeed, there is no obvious reason why such a prolific iron industry should have failed to develop over so long a period. If it were not for the conventional chronology the metalwork would probably have been allocated a considerably shorter time-span.

While the trend of recent work has been to reduce the overall dates for the Balkan Complex relative to the accepted chronology for Greece – moving it away from the Bronze Age and down into the Iron Age – the issue is not so simple.

Evidence against a lowering of the Balkan Complex *en masse* comes from Troy VIIb. Both the coarse ware found throughout this level and the Knobbed Ware from its latest phase have been compared to the so-called Barbarian Ware found in LHIIIC deposits at settlements in southern Greece.[33] This suggests that LHIIIC-style pottery was still being produced at a time when Balkan Complex pottery was in circulation. However, even the claimed similarity between these various groups of coarse wares is itself a matter for debate. Sandars reasonably concluded:

> I am pessimistic about finding particular sources for the pots from, for instance, Korakou, or Tiryns, or Sparta, or Aigeira, in any one society outside Greece. They could be found almost anywhere from the Neolithic to the Roman Iron Age.[34]

Better evidence involving actual associations is provided by the recent finds from the hillside cemeteries of Kastri on Thasos, where excavations have recovered stratified burials. In the lower level skeletons were found with local copies of LHIIIC pottery, while the upper group of inhumations was accompanied by Balkan Complex channelled vessels and occasional LHIIIC and Submycenaean imitations.[35] Clearly, no great gap in time existed between the end of the use of copies of Mycenaean pottery and the adoption of Balkan wares at Troy and Thasos. Wardle's attempt to push the whole Balkan Complex down into the Iron Age therefore cannot work.

Although we now have a better notion of the beginnings of the Balkan Complex, an outstanding difficulty is the scarcity of firm correlations between its final phases and the reasonably well dated Archaic Greek pottery sequence of the 7th century BC. All too often classical archaeologists have shown little interest in the local wares of areas affected by the great wave of Greek colonization at this time. This lack of concern is particularly unfortunate, given that the cultural stimulus provided by the colonies may have been critical in the formation of the Macedonian kingdom. Perdiccas, the first King of Macedon, seems to date to the mid-7th century BC.

An important exception is the colony planted by the Milesians at Histria, near the mouth of the Danube, excavated by Rumanian archaeologists. One of the earliest Greek settlements on the Black Sea coast, its foundation was dated by the 4th-century AD Church historian Eusebius to 657 BC. Miletus, on the Aegean shore of Turkey, was itself an early Greek colony, traditionally associated with refugees from Pylos in the Peloponnese. From the excavation of the dwellings and cemeteries at Histria came native pottery related to the latest Balkan Complex material including some with pie-crust and channelled decoration. These crude local wares were found with late 7th-century East Greek pottery imported from Rhodes and Chios by the colonists, the delicate execution of the latter providing a vivid contrast in quality.[36]

A dependency culture

Overall, the picture for the chronology of the Late Bronze and Early Iron Age Balkans is one of complete dependence, either directly or indirectly, on the agreed historical dating for Greece. As with the other European areas reviewed above, this reliance on outside sources has contributed to a highly unsatisfactory and problematic state of affairs.

The difficulties over absolute dating are in no way relieved by an almost total absence of radiocarbon results.[37] The fixed points given by Greece at either end of the sequence leave us with a complex of material which, within the present chronology, is required to cover at least four centuries. During this long period there is little sign of change in either metallurgy or pottery, both of which developed rapidly in the Late Bronze Age but apparently stagnated after the introduction of iron-working and the coming together of the Balkan Complex. Once the length of this cultural depression is fully accepted by archaeologists it will prove extremely difficult to explain, and may well lead to the creation of a Balkan 'Dark Age' to match those elsewhere across the Mediterranean. To see how these widespread problems have arisen, we need to take a long hard look at the chronology of Greece itself.

CHAPTER 4

The Dark Age Mysteries of Greece

So far we have reviewed a considerable range of difficulties in understanding the prehistoric cultures of Central, Eastern and Southern Europe, which depend for their dating on synchronisms with the accepted chronology of Late Bronze and Iron Age Greece. These problems are usually dealt with in a piecemeal fashion, treating individual cultures or geographical areas separately. When they are considered together a disturbing pattern is seen to repeat itself – one involving frequent lacunae in stratigraphy, serious dating conflicts involving differences of some 200 years or more and recourse to models postulating the abandonment of sites and their reoccupation after equally long periods of time.

At present, all research is carried out in the belief that these 'Dark Ages' represent a real span of time. It is assumed that the overall chronology, for all its 'gaps' and other tensions, has been built on a framework of fixed and reliable absolute dates. Yet it is conceivable that, without the synchronisms provided by the Aegean Late Bronze Age, many areas of ancient Europe would have developed more consistent, hiatus-free chronologies for the Bronze to Iron Age transition. This could be done by giving phases preceding the Dark Ages a much lower dating.

For example, were no Mycenaean pottery found with the material of the Late Apennine, Sub-Appenine and Proto-Villanovan in Italy, these phases might be substantially overlapped, easing numerous chronological and stratigraphical problems. Similarly, were the bronzes of Sardinia to be freed from the limits set by parallels with 12th to 11th-century Cypriot metalwork, greater weight could be given to the 9th to 6th-century date-range suggested by Italian comparisons and contexts. Likewise, the present trend to lower the dates for the Balkan Complex and Troy VII is constrained only by links with Late Bronze Age Greece.

The fact remains, however, that the established synchronisms between these European cultures and Late Mycenaean civilization (14th–12th centuries BC) can no more be ignored than those during the Late Geometric to Archaic periods (8th–6th centuries BC), when

actually had a wider distribution. This fact is taken as the main indication for a supposed shift of population to the coasts, the Ionian and Aegean islands and even as far as Cyprus.[3]

By the beginning of the 11th century BC Mycenaean civilization had collapsed. Many theories have been put forward to explain this dramatic downfall. Explanations vary from the straightforward, exemplified by the ever popular hypothesis of an invasion of Dorians, incomers from the north, through to attempts to apply extremely complex and abstract mathematical models. They take in a variety of other ideas that include natural catastrophes such as a series of earthquakes, climatic changes and droughts and the effects of famine and epidemic on the Mycenaean economy. Some adopting Marxist stances have suggested class warfare and the overthrow of the aristocracy.[4]

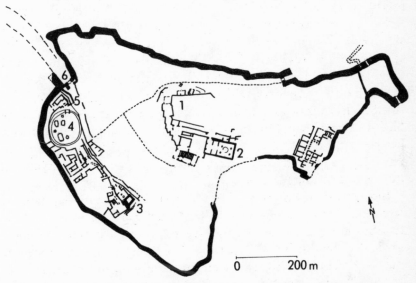

FIG. 4:1   Plan of the citadel of Mycenae: 1. Palace complex; 2. Megaron; 3. 'Shrine'; 4. Grave Circle A; 5. Granary; 6. Lion Gate (*after Hawkes 1974*).

Weighing up all these theories, it becomes clear that a combination of factors would make most sense. For example, climatic change could lead to crop failures; the resulting food shortages may have sparked off wider social unrest. Alternatively it can be argued that massive earthquakes hit most Mycenaean centres at a time when there were already severe economic problems.[5] Whatever the answer may be, Greece slid into decline, entering an eventless and mysterious Dark Age. The archaeological record for the following centuries is poor indeed by comparison to periods both before and after. This documented fall in the number of sites following the end of Mycenaean civilization is almost universally translated into a dramatic decline in population. While LHIIIB, lasting 100 years on the conventional chronology, has produced 462 sites for the entire Mycenaean world, the LHIIIC period of 125 years' duration has only 238 sites to its name.[6]

Vincent Desborough, author of a seminal work on the Greek Dark Age, summarized the curious nature of the period:

> . . . the changes that come about are little short of fantastic. The craftsmen and artists seem to vanish almost without trace: there is very little new stone construction of any sort, far less any massive edifices; the metal-worker's technique reverts to the primitive and the potter, except in the early stages, loses his purpose and inspiration; and the art of writing is forgotten. But the outstanding feature is that by the end of the twelfth century the population appears to have dwindled to about one-tenth of what it had been little over a century before.[7]

Recovery was a very long time in coming. However, when the recession finally ended the new Greek society displayed many 'old' Mycenaean features preserved through a supposedly considerable time-span. The problem of continuity across this 'Dark Age' begins the following review of the major features of Greek archaeology between 1200 and 700 BC.

The reappearance of ivory-working

It is remarkable that most examples of continuity occur in luxury goods of the sort one would have expected to disappear during the cultural Dark Age generally envisaged. As Bernhard Schweitzer remarked: ' . . . the real media in which Mycenaean art survived were jewellery, utensils of gold, silver, bronze and ivory inlay, and probably weaving and carpets'.[8]

In Mycenaean times there was a flourishing industry of ivory-carving which, although originally derived from the East, came to have a strong influence on Levantine schools. At the end of the Late Bronze Age, ivory manufacture ceased in Greece, reappearing again only around 850 BC.[9] It is usually assumed that the techniques of ivory-carving were preserved in the Levant during the Dark Age and then exported to Greece for a second time.[10] Yet the Levant itself has an equally puzzling hiatus in its ivory-working tradition between 1175 and 850 BC (see Chapter 8), on either side of which the motifs on the ivories are remarkably similar. The same problem is apparent when specific examples of Greek ivories are considered.

On the island of Delos, traditional birth-place of Apollo and Artemis, excavations in the 1940s discovered a rich cache of ivories beneath the much later Hellenistic Temple of Artemis.[11] The ivories and much else in the deposit were dated to the Mycenaean period on stylistic grounds and were clearly associated with Levantine schools of production, particularly that known from Megiddo. There is a curious connection with much later material in the Near East (see Fig. 11:4), on which Helene Kantor commented:

> When details of the animals on the Delos and Mycenaeanizing Megiddo plaques are compared with those of the North Syrian ivories and the Tell Halaf orthostats the patterning is seen to be well nigh identical despite the passage of three centuries without any known links.[12]

An answer may lie in the context of the Delos material. As only became clear later, there was Geometric pottery in the deposit, which should date its formation to the 8th century, although the stylistic dating of the ivories is unquestionable.[13] It is conceivable that this material was preserved as heirlooms throughout these centuries, but it is hard to see where. There is a hiatus in building activity on Delos after the Bronze Age (although not matched by the pottery found on the island, which continues uninterrupteed). The excavator suggested that this was an earlier deposit, disturbed during levelling operations on the site, and then reburied.[14] Alternatively, could the time-lapse between the two periods be much shorter than is generally agreed?

A similar puzzle concerns the five female figurines in ivory from the Dipylon Gate cemetery of Athens.[15] These were inspired by Syrian ivories, of which the closest in style come from Nimrud and date to the 9th century BC. Richard Barnett, the publisher of the Nimrud ivories, noted that the Syrian school had an artistic vocabulary that 'incorporated as a residue many of the shapes, subjects and devices of the Canaanite-Mycenaean tradition'.[16] This is a remarkable feat if there really was a two- or three-century break in production (see frontispiece).

To account for the continuity of ivory-working in the Levant, Sir Max Mallowan argued that during the interval the Phoenicians had transferred their skills from ivory to perishable materials such as textiles and wood.[17] This is a hypothesis often wheeled out to explain similar lacunae in other fields of material culture.

Continuity in painted pottery motifs

The perishable materials theory has also been employed to explain some striking resemblances between the painted pottery of the latest Mycenaean phases (13th–12th centuries BC) and that of the mature Geometric (late 9th–8th centuries BC) and the 7th-century 'Proto-Attic' styles. In his classic study of the problem of survival and continuity in Greek art between these periods, J. L. Benson summarized the work of a number of specialists:

> . . . various scholars who in actual fact have worked quite inten-sively with Attic Late Geometric and Proto-Attic pottery (R. S. Young, K. Kubler and E. Brann) have found and recorded evidence for the continuing and recurring influence of the Myce-naean tradition (not specifically in figure style); M. Pallottino, I. Charbonneaux, T. B. L. Webster, A. Snodgrass and others have explored aspects of the influence of that same tradition on figure style itself. In a quite different frame of inquiry a recent investiga-tor of the symmetrical principle in Greek pictorial composition has been forced to recognition of a persistent substratum of Mycenaean influence on early Greek art . . . Yet another investi-gator found the origin of nearly all motifs of Rhodian Orientaliz-ing to be Mycenaean and had to postulate their survival on textiles and metal ornaments.[18]

The theory that the motifs of painted pottery survived through a different medium has to be brought into play because no pictorial pottery is known in the period between the Mycenaean originals and their derivatives several hundred years later. To account for this recurrence of motifs in the figured pottery of the 8th century BC, Benson felt that there must have been some contact between Geometric artists and the products of Late Bronze Age Greece. This, he argued, could have taken place in Attica, thought to have been a rallying place for refugees after the disturbances at the end of the Bronze Age, bringing with them treasured possessions such as carpets, jewels and possibly vases.[19] If Benson's thesis were correct, one might expect clear evidence of the survival of Mycenaean fashions in Attica. Yet despite his exhaustive search, the area provides very few convincing examples of continuity between the Mycenaean and Geometric ages – hence the recourse to the textiles theory.

From another perspective, pottery motifs play a crucial role in our understanding of the demise and apparent reappearance of chariotry. Unfortunately, no physical traces of chariots have ever been recovered either from the Mycenaean period or the Early Iron Age in Greece. Chariots are mentioned on the Linear B tablets and illustrated on Mycenaean pottery and frescoes; likewise, during Geometric times, painted pottery and models are the primary sources of evidence for their existence. However, between the last depiction on Late Helladic vases and the Late Geometric period, when pictorial art flourished again, no chariot illustrations are known. Hilda Lorimer noted that despite this gap there was a very close similarity between the Bronze Age and Geometric vehicles.[20] Snodgrass, in a more detailed examination, recognized changes in form but seemed to be swayed more by the difference in date indicated by the standard chronology. He concluded that:

. . . since there is no sort of evidence from the Late Helladic III period down to the later eighth century for the use of chariots in the Aegean, it seems unwise to assume any continuity between the Mycenaean and Geometric chariots until this can be proved.[21]

By comparing individual features such as four-spoked wheels and centrally placed axles on Near Eastern examples with Geometric representations, Snodgrass explained the reappearance of the chariot in Greek art as an importation. However, nowhere are the features witnessed together in Greek representations actually seen combined in a single Near Eastern scene. Snodgrass cautiously offered an alternative hypothesis: the chariots on Geometric vases could have been inspired by the epic poetry of Homer and a few surviving Mycenaean painted pots. He felt it was unreasonable to believe that these early Greek warriors could have afforded the luxury of a vehicle from which they would seldom have fought! Snodgrass was thus unclear whether or not the chariot really existed in the 8th century BC.[22]

The problem of continuity has been considered more recently by
Joust Crouwel. He felt that Late Geometric depictions of chariots
were direct descendants from Mycenaean examples. Furthermore,
he noted that the characteristics of 8th-century Near Eastern chariots differed significantly from the Greek, thus negating the import
theory. He preferred to see the characteristic features of the most
common form of 7th-century Greek chariots as ultimately derived
from the local chariots of the Bronze Age.[23]

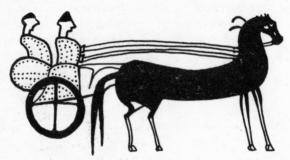

FIG. 4:2   (Above) A Mycenaean 'dual' chariot from a pictorial vase found in
Cyprus (*after Vermeule & Karageorghis 1982*). This type of vehicle should be
considered the ancestor of the Geometric high-fronted chariot as depicted
(below) in 8th-century vase painting (*after Crouwel 1981*).

Indeed, it is difficult to understand the development of the chariot
unless a Mycenaean predecessor existed. It seems to be only the
four-century gap that prevents archaeologists from seeing an indigenous development.

Our understanding of other items of military equipment is
similarly blighted. Two distinctive shield types are shown in the
same scenes as chariots on many Late Geometric vases: the 'Dipylon', named after a distinguished vase-painting workshop in

Athens; and the 'Boeotian' after the region in central Greece. No actual remains have been recovered. Ultimately, both can be seen as derivatives of the man-enclosing figure-of-eight shields from the Bronze Age.

There is even a single example of the Dipylon shield that dates to the late Mycenaean period on a vase from Iolkos.[24] This shows that the ancestor of the Dipylon type was Mycenaean. Snodgrass, having suggested that the chariot depictions of Late Geometric art did not represent contemporary objects, was forced to argue the same for the Dipylon shield – that it was some sort of throwback with heroic associations. His argument was based on the over stylization of the shield on Geometric pottery.[25]

FIG. 4:3   Fragment from a Geometric vase found in Athens – the middle figure carries a Dipylon shield type (*after Greenhalgh 1973*).

Peter Greenhalgh disputed this in his book on early Greek warfare. He pointed out that ordinary round and rectangular shields also shown on Late Geometric vases were clearly in use at the time (a fact also acknowledged by Snodgrass). This implies that the Dipylon shield was also real. However, Greenhalgh could not believe that they were derived from the Bronze Age because of the gap in time. He ignored the evidence of the Iolkos vase, stating that the small round shield was the most popular at the end of the Mycenaean period, an argument which hardly refutes the existence of the Dipylon type in the Late Bronze Age. He put forward the idea that their design was new, dictated in particular by their use in conjunction with the spear.[26]

The antecedents for the Boeotian type were clearly in the Bronze Age. According to Reynold Higgins, representations of figure-of-eight shields on beads from the Late Bronze Age compare closely to the Boeotian type.[27] The problem is obvious and clearly stated by Snodgrass:

If the Boeotian shield was an actuality in Geometric Greece, then we have to assume either that it was modelled, more or less slavishly, on the bead-miniatures of LHIII; or that the 'figure-of-eight' shield, having actually developed into this form, then remained in use, unchanged, for centuries; or else that it was revived by pure coincidence in identical form, after an equally long lapse.[28]

FIG. 4:4   Middle Protocorinthian vessel from Lechaion showing a warrior with hoplite round shield (left) in combat with others using the 'Boeotian' type (*after Snodgrass 1964*).

There seems little hope for an answer to these questions in the current chronological framework. It is difficult to believe that the chariots and shields could have designs so closely related to earlier forms by total chance. On the other hand, there remains a gap of several centuries for Bronze Age traditions to leapfrog. This problem is not confined solely to pottery.

Bronzes, ceramic models and heirlooms

Along with pottery and the vase painters, the bronze workshops also continued to function after the end of the Mycenaean period. With a few exceptions, the only surviving products of these workshops are tripods.[29]

Despite Schweitzer's confident statement regarding continuity in the bronze industry, the tripods he cites are themselves the focus of a classic chronological debate. Unlike the question of chariots and shields, where some see the Dark Age as an impenetrable barrier to local development, the descent of Geometric tripods from those of the Mycenaean period is generally accepted. For example, Snodgrass has noted the 'close resemblance of the earliest Iron Age tripods to the few known examples from the latest Bronze Age'.[30]

But despite attempts to link the two groups by raising the date of the earliest Geometric examples, a large void still remains in the sequence. With tripod-cauldrons, a form where the container and stand are moulded together, Schweitzer discussed the earlier view that there was 'a slow continuous development of the tripod type through three centuries, from about 1000 B.C. to the end of the eighth century', based on comparison of the decorations on tripods with those on Attic pottery. Schweitzer, however, dismissed these decorative links and further noted that all the ceramics involved belong to the 8th century. Pierre Amandry and Sylvia Benton, who studied the tripod-cauldrons of Delphi and Ithaca respectively, agree with this assessment, the latter citing 'the almost complete lack of rich finds between the Mycenaean epoch and about 800 B.C.'.[31]

At present, the earliest trace of tripod manufacture in Greece after the Mycenaean period comes from a deposit dated to c. 900 BC at Lefkandi on Euboea, containing fragments of moulds for casting sturdy rectangular strips of bronze decorated in relief, thought to be the legs of tripod stands or cauldrons.[32] As there is no earlier evidence, Snodgrass was forced to take a very different view from Schweitzer's: 'I still remain sceptical as to the existence of a continuous industry for the casting of bronze tripods throughout the dark age of Greece.'[33]

The apparent absence of large bronzes during the 'Dark Age' has given rise to the view that the bronze industry in Greece sank into a complete recession due to a lack of raw materials, following the collapse of the old Mycenaean markets.[34] Such an understanding would only put more distance between Late Bronze and Geometric bronzework, further aggravating the problem of their relationship. Like the textiles argument applied to continuity in ivory-carving and pottery motifs, it has sometimes been argued that the forms of Late Bronze metalwork were preserved in ceramic models over three centuries.

The ceramic theory has been applied, in particular, to the complex question of the relationship between the major tripod series of Geometric Greece and their Cypriot prototypes from the end of the Bronze Age.[35] Hector Catling notes that there are no ceramic copies of tripod stands from Mycenaean or Submycenaean times; and furthermore:

. . . surprisingly, there are none of Protogeometric date, when potters seem to have been at their fondest for copying in clay objects normally made in other materials. It is not until the period of the fully developed Geometric that the copies appear.[36]

FIG. 4:5   Rod tripod of 12th-century Cypriot
type, discovered in an 8th-century grave in
the area of the Pnyx, Athens (*after Snodgrass
1982*).

Actual examples of tripods of Late Cypriot form are also found in
much later deposits in Greece.[37] Regarding the style of these finds,
Catling stated:

> None of the stands from contexts later than the twelfth century
> have features either of form, technique, or ornament which
> obviously distinguish them from the others. One cannot, in fact,
> speak of a stand as being 'of tenth-century type', 'of eighth
> century type'.[38]

He therefore concluded that the late examples were actually highly
prized heirlooms. Schweitzer, however, held that the examples
found in the 9th to 8th-century contexts were of contemporary
manufacture, citing in support the ceramic models known from this
period.[39]

A related problem concerns the wheeled, four-sided stands of
12th-century Cypriot type found in 8th to 7th-century Greek
contexts. Catling argued that they were exported from two specific
workshops in Cyprus which were broken up at the end of the
Bronze Age:

> Our stands, I believe, were prized long after they were made
> because of their great technical virtuosity. They were also prized
> because they could not be repeated – they were marvels
> . . . They became treasured, personal belongings . . . passed
> from hand to hand, generation after generation, acting always as
> a reminder of the achievements of the past.[40]

James Muhly disputed Catling's heirloom theory, feeling that it
is unreasonable to deny Dark Age craftsmen the skill necessary to

manufacture such complex stands (see Plate 12). Further, he noted that the excavators of the examples from Delphi and the Heraion at Samos saw no reason to assume that the Cypriot-style stands were not contemporary with the other material in the deposits. Indeed, at the Heraion, which produced 'a remarkable array of imported objects', nothing else was found which was 'so totally out of context'.[41] Nevertheless, Muhly could not produce any hard evidence of sophisticated bronze manufacture in Dark Age Greece before the Lefkandi finds of around 900 BC.

We are left with the strange picture of late 10th to 8th-century craftsmen copying antique styles of Cypriot bronzework, with no intermediate forms (either in bronze or clay) to serve them. One is inevitably reminded of the related problem of the Sardinian bronze tripods, placed in the 9th to 7th centuries by the evidence of Italian contexts but in the 12th century BC by Cypriot parallels (see Chapter 2).

The introduction of the alphabet

A similar mystery concerns the supposed eclipse of literacy between the close of the Mycenaean palace period, early in the 12th century BC, and its re-emergence in the 8th century.

The major Mycenaean centres employed skilled bureaucracies to keep administrative records – such as inventories of available goods, notes of taxes and lists of offerings made to the gods. Their script, known today as 'Linear B', was used not only on clay tablets but also in brief inscriptions on pots. It was ultimately derived from an ancient Cretan system of hieroglyphics, adapted into a system of eighty-seven signs to represent syllables. Yet compared to an alphabet which can express sound-values by as few as twenty characters, Linear B was extremely cumbersome. Its complexity meant that it would not have been easy to master; by the same token its decipherment proved to be a difficult task.

The first examples were discovered by Sir Arthur Evans at Knossos in 1900, followed by other tablets which came to light on the Greek mainland, notably the large archive discovered at Pylos in 1939. But it was not until 1952 that the script was cracked, by the brilliant efforts of the young English architect Michael Ventris. He demonstrated, to the surprise of many scholars, that the language behind Linear B was Greek. Scholars of the 'old school', following

Evans, thought that Mycenaean civilization was merely an offshoot of the non-Greek Minoan. If this were the case, the language of the Mycenaeans, especially as it was written in an adapted Cretan script, would not have been Greek.

The decipherment of Linear B threw a completely new light on the Mycenaean world. For example, it is now known that the Olympian gods familiar from Homer (including Zeus, Hera, Poseidon, Athena, Artemis, Hermes and Dionysos) were worshipped during the Late Bronze Age. Such discoveries suddenly brought the Mycenaeans into a much closer cultural relationship with the Greek world of historical times. Yet despite this evidence of continuity, on the presently accepted chronology Linear B is thought to have totally fallen out of use by the early 12th century BC. There are no inscriptions to fill the gap between that date and the 8th century, when the earliest Greek alphabetic texts begin to appear.[42]

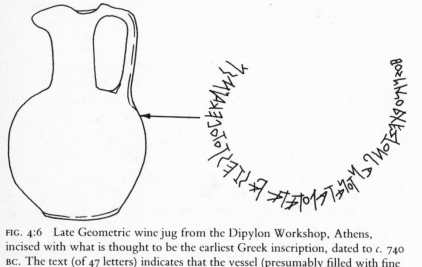

FIG. 4:6   Late Geometric wine jug from the Dipylon Workshop, Athens, incised with what is thought to be the earliest Greek inscription, dated to c. 740 BC. The text (of 47 letters) indicates that the vessel (presumably filled with fine wine) was an award for the winner in an Athenian dancing competition (*after Boardman 1980*).

It has been supposed that literacy continued in Greece during the Dark Age, but that the writing medium changed from clay to a perishable material such as wood[43] – a theory reminiscent of that used to explain the disappearance of ivory carvings, bronzework and figured pottery in the Aegean during the same period. Current scholarship generally accepts an apparent lapse into illiteracy, and explains it as follows: with the fall of the palaces the need for writing ceased and the script was thus soon forgotten; Greece remained illiterate until some time during the 8th century BC, when her traders on the Syrian coast met a people using, not a syllabary, but an alphabet.[44]

Such a model has been undermined by the observation that early '11th-century' Levantine forms apparently served as the prototypes for the 8th-century Greek alphabet (see Table 4:1). The detailed arguments have been forcefully presented by Joseph Naveh, a leading Semitic palaeographer.[45] The earliest Greek writing closely resembles examples from Syro-Palestine conventionally dated to c. 1050 BC, not only in the shapes of the letters, but also in the direction of writing and the use of word-dividers. Thus, instead of the traditional idea of the Greek alphabet being borrowed from that of the Phoenicians, both would have developed from a common parent script, termed 'Proto-Canaanite'.

Still, a plausible mechanism for the transference of 11th-century Levantine forms to 8th-century Greece remains elusive. Pyle McCarter has suggested:

> . . . that the Greeks, though their script did not diverge as an independent tradition before c. 800, had experimented with the Semitic alphabet as early as c. 1100 . . . The memory of the earlier experimentation survived long enough . . . to exert a limited influence upon the final formulation of the Greek alphabet years later.[46]

Naveh rightly described this as an 'impossible formula'.[47] Preferring to take the evidence at its face value, he argues that the Greeks adopted and used the contemporary Proto-Canaanite script during the 11th century BC.

The recent discovery of a 'late 11th-century' Phoenician inscription on a bronze bowl from Crete has been taken by some as convincing support for Naveh's arguments. The renowned American palaeographer Frank Cross, accepting the case for the early adoption of the alphabet by the Greeks, dated the bowl to the 11th century BC by the style of the writing,[48] but ran into problems with the local archaeological evidence. The bowl was found in an unplundered tomb at Tekke near Knossos, together with Cretan pottery dated to the early 9th century BC. According to the excavator this assemblage represented a second burial, since nearly half of

Table 4:1

LATE PROTO-CANAANITE 1200-1050 BC	ARCHAIC GREEK 8th cent. BC	CLASSICAL GREEK NAMES	PHOENICIAN 8th cent. BC
		Alpha	
		Beta	
		Gamma	
		Delta	
		Epsilon	
		Digamma*	
		Zeta	
		Eta	
		Theta	
		Iota	
		Kappa	
		Lambda	
		Mu	
		Nu	
		Xi	
		Omicron	
		Pi	
		Qoppa*	
		Rho	
		Sigma	
		Tau	
		Upsilon	
		Phi	
		Chi	
		Psi	
		Omega	
		Sampi*	

Was the Greek alphabet borrowed from the Levant in the 11th or 8th century BC? It has been argued that the 'Proto-Canaanite' rather than Phoenician script provided the inspiration for the earliest Greek alphabet. The letters compared are shown in the Greek order; those marked with an asterisk were becoming obsolete as phonetic characters by classical times (*after Naveh 1982 and Garbini in Moscati ed. 1988*).

the pots on the floor of the tomb were Attic Late Protogeometric, apparently belonging to an earlier burial of the late 10th century BC. Cross assumed that the Phoenician bowl was associated with the earliest material, and, guided by his dating of the inscription, argued that the dates for the Protogeometric period as a whole should be raised.[49]

Aegean archaeologists remain largely unconvinced by these arguments. As Professor Nicolas Coldstream put it:

> . . . it is tantalizing to know that the Phoenician alphabet was on view to Knossians well before 850, and over a century before the earliest known use of the Greek alphabet. Nevertheless . . . the new Phoenician graffiti have not shaken the orthodox view that Greek alphabetic writing began in the eighth century.[50]

The origin of the Greek alphabet thus provides an almost perfect paradox. While Near Eastern experts, using palaeographic arguments, are increasingly drawn to the view that the Greeks borrowed the alphabet as early as the 11th century BC, there is still a genuine absence of datable examples from the Aegean before the 8th century. Ultimately the question must hinge on the absolute dating of the 'Proto-Canaanite' examples from Palestine (see Chapter 10). Is the gap between the archaeology of the '11th' and 8th centuries a real one?

Palaces, fortifications, houses and temples

The architectural history of the Greek Dark Age amply demonstrates the post-Mycenaean collapse. On the mainland south of Thessaly, as well as the Aegean islands, construction in stone and brick almost entirely ceased. In Desborough's words 'the extreme rarity of any stone construction for a period of centuries after LHIIIC strongly supports the view that the skill had been lost . . .'[51]

There is very little new building construction during LHIIIC, especially on the grand scale of the preceding period. At the major sites the main characteristic of the architecture is the reuse of LHIIIB housing. *Megaron* plan structures, thought to be the throne-rooms of palaces, continued in use at Iolkos in the north and at Phylakopi on the island of Melos, but no new examples were built – with the possible exception of an enigmatic structure at Tiryns, erected over the foundations of the old *megaron* but of considerably reduced size.[52]

Monumental architecture, typified by the famous Lion Gate at Mycenae, was not attempted after LHIIIB. Similarly the skill of building with saw-cut blocks (ashlar masonry) seems to have been forgotten for several centuries. While some of the old cyclopean fortifications doubtless continued in use much later, no new city walls were built anywhere after LHIIIC. It is only in the Geometric period that defences were constructed once more – and even then not on the mainland but in the Cyclades.[53]

The figures (see Table 4:2) for sites producing possible evidence of building activity have been drawn from Konstantine Syriopoulos's catalogue of the archaeology of the Greek world from 1200 to 700 BC.[54] He lists 273 Dark Age sites for the area of mainland Greece, excluding the north (Thessaly, Epirus, Macedonia, Thrace and the Ionian Islands) but including the islands as far as the Cyclades, grouped into four periods: Late Helladic IIIC (1200–1075 BC), Submycenaean (1075–1025 BC), Protogeometric (1025–900 BC) and Geometric (900–700 BC). The table illustrates the sharp decline that Greece suffered and the sparse and uneven nature of the architectural record when compared with the Mycenaean past.

In interpreting these figures it should be noted that the existence of Submycenaean as a separate chronological phase in all areas

Table 4:2

Known Dark Age sites in area (1200–700 BC): 273

Phases	Number of sites in area	Architectural remains in area
LHIIIB	*c. 230*	*c. 125 (54.3% of LHIIIB sites in area)*
LHIIIC	118 (43.2% of total sites in area)	22 (18.6% of LHIIIC sites in area)
Submycenaean	45 (16.4% of total sites in area)	6 (13.3% of SM sites in area)
Protogeometric	92 (33.6% of total sites in area)	15 (16.3% of PG sites in area)
Geometric	195 (71.4% of total sites in area)	39 (20% of G sites in area)

Statistics for Greek sites from the Dark Age and LHIIIB compared.

remains *sub judice* (see below, p. 90). An additional factor to be taken into account when assessing the intensity of building activity attributed to the Submycenaean and Protogeometric periods is the fact that a number of structures could date to either phase due to the occurrence of both Submycenaean and Protogeometric sherds or the difficulty of distinguishing between the two styles; they therefore appear twice in the figures.[55]

Despite the long-standing lack of excavation of sites from certain periods, it is clear that there was a slump in building activity, be it in stone or other material, from the end of LHIIIC until the later Geometric period.[56] The picture for the Protogeometric is somewhat improved by comparison with the Submycenaean but is still meagre when set against the statistics for the late Mycenaean period. As Snodgrass has pointed out:

> When we turn to the architectural features of the period, we see the full extent of the fall in standards which the years of depopulation had brought. Only at one or two places in Greece is there any sign that good stone-built constructions of eleventh or tenth-century date existed . . .[57]

The architectural record continues to remain poor well into the Geometric period. Coldstream notes that:

> Whereas eighth-century burials have been excavated at well over a hundred sites throughout the Greek world, fewer than fifty have produced any evidence of settlement. At most of these places the architectural remains are either negligible or missing altogether, the evidence being confined to a handful of Geometric sherds found in later contexts.[58]

The rarity of architectural remains between the Mycenaean and Late Geometric periods is usually accounted for by the assumption, reminiscent of explanations for the recessions in other skills, discussed above, that houses in the intervening time were constructed exclusively, or to a large extent, of perishable materials such as mud-brick, wood or clay.[59] Such arguments, perhaps plausible with regard to ivories and metalwork (which could have been scarce during a genuine Dark Age), might seem a little strange when applied to an area as rich in stone as Greece. It is more worrying overall that there is so little evidence of any sort of building during this long period of time.

Snodgrass suggested, as part of a wider explanation for the Dark Age, that the paucity of architecture could be explained by a shift to greater dependence on pastoralism, with stock-rearing replacing mixed farming, as a response to the collapse of the centralized Mycenaean palace economy. He argued that this less sedentary way of life would have resulted in semi-permanent settlements with more makeshift buildings of mud-brick and wood. He cited the apsidal structures found below the Geometric buildings at Lefkandi and the outlines of circular huts underneath houses of the same period at Eretria, interpreted as evidence of seasonal occupation.[60] While Snodgrass has provided a plausible model for society in the immediate post-palace period, it is difficult to see why it took so long for the economy to recover.

Despite the apparent dearth of building activity during the Dark Age, there is a curious continuation of Mycenaean elements in the architecture of the Late Geometric and Archaic periods, when construction in stone began to flourish again. Coldstream considers that the plans of 8th-century BC temples have undeniable precedents in the Bronze Age. The apsidal type seen in the Geometric temple at Eretria and the models from Perachora preserves the porch and main-room arrangement of the *megaron*. The ancestors of the Doric and Ionic temples familiar from classical Greece are even closer to the *megaron*, with their long rectangular plan and single entrance.[61]

In view of the certain knowledge that Olympian deities existed in the Bronze Age and survived the Dark Age, as well as the possibility that the Mycenaean *megaron* functioned as a centre of religious ritual rather than a throne-room, we seem to be confronted again with a remarkable case of survival.[62] But the strange thing is that no actual temples survive from the Dark Age; indeed it has to be assumed that 'almost all worship took place in the open air'.[63] Thus, on the accepted chronology, the use of temples, along with later derivatives of Mycenaean architecture, the reappearance of widespread building in stone, ashlar and other fine masonry and the whole repertoire of skills needed to produce it, all have to be seen as curious 'revivals'.

The stratigraphic record

The disappearance and reappearance of such a wide range of skills provides circumstantial evidence suggesting that the current chronology is overstretched – particularly when seen in conjunction with the patchy nature of the stratigraphy for the Greek Dark Age. A brief review follows of the stratigraphic evidence from LHIIIC until Geometric times, considering the relationship of each phase with those preceding and succeeding it, in order to show how the relative chronology has been shaped.

The situation is not straightforward because of the regionalism in pottery styles throughout the Dark Age period. The standard pottery sequence for Early Iron Age Greece is drawn from Attica: the Protogeometric, for example, being defined by the material from the Kerameikos cemetery in Athens. Elsewhere, different regional styles developed independently. Local variations began in the LHIIIC period with the dislocation of Mycenaean culture, developing into distinct local styles in the following periods. Correlating these with the Attic sequence within a single general chronology is fraught with difficulty. Since Attic vases are often found together with local pottery of a less developed style, this is taken to indicate a considerable time-lag in the spread of Attic influences, for which the standard chronology attempts to allow.

The initial problem is to decide whether a 'Submycenaean' style followed LHIIIC and existed as a separate phase at all. In 1978 Jeremy Rutter suggested, on the basis of his study of the pottery from Corinth, that Submycenaean was the funerary material belonging to the last phase of LHIIIC, and that the two were actually contemporary. He therefore made a plea for the abandonment of

FIG. 4:7 Submycenaean vessel from the Kerameikos, Athens.

the term.[64] This was unsuccessful, as Submycenaean has subsequently been found stratified above LHIIIC at Mycenae and Tiryns and beneath Protogeometric strata at Asine. The identification of Submycenaean as a separate phase at these sites is now accepted. In Athens, where settlement information is lacking, material from the Kerameikos burials is thought to suggest the same.[65] However, in other areas it seems that 'Submycenaean' as such did not occur. In Thessaly, for example, the local Protogeometric style evolved directly from late Mycenaean wares, as demonstrated by the Iolkos stratigraphy and pottery.[66]

This phenomenon can create tensions, none more troublesome than those of the Laconian sequence of the Peloponnese. At the sanctuary of Apollo at Amyclae, near Sparta, the excavators noted that the latest Mycenaean material was mixed with Laconian Protogeometric pottery in a stratum entirely distinct from the succeeding Geometric level (late 9th and 8th centuries BC). They gave this deposit an 11th to 10th-century date in line with the conventional chronology.[67] The date has since been lowered by Desborough and Snodgrass, who start the local Protogeometric in 950 or 900 BC respectively, on the basis of stylistic correlations with the Attic series.[68] Nicholas Hammond recognized the problem this creates, as it introduces a time-gap into an apparently continuous stratum.[69] Paul Cartledge, however, argued that the stratigraphy was deceptive: although preserving the correct progression, the sequence was formed by material washed downhill from the sanctuary. According to him there was a genuine stylistic break between the LHIIIC and Protogeometric styles.[70]

Although accepting a gap in the stratigraphy, William Coulson objected to Cartledge's analysis. In his opinion Late Mycenaean influence could be clearly discerned in the Protogeometric pottery.[71] Basing his understanding on the evidence of neighbouring Nichoria in Messenia, Coulson created a local 'Dark Age' pottery sequence which he felt could also bridge the gap at Amyclae. His 'Dark Age' phases correlate with developments in the west Greek pottery tradition, which, evolving separately from that of Attica, is thought to have preserved the LHIIIC style into the 10th century BC.[72] In an admittedly arbitrary fashion, Coulson placed his Dark Age (DA) I between 1075 and 975, with DA II lasting until the close of the 9th century.[73] Coulson's DA II pottery has traits in common with the Amyclae Protogeometric material, which would thus be separated by a century from the latest Mycenaean finds.[74]

Kare Fagerström, however, was highly critical of the Nichoria evidence on which Coulson based his 'Dark Age' sequence:

> Repeatedly, however, there occurs an admixture of LHIII material in what seems to be regarded as uncontaminated DA I or DA II strata. The distinction between DA I and DA II is not a clear one – a rather natural thing, seeing that one of the reasons for choosing the term Dark Age was that the pottery is obscure as to classification. In these murky backwaters of Messenia it may well be that LHIII shapes in some cases were preserved, perhaps through centuries, especially as there are no clear signs of disruption at the end of LHIII.[75]

Amyclae and Nichoria therefore throw no real light on the gap in time, if any, between the Mycenaean and Protogeometric periods outside Attica. Certainly there is no solid basis for Coulson's claim that 100 years separate the two.

Initial hopes that Lefkandi on Euboea, by virtue of its deep stratigraphy, would provide many of the solutions to understanding the Dark Age sequence have proved to be unfounded. The evidence for the Submycenaean and Early Protogeometric phases comes exclusively from tombs, and the two seem to be confused both stratigraphically and stylistically. In one case a tomb that would normally have been attributed to the Protogeometric had to be dated to the Submycenaean, simply because it was overlain by another which contained a Submycenaean oil flask.[76] Other deposits, and even single pots, show a mixture of Submycenaean and Early Protogeometric styles suggesting a considerable overlap between the two at Lefkandi.[77]

The site also posed difficulties in defining the difference between the later Protogeometric and the 'Sub-Protogeometric' – an unfortunately cumbersome term for the local styles equivalent to the Early and Middle Geometric of Attica. Even after the development of a detailed typological sequence based on tomb finds, the distinction between Protogeometric and Sub-Protogeometric material remained blurred. Thus, for example, the terminal date for the deposit beneath the 'Yard Floor' was hard to determine because of the 'nebulousness of the frontiers between LPG and SPG I'.[78]

The main stratigraphic evidence for the Sub-Protogeometric comes from three superimposed deposits: two successive pits covered by material laid down to level up the site for building work. Together, these are supposed to represent the period between *c.* 900 and 750 BC. The finds in the three deposits were so mixed that in the case of the uppermost it was felt that: 'The material could represent all stages from LPG to SPGIII.'[9] The presence of Late Proto-geometric material in all three levels worried the excavators and had to be explained as an 'admixture, in unknown quantity, in the two upper deposits of earlier material – undeniable in view of the number of joins made between one deposit and another'.[80]

A striking feature at Lefkandi is the overall homogeneity in the pottery styles between *c.* 900 and 750 BC, attributed by the excavators to the conservatism of the inhabitants, 'traditional to an extreme in their unusual burial practices and in their adherence to a pottery style which once evolved was clung to for over 150 years'.[81]

Amyclae, Nichoria and Lefkandi are all well excavated sites, and indeed the best representatives of Greek 'Dark Age' archaeology. Yet their stratigraphies clearly highlight the problem of dating the regional pottery of the Protogeometric and Geometric periods. At a time when some areas of Greece are considered to have entered the Geometric phase, in others (particularly in the north) the styles are still, strictly speaking, Protogeometric. Thus Snodgrass allows Attic Protogeometric to run from *c.* 1050 to *c.* 900 BC. Yet in places such as Euboea, Elis, Phocis, Locris, Achaea, Messenia and Laconia, he has Protogeometric beginning much later and continuing as late as 750 BC, when the Attic Middle Geometric was ending. In these areas the Protogeometric style seems to have given way immediately to a Late Geometric phase without intervening equivalents to Attic Early and Middle Geometric.[82]

Overall, the conventional chronology allows Protogeometric styles an extremely long currency. Internal controls on the length of the Protogeometric are hard to establish, but the frequent superim-position of Geometric deposits over late Mycenaean material offers no support for the idea that the Protogeometric was of any great duration.[83] Unlike instances where Protogeometric strata directly overlie Mycenaean, the lack of intervening levels between Geomet-ric and Mycenaean material is somewhat surprising. What makes these cases especially puzzling is not so much the absence of occupational debris as the lack of any natural accumulation of sediment or silt over the centuries.

Indeed, at a striking number of sites throughout Greece, the

Protogeometric is represented only by tomb finds. Thus, at Lefkandi there is a gap in the settlement record following the extensive LHIIIC occupation: after about 1100 BC there are no traces of habitation until the Late Protogeometric shortly before 900 BC.[84] The missing periods (Submycenaean, Early and Middle Protogeometric) are indicated only by finds from nearby cemeteries.

To produce a full survey of the anomalies in the stratigraphy and cultural history of Dark Age Greece is far beyond the scope of the present book. It is unfortunate, nevertheless, that the many different aspects of the whole Dark Age problem are rarely, if ever, considered together.

Ironically, many scholars of the 19th and early 20th centuries would have seen the above difficulties in Greek archaeology as quite illusory, the products of an artificially long chronology. They saw no need to accommodate a Dark Age between the Mycenaean and Geometric eras. William Ramsay, A. S. Murray, Cecil Torr and many others were happy, from the evidence at their disposal, to date the end of Mycenaean civilization as late as the 9th or even 7th century BC! Ramsay, for example, saw a connection between 9th to 7th-century Phrygian rock-carvings and the sculpture of the Lion Gate at Mycenae.[85] Murray was a staunch supporter of a low dating for Mycenaean civilization, associating it with the period of col-

FIG. 4:8 (Left) The famous Lion Gate at Mycenae, presently thought to have been constructed in the 13th century BC (*after Kantor 1956*). (Right) 8th–7th century façade with lions from a Phrygian tomb at Arslan Tash, central Anatolia (*after Ramsay 1888*).

onization and the early tyrants, during the 8th and 7th centuries BC.[86] Torr drew attention to, amongst other things, the close resemblance between the carved gemstones of the Mycenaean and Geometric ages.[87] He questioned the validity of the Egyptian Sothic chronology and fiercely resisted the attempts of Petrie and others to raise the dates for Mycenae into the 2nd millennium BC (see Chapter 1).

No one today could seriously contemplate the lowest dates for Mycenaean civilization experimented with by late 19th-century scholars. Nevertheless, the force of their arguments regarding some continuity between the Mycenaean and Geometric ages cannot be ignored. Nor can one fail to be struck by the similarities between the Dark Age of Greece and those of Eastern and Southern Europe between 1200 and 800 BC, especially as those areas depend on Greece for their chronology. In Greece itself so many questions surround the nature and duration of the Submycenaean, Proto-geometric and Geometric periods that there is good reason to doubt whether they really occupied the generous lengths of time usually assigned to them. To cite Snodgrass, one of the leading authorities on the archaeology of Dark Age Greece:

> . . . why did it come about that some four centuries elapsed during which Greek material culture appears to have changed so little? Why did it take so long for literacy, representational art, monumental architecture, and other attributes to appear, or reappear, in the form in which they eventually did?[88]

CHAPTER 5

The Foundations of Geometric Chronology

The previous chapter has shown the kinds of problems that crop up time and again within the conventional chronology for the Greek Dark Age. The questions raised by Snodgrass now need to be considered against the background of the interminable difficulties involved in dating the pottery of these centuries. It has already been suggested, on the basis of internal evidence, that the lengths of time assigned to some of the Early Iron Age cultural phases may be over-generous. How and why did archaeologists arrive at these figures?

The span which the Dark Age occupies seems to be clearly defined by two fixed points. The first is provided by associations between Mycenaean finds and Egyptian New Kingdom material, the last being the occurrence of early LHIIIC pottery with objects bearing the name of the 20th Dynasty Pharaoh Ramesses III (1184–1153 BC) in Palestine.[1] The second fixed point is the historical record of Late Geometric and Archaic colonization in Italy and Sicily towards the close of the 8th century BC.

Between these two parameters the situation is much less clear. It is often with some reluctance that specialists have accepted the necessity of spinning out the limited amount of ceramic evidence for the LHIIIC, Submycenaean, Protogeometric and Geometric phases, to cover the period between the 12th and 8th centuries BC (see Table 5:1). Indeed, these are sometimes made to occupy bewildering lengths of time. As Snodgrass wrote:

> . . . this brief sequence of periods must be extended over probably about 400 years or more. It is clear that we are dealing with a very slow rate of development in the potter's art in Greece. If we make a provisional hypothesis as to the duration of the styles, and assume about 150 years for the residue of Mycenaean IIIC, 150 for the Attic Protogeometric, and 50 years each for Attic Early and Middle Geometric, we shall be taking a wholly arbitrary step; but we shall arrive at approximately the right total, without

Table 5:1

Early Protogeometric		1025–980 BC*
Middle Protogeometric		980–960 BC*
Late Protogeometric		960–900 BC*
Early Geometric	I	900–875 BC
	II	875–850 BC
Middle Geometric	I	850–800 BC
	II	800–760 BC
Late Geometric	I	760–735 BC
	II	735–700 BC

The standard system for Greek Attic pottery of the Dark Age, as developed by Desborough (1952) for the Protogeometric and Coldstream (1968) for the Geometric. Where dates are marked with an asterisk, Desborough has allowed the possibility that they might be raised by some fifty years, depending on the chronology assigned to Stratum III at Tell Abu Hawam.

unduly straining credulity in any one case. We can also be virtually certain that no reduction in any one of these figures is possible without a compensatory lengthening elsewhere . . .[2]

A good example of the knock-on effect described by Snodgrass can be seen in the recent redating of LHIIIC by Penelope Mountjoy, in which the converse is happening – the lengthening of one period demands the shortening of another. The many phases of building activity at both Mycenae and Tiryns during LHIIIC prompted her to suggest that a longer span should be ascribed to this period, pushing it into the mid-11th century BC. Allowing two generations for the Submycenaean, she had to lower the start of Protogeometric by some fifty years.[3] As a consequence, the time allowed for the Geometric as a whole would have to be shortened. In cases like this chronology becomes little more than a juggling act.

Reassessing the Archaic

The only way of escaping this dilemma is to tie the relative chronology for pottery to a framework of absolute dates. The logical procedure is to work back in time from the known to the unknown, in this case starting from the earliest certain points in Greek history. These fall in the Archaic period which preceded Classical civilization.

The method by which the archaeological chronology has been

established is to use 'a few fairly reliable fixed points to which the stylistic sequence can be pegged'. These are the rare historically dated events with which pottery can be associated, such as the finds under the burial mounds believed to have been raised over the Athenians and Plataeans who fell at the battle of Marathon in 490 BC.[4] Given the richly documented history of Greece from the 7th century BC onwards, one might think that archaeological dating in Greece had been established without question for the whole of the Archaic period. Surprisingly, this is not the case.

Over the last few years a series of studies by the late David Francis, a specialist in Persian–Greek relations, and Michael Vickers, Assistant Keeper of Antiquities at the Ashmolean Museum, Oxford, has challenged practically all the major criteria for dating Greek art and architecture even as late as the early 5th century BC. Indeed, in Vickers's opinion: 'The first incontrovertible "fixed point" in the Greek [archaeological] chronology is the Parthenon, begun in 447.'[5]

FIG. 5:1   Burial mound at Marathon identified as that raised over the Athenians killed in the famous battle with the Persian invaders in 490 BC. Excavated in 1890 it covered the remains of 192 bodies, buried with weapons and Black Figure vases (*from Breasted 1916*).

For example, they would give a date in the 470s BC, after the Persian Wars, to the Siphnian Treasury at Delphi, once thought to provide 'our best fixed point in all the history of archaic art', around 525 BC.[6] Further, Francis and Vickers do not accept that the boom in Athenian wealth, art and architecture known from the archaeological record should be attributed to the years before and during the Persian Wars (494–479 BC); they would see it instead as a consequence of the Greek victory.[7] Their revision does indeed agree with the statements of classical authors such as Diodorus of Sicily in the 1st century BC regarding the healthy economy of Athens after its defeat of the Persian invaders and the looting of their camps:

> . . . every Greek city was filled with such abundance that everyone was amazed at the change for the better. For the next fifty years, Greece enjoyed great progress towards prosperity. During this time the crafts increased owing to prosperity, and the greatest artists are mentioned as having flourished at that time.[8]

When one contrasts this statement with a modern assessment, based on the conventional dating of the archaeological remains, that 'Athens was not a wealthy state in the 470s and 460s',[9] Francis and Vickers's argument certainly becomes attractive.

In some instances the standard dating is certainly wrong. For example, David Gill has demonstrated that, even using conventional dates, the pottery found beneath the Temple of Aphaia on Aigina shows that its construction has been dated too high at 510 BC, and that it was actually built later than 480 BC.[10]

In step with their reduction of many of the 'fixed points' in Greek art history, Francis and Vickers have proposed a radical compression of Archaic pottery chronology. For example, they have offered a 'recalibration' of Greek ceramic chronology which would involve lowering dates presently given as 550–525 BC by some forty-five to seventy years, and those around 620–600 BC by as much as eighty years. The debate about the value of their revision is ongoing. Certainly some lowering of Archaic dates seems to be in order, but exactly how much remains a moot point.[11] On balance, their revision of 7th-century material seems too drastic. The wider issues involved in the debate bring us to the controlling evidence for the dating of earliest Archaic pottery provided by the first Greek colonies in the West.

Western colony dates and the end of the Geometric

The basic information for calculating the precise dates of the foundation of the western colonies (see Map 2) is provided by the greatest of classical historians, Thucydides. In his *Peloponnesian War*, he wrote that Megara Hyblaea in Sicily was founded 245 years before its destruction by Gelon of Syracuse, an event fixed by information in Herodotus to *c.* 483/482 BC. Accordingly, Megara would have been established around 728 BC. Thucydides also states that Megara was founded at about the same time as Leontini, itself established five years after Syracuse, the first colony in Sicily. Thus the usually accepted date for Syracuse is 734 or 733 BC.[12] Thucydides' colony dates are tied in to the Greek pottery chronology by the belief of archaeologists that the earliest finds (Late Geometric and Protocorinthian) at Greek colonies will date to the time of their foundation. As Robert Cook noted:

> . . . the foundation dates given by Thucydides are accepted as a necessary assumption. However, in history and literature these foundation dates are equally assumed, so that archaeology sinks or swims with them.[13]

There are two elements involved in this 'necessary assumption'. First, the nature of the dates that Thucydides has in effect provided; and, second, the reliability of the association of the Greek pottery on these sites with the colony dates.

It is generally felt that Thucydides' colony dates are sound. Thucydides showed himself in his recording of the Peloponnesian War to be a rigorous critic of any claims which lacked substance. In his introduction, he prides himself on being sceptical of traditional sources for history, with their tendency to exaggerate.

Unfortunately there is almost no controlling material against which to check the dates given by Thucydides. One exception is the case of Akragas in Sicily, according to Thucydides established 108 years after the city of Gela, itself founded forty-five years after Syracuse. This gives a date of about 581/580 BC for Akragas.[14] An ode by the 5th-century BC poet Pindar, celebrating the victory of Theron the Emmenid, tyrant of Akragas, at the Olympic Games of 476/475 BC, claims that no city 'in these hundred years' had produced such a man as Theron.[15] This has been thought to imply a foundation of Akragas a century earlier, perhaps based on a local tradition about the city's antiquity, one presumably favoured by Theron himself. It has often been taken to give an approximate date for the foundation of the city around 575 BC, giving a fair enough agreement with Thucydides by any standards.[16]

However, it seems a little strange to use the very type of source that Thucydides himself would have rejected to support his dating. Pindaric scholars of modern times generally accept that a 'hundred years' meant little more to the poet than 'a long time'.[17] It is difficult to accept Pindar as a confirmation of Thucydides. Even if they both used the same traditional evidence for the founding of Akragas, this apparent consistency is no substitute for knowing if their common source was accurate.

Here lies the nub of the problem: where might these dates come from? Again, most commentators agree: Thucydides relied on the slightly earlier chroniclers Antiochus of Syracuse and Hellanikos of Mytilene. It is presumed that they were the recipients of an oral tradition which preserved dates in the form of family trees – i.e. that such and such occurred so many generations after a certain event. Some historians have assumed that the dates given by Thucydides were calculated using a standard generation length, but it is clear that there was never an agreed unit in classical times.[18] It is also clear that there was a considerable element of exaggeration in many ancient calculations (see Appendix 2). Whether, and by how much, these factors would have affected the dates arrived at by Thucydides is unknown; for all his caution, the possibility remains worrying when we are forced to rely so heavily on his figures.

Nicolas Coldstream, author of the definitive work on Geometric pottery, found that his ceramic chronology for the western colonies provided a good match with the Thucydidean dates: 'this agreement should help restore faith in Thucydides as an accurate chronographer'.[19] A more realistic view might see this agreement as, at best, a happy coincidence, and one also involving a degree of circular reasoning.[20] Andrew Burn astutely pointed out fifty years ago that:

It is not . . . possible to check the accuracy of Thucydides' western chronology by means of the archaeological data – all the less so since . . . the existing system of dating for early Greek pottery rests largely on Thucydides' chronology itself.[21]

Table 5:2

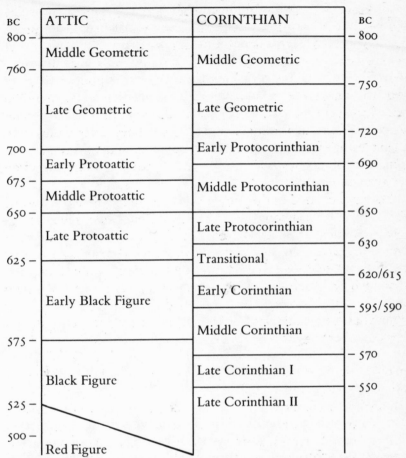

BC	ATTIC	CORINTHIAN	BC
800 –			– 800
	Middle Geometric	Middle Geometric	
760 –			– 750
	Late Geometric	Late Geometric	– 720
700 –		Early Protocorinthian	– 690
	Early Protoattic		
675 –		Middle Protocorinthian	
	Middle Protoattic		– 650
650 –		Late Protocorinthian	– 630
	Late Protoattic		
625 –		Transitional	– 620/615
	Early Black Figure	Early Corinthian	– 595/590
		Middle Corinthian	
575 –			– 570
	Black Figure	Late Corinthian I	– 550
525 –		Late Corinthian II	
500 –	Red Figure		

Relative chronology of the Attic and Corinthian pottery sequences during the Late Geometric to Archaic periods (*after Coldstream 1968; Cook 1969 & 1972; Boardman 1974; Amyx 1988*).

It is ironic, then, that Coldstream's justification for his chronology was partly dependent on the Thucydidean colony dates; these would suggest that the Late Geometric style as found at Naxos, Syracuse and elsewhere in the West was current in the second half of the 8th century BC. His confidence in the traditional dates was strengthened by one independent piece of evidence. The date for the end of the Late Geometric is determined by firm associations (in Greece) with pottery of the Early Protocorinthian style. Coldstream's starting point for the latter depends on a discovery at the

Greek colony of Pithekoussai, which though it has no traditional date is generally thought to be the first in the West. In Grave 325 very early Protocorinthian vessels were associated with an Egyptian scarab of Pharaoh Bocchoris, whose reign is usually dated between 720 and 715 BC.[22] Nobody can know how old this scarab was when it was buried: it might easily have come to rest there many years after its manufacture. To hang the Protocorinthian sequence from a date based upon a single find is a dangerous, though currently expedient, exercise.

FIG. 5:2   An unusual scene of a shipwreck, from a Late Geometric vase discovered at the Greek colony of Pithekoussai, Italy (*after Boardman 1980*).

Not only is the evidence from the colonies difficult to accept on practical grounds; the interpretation given to it is far from consistent. At Gela the excavators wanted to keep the date of 700 BC for the end of Early Protocorinthian set by Humfry Payne, the first to develop a chronology for Corinthian pottery. They argued that the Early Protocorinthian pottery from Gela must have come from a precolonial settlement and not the colony itself, founded in 688 BC. Coldstream rejected this proposal, feeling that 'if such an argument were admitted, it would be difficult to interpret any of the Western dating evidence with complete objectivity'.[23]

As a result, he lowered the date of the end of Early Protocorinthian to 690 BC. But Coldstream's ground rule for pottery dating seems to have fallen out of use. Even though earlier material is now known from other colony sites, this has *not* led to any change, i.e. to a lowering of dates. What was overlooked in 1931 when the colony dates were first used to set the pottery chronology was that the earliest remains were unlikely to have turned up readily in the small-scale excavations originally undertaken. It should come as no surprise that as further work takes place earlier material is encountered at more of these Greek settlements. For example at Syracuse (Thucydidean date 733 BC) mid-8th-century Euboean pottery has been found.[24] Each time such finds are uncovered the logical consequence would be to adjust the pottery chronology downwards to fit the colony dates. Unfortunately, the system has ossified and no changes have been made in the last twenty years.

The colony dates given by Thucydides remain the best available. Yet attempts to apply them to the pottery chronology have been woefully inconsistent, with a tendency to cling to the highest possible estimates. The recent finds, combined with the possibility that Thucydides' dates may be slightly too old, suggest that a reduction of pottery dates in the order of twenty-five years is feasible. This comes some way to meeting the 'recalibration' of Archaic chronology proposed by Francis and Vickers, but to go further would require a wholesale rejection of the colony evidence.

Hamath: full of eastern promise

Before the period of western colonization, archaeology and the traditional history of Greece follow separate paths. While the ancient authors provide a chronology for the lineage of the Spartan kings going back to Heracles himself, and some suspiciously precise placements for events such as the Trojan War and the subsequent 'Return of the Heraclids', none of their calculations, frankly, can be trusted (see Appendix 2). The innumerable attempts to derive dates for the archaeological record from this semi-mythological material have been to no avail. That the impossibly high dates for Phoenician colonies in the West (see Chapter 2) were drawn from these same sources should in itself be sufficient warning against relying on them.

Attempting to find more solid ground, archaeologists have turned to the Near East. Indirect links via Cyprus exist, but they are generally ignored because of the extreme difficulty of producing an agreed chronology between Cyprus and Palestine (see Chapter 7). More directly, Geometric pottery has been discovered at many sites in Syria and Palestine, where dates for the stratigraphy are thought to be sound because they are historically based. This controlling evidence, the essential criteria for dating the various Geometric phases, comes from a few key sites in the Levant – namely Hamath, Samaria, Megiddo, Tyre and Tell Abu Hawam (see Map 10).

Unfortunately, firm agreement among Near Eastern archaeologists over the dating of the strata in which Geometric exports occur is rare, a fact which has always been a matter of great concern to Aegean specialists. The case involving the ancient city of Hamath (modern Hama) in Syria is generally thought to be certain and is therefore often used as a starting point. With this in mind Cook wrote:

> It is different with Hama, which was destroyed by the Assyrians – as their records tell us – in 720 B.C.: so the one example of the Attic Middle Geometric II and the three Late Geometric fragments must be earlier.[25]

A review by Francis and Vickers reached a very different conclusion. Although they accepted that one Middle Geometric sherd[26] was found in a burnt deposit attributed to the Assyrian conquest of 720 BC, they stressed the fact that the three Late Geometric examples found at the site were strays, which could not be associated with any particular stratum. Coldstream's assumption that 'the three LG fragments . . . cannot be later than 720' because Hamath 'lay desolate' after the Assyrian conquest is contradicted by Sargon II's own statement that he recolonized the land with Assyrians and

FIG. 5:3   Typical Middle Geometric II vessel from the Kerameikos, Athens.

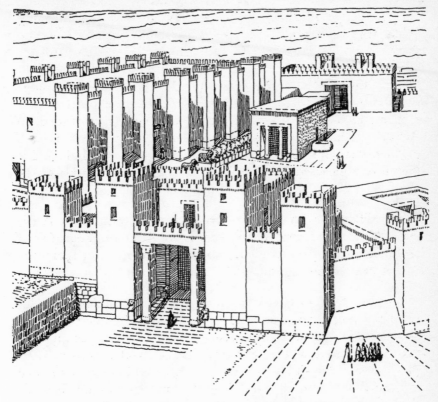

FIG. 5:4   A reconstruction of the 8th-century Aramaean citadel of Hamath (*from Fugmann 1958*).

Medians,[27] and by archaeological evidence for a reoccupation.[28] Francis and Vickers concluded that there is:

> . . . no compelling reason to believe that any of the LG trio belongs to vessels already at Hama when Sargon II destroyed it . . . On the evidence presented in the excavation reports they may equally be attributed to a later occupation . . . since so much depends on the interpretation of these finds, we suggest that they continue to remain *sub judice* until a sealed deposit of pre-720 LG comes to light in the Syro-Palestinian region.[29]

It seems that Hamath can be used as a *terminus ante quem* only for the manufacture of Middle – certainly not Late – Geometric pottery. Moreover, even the cut-off point of 720 BC for the earlier style is questionable. It relies on the assumption that the city was destroyed by Sargon. While he boasted his destruction of the 'land of Hamath', specifying that he burnt the city of Karkar, any reference to Hamath the city is conspicuously absent from his records.[30] Thus the promise once offered by Hamath, of providing the most reliable chronological fix after the Mycenaeans, seems to melt away.

Samaria and Megiddo: Geometric finds in Israel

Fragments of Greek pottery exported to Israel during the Dark Age are usually held to provide invaluable pointers to the dating of the Middle Geometric style. Six sherds were discovered at Samaria, capital of ancient Israel, by a British team. Unfortunately, the crucial Middle Geometric II pieces came from 'adjoining strips . . . in a disturbed area which were labelled respectively Period V, Period VII, Hellenistic and Late Roman! The find-spots therefore throw no light on the date . . .'[31] Nevertheless, one of the excavators, Kathleen Kenyon – albeit working from memory – seemed confident that at least one Middle Geometric piece was found in 'undisturbed stratification' of Period V.[32] On the strength of this same sherd Coldstream declared that:

> The end of MG II must be placed not later than c. 750 B.C., since the dating of Period V at Samaria to the early eighth century is generally accepted.[33]

The value of this single sherd has been queried by Francis and Vickers. Stressing the uncertainties involved in the 'notoriously confused' stratigraphy of Samaria, as well as the possibility mooted by Olga Tufnell that Period V's structures may have been sealed as late as the Assyrian sack in c. 722 BC (see Chapter 8), they concluded:

> The excavation reports themselves provide no objective stratificational basis for attributing the one critical MG II sherd . . . to 'the early eighth century' and, in default of stratigraphically definite information regarding the sherd's precise locus, we think it only prudent to accept the Assyrian destruction as the earliest *terminus ante quem* for MGII at Samaria.[34]

In the Jezreel Plain north of Samaria lies Megiddo, one of the most extensive city mounds of ancient Palestine. Here, two Middle Geometric sherds were discovered by an American team in the

1930s, and reported as coming from Stratum V. The stratigraphy of the site is particularly complex, and many corrections to it were made during the time between the original excavations in the 1930s and the Israeli work of the 1960s. A major revision was the conflation of the upper part of Stratum V with the lower parts of its successor Stratum IV – resulting in the definition of a new composite level, VA/IVB. Further, dates assigned by biblical archaeologists to the end of this new stratum varied considerably, ranging from 925 to 850 BC.

Reviewing the various schemes on offer, Coldstream wisely opted for the lowest available dating. Classifying the two Greek sherds in question as Attic MGI, he concluded that this period must have begun by the mid-9th century BC:

> The closing of this composite stratum must now be taken as the *terminus ante quem* for the date of our MGI sherds . . . at all events, they cannot be *later* than the latest possible date for the end of the new Stratum VA/IVB.[35]

However, after a period of relative certainty, serious doubts arose about the exact find-spots of the pieces. An investigation by A. J. Hoerth of the Oriental Institute of Chicago showed that the facts regarding the Geometric sherds had been incorrectly reported in the first place: 'at least one of the fragments was unearthed in stratum IV', with the second piece probably coming from the same level.[36] Stratum IV at Megiddo is generally thought to have been destroyed by the Assyrian conqueror Tiglath-pileser III in 733 BC, which would considerably lower the date of the Geometric sherds.[37] Worse still, the first fragment is associated with a building which, on the most recent analysis, stood until 609 BC.[38]

It is simply impossible to accept any longer that the Megiddo finds prove that Middle Geometric I had begun by the middle of the 9th century BC.

The Phoenician contribution: Tyre and Tell Abu Hawam

The wealthy Phoenician city of Tyre, situated on an island off the Lebanese coast, is the richest source of Early Iron Age Greek pottery in the Levant. Hundreds of examples are known but only a few have been found in undisturbed contexts. From her 1973–4 excavation at Tyre, Patricia Bikai published about fifteen stratified

Greek Dark Age sherds, ranging from the Late Protogeometric to Late Geometric periods.[39]

These fragments could have been given absolute dates were Tyre capable of producing an independent local chronology. Unfortunately this is not the case. Although a sound historical chronology for the Kings of Tyre can be established back to the time of Hiram in the early 10th century BC, at no point can this be tied to the archaeological material known from the city.[40] Dates for the Tyrian stratigraphy can be estimated only from finds of foreign objects. There are two major pegs. The beginning of Stratum XIII, the lowest Iron Age level, is dated to 1070/1050 BC by the occurrence of Cypriot 'White Painted Ware'. The next chronological marker is more certain; from the end of Stratum III an inscribed Egyptian urn of the 25th or 26th Dynasty was found, dating no earlier than 750, and possibly after 700 BC.[41] Accordingly, Bikai chose to place the close of Stratum III c. 725 BC.[42]

FIG. 5:5 Hieroglyphic text inscribed on a fragmentary urn unearthed at Tyre. It mentions an Egyptian priest 'Pasheri [. . .]' with 25th-26th Dynasty titles: 'Prophet of Amun-Ra, King of the Gods, Seal-bearer of the Lord of the Two Lands' (after Bikai 1978b).

Between these two pegs, all other strata (XII to IV) had to be spaced out to fill the available time, with the help of a few general Palestinian correlations, but, more important, with reference to the accepted Greek pottery chronology itself – a completely circular methodology since the latter can be dated only by Near Eastern connections! It is therefore not surprising that some of the Late Protogeometric and Middle Geometric I finds occur in contexts whose dates agree with the standard Greek pottery chronology.

Only one fragment of Middle Geometric II (conventionally 800–760 BC) is known from Tyre. This was found in Stratum III, dated by Bikai to c. 750–725 BC, which would make the Greek sherd slightly too old for its context. As a single find this is of no great importance, but it does seem to fit into a wider pattern of

MGII material being found in Eastern Mediterranean contexts half a century too late. Cases already noted are Hamath and Samaria. Further examples come from late 8th-century Cypriot tombs – a vase from Amathus, and at Salamis even a twenty-one piece royal 'dinner set'.[43]

It is curious that while Bikai took the traditional dates of LPG and MGI as a guideline for the earlier levels at Tyre, she could not do the same for MGII, as this would clash with the Egyptian evidence for dating Stratum III. Two points need to be underlined. First, it is dangerous to employ Greek material for dating purposes in this circular fashion. Second, there is now no firm evidence from any Near Eastern site to support the present high dating for the Middle Geometric II period.

For outside help in dating Dark Age pottery earlier than MGII Aegean archaeologists have always relied on the finds from Tell Abu Hawam, a southern Phoenician port near modern Haifa. The dates assigned to the destruction of its Stratum III provide the crucial benchmark. Indeed, for many decades the chronology of early Greek Geometric pottery has rested on two sherds from Tell Abu Hawam belonging to the Early Geometric II and Middle Geometric I periods.[44]

The destruction of Stratum III was variously dated by biblical archaeologists to between 925 BC and 815 BC.[45] When Coldstream examined the evidence in 1968 he chose the lowest estimate available, concluding that the Middle Geometric I style had already begun by the second half of the 9th century BC.[46] Clearly the Early Geometric must have started even earlier, a date of around 900 BC being extrapolated from the Tell Abu Hawam evidence, thus providing the terminal date for the Attic Protogeometric. As Desborough noted: 'A great deal, therefore, hinges on the two pieces found at Tell Abu Hawam.'[47]

However, the local problems involved in dating the destruction

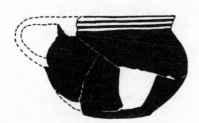

FIG. 5:6 Glazed cup, perhaps of Cycladic origin, found in Tell Abu Hawam Stratum III and attributed to the early Middle Geometric period (*after Coldstream 1977*).

of Stratum III remained acute. Placing its end in the 10th or 9th century BC created a considerable gap in occupation on the site before the next traces in Persian times. This apparent hiatus has now been considerably reduced by a revision carried out by Jacqueline Balensi, the latest excavator of Tell Abu Hawam. In her opinion Stratum III must have lasted to at least 750 BC[48] – a conclusion based on comparisons with the pottery of nearby Phoenician sites, including Tyre.

Balensi's work removes at a stroke the linch-pin of Greek Middle Geometric chronology. Tell Abu Hawam can certainly no longer be taken to uphold a 9th-century BC date for the beginning of this phase.

The 'compulsion of unaccountable time'

Far from supporting the high chronology current for Greek Dark Age pottery, the Near Eastern sites where it is found actually point to radically lower dates. The conventional placements for the beginning of Late Geometric (c. 760 BC), Middle Geometric (c. 850 BC) and Early Geometric (c. 900 BC) are thus completely unsubstantiated. The only other means of providing a chronology for these periods is simply to work backwards from the Archaic, using guesstimates based on internal criteria for their duration. But any adjustments this method would produce have always been constrained by the parameters of the absolute chronology.

Early attempts, for example that of J. M. Davison, considered that the Early Geometric began no earlier than 850 BC. She argued that the development of the styles employed by individual Attic workshops must have been rapid. Indeed, were it not for the limits set by the overall chronology she felt that 'not more than 100 or at most 150 years would have been proposed for the development of the whole Geometric style'. Davison lamented the conclusions resulting from:

> the compulsion of unaccountable time – there are presumably 200 years to be filled by Geometric pottery; therefore, the extant Geometric pottery must be so categorised and arranged as to fill out this preconceived framework.[49]

Coldstream objected to such low dates on the grounds of correlations with Levantine archaeology:

> At this stage we can only conclude that any attempt to compress Middle Geometric into . . . the first half of the eighth [century] will run counter to all the rival systems of Palestinian chronology.[50]

Such reasoning is clearly no longer supported by the Near Eastern evidence.

Similarly, a much shorter period of time could be allowed for the Protogeometric than the 125–150 years usually prescribed. Desborough expressed the opinion that the Protogeometric period should be made as 'short as possible'.[51] On the basis of the pottery sequences of Athens and Lefkandi, Mervyn Popham felt that the duration allocated is 'long for the degree of development and change in the pottery that can be discerned' and allowed that 'some shortening of the period could be sustained', perhaps to 100 years.[52]

Using the minimum estimates already available for the key periods would produce a dramatically lower chronology. The evidence from the western colony foundations suggests that the end of the Late Geometric period could be lowered by a couple of decades. As an experiment, if one placed the close of the Late Geometric about 675 BC and adopted Davison's figure of 100 years for the whole Geometric style, the end of the Protogeometric would fall around 775 BC. Following Popham's estimate of a century for the Protogeometric would put the end of Submycenaean at c. 875 BC. Allowing one generation for the Submycenaean[53] brings us to a date for the end of LHIIIC around 900 BC, nearly two centuries later than its conventional placement.

While reasonable, a reduction of this order would have to stretch the last Mycenaean phase, LHIIIC, to an impossible degree to avoid introducing an absolute hiatus into the archaeological record. In the last analysis Greek chronology before the Archaic period still hangs pendant-like from the Egyptian 'high point' for Mycenaean civilization fixed by Petrie a century ago (see Chapter 1). Problems in Mycenaean dating are still largely considered to be a matter of fine-tuning, due to an implicit faith in the accuracy of Egypt's absolute chronology.[54] It was only the application of Egyptian dates that inserted the long Dark Ages into the history of Greece, and, by extension, into that of Southern Europe.

Is it possible that a false turn was taken at the end of the last century, leaving us with a faulty chronology for the Mediterranean

Bronze Age? At first glance this would seem unlikely, given the established pattern of synchronisms between the Aegean, Anatolia, the Levant and Egypt during the Late Bronze Age. However, a review of these areas actually seems to confirm, rather than dispel, our doubts.

CHAPTER 6

Redating the Hittite Empire

Until the late 19th century the Hittites were a truly 'lost' civilization. The idea that they had ruled an empire dominating most of Anatolia and northern Syria during the Late Bronze Age was unheard of. The credit for rediscovering them belongs to one William Wright, an Irish missionary to Damascus who, in 1872, was shown some curious stone blocks in the bazaar of the Syrian town of Hamath. They were carved with intricate symbols bearing enough superficial resemblance to Egyptian hieroglyphics to indicate that they represented a system of writing; in all other respects, however, they were completely unintelligible. Nevertheless, Wright correctly ascribed the inscriptions to the Hittites[1] – a shot in the dark since the Hittites were, at the time, known solely from a few oblique references in the Old Testament. From these it could be said, at most, that the Hittites were one constituent of the highly mixed population of the ancient Levant and that Hittite kingdoms had existed to the north of Israel during the age of Solomon and his successors (10th–9th centuries BC).[2]

The 'Hamath Stones' were not the first Hittite monuments to be examined. During the mid-19th century a number of European explorers had already investigated many of the visible remains at Boghazköy (once Hattuša, the capital of the Hittites) and other sites in central Anatolia, such as the picturesque rock sanctuary at Yazilikaya, but without correctly understanding their nature. The sculptures were mistakenly attributed to the Medes, Persians, Assyrians or even the Egyptians. The real identity of their creators, the inventors of the hieroglyphic writing found on stelae and rock-carvings scattered throughout Turkey, Syria and Mesopotamia, remained a mystery.

Wright's contribution was to link this script with the biblical Hittites. His case was taken up in 1876 by the noted orientalist Archibald Sayce, who propounded the bold hypothesis that the Hittites had once ruled an empire reaching from the coasts of the Black Sea and the Aegean to northern Syria. Egyptian records seemed to allude to such an entity – the armies of a people known as the 'Kheta' repeatedly confronted 18th and 19th Dynasty Pharaohs

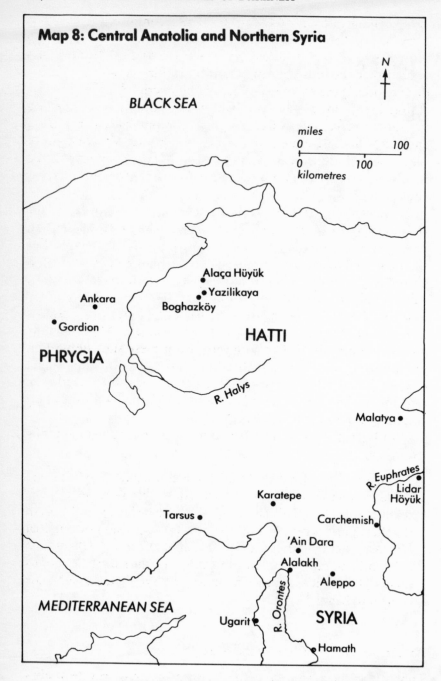

Map 8: Central Anatolia and Northern Syria

campaigning in Syria. Assyrian texts also commonly referred to Syria as the 'land of Hatti', a name equivalent to the Egyptian term Kheta. Sayce identified both with the biblical Hittites, and argued that the existence of a Hittite Empire could explain the distribution of the mysterious hieroglyphic script.[3]

Initial reactions to Sayce's theory were distinctly cool. The idea that an extensive, but entirely forgotten, empire had existed in the ancient Near East grated on the preconceptions of 19th-century scholarship. Indeed, there seem to be only two references in the whole of classical literature which, with the benefit of hindsight, could conceivably relate to the Hittite Empire.[4]

With such meagre support from the received knowledge of the classics Sayce had great difficulty in convincing his contemporaries. A further major objection concerned the time-scale involved. The Egyptian references to the 'Kheta' are dated to the 15th–13th centuries BC. On the other hand, Assyrian records mentioning the 'land of Hatti' came largely from the 1st millennium BC: they describe a group of prosperous city-states in south-east Anatolia and northern Syria, notably Carchemish, Hamath, Malatya, Gurgum and Kummukh. The sculptures from these sites showed an unmistakable relationship with Late Assyrian art, particularly that of the 9th and 8th centuries BC. What relevance, then, could the remains of these much later Hittite states have to a hypothetical empire of the 2nd millennium BC?

Otto Puchstein, a German art historian, summarized the problem in 1890:

> . . . neither here [in Asia Minor] nor in northern Syria is there evidence that so-called Hittite sculpture already existed in the tenth century B.C. This fact seems to me to be incompatible with the views of Sayce. For him the greatest expansion of Imperial Hittite power, and thus the flourishing of Hittite art, falls almost half a millennium before the time in which the surviving monuments of ancient Commagene [northern Syria] and Asia Minor came into being.[5]

An empire without an archaeology

Thus, from the very outset, the major problem of Hittite studies was one of chronology. The fruitful years of Near Eastern archaeology at the end of the 19th century produced only further confusing results. Most of the Hittite monuments under study, largely relief carvings and other sculpture, lay in south-east Anatolia and northern Syria. While much of this art clearly borrowed from Late Assyrian styles, the date of the remains from the central Anatolian plateau (such as those at Alaça Hüyük, Boghazköy and Yazilikaya), which showed less direct Mesopotamian influence, was more open to question. Some archaeologists felt they could even detect parallels with Egyptian and Mycenaean art of the 14th to 13th centuries BC.[6]

FIG. 6:1   Nineteenth-century sketch of the winged sphinx from the Hittite city of Alaça Hüyük, central Anatolia. The sculpture betrays the influence of Egyptian New Kingdom art (from Maspero 1896).

Nevertheless, around 1900 the consensus remained that the majority of the central Anatolian monuments, like those in Syria, belonged to the 1st millennium BC. Even H. R. Hall, a doughty adversary of the low chronologist Torr (see Chapter 1) and a leading proponent of high dates for Mycenaean and Minoan civilizations, agreed. Denying any of the proposed links between the Mycenaean and Hittite cultures, he insisted on placing the former in the 14th–13th centuries BC, while giving a date no earlier than the 9th century BC for the latter.[7] In such a climate of opinion the Hittite regime envisaged by Sayce seemed to be an empire without an archaeology. Two sensational developments, however, were to vindicate his theory.

The first was the discovery of the royal Egyptian archive at El-Amarna. In 1887 a peasant woman rummaging through its ruins turned up some clay tablets. News soon reached local antiquities dealers, and hundreds of tablets had escaped into private collections by the time that archaeologists had taken a serious interest in the matter. Excavations of the site eventually took place, including work by Petrie between 1891 and 1892 which recovered twenty-two fragments.[8] Meanwhile, European and American museums had begun the long task of bringing together and reconstructing some 300 letters, comprising one of the most important groups of documents known from the entire ancient world.[9] The tablets were inscribed with cuneiform Akkadian, the already deciphered language of ancient Babylonia, which evidently served as the *lingua franca* of the Near Eastern Late Bronze Age. The texts proved to be the diplomatic correspondence of Pharaohs Amenhotep III, Akhenaten and Tutankhamun, not only with their vassals in Palestine and Syria, but also with the other great powers adjacent to, and often vying for possession of, these territories.

Thus as well as giving a vividly detailed snapshot of the workings of the 18th Dynasty Egyptian Empire, the El-Amarna archive provides an invaluable source of political information regarding contemporary Western Asia (see Chapter 12). Among the letters were two from Suppiluliuma I of Hatti, a 'Great King' evidently on an equal footing with the Pharaoh himself. The latest El-Amarna correspondence, from the time of Tutankhamun, revealed the extent of Suppiluliuma's power: after eliminating the Kingdom of Mitanni (Egypt's ally) in a contest for the control of northern Syria, Hittite armies marched as far south as the Lebanon, and severely weakened Egyptian power in the area.

The second major development came in 1906 when Hugo Winckler began his excavations at Boghazköy, uncovering an even greater archive of cuneiform tablets (more than 10,000 in number), many in Akkadian; others were in the Nesite branch of the Hittite language group, which was deciphered by 1915. These discoveries revealed that Boghazköy, with its palaces, temples and magnificent defence-works, was Hattuša, the long-sought centre of the ancient Hittite Empire, which had, at its peak, dominated Anatolia and Syria.

FIG. 6:2   Ramesses II lays siege to the town of Dapur in northern Syria. His records say that he seized it from the Hittites in his year 8.

The Boghazköy records provided an unexpected wealth of detail on the complex relations between the Hittites and Egypt, the annals of Great King Suppiluliuma I completing the story begun in the El-Amarna letters. On the death of Tutankhamun, his widow wrote to Suppiluliuma requesting a Hittite prince for a husband. Suppiluliuma sent one of his sons to marry her, but he was murdered on arrival.[10] After this extraordinary episode, during which Hatti and Egypt came close to dynastic unification, war was renewed. It continued sporadically until the time of Suppiluliuma's grandson, Hattusili III, who launched an offensive against Pharaoh Ramesses II, culminating in the famous battle of Kadesh on their Syrian frontier. Eventually the combatants, both under pressure from the Assyrians and, perhaps, the rise of nationalist states within Syro-Palestine, signed a treaty; the copy belonging to Hattusili was found at Boghazköy, paralleling the Egyptian version carved on the walls of the Ramesseum and the Temple of Amun at Karnak.[11]

Peaceful relations continued throughout the 19th Dynasty,

Ramesses' son Merneptah even sending supplies of corn to the Hittites.[12] The Boghazköy archive dries up after the reign of Suppiluliuma II, who must have been a contemporary of Ramesses III in Egypt. The records of both countries suggest that the Hittites were, by then, in difficulties, and it is assumed that the destruction of Boghazköy and other Late Bronze Age centres took place not long afterwards.

The discovery of these detailed records left absolutely no doubt about the relative chronology of the Hittite Empire. It could now be firmly synchronized with the 18th and 19th Dynasties, and hence dated, by the accepted Egyptian chronology, to the 15th–13th centuries BC. The fall of the Empire would then have taken place between 1200 and 1175 BC. Accordingly, the dates for the remains at Boghazköy, Yazilikaya and related sites in central Anatolia were sharply raised by several centuries.

A Hittite 'afterglow'

The establishment of an Egyptian-based chronology for the Hittite Empire had some curious effects on the interpretation of its archaeology. The Hittite world became divided into two chronological, and to some extent geographical, parts: (a) the original area of Hittite civilization in central Anatolia, together with some major dependencies (such as Tarsus in southern Anatolia and Ugarit on the north Syrian coast), whose relationship to 14th to 13th-century BC Egypt is well documented;[13] and (b) the lesser Hittite states to the south, dated by their links with 10th to 8th-century Assyrian history. These two groups shared the use of Hittite hieroglyphics and the same basic cultural and artistic traditions, but they appeared to be separated in time by a gulf of 200–300 years.

Thus, although the theory of a Hittite Empire had been confirmed, the simple interpretation of Sayce, Wright and other scholars – that the distribution of Hittite hieroglyphics and art mirrored the extent of its political control – had to be abandoned. The original model was replaced by a significantly different one, the broad lines of which run as follows.

During the Late Bronze Age the Hittites extended their sway over south-east and eastern Anatolia and northern Syria. Then, around 1200 BC, beset by economic troubles, the Empire collapsed under pressure from 'barbarian' invaders, including the so-called

Sea Peoples (see p. 18). The invaders sacked the main centres (most of which show signs of burning) and plunged Anatolia into a Dark Age of several centuries' duration. The Empire was forgotten and its capitals abandoned until they were reoccupied by the Phrygians, immigrants from the Balkans, some 400 years later. In the meantime, however, Hittite civilization had begun to flourish again to the south-east, in what has been described as a 'strange afterglow which lasted for no less than five centuries'.[14] This 'afterglow' is so pronounced that most scholars believe that there was a migration of 'Hieroglyphic Hittites' (speakers of the Luwian branch of the language) fleeing southern Anatolia after the fall of the Empire.[15] Founding 'Neo-Hittite' states in areas once ruled by the Empire they perpetuated Hittite customs, religion, names, hieroglyphic writing and styles in art and architecture until the Assyrian conquest of the 8th century BC.

To date, not a shred of hard evidence has been produced to confirm the major outlines of this model. The Egyptian texts of Ramesses III, usually invoked to support the theory that the Hittite Empire was destroyed by a sweeping invasion of Sea Peoples, actually say nothing of the sort, although they do obliquely refer to a war in which the Hittites were involved.[16] Likewise, there is no historical evidence for a movement of Hieroglyphic Hittites, under pressure from invading Sea Peoples or otherwise, in the following years. There are other grounds for seeing the whole hypothesis as unnecessary. Hieroglyphic writing was already in use in northern Syria under the Empire, while the languages reflected in the choice of personal names of Iron Age Syria provide no support for the previous arrival of new peoples.[17]

The simplest explanation would still seem to be that the civilizations of south-east Anatolia and northern Syria received their Hittite stamp during the centuries when the Empire dominated those regions. But this apparently logical model seems impossible to reconcile with the presently accepted chronology for Hittite history. Some north Syrian cities reflect direct Imperial Hittite control, seen from both historical and archaeological evidence: for example, Imperial Hittite correspondence and seals have been discovered at Ugarit in 14th–13th-century levels,[18] while similar finds at Alalakh (including a relief of Great King Tudhaliya IV) reveal increasing Hittite influence over the same period.[19] Neither of these cities, however, survived into the Iron Age. On the other hand, where the 'afterglow' in northern Syria and south-east Anatolia persisted into the Iron Age, its beginning is generally dated two centuries too late to be linked with the Empire.

Dark Age or Golden Age?

This dilemma seems to have come about because, as already discussed, the archaeology of the 'Neo-Hittite' states has been dated principally by links with Mesopotamian rather than Egyptian chronology. Assyrian history can be firmly dated from about 900 BC onwards (see Chapter 11), Late Assyrian art being one of the most richly documented of the ancient world.[20] From the mid-9th century onwards its Empire began to control the city-states of northern Syria and south-east Anatolia, which soon started to emulate the art of their masters.[21] By the second half of the 8th century BC the area was finally absorbed by Assyria.

Thus the degree of Assyrian influence on a particular Neo-Hittite sculpture provides a useful yardstick for dating. Yet Imperial Hittite styles and motifs can still be detected in much of the art, despite the low dates derived from Assyrian comparisons. The application of two systems of stylistic criteria to the art of the Neo-Hittite states has resulted in a chronological tug-of-war, horribly reminiscent of those in the Dark Age controversies elsewhere.

FIG. 6:3　Fragment of relief from Carchemish showing a winged genie. Details such as the wings, costume, and small bucket, betray the influence of Late Assyrian art and place this sculpture in the 8th century BC (drawing by David Hawkins).

The basic sequence of Neo-Hittite art was outlined in the 1940s by Ekrem Akurgal, the doyen of Turkish archaeology. He defined an 'Early' phase between c. 1100/1050 and 900/850 BC.[22] There were difficulties, however, as his principal examples for this stage, from the Lion Gate at Malatya, were ascribed by their excavator to an 8th-century BC building complex (see below). Still, Akurgal felt obliged to accept an earlier date: 'no other conclusion is possible since the artists had direct knowledge of the art of the Hittite empire'.[23]

Akurgal's 'Middle Neo-Hittite' phase, c. 900–750/730 BC, is characterized by the introduction of Assyrian motifs. He also defined a 'Late Neo-Hittite' period following the Assyrian conquest – during which the remaining Hittite element in the art was swamped by Assyrian, Aramaean (Syrian) and Phoenician styles and practically disappears altogether.[24] (Winfried Orthmann's more recent classification is also shown in Table 6:1.)

Akurgal's chronology was energetically attacked by Henri Frankfort, then the foremost expert on ancient Near Eastern art.

Table 6:1

Akurgal	*Orthmann*	*Examples*
Early Neo-Hittite c. 1100/1050–900/850 BC	**Late Hittite I** c. 1000–950 BC	Carchemish Water Gate; 'Ain Dara (nr Unki)
Middle Neo-Hittite c. 900/850–750/730 BC	**Late Hittite II** c. 950–850 BC	Carchemish Suhis to Katuwas group; Malatya Lion Gate; Marash Palalam stela
	Late Hittite IIIa c. 850–750 BC	Carchemish Yariris & Kamanis group; Malatya and Marash – miscellaneous pieces
Late Neo-Hittite c. 730–700 BC	**Late Hittite IIIb** c. 750–700 BC	Carchemish Pisiri style; Malatya colossus; Karatepe, late (?) material

The generally accepted dating scheme for Late or Neo-Hittite sculpture, following the work of Orthmann (1971; cf. Hawkins 1982, 436); the earlier system of Akurgal is given for comparison (1946, 1968). Some of the main examples of Neo-Hittite art within Orthmann's classification are given.

Regarding the sculptures of the Lion Gate at Malatya, he agreed that Akurgal had established 'their close affinity to imperial Hittite art':

> But he does not dare to draw the conclusion that they belong to the second millennium, as his own evidence suggests to me. This is due to his overrating the continuity between Hittite art and the sculptures of the ninth–seventh century B.C. . . . His argument that the lions cannot belong to the imperial period is not convincing . . . the lions are certainly not closer to those of the first than those of the second millennium. They share, moreover, with the god at the Royal Gate of Boghazköy the most peculiar device of hair rendering by a network of single linear spirals.[25]

Frankfort was prepared to follow to the letter the indications of Imperial Hittite influence on the one hand, and Assyrian and Aramaean influence on the other, effectively dividing all Hittite art into two blocks: one ending in the 13th century BC, the other beginning in the 9th. He insisted that there was no continuity between the two, asking how the latter could possibly have preserved 'intact a detailed iconographical tradition throughout the period of the migrations of the Sea-People which utterly destroyed the Hittite Empire'.[26]

In Frankfort's view, the 12th to mid-9th centuries in south-east Anatolia and northern Syria were a cultural Dark Age.[27] What he failed to explain, logical as he may have been in his chronological conclusions, was the obvious evidence of continuity between the two ages. Stressing this, his opponent Albright arrived at a diametrically opposite conclusion:

> . . . the refusal of an earlier authority to recognize the existence of any monumental art or architecture in the neo-Hittite states between 1200 and 850 B.C. was entirely wrong . . . the eleventh and tenth centuries were the golden age of Syro-Hittite art and architecture.[28]

It is a striking testimony to the confusion inherent in the chronology that two eminent authorities could describe the same period of time as a 'Dark Age' and a 'Golden Age' respectively. The problem remains as desperate today as it was at the time of Frankfort and

Albright. David Hawkins, the leading authority on the Neo-Hittite states of the 12th to 10th centuries, despairingly concluded that:

> During these three centuries, such archaeological remains as have been discovered in Syria float in a chronological vacuum . . .[29]

Carchemish: Hittite capital of Syria

The examination of two key sites may provide some clues to the conundrum of Hittite chronology. These are Carchemish and Malatya, where excavation has uncovered the richest sequences of Neo-Hittite inscriptions and art. The two cities figure prominently in the historical records from both the Late Bronze and Iron Ages; their remains might, then, hold the vital evidence needed to clarify the relationship between the Empire and its dependencies to the south-east.

Carchemish on the Euphrates was conquered by the Hittites in the very year that Tutankhamun died, as we know from the extraordinary fact that his widow wrote to 'Great King' Suppiluliuma I as he laid siege to the city. The capture of Carchemish can thus be dated c. 1325 BC by the conventional Egyptian chronology. Thereafter the city remained firmly in Hittite hands and was the seat of the cadet branch of the royal family responsible for governing Syria. The imperial dynasty at Carchemish is well known – through letters, treaties, seals and other texts – from Piyasili the son of Suppiluliuma to his descendant Talmi-Teshub, who must have lived a generation or so before the collapse of the Empire at the beginning of the 12th century BC. Then, after a grey period of some centuries, Carchemish reappears in the Assyrian records of the 9th century onwards, as a vigorous and rich (particularly in metals) independent kingdom, the apparent leader of the Neo-Hittite states.[30]

After some preliminary trenching in the 1870s, work at Carchemish was resumed by the British Museum in 1911, directed by David Hogarth with Leonard Woolley and T. E. Lawrence ('of Arabia'). The excavation may originally have doubled as a spying operation, the site lying close to the German-built Istanbul to Baghdad railway; the First World War interrupted the work, and subsequent hostilities meant that the project had to be abandoned in 1920. Conditions were hardly ideal: many notes and finds were lost during these troubled years, and the final publication of the site, left

Table 6:2

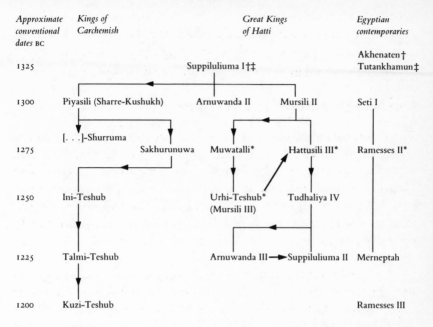

Approximate conventional dates BC	Kings of Carchemish		Great Kings of Hatti		Egyptian contemporaries
					Akhenaten† Tutankhamun‡
1325			Suppiluliuma I†‡		
1300	Piyasili (Sharre-Kushukh)		Arnuwanda II	Mursili II	Seti I
	[. . .]-Shurruma				
1275		Sakhurunuwa	Muwatalli*	Hattusili III*	Ramesses II*
1250	Ini-Teshub		Urhi-Teshub* (Mursili III)	Tudhaliya IV	
1225	Talmi-Teshub		Arnuwanda III→Suppiluliuma II		Merneptah
1200	Kuzi-Teshub				Ramesses III

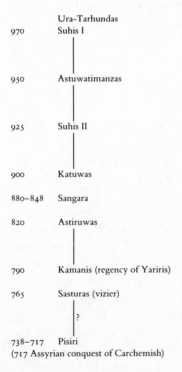

GAP IN HITTITE RECORDS

	Ura-Tarhundas
970	Suhis I
950	Astuwatimanzas
925	Suhis II
900	Katuwas
880–848	Sangara
820	Astiruwas
790	Kamanis (regency of Yariris)
765	Sasturas (vizier)
	?
738–717	Pisiri
(717 Assyrian conquest of Carchemish)	

Chart showing the known Hittite kings of Carchemish. Dates for the first sequence are based on those for the Great Kings of Hatti (Hittite Emperors), whose chronology is linked to that of Egypt. The line of succession in the two houses is shown by arrows. Synchronisms with specific pharaohs are indicated by symbols. After about 1200 BC there is supposed to be a gap in documentation. Assyrian records from the reign of Tiglath-pileser I (conventionally dated *c.* 1100 BC) contain a reference to a Hittite king called Ini-Teshub, generally assumed to be a king of Carchemish and the second ruler of that name; such an individual, however, is unattested at Carchemish. Apart from this problematic reference the records are completely silent regarding Carchemish between the early 12th and 10th centuries BC. Thereafter a line of kings can be reconstructed from the native monuments and Assyrian records (Woolley and Barnett 1952, 240, 259–66; Mallowan 1972, 64; Hawkins 1974, 70; 1986, 260).

to Woolley, appeared only in 1952. Nevertheless, the archaeologists involved were among the best of their day, and keenly
interested in the chronological potential of the site.

The limited excavation concentrated on the palace complex and
monumental gateways, bringing to light an invaluable collection of
stone sculptures, many of which bear inscriptions. Most of the
material can be securely arranged in chronological order not only
by style but by the clues in the texts. All analyses, from Woolley's
onwards, agree on the same basic sequence and dating (see Table
6:2): beginning with a dynasty founded by Suhis I in the early 10th
century, the information takes us down to the time of Pisiri, last
independent King of Carchemish before its capture by the Assyrians in 717 BC. Woolley established that these monuments were
associated with a style of Iron Age pottery which he named
'Yunus', after a nearby cemetery. Preceding this was an 'Amarna'
Late Bronze Age ware, also known from graves.[31] By contrast the
excavation of the city itself barely penetrated the Late Bronze Age
levels and the bulk of the excavated material seems to date from the
10th to 8th centuries BC.

Despite this fact, the excavators assigned several of the unin-
scribed reliefs to the Bronze Age, on grounds of style. In 1911
Hogarth noted the resemblance of those on the 'Herald's Wall' and
the 'Water Gate' to the Hittite sculptures from central Anatolia,
particularly those from Alaça Hüyük, and suggested a date in the

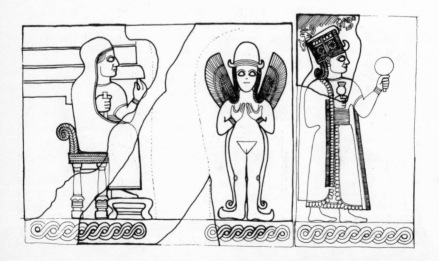

14th and 13th centuries BC.[32] He met strong opposition from art historians, who stressed the Late Assyrian influence visible in the same sculptures. By 1924, Hogarth had retreated from his original position and denied that there was any artwork or inscription from Carchemish which could be dated before the 12th century BC.[33] Woolley, however, held out longer. Following Hogarth's original impressions, he dated the reliefs of the Herald's Wall (see Plate 13) to the Late Bronze Age, arguing that much of its iconography derived from the art of the Mitanni Empire, which had dominated north-eastern Syria before its conquest by Suppiluliuma I.[34] Likewise, the sculptures of the Water Gate were, according to Woolley, 'on archaeological grounds definitely assigned to the Middle Hittite period, before 1200 B.C.'.[35] Nevertheless, later scholarship, as summarized by Max Mallowan, had to dismiss his estimates:

> The chronology and sequence dating of the rich series of sculptures discovered at Carchemish remains a problem, even after 60 years of investigation, but it is generally recognised that Leonard Woolley exaggerated the antiquity of some of the orthostats and

FIG. 6:4   A portion from the Long Wall of sculpture at Carchemish. The reliefs, depicting a procession of gods, were commissioned by a King Suhis, whose wife is shown on the left. He is generally agreed to be King Suhis II, who reigned at the end of the 10th century BC (drawing by David Hawkins).

it is no longer possible to assign any of them to the second millennium B.C. On the contrary, many critics will now support Frankfort's view that none of this particular series of sculptures could have been executed without an awareness of Neo-Assyrian art.[36]

The idea that the sculpture could reflect the influences of 'both' periods (13th-century Imperial Hittite and 10th-century Late Assyrian) was, of course, never entertained – such a concept would have been a chronological impossibility.

The controversial sculptures aside, many artefacts of much earlier date *were* discovered in the Neo-Hittite city. Near the Water Gate was found a stone mace-head bearing a Pharaoh's name, probably Ramesses II.[37] On a pavement which he dated no earlier than the 9th century BC, Woolley identified 'several late Mycenaean sherds and a piece of Cypriot Iron Age ware . . . These must have come from the Temple Treasury where they had been preserved for many generations.'[38] Excavating the Temple of the Storm God, he discovered a basalt stela which, as well as mentioning a 'Great King', is surmounted by a winged disc, the symbol of imperial power – it was evidently a relic from the Empire (see Fig. 6:7).

FIG. 6:5   (Left) One of the figures from the 7th-century BC 'Gold Tomb' at Carchemish. (Right) The Sun God as represented on the rock frieze at Yazilikaya in central Anatolia, conventionally dated to the 13th century BC.

In a tomb securely dated to the 7th century BC, Woolley found a series of small gold figures[39] which bear a striking resemblance to the pantheon on the frieze at Yazilikaya, conventionally dated to the 13th century BC. Hans Güterbock noted that this discovery 'links the Late Hittite period with the time of the Empire . . . There is no doubt that both in style and in subjects these figures . . . are Hittite in the sense of the Hittite Empire at Boghazköy.' Yet he wondered: 'How did carvings of the thirteenth century get into a tomb of the seventh?'[40] Woolley himself considered that the jewellery was manufactured during Neo-Hittite times, but in a style which had, somehow, been preserved for 500 years. Güterbock preferred to see them as heirlooms, brought to Carchemish by the Imperial Hittites and 'kept in the treasury in spite of the change in domination', or, alternatively, that they had been carried there by migrating Hieroglyphic Hittites who had joined in the looting of the Late Bronze Age centres when they were sacked by barbarian invaders around 1200 BC.

With so many 'heirlooms' at Carchemish it may seem surprising that Woolley was not tempted to explain them by simply backdating the construction of the Neo-Hittite city to the time of the Empire. The pottery sequence, established by the evidence of the nearby Amarna and Yunus cemeteries, prevented him taking such a step. Woolley initially considered setting the boundary between the Amarna and Yunus styles as late as c. 720 BC, when the city was conquered by the Assyrians.[41] But after reflecting on the essentially Hittite character of the Yunus grave material, plus the association of Yunus pottery with the construction of the Neo-Hittite city, he concluded that it must represent a pre-Assyrian phase. Its beginning he set at the transition from the Late Bronze to Iron Ages, when the city was destroyed and rebuilt, between the time of the Sea Peoples invasion c. 1200 BC and the migration of Hieroglyphic Hittites to Carchemish, c. 1100 BC.[42]

In one sense Woolley was right: he insisted that a date of 1200/1100 BC was 'certainly the *terminus post quem* of the Yunus cemetery'.[43] To raise it higher by stretching the time-span of Yunus Ware any further would have been most unlikely. Indeed, recent studies suggest that his date could be reduced considerably. It has been argued that the Yunus cemetery actually began at the end of the 9th century;[44] further, pottery expert Kenneth Sams has drawn many comparisons between the Yunus painted ware and the Phrygian decorated ware known from central Anatolia in the 8th–7th centuries BC.[45] He therefore found 'puzzling' Woolley's association of Yunus Ware with a reconstruction of Carchemish c. 1200–1100 BC, and wondered 'whether, in reality, a considerable gap might have existed between the destruction and the resettlement'.[46]

The fallout from Sams's dating of the pottery would be the introduction of an archaeological 'Dark Age' at Carchemish, lasting from the early 12th to the late 9th century. But a gap of such length is contradicted by the historical evidence: securely dated references to Carchemish appear in Assyrian texts from the early 9th century, while the hieroglyphic inscriptions from the city itself allow the reconstruction of a local dynastic history back to the early 10th century BC. This still leaves, of course, an undocumented period of more than 200 years between the first Neo-Hittite dynasts and the last kings of Bronze Age Carchemish c. 1200 BC (see Table 6:2). So, to a limited degree, Sams's suggestion regarding a desertion of the site might seem to be supported.

Nevertheless, the idea that the site was abandoned for over two centuries fails to square with the evidence, from so many features, which demonstrates continuity from the Imperial to Neo-Hittite phases at Carchemish. In particular, Woolley noted that the Amarna and Yunus pottery phases, far from being separated by any gap, actually seem to overlap.[47] Since Sams's analysis shows that the Yunus pottery cannot be significantly raised in date, the only alternative would be to lower the dates for Amarna Ware.

Carchemish leaves us with a bizarre dichotomy: while the local material, from sculpture to pottery, suggests direct continuity between the Imperial and Neo-Hittite periods, the external evidence for dating actually suggests a considerable gap in its occupation.

The enigma of the 'Lion Gate'

The other main site where continuity has been sought is Malatya. Its excavation, by the French in the 1930s and by an Italian team since the 1960s, has uncovered buildings and fortifications reflecting a long history. Beneath an Assyrian palace was a monumental Neo-Hittite complex with a rich series of reliefs and inscriptions centring on the 'Lion Gate'; below these were the Late Bronze Age levels of the Hittite Empire. One might imagine Malatya, with the benefit of more extensive excavations, could hold some firmer clues to the relationship between the Imperial and Neo-Hittite periods.

The Lion Gate sculptures featured prominently in the wide-ranging controversy between Albright and Frankfort over the dating of ancient Near Eastern art (see Chapter 8). While Frankfort made a strong case for seeing these sculptures as a provincial product of Imperial Hittite art, his dating is impossible to reconcile with the stratigraphic evidence. Louis-Joseph Delaporte, who first excavated the Lion Gate, placed its construction in the 8th century

FIG. 6:6 (Above) Relief from the Lion Gate complex at Malatya, depicting a king (*PUGNUS-mili I) offering a libation before the gods (*after Frankfort 1969*). Until recently this carving was dated to the 10th century BC. Despite this, the close similarity in iconography and treatment to Hittite Imperial sculpture is conspicuous. (Right) Scene from the '13th'-century carvings at Yazilikaya showing King Tudhaliya IV embraced by the god Sharruma (*after Akurgal 1968*). Compare the shoes, swords with crescent pommels, the king's robes and curved staff, the god's short kilt, multi-horned crown and other details with those on the Malatya relief.

BC.[48] A late 10th to 9th-century date is currently preferred, and satisfies all the available criteria:

1 The Lion Gate lies below an Assyrian palace, presumably built soon after 713 BC, when the Assyrians conquered Malatya.[49]
2 It overlies a gateway dated by the Italian excavators to the late Hittite Empire[50] and is therefore later than *c*. 1200 BC.
3 Two radiocarbon tests on charred wood lying above the Imperial gateway give a date-range of 1040–910 BC.[51] The construction of the Lion Gate must postdate this burning.

4   The earliest sculptures from the Gate show a number of re-
    semblances to the Suhis group of sculptures from Carchemish
    (see Tables 6:1, 6:2 and Fig. 6:4), which can be dated indepen-
    dently between about 970 and 900 BC.

All things considered, it seems reasonable to date the main group
of sculptures decorating the Gate, along with its construction, to
some time after 950 BC. Yet their striking resemblance to works of
the Empire period remains worrying. Orthmann, while placing the
sculptures in the late 10th century BC, was puzzled by numerous
details of antiquated style.[52] Hawkins followed Orthmann, but
noted that:

> The Malatya sculpture forms a somewhat anomalous group
> within the Neo-Hittite assemblage. Stylistically it has closer
> affinities to the art of the Hittite Empire than with the rest of the
> Neo-Hittite group.[53]

A way out of this dilemma was offered by Frankfort, who
suggested that the Lion Gate sculptures were genuine products of
the Imperial age, *reused* in a much later building. The idea was
discounted by Orthmann, who, from a thorough first-hand examination of the reliefs, concluded that their arrangement and
dimensions fit perfectly with the available wall space in the Lion
Gate; they do not, on the other hand, suit the plan and scale of the
underlying Imperial gateway. Further, as Orthmann stressed,
'archaic' as the sculptures may be, they still stand at the beginning of
the stylistically related series of Neo-Hittite sculptures from
Malatya.[54]

Somehow it seems that two or three superfluous centuries inter-
vene between Imperial Hittite sculpture and its reflection at
Malatya. It is indeed remarkable that such a detailed stylistic and
iconographic tradition could have been faithfully preserved for so
long after the fall of the Empire. A similar continuity over the same
period of time can be seen in the small finds and pottery from
Neo-Hittite Malatya. As the latest excavators noted: 'the general
character of this material, especially of the pottery, does not differ
fundamentally from the Imperial Hittite production'.[55]

Kingship and continuity

The Malatya sculptures might have remained just another vague enigma of Dark Age chronology, were it not for a recent discovery which has brought the whole problem into much sharper focus. In 1985 two seal impressions were found in the final Late Bronze Age level at Lidar Höyük on the upper reaches of the Euphrates. Their inscriptions, in both hieroglyphic Hittite and cuneiform, give the owner's name as 'Kuzi-Teshub, king of the land of Carchemish, son of Talmi-Teshub, king of Carchemish'.[56]

The information is invaluable, as it extends the genealogy of the Late Bronze Age Kings of Carchemish by another generation, showing that Talmi-Teshub was not the last representative of Hittite imperial power in Syria. His son Kuzi-Teshub must have ruled in Carchemish very near the time that the Empire collapsed.

But the full consequences of this discovery began to unfold only in 1987, when David Hawkins re-examined the Lion Gate inscriptions. Two of the Malatyan kings claimed to be grandsons of 'a Great King, King of Carchemish' by the name of Kuzi-[X], the reading of the second hieroglyphic element being uncertain. The new seal impressions enabled Hawkins to establish a definitive reading of the name as Kuzi-Teshub. He immediately recognized the significance of this discovery:

> Given the discovery of the seal of Kuzi-Tešub king of Karkamiš, we are surely forced to read the name of the Melidian [Malatyan] grandfather as Kuzi-Tešub(as), and because of his titles . . . actually identify him as that king of Karkamiš, the son of Talmi-Tešub. A long sought piece of evidence for continuity between the Hittite Empire and the Neo-Hittite successor kingdoms is thus available . . .[57]

This 'surprising new evidence', as Hawkins described it, leaves little doubt that one of the major Neo-Hittite dynasties was directly descended from the imperial line. By itself it is enough to dispense, once and for all, with the absurd theory of Hieroglyphic Hittites who, on the collapse of the Empire, migrated to northern Syria where they resurrected Hittite civilization more than two centuries later.

The chronological consequences are even more profound. Following the generally accepted time-scale for the Late Bronze kings (which places Kuzi-Teshub shortly after 1200 BC), and assuming a generation length of between twenty-five and thirty years, Hawkins calculated new dates for his descendants at Malatya. Most of the Lion Gate sculptures bear inscriptions of a king whose name can be partially read as *PUGNUS-mili, a name borne by both a son and a great-grandson of Kuzi-Teshub:

> The author of the Lion Gate could be identified with either, which would date the Lion Gate to the early or late XIIth century B.C., a date up to two centuries earlier than recent opinions favour.[58]

To achieve this major shift, Hawkins had to reject the case for placing the Lion Gate in the late 10th–9th centuries, which he had once accepted. The stratigraphical and stylistic reasons for the low dating, as noted above, are supported by the radiocarbon dates on material found under the Gate giving a *terminus post quem* for its construction of 1040–910 BC. Aware of this difficulty, he suggested that the sculptures were 12th-century works reused in a much later building. Yet there are no earlier Neo-Hittite structures from which the sculptures could have come – the Lion Gate lies directly above the destruction level of the Late Bronze Age gateway.

The discovery of Kuzi-Teshub – the 'missing link' between the Hittite Empire and its offshoots – thus proves to be something of a problem. On the conventional chronology, well over 200 years separate the Hittite Empire of the 13th century BC from the Neo-Hittite kingdoms of the late 10th–9th centuries. Yet they are now connected, not only by the intimate resemblance of their art, pottery and culture, but also by a genealogical link! The strategy of redating the Lion Gate kings to the 12th century BC can be firmly rejected on the grounds of stratigraphy, art history and radiocarbon dating.

Yet there is an alternative, although a radical one. This is to question, not the accepted dates for the Iron Age sculptures of Malatya, but those for the Late Bronze Age as a whole. Following the generally agreed placement for the sculptures, and allowing twenty-five years per generation, we can allow a date for Kuzi-Teshub around 950 BC (see Table 6:3). This automatically reduces the dates for his father Talmi-Teshub and grandfather Ini-Teshub, together with those for the Hittite Emperors Tudhaliya IV and Hattusili III, with whom they are inextricably linked. The result would place the end of the Empire 225–250 years later than usual.

This experiment with the chronology of Malatya works, of course, only if one ignores the Egyptian-based chronology for the

Table 6:3

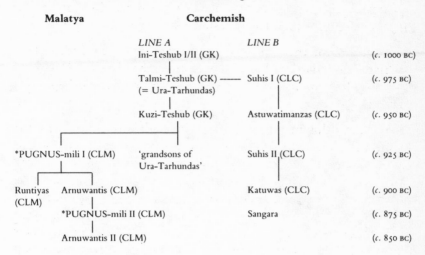

Malatya	Carchemish	
	LINE A	**LINE B**
	Ini-Teshub I/II (GK)		(*c.* 1000 BC)
	Talmi-Teshub (GK) ----- Suhis I (CLC)	(*c.* 975 BC)
	(= Ura-Tarhundas)	
	Kuzi-Teshub (GK)	Astuwatimanzas (CLC)	(*c.* 950 BC)
*PUGNUS-mili I (CLM)	'grandsons of	Suhis II (CLC)	(*c.* 925 BC)
	Ura-Tarhundas'	
Runtiyas Arnuwantis (CLM)	Katuwas (CLC)	(*c.* 900 BC)
(CLM)	
*PUGNUS-mili II (CLM)	Sangara	(*c.* 875 BC)
Arnuwantis II (CLM)		(*c.* 850 BC)

GK: 'Great King'
CLM: 'Country Lord' of Malatya
CLC: 'Country Lord' of Carchemish

The early Iron Age kings of Malatya and Carchemish – alternative scheme.
New evidence suggests that 'Great Kings' of Carchemish, members of the
Imperial Hittite family (Line A), ruled concurrently with local 'Country Lords'
at Carchemish (Line B) during the 10th century BC. The territory ruled by the
'Great Kings' also seems to have included Malatya, where their descendants
later held power.

Hittites. All the same, it receives some striking support from the
Carchemish evidence.

The Lion Gate sculptures find their closest parallels in those
produced by the 'Suhis dynasty' at Carchemish (Tables 6:1, 6:2),
dated to the mid to late 10th century BC. Suhis and his descendants
clearly commissioned and inscribed these sculptures, yet their role
as rulers of Carchemish remains mysterious. The titles they gave
themselves were restricted to the relatively modest tag: 'Lord of the
country of Carchemish'. Hovering alongside them, a presence
which Hawkins has increasingly noted during his collation of all
available Neo-Hittite inscriptions, is another line of kings who
seem to claim greater titles.

The key figure is a monarch known from the stela discovered by
Woolley in the Temple of the Storm God, always regarded as
problematic due to its 'archaic' style. The dedicator of the stela,

FIG. 6:7　Stela A4b from the Temple of the
Storm God, Carchemish (*after Woolley 1952*).

Ura-Tarhundas, as his name is usually read, described himself as
'Great King, King of Carchemish'.[59] Despite its imperial connotations, the stela was discovered among the Neo-Hittite remains at
the site (see above), while Ura-Tarhundas can be dated to approximately 970 BC by his apparent connections with the Suhis line. The
stela mentions a Suhis, presumably the first ruler of this name in the
dynasty of 'Country Lords'. More important, Katuwas, who
reigned *c.* 900 BC, appears to refer in a fragmentary inscription to a
struggle for power in the city with the 'grandsons of Ura-
Tarhundas'. A further inscription from the Suhis period refers to
the preparations made for the marriage of Great King Tudhaliya.[60]

Taken together, these fragments of information suggest that the
10th-century BC 'Country Lords' of Carchemish shared power with
another line of rulers who were reckoned to be Great Kings. Yet the
Great Kings of Hatti (and the cadet branch at Carchemish) supposedly disappeared together with the Empire around 1200 BC. It is

hard to imagine that the title was resurrected two centuries later at a time when Carchemish had its own local rulers.

Following the provisional low chronology described above, Kuzi-Teshub, ancestor of the kings of Malatya and Great King of Carchemish, would have reigned c. 950 BC, and his father, Talmi-Teshub, c. 975 BC. This family, then, could have formed a senior line of rulers parallel to the Suhis dynasty, and it can surely be no coincidence that the hieroglyphics for the name of the Great King Ura-Tarhundas can also be read (in the Hurrian rather than Luwian language) as Talmi-Teshub.[61] If we identify the two, the history of Carchemish can be rationalized straight away. The void between the Empire and the 10th century BC would be removed; the mysterious Great Kings are explained as the last incumbents of Hittite imperial power in the area; and, above all, continuity in art and archaeology between the two periods is restored. The problems of the long-surviving Bronze Age heirlooms, the 'archaic' sculptures and the dating of Yunus pottery would all melt away. Lowering the terminal date for the Late Bronze Age of south-east Anatolia and Syria seems to be a much more rewarding approach than the introduction of another Dark Age.

The Dark Age of central Anatolia

The archaeology of central Anatolia provides the capstone to the dilemma of Hittite chronology. While Hittite civilization is supposed to have replicated itself to the south-east some two centuries after the fall of the Empire, the same period is matched in the old heartland by a complete blank in the cultural record.

After the end of the Late Bronze Age, currently dated to the beginning of the 12th century BC, the earliest datable finds from central Anatolia belong to the 8th-century BC Kingdom of the Phrygians, familiar from classical sources. Greek tradition relates many stories about the avaricious King Midas (he of 'the golden touch') and his father Gordius, who left, at the city to which he gave his name, an impossibly complex knot on the pole of an ox-cart. Preserved by the priests of Gordion, it was destined to be unravelled by a future conqueror of 'all Asia'. Centuries later the impetuous Alexander the Great arrived at Gordion and solved the puzzle by simply slicing through the knot with his sword.[62]

The legends suggest a fairly close acquaintance between ancient

Phrygia and Greece, and this is reflected in the archaeological record. Phrygian ceramic, ivory and metalwork styles provide numerous comparisons with Greek products of the Geometric to Archaic periods. These give some general synchronisms, refined by more precisely datable links with the Urartian civilization of eastern Anatolia and the Assyrians of Mesopotamia. Mitas of Mushki (Midas of Phrygia) is mentioned by the Assyrian King Sargon as his main rival in Anatolia. He appears to have instigated the rebellion of Pisiri, last independent king of Carchemish, which was crushed by his Assyrian masters in 717 BC.[63] During the early 7th century the short-lived Phrygian kingdom was destroyed by an invasion of the nomadic Cimmerians from Russia. According to Greek tradition, King Midas poisoned himself rather than submit.[64]

The archaeology of the Phrygians is thus reasonably well dated, with their first remains placed no earlier than the end of the 9th century BC. But as the preceding Hittite settlements are dated by Egyptian links no later than the early 12th century BC, a considerable gulf lies between the two cultures. The enormity of the problem was described succinctly by Akurgal:

> . . . it is striking that up to date not only no Phrygian, but no cultural remains of any sort have been found which might belong to the period between 1200 and 800 B.C. This could indicate that Central Anatolia at that period was either very thinly populated or occupied by nomad tribes who left no material remains in the dwelling mounds.[65]

Akurgal wrote this in 1962 and nothing has been discovered since to alter his assessment substantially. Indeed, much the same still applies throughout most of western and north-western, as well as central, Anatolia.[66] Efforts have been made to supply information for the 'missing' centuries. The excavator of the imperial capital at Boghazköy, Kurt Bittel, noted the absence of sedimentation between the Hittite and Phrygian occupations:

> The earliest constructions were undertaken at a time when Hittite ruins still lay visible above the surface. On top of them there is no trace of a sterile stratum as would have been formed by natural sedimentation. This stratigraphic observation as such does not give a measure of time, but it tends to limit the interval between the end of the Hittite citadel and the beginning of Level II.[67]

1–4 Four leading protagonists in the 20th-century debates on ancient chronology – Sir William Matthew Flinders Petrie, 1853–1942 (*above left*); William Foxwell Albright, 1891–1971 (*above right*); Einar Gjerstad, 1897–1988 (*below left*); Dame Kathleen Kenyon, 1906–1978 (*below right*).

5 *opposite above* Weapons, tools, vessels and ornaments from the burials of the Hallstatt salt-miners, depicted against the background of the Austrian Alps (*from Hoernes 1925*).

6 *opposite below* Heinrich Schliemann (1822–1890), the adventurer who discovered Troy and the Mycenaean civilization.

7 *above* Typical *nuraghe* at Santa Barbara, Sardinia.

8 *right* Bronze figurine of a warrior or chieftain from Monte Arcosu, Sardinia, 9th–7th century BC.

9 *above* Mycenaean vase (13th century BC) from Enkomi, Cyprus.

10 *below left* Typical Protogeometric vase.

11 *below right* Late Geometric vase of the Athenian Dipylon style.

12 Bronze four-wheeled stand from Cyprus. Panels on the other sides depict musicians, a winged sphinx and a hunting lion.

13 Hittite Storm God from the Herald's Wall, Carchemish, dated by the excavators to the 14th–13th centuries BC but by most art historians to the 10th–9th.

14 *above* Hunting scene on a Cypro-Mycenaean ivory gaming box from the Late Bronze Age tombs of Enkomi, Cyprus. The tombs contained Mycenaean pottery of the 12th century BC but the excavator, A. S. Murray (1900, 14), resisted such a dating, pointing to similarities between the art of the grave-goods and that of 9th–7th century Greece and Assyria. The problem still remains. Irene Winter (1976, 9–10) noted that the Enkomi scene 'so closely resembles a similar hunting scene on one of the pyxides from Nimrud that only details such as the hairdo of one of the chariot followers or the flying gallop of the animals mark the Enkomi piece as a work of the second millennium B.C., separated by some four centuries from the Nimrud pyxis'.

15 *below* The box (*pyxis*) from Nimrud, belonging to the 9th to 8th-century school of Syrian ivory carving.

16   Bust of Pharaoh Osorkon I (22nd Dynasty) from Byblos with
Phoenician alphabetic inscription.

17 *above* Ivory box from the Late Bronze Age cache at Megiddo.

18 *below left* Red granite relief from Bubastis depicting Pharaoh Osorkon II (22nd Dynasty) and his wife, Queen Karoma.

19 *below right* Relief of griffon from the 9th-century palace at Tell Halaf, northern Mesopotamia.

In order to reduce the chronological gap, Bittel wondered whether the dating of the Phrygian Level II might be raised, but concluded that present evidence allowed a date for the earliest Phrygian wares no earlier than the late 9th century BC.[68] He summed up:

> It has to be admitted that thus far Boğazköy has contributed little to the illumination of what we call the Dark Age. Not a single find has turned up which can be attributed safely to the centuries immediately following the fall of the Hittite capital. The Assyrian seal . . . and a good deal of the pottery, which has parallels in Gordion of the Midas period, point to the second half of the 8th century B.C. How much earlier the occupation may have been is as yet difficult to determine, but we should emphasize again that the stratigraphic situation does not suggest too long a gap after 1200 B.C.[69]

Bittel could not, however, reconcile his judgment that the gap was minimal with the external evidence for dating the ceramic material, which places over 300 years between the Hittite and Phrygian levels at Boghazköy.

Cutting the Gordian Knot

Paradoxically, remains of both cultures, supposedly separated in time by several centuries, have actually been found together at one site. This is Gordion, a Hittite settlement before it became the seat of the Midas dynasty. The final publication of the excavations is still awaited, but preliminary reports, together with extensive published analyses of the pottery, tell an intriguing story.

Gordion is generally agreed to have been sacked by the Cimmerians in the early 7th century BC. From before the destruction three phases of painted Phrygian ware were discerned by the excavators, representing 100 years or so, and covering the period of the great Phrygian kingdom. Soundings taken from the underlying strata of earlier phases produced completely unsuspected results. Most Hittite settlements are sealed with a clear destruction level, separating them from any traces of subsequent occupation. No archaeological relationship between the Hittites and Phrygians had therefore been envisaged. At Gordion, however, there was no such break. Instead, the two cultures appear to have co-existed for a considerable time.

This process was clearly reflected in the successive levels at Gordion. The topmost contained mainly Phrygian pottery, including two painted sherds, but also 'a large admixture of late Hittite'. The next 'produced pottery about half Hittite, half Phrygian'; the third layer 'produced again about half Hittite and half Phrygian pottery', the Phrygian ware being a mixture of wheel-made and hand-made; the fourth level contained 'Hittite pottery with a minimal representation of Phrygian, both wheel-made and hand-made'; 'all the layers below were of Middle and Late Bronze Hittite times'.[70]

The occurrence of Hittite pottery together with two painted sherds in the uppermost level is the most surprising result, as Phrygian painted ware is generally considered to have begun no earlier than the late 9th century BC.[71] Likewise Phrygian pottery, according to the conventional chronology, should never have been found at all in the deeper levels. Bittel, however, welcomed these finds as the evidence needed to bridge the Dark Age gap, arguing that the first Phrygian pottery at Gordion was indeed as early as the 12th century BC.[72] Yet how could this be when the same material elsewhere is always dated three centuries later?

Another possibility, considered by Sams, is that the controversial levels at Gordion were somehow 'telescoped', creating the false impression of an overlap.[73] It is not uncommon for material from two levels to become mixed together by activities such as pit-digging. In this case, however, it is hard to conceive how such a process could have involved four levels, and how the resulting admixture would have produced such a steady increase in amounts of Phrygian finds the higher one goes in the sequence. Moreover, this gradual increase went together with a technological progression, shown by the 'growing proportion of wheel-made to hand-made vases among the Phrygian pottery'.[74]

The alternative, as seen by Anatolian expert James Mellaart, was to reconsider the chronology. Judging the top two levels in the sequence as 8th-century, and the fifth as possibly of Imperial Hittite date, Mellaart noted that the two intervening levels with mixed pottery 'previous to 800 B.C. are unlikely to stretch back to 1200'.[75] To resolve this specific problem, as well as the wider question of the lacuna in the Early Iron Age of Anatolia, Mellaart suggested a radical solution:

. . . the disintegration of the Hittite New Kingdom should not, outside the immediate area around the capital Hattuša which was burnt and deserted, be equated with the end of the Anatolian Late Bronze Age, and the old idea that the Early Iron Age started *c.* 1200 B.C. must be repudiated as unrealistic. A date of *c.* 1000 B.C. plus or minus 50 years seems a fairer estimate for the transition from the Late Bronze Age to Early Iron Age . . .[76]

Yet Mellaart's Solomonic judgment, dividing the Anatolian Dark Age into two halves and allocating the earlier part to the Bronze Age, does little to resolve the problem. He adduces no firm evidence that other Late Bronze centres survived as long as 200 years after the destruction of Boghazköy.[77] His model introduces two unsubstantiated ghost centuries into the history of Late Bronze Age sites. It also fails to deal with the remaining gap on the Phrygian side of the line, which he draws *c.* 1000 BC. There is still at least a century and half on this side of his transitional point unaccounted for before the arrival of Phrygian pottery.

Setting aside all the speculative solutions which have been suggested to solve the Gordion problem, one strategy has been consistently overlooked. This is the lowering of Late Bronze Age chronology for which the Neo-Hittite evidence discussed earlier so strongly argues. Mellaart's claim that the latest material from the Hittite capitals does not necessarily finish precisely at the time of the Empire's presumed collapse is not unreasonable. A few generations may have elapsed before the last hangers-on deserted, or were driven from the now redundant capitals. If the Empire gradually fragmented in the second half of the 10th century BC, as argued above, then Boghazköy, Alaça Hüyük, Yazilikaya and the other old centres may have been finally deserted as late as the mid-9th century. With early Phrygian material dating to *c.* 825 BC, the centuries-long abandonment of central Anatolian sites can now be seen as a short interim period. At Gordion, eventual capital of the Phrygians, an early wave of the newcomers seem to have entrenched themselves while the city was still under Hittite control.

The paradoxical overlap of Hittite and Phrygian pottery at Gordion might be reasonably explained after all. To take a lead from Alexander, perhaps the tangled knot of Gordian archaeology can be unravelled only by cutting the chronology.

CHAPTER 7

Cyprus, Ceramics and Controversy

Cyprus plays a pivotal role in the archaeology and chronology of the Eastern Mediterranean. Its central geographical location contributed to the development of a lively history, making this copper-rich island an inviting stepping stone, upon which the great ancient cultures met and intermingled. During the Late Bronze Age it was a flourishing centre for commerce between the Aegean, Anatolia, the Levant and Egypt. Close links with the Greek world, both during the Mycenaean period and then again in the Archaic, have inevitably embroiled the island in Dark Age questions. Yet there is a significant difference: the problem here has an added dimension. The trading relationships between Cyprus and its neighbours serve as a measure of dating control – this is where the Greek and Palestinian systems of chronology are forced into direct confrontation. Could this be the place to throw light on the centuries of darkness seen throughout the Mediterranean world?

The end of the Bronze Age: appointment with catastrophe

Towards the end of the Bronze Age, the archaeological period known as Late Cypriot IIC (usually thought to terminate in 1225 BC) saw the destruction of sites throughout the island and a sharp fall in population. This is commonly attributed to an invasion of Mycenaeans, who had strongly influenced Cyprus in the past. In the succeeding period, Late Cypriot III, the intruders settled down and, although not necessarily welcome, co-existed with the local inhabitants. The site of Enkomi amply illustrates their impact (see Plate 14). Immediately after the destruction of its Late Cypriot IIC settlement, Enkomi was rebuilt on a rearranged plan, using fine ashlar masonry and a massive fortification resembling those of Mycenaean citadels. Associated with this new town are large quantities of LHIIIC pottery.[1] During the next 100 years several other waves of Aegean people are thought to have arrived in Cyprus, including a distinct Minoan group, as well as a final batch of Achaeans c. 1075 BC.[2] There are also some important Levantine influences on the culture of this period, to which relatively little attention has been paid by Cypriot archaeologists.[3]

The evidence is difficult to interpret with precision. However, the accepted scenario is not totally unreasonable. In the words of Catling:

> On the one hand . . . there was a terrifying diminution in the population and abandonment of large parts of the island. On the other, at those sites where occupation persisted until the threshold of the Iron Age, there is evidence of reasonable prosperity and a fairly vigorous material culture, in which the native Cypriot elements were heavily overlaid by cultural traits for which the Achaean colonists were responsible.[4]

Some fourteen sites have produced Late Cypriot III archaeological material, a fact which supports Catling's assessment.[5] But it must be noted that the great majority of these places flourished only in the earlier part of this period, LCIIIA–B (1225–1150 BC). The later part, LCIIIC (1150–1050 BC), is sparsely represented by settlements, although the excavation of wealthy 11th-century burials (such as those at Palaepaphos and Kourion) creates a strange contrast. Vassos Karageorghis, the doyen of Cypriot archaeology,

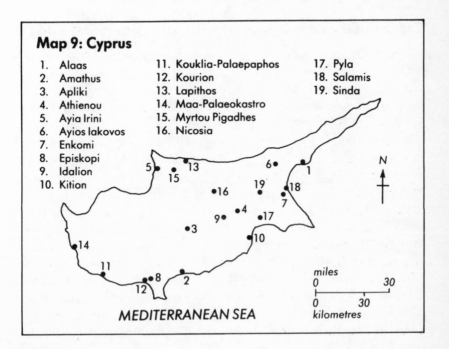

Map 9: Cyprus

1. Alaas
2. Amathus
3. Apliki
4. Athienou
5. Ayia Irini
6. Ayios Iakovos
7. Enkomi
8. Episkopi
9. Idalion
10. Kition
11. Kouklia-Palaepaphos
12. Kourion
13. Lapithos
14. Maa-Palaeokastro
15. Myrtou Pigadhes
16. Nicosia
17. Pyla
18. Salamis
19. Sinda

MEDITERRANEAN SEA

miles
0   30

0   30
kilometres

FIG. 7:1 Impressions from two Late Bronze Age Cypriot cylinder seals, illustrating the cosmopolitan culture of the island during this period. The techniques of cylinder seal manufacture were developed in Mesopotamia, whose artistic influence is detectable in the example above. The scene below, however, exhibits strong Mycenaean influence, particularly in the depiction of the 'Master of Animals' at the centre of the scene (*after Schaeffer 1983*).

was prompted to assert that 'the Greeks of Cyprus, unlike their kinspeople on the Greek mainland where there was illiteracy and poverty . . . had formed prosperous communities which were trading with the Near East'.[6]

In the conventional view a horrific disaster was yet to follow: the Late Bronze Age came to a sudden end between 1075 and 1050 BC.

A violent destruction is evident in the fortifications of Enkomi, while the cyclopean walls and bastions of the famous city of Kition tumbled down. This fate was shared by the towns of Sinda and Maa-Palaeokastro. The causes of the catastrophe are not known, though a great earthquake has been proposed.[7] From then on a veil of darkness covers the history of the island.

The widespread disruption following the 13th century BC was summed up by Lawrence Stager:

> In the 12th–11th centuries nearly 90 percent of the settlements of Cyprus are abandoned. Practically all of our evidence for what is happening on the island comes from the coastal sites: Enkomi, Kition, Episkopi, and Kouklia . . . By the end of the 11th century, even the seaports cease to exist.[8]

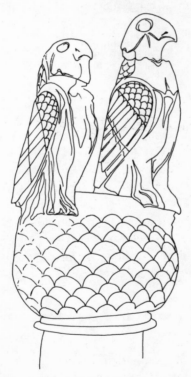

FIG. 7:2 Gold sceptre (height 16.5cm) topped by a globe on which stand two falcons, inlaid with white and blue enamel. It was found in a Late Cypriot IIIC 'royal' tomb at Kourion, conventionally dated to the early 11th century BC (*after Karageorghis 1982a*).

The earliest Iron Age: why seek the living among the dead?

As Karageorghis remarked: 'The history of Cyprus after about 1050 BC is clouded by what is usually called the "Dark Age" in Greece.'[9] Indeed, the island is thought to have suffered a cultural recession. Widely differing opinions have been expressed as to its duration, but it is usually supposed that it lasted over two centuries, well into the Iron Age. Contacts with mainland Greece reached a low ebb: during the periods called Cypro-Geometric I and II (1050–850 BC) only an extremely limited number of ceramic correlations can be made between the two areas (see below, p. 157).

FIG. 7:3   A unique seven-mouthed Bichrome Ware vessel (height 15cm) from a Cypro-Geometric I tomb at Kition, conventionally dated to 1050–950 BC (*after Karageorghis 1978*).

The evidence from the Early Iron Age dwindles dramatically, with most of the finds coming from burials: some ten cemeteries are known. The sanctuaries of Ayia Irini, Ayios Iakovos and Myrtou-Pigadhes were constructed at this time, but the only site which can claim even minor domestic building activity is Kition, and even this was abandoned c. 1000 BC.[10] Hence the conventional picture of Cyprus at the beginning of the 1st millennium BC can be described as one with an entirely homeless population. Since tombs are for the dead, we are asked to believe that it is simply not known where the inhabitants lived during this period. Stager has posed the appropriate question:

> During this supposed Dark Age, 'only a few cemeteries are known but no settlements'. Why is there a gap between the 11th and 9th centuries in the history of settlement throughout the island?[11]

In the case of Kition the gap is particularly hard to understand. According to literary tradition, early in his reign Hiram I, King of Tyre, had to suppress a revolt here. This information, if correctly interpreted, shows that the 'Kitians' were under Tyrian rule in the 10th century BC, at least from the time of Hiram's father Abibaal.[12] Yet, in complete contrast, the present archaeological dating has the city unoccupied between 1000 and 850 BC! Strangely enough, a similar situation prevails in Phoenicia itself (see Chapter 8).

Qrthdst and the coming of the Phoenicians

Even during Cypro-Geometric III (850–750 BC) the main evidence continues to be that of pottery found with burials, although this now comes from nearly twenty cemeteries. In terms of architectural remains, apart from the religious complex at Kition and the sanctuaries at four other sites,[13] only Kourion has produced evidence of a modest settlement, but its precise dating is still disputed.[14] Overall, it is still true that the archaeological search for the living population of Cyprus has to be carried out amongst the dead.

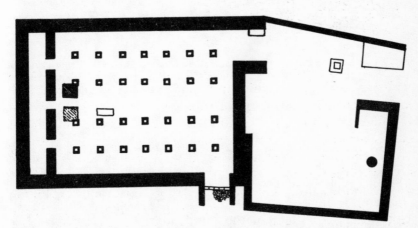

FIG. 7:4   The temple of Astarte at Kition, one of the largest in the Phoenician world (35.5 × 22m), dated by its excavator to *c.* 850–800 BC. It was built directly on top of the Late Bronze Age temple, abandoned *c.* 1000 BC (*after Karageorghis 1978*).

Nevertheless, Cypro-Geometric III is supposed to have witnessed the definite establishment of Phoenician rule on the island, with the foundation by Tyre of an urban centre called *qrthdst*, i.e. the 'new city'. The name is known from two inscriptions dated shortly after the end of the period (*c.* 735 BC), and generally identified with

Kition.[15] Although earlier Phoenician pottery has been collected from Cypriot tombs, it is the substantial quantity at Kition which is taken to indicate some form of colonization.[16] Thus Kition seems to be the first Phoenician colony at the beginning of the westward expansion of this remarkable seafaring nation (see Chapter 2).

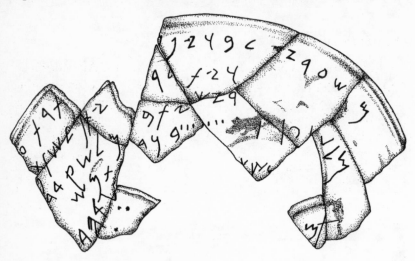

FIG. 7:5   Inscribed Phoenician Red Slip Ware bowl found on the earliest floor of the temple of Astarte at Kition. The text is enigmatic – according to one translation the first line reads: '. . . Incantation. Poke the dog so that it slumps [before As]tarte, and p[oke . . .]' (after Coote 1975).

A highly significant discovery was made during Karageorghis's excavations at Kition, when fragments of a famous bowl bearing a Phoenician inscription were unearthed. It was found in the destruction level, dated by him c. 800 BC, of the Cypro-Geometric III temple of Astarte, built on the foundations of its Late Bronze Age predecessor. However, some serious objections have been put forward which affect the local chronology – for example, the Phoenician plates found in the same level as the Kition bowl have been dated by Bikai to c. 750–700 BC, following her Tyrian pottery sequence.[17] A related problem was raised by Robert Coote, who examined the Phoenician inscription and suggested that its date should be reduced on palaeographic grounds:

> Unless the script represents an otherwise unknown (but not necessarily unexpected) Phoenician cursive of the 9th or the 8th

century, to all appearances it belongs as late as the early 7th century.[18]

Other palaeographers, such as Cross, have adopted slightly higher estimates, but they nearly all fall in the mid-8th century and so are still lower than Karageorghis's archaeological date for the deposit.[19]

The bard's syllabary?

The great cities of Cyprus during the Late Bronze Age adopted a script, presumably to administer local industry and international trade, as well as for general communication. A fragment of a baked clay tablet with engraved signs, dated by the excavator of Enkomi to *c.* 1500 BC, is the earliest written document from the island and has yet to be deciphered.[20] The fact that the script can be compared with Cretan Linear A has led it to be termed 'Cypro-Minoan' since the time of Sir Arthur Evans. Its language is thought to be non-Greek, possibly the native Eteocypriot,[21] in sharp contrast to its transformation a few centuries later into the so-called Archaic Cypriot syllabary, which was clearly used for writing Greek.

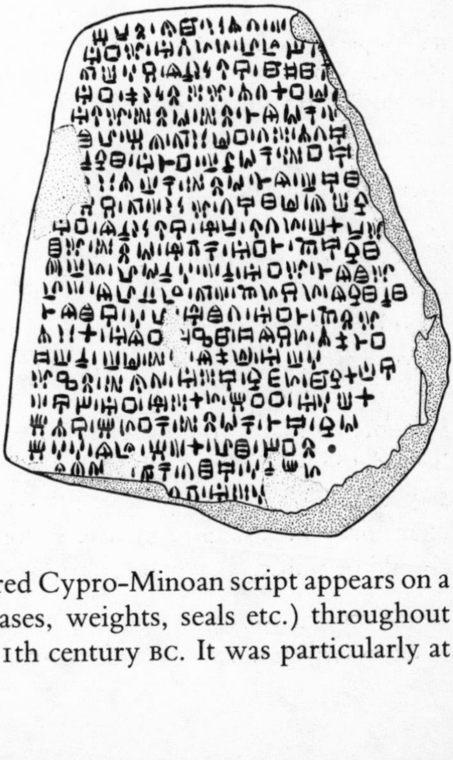

FIG. 7:6 Fragmentary Cypro-Minoan cushion-shaped clay tablet (10 × 9cm) from Enkomi, conventionally dated to the end of the 13th century BC. Unlike the inscribed tablets from the Aegean, which were unbaked, the Cypro-Minoan ones were baked, in accordance with Near Eastern fashions (*after Dikaios 1971*).

The still largely undeciphered Cypro-Minoan script appears on a variety of objects (tablets, vases, weights, seals etc.) throughout Cyprus, down to the early 11th century BC. It was particularly at home in the urban centres of the 12th century. At the end of the Bronze Age the script completely vanishes. With regard to literacy, one could justifiably imagine that from then until the 8th century BC Cyprus had vanished under the waters of the Mediterranean. Yet the traditional understanding of archaeology would have us believe that after this prolonged break writing miraculously flourished again – in the form of the Archaic/Classical Cypriot syllabary, clearly evolved from Cypro-Minoan, known from the 8th to the 1st centuries BC.[22]

Although analogous to that of the Greek mainland and Crete, the lacuna in literacy among the Cypriots during the Dark Age has much more serious implications. At least Linear B was succeeded after the gap by a totally different form of writing: the alphabet. In Cyprus the same general script reappears without any trace of its transmission across the centuries of darkness. As Sterling Dow once observed uneasily:

> The instance of Cyprus is perhaps the clearest, most neglected, and most astonishing . . . during the intervening . . . centuries . . . the Cypriots wrote largely, perhaps exclusively, on perishable materials.[23]

Once again the by now familiar 'perishable materials' theory is encountered, which becomes ever more suspect each time it is employed in a different region. Because of the weaknesses inherent in this explanation, other theories have been put forward to explain the resurrection, but they are even more implausible. S. Casson once suggested that 'the knowledge of the script reverted to the hands of bards'![24] Certainly bards passed on heroic tales (such as the Homeric cycle), but surely their particular fame lay in their ability to do so orally.[25] How could they transmit 'a script' without writing it down? Had they done so, where are the examples?

Indeed, only one inscription in the Archaic syllabary exists to fill the void in literacy between the early 11th and 8th centuries BC. This is the bronze spit from a rich tomb at Palaepaphos, dated to the second half of the 11th century BC. The inscription on it reads *o-pe-le-ta-u*, the genitive in the Arcadian Greek dialect of the name Opheltes. Interestingly, this fact agrees with the legend acknowledging Agapenor, leader of the Arcadians in the Trojan War, as the founder of Paphos.[26] It is clear that the Archaic syllabary had already begun to develop, since the signs are no longer Cypro-

Minoan in form. The inscription has been announced as the 'missing link' in near triumphal terms by T. Mitford and O. Masson:

> Thus, the old problem of the supposed existence of a 'Dark Age' characterized by centuries of illiteracy, is now satisfactorily solved. We may infer that the syllabary already existed at the end of the eleventh century: the absence of texts until the eighth century could result from a general diminution of literacy in these times . . .[27]

This single find has merely shifted the problem, from one concerning the transmission of Cypro-Minoan to Archaic Cypriot over the Dark Age without intermediate examples, to one within the development of the Archaic syllabary. A gap of several centuries still remains. The loss of literacy during the Dark Age continues to be a thorn in the side of the conventional dating of Cypriot archaeology.

Gjerstad and the birth of Cypriot chronology

The solid foundations for Cypriot chronology were laid by the Swedish Cyprus Expedition in its archaeological work between 1927 and 1930. The mastermind behind the project was Professor Einar Gjerstad, who was later to explore the early history of Rome (see Chapter 2). In the 1930s he began the pioneering task of dating the island's archaeology.

From the mid-7th century BC onwards, imports of Attic pottery and Egyptian scarabs furnished abundant correlative material for dating Cypriot pottery. For earlier periods, and in the absence of stratigraphy, a statistical method was employed by which a local ceramic typological sequence could be constructed back to the beginning of the Iron Age.[28] On the basis of this internal, non-absolute chronology, Gjerstad estimated that the start of the Iron Age could not be pushed back as early as Mycenaean scholars required at that time, i.e. to the mid-12th century BC. His aim in this was apparently to avoid the danger of creating a huge Dark Age.

Whereas direct connections with Egypt established the dates for most of the Late Bronze Age in Cyprus, its last third was synchronized with Greece. At the end of Late Cypriot IIC most sites were destroyed and the native Cypro-Mycenaean pottery was replaced by LHIIIC of the mainland Greek type. This marked the beginning

of the succeeding period, Late Cypriot III, which was thus dated to
c. 1225 BC (recently altered to after 1200 BC).[29] The next stage was to
determine when Late Cypriot III ended, and hence when Cypro-
Geometric I began.

Even before Gjerstad had published his conclusions, Arne Furumark, the leading authority on Mycenaean pottery chronology,
had already argued that Cypro-Geometric could not have started
later than about 1150 BC.[30] Feeling intuitively that this date was too
high, Gjerstad arbitrarily reduced it by a century, to c. 1050 BC, and
launched a lengthy attack on Furumark.[31] Although, in terms of the
evidence as it stood, Gjerstad's arguments were not convincing,
Furumark felt inclined to accept most of them, evidently in view of
his opponent's superior grasp of Cypriot matters. This acceptance
had the drastic result that the later part of Mycenaean chronology
was now dated by Cyprus – against all previous expectations.[32]
Having 'succeeded' in placing the beginning of Cypro-Geometric I
at c. 1050 BC, Gjerstad's second step was to look for connections in
mainland Levant in order to demonstrate that his low chronology
was to be trusted.

The main Cypriot ware from that period, known as White
Painted I, had been found in Palestine at several sites (including
Megiddo Stratum VI, Gibeah and Tell Fara South). Unfortunately,
the understanding of Palestinian stratigraphy was in such a chaotic
state (and still is; see Chapter 8) that only Megiddo VI was thought
important enough to discuss. Yet even this site was variously dated,
and Gjerstad decided to pick the very lowest date proposed for this
level (1050–1000 BC), which suited his own scheme.[33]

In effect Gjerstad's low chronology, although violating certain
archaeological standards, had the merit of reducing the length of the
Dark Age when compared with Greece and other lands – but at the
expense of stretching out the Late Bronze Age. Even so, a considerable gap remained which stood in need of definition. The duration
of the Cypriot Dark Age ultimately depends on the time allowed
for the various phases of the Iron Age (c. 1050–325 BC). The dating
of these presents a complex problem which has so far defined a
satisfactory solution. The basic system of Gjerstad runs thus:

Cypro-Geometric	I	1050–950 BC
	II	950–850 BC
	III	850–700 BC

Cypro-Archaic	I	700–600 BC
	II	600–475 BC
Cypro-Classical	I	475–400 BC
	II	400–325 BC

This chronological scheme, with only a single amendment, is still adhered to by Cypriot and Aegean archaeologists.[34] The alteration concerns the date of the beginning of Cypro-Archaic I, which Karageorghis raised from 700 to 750 BC, and which Gjerstad, by way of compromise, placed at 725 BC.[35]

In the early 1960s Judy Birmingham attempted to revise this scheme, redefining its internal ceramic categories, but her work has had only a limited impact on Cypriot archaeologists.[36] Although she was obliged to follow the same overall parameters in terms of absolute chronology, her model, among other differences, set the beginning of Cypro-Archaic II in 725 BC and that of Cypro-Classical I as early as 600 BC, a quite extraordinary result:[37]

Early Iron	(= CGI)	1050–900 BC
Middle Iron 1	(= CGII, CGIII & CAI)	900–725 BC
Middle Iron 2	(= CAII)	725–600 BC
Late Iron	(= CCI & CCII)	600–325 BC

Gjerstad at first ignored the challenge, and later briefly dismissed it:

> . . . by disregarding the results obtained by numerous, methodical archaeological excavations carried out both by Cypriote and foreign expeditions, she has evidently convinced herself of having made a positive contribution to the study of Cypriote culture.[38]

Birmingham's relatively short length of 175 years (compared to Gjerstad's 350) for the Cypro-Geometric II, III and Cypro-Archaic I periods combined seems reasonable, given the obvious lack of archaeological evidence for the first two of these phases. Yet her revision cannot be sustained if the effect is to raise the date of Cypro-Archaic II (firmly tied to the 6th century BC by Greek connections), which, if anything, could only be downdated.

A challenge with greater impact came from archaeologists working in the Levant, among whom Gjerstad's chronology created pandemonium. In the first instance the attack came from Albright, the giant of biblical archaeology.[39] But it was really Albright's doctoral student, Gus Van Beek, who, after adducing strong evidence from sites in Palestine, led the opposition to the 'low' Cypriot chronology:

> Geometric I cannot begin as late as 1050 B.C. but must go back to 1100 BC, and in all probability to a few decades earlier . . . Geometric II appears to be only a transitional phase in which the forms of I give way to those of III and may be dated about the latter half of the 11th century B.C. The beginning of Geometric III, then, must be placed at the end of the 11th century B.C. . . . Forms of Archaic I begin to appear in the third quarter of the 10th century and continue through the ninth century.[40]

On the basis of Palestinian correlations Van Beek raised the dates for Cypro-Geometric I and all succeeding periods. He did not alter the dating of Cypro-Archaic II, presumably because he was aware of its Greek connections. At its greatest extent Van Beek's revision required the redating of Archaic I to 950/925–800 BC, as opposed to Gjerstad's 700–600 BC: a difference of some 225 to 250 years. The chronology resulting from Van Beek's scheme would be as follows:

Cypro-Geometric	I	1130/1100–1050 BC
	II	1050–1000 BC
	III	1000–950/925 BC
Cypro-Archaic	I	950/925–800 BC
	??	*800–600 BC*
	II	600–475 BC
Cypro-Classical	I	475–400 BC
	II	400–325 BC

A grey area between 800 and 600 BC was left by Van Beek, who gave no indication of whether it was a new, later Dark Age, or if the Cypro-Archaic I was to be extended to cover 325 or even 350 years – an incredibly long period of time for this single ceramic phase. Van Beek himself must have recognized the problem, as he subsequently modified his scheme by allowing Cypro-Geometric III to end in 900 BC and Cypro-Archaic I in 750 BC.[41] Even so, this still leaves a hiatus of 150 years (750–600 BC) in a period well represented throughout the rest of the Greek world.

The dilemma of Black-on-Red Ware

The occurrence of Cypriot 'Black-on-Red Ware' in the wrong Palestinian strata forms the focal point of the disagreement between the Gjerstad and Van Beek schools of thought. While its first appearance was placed by Gjerstad in the Cypro-Geometric III phase (*c.* 850 BC onwards), the same pottery was consistently found in Palestinian contexts dated to the 11th–10th century BC. As Van Beek noted:

> The most troublesome problem of Cypriote Iron-Age chronology is B.R. [Black-on-Red] ware as represented by the ubiquitous handle-ridge juglet or ointment bottle. Gjerstad has dated B.R. I about 850–700 B.C. . . . In doing so, he has been forced to deny the Cypriote origin of the juglets which are found in almost every 11th–10th-century site in Palestine, although most of these are identical in form and decoration with those found in Cyprus.[42]

Gjerstad, however, was not prepared to abandon his dates unless two conditions were met: first, it had to be proved that the Black-on-Red of 11th to 10th-century Palestine was the same as that from Cyprus; second, given that the same ware was involved, all possibilities of lowering Palestinian chronology should be exhausted prior to raising the Cypriot dates.[43]

Van Beek insisted that Gjerstad 'cannot arbitrarily deny the Cypriote origin of the ware found in Palestine simply because it is earlier than 850 B.C.'.[44] Indeed, the Black-on-Red found in 11th to 10th-century Palestine looked identical to the Black-on-Red found in Cypro-Geometric III sites on Cyprus. Further, it seemed impossible to lower the date of the Palestinian examples, since they were firmly correlated with 11th-century local ceramics, such as 'Philistine Ware', the dates for which are linked to the accepted Egyptian chronology.[45]

Nevertheless, Gjerstad's point regarding the provenance of Palestinian Black-on-Red Ware still had to be answered. Recently the application of Neutron Activation Analysis has added a new perspective to the debate. Examination of Black-on-Red sherds discovered at Tel Mevorakh in the Sharon Plain of Israel has shown that its origin 'is to be sought in Eastern Cyprus'.[46] Other analyses have produced different though inconclusive results, which tend to suggest that although some Black-on-Red Ware found in Palestine

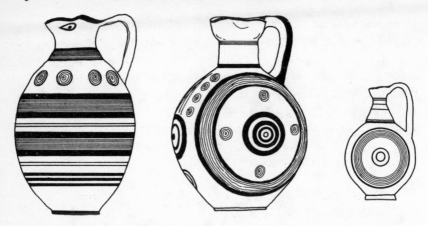

FIG. 7:7 'Black-on-Red Ware' jugs from Cyprus. The first from the left (BoR
I) belongs to the Cypro-Geometric III period, the second (BoR II) to Cypro-
Archaic I and the third (BoR III) to Cypro-Archaic II. Black-on-Red Ware
(bowls, jars, juglets and amphorae of various sizes) was made of reddish-brown
clay, red-slipped and decorated with black paint (*after Gjerstad 1948*).

was made in Cyprus, another group may have had a different
provenance, most likely on the Syro-Palestinian coast.[47]

In any case, Neutron Activation Analysis cannot by itself resolve
the chronological question. Whatever the origin of this pottery (in
Cyprus and/or Syro-Palestine), a choice still has to be made between the relative merits of the high and low chronologies for these
two areas. The high chronology is seemingly supported by the
conventional dates for Palestinian stratigraphy. It also has, in
Stager's opinion, the advantage of providing a solution to the Dark
Age dilemma:

> A further possibility to be investigated is that the two to three
> century 'Dark Age' of Cyprus is largely illusory – created by
> modern scholars, not ancient disasters – hinging on the dating of
> the Black-on-Red pottery of the Cypro-Geometric [III]
> period . . . If it can be shown that Cypro-Geometric I–II occu-
> pied merely a short span in the 11th to 10th century and was
> immediately followed by the greater prosperity of Cypro-
> Geometric III, then the so-called Dark Age is largely
> eliminated.[48]

However, this view overlooks a fundamental objection to the

application of the high chronology. Raising the dates for the Cypro-Geometric to close the 11th to 9th-century Dark Age gap can be carried out only by creating a new 'Dark Age' later in the pottery sequence. The disastrous effects of this anomaly on Van Beek's scheme have already been noted.

The high chronology also poses an insuperable problem when set against Aegean material. Generally accepted synchronisms with Attic and Cycladic pottery (see Table 7:1) make the following periods approximately contemporary:[49]

1   Final Late Helladic IIIC to Submycenaean with the later part of Late Cypriot III
2   Late Protogeometric with later Cypro-Geometric II
3   Middle Geometric with later Cypro-Geometric III
4   Late Geometric with Cypro-Archaic I

Van Beek's revision of Cypriot chronology would inevitably raise the dates for the Greek Protogeometric, and therefore the beginning of the Geometric, further intensifying the Greek Dark Age. Desborough described the consequences of Van Beek's high system from the standpoint of Aegean archaeology:

> If the end of Attic Protogeometric is to be dated *c.* 1025 B.C., then one must fit in between this date and *c.* 1150 B.C. (which I reckon to be about the time of the destruction of Mycenae) the remainder of the LH:III C1b period, LH:III C1c, LH:III C2 (sub-Mycenaean) and Attic Protogeometric. Furthermore, the duration of Attic Geometric, whose terminal date is fairly securely fixed at the end of the eighth century, will be a matter of over 300 years. These may appear at first sight rather startling deductions, but if one follows the higher dating to its logical end such are the consequences. I doubt whether any Greek archaeologist would be prepared to accept them, and yet, if this dating is founded on fact, they have to be accepted.[50]

Desborough's doubts still hold good today. During the last thirty years only one Greek archaeologist has attempted to raise the dates for the Protogeometric using a 'new' relative correlation, but apparently on the basis of a misunderstanding of the finds from the Cypriot site of Alaas.[51] In fact the more general trend is to lower them (see Chapter 5). But this area of research is fraught with

Table 7:1

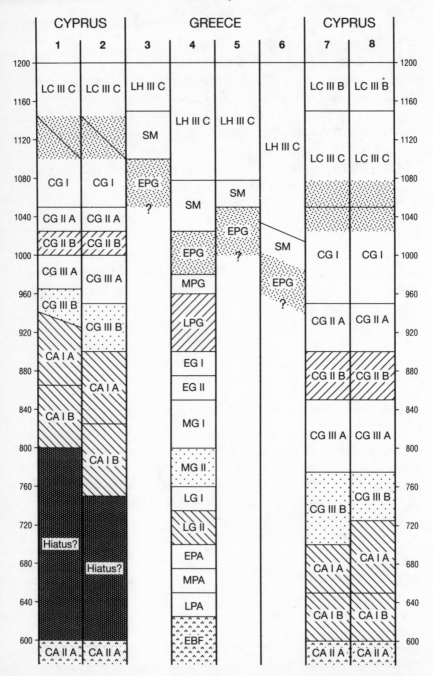

difficulties and almost inevitably involves a large measure of circular reasoning.

It is useful to remember the words of Robert Merrillees (referring to the Bronze Age, but equally valid for the Early Iron Age) warning against borrowing Cypriot chronology:

> It is in fact not uncommon to find that the Bronze Age strata of Syria and Palestine, and even incredibly deposits in Egypt . . . have been dated according to the imported Cypriote pottery, whose absolute chronology in turn depends on theirs! As a result the dates of part of, or even whole Bronze Ages come to be built up like houses of cards, with all the stability and longevity which characterise that kind of monument.[52]

Cyprus versus Palestine

The 'higher dating', which Desborough felt would lead to 'startling deductions' in the Aegean, ultimately depends on Palestinian stratigraphy. Recent work at Tel Mevorakh has positively resolved this problem, in the opinion of its excavator Ephraim Stern. Stratum

---

The 'high' and 'low' chronologies for Iron Age Cyprus. The first two columns show the development of Van Beek's scheme, based on links with the 'high' Palestinian chronology. The last two show Gjerstad's scheme, a local relative sequence tied to a 'low' Palestinian chronology at its beginning, and a combination of Greek and Egyptian synchronisms at the later end. The middle columns show the varying dates offered by Aegean archaeologists for the Greek Iron Age, which fall uncomfortably between the two Cypriot extremes. Shaded areas indicate those pottery phases which should be partly contemporaneous. Van Beek's dates, while consistent with those currently preferred by the majority of archaeologists in Israel, would have drastic consequences if applied to Greece, as well as introducing a 'dark age' in the Cypriot sequence during the 8th and 7th centuries. A solution to this quandary can be found by a reduction in the Iron Age dates for Palestine (see Chapter 8).

1 = Van Beek 1951
2 = Van Beek 1955
3 = Furumark 1941
4 = Furumark 1944, Desborough 1952, Coldstream 1968, Cook 1972
5 = Iakovidis 1979
6 = Mountjoy 1988, Hankey 1988
7 = Gjerstad 1948
8 = Gjerstad 1974

VII, which produced Black-on-Red and other Cypriot wares, was confidently assigned to the 10th century BC. Thus Stern declared:

> . . . the old debate, which began in the mid-fifties, in which the validity of Gjerstad's chronology was challenged, seems now, in the light of the latest studies, to have found its solution in favour of the earlier dating of the Palestinian material, as was first suggested by G. Van-Beek.[53]

Yet Stern's dating of Stratum VII would assume a subsequent hiatus at Tel Mevorakh of a similar order to the gap (or extension) which Van Beek's high dating would produce in the Cypro-Archaic pottery sequence:

> . . . our study of the local pottery of stratum VII at Tel Mevorakh led us to assign it to the tenth century B.C. . . . If this conclusion is correct and stratum VI began only in the fifth century, the approximately four-hundred-year gap between these two strata creates a unique situation that can contribute greatly to the long-standing debate concerning the initial appearance of these imported pottery groups in Palestine.[54]

A 'unique situation' is certainly created, and may even contribute to the 'long-standing debate'. But how Stern can feel this favours the high chronology remains something of a mystery. If Gjerstad's low dates were applied to Tel Mevorakh the gap would be substantially reduced.[55] Any such revision, while it could certainly make better sense of the Tel Mevorakh evidence (and that from contemporary sites), would be wildly at variance with accepted Egyptian chronology, the backbone of Palestinian archaeological dating.

As long as no questions are raised concerning the validity of the absolute dates borrowed from Egypt, and as long as Cypriot archaeologists turn a blind eye to the Cypro-Palestinian debate, the problem will never be resolved. The remarks of the excavators at Tel Qiri, another northern Israelite site, illustrate the situation:

> This coherent set of chronological evidence [i.e. from Palestine] is unfortunately at odds with the accepted date of the Black-on-Red ware in Cyprus. The chronological range in Cyprus is fairly consistently a century or more later than their dates in Palestine. This dispute has raged since the 1930s. It is clear, given the NAA

[i.e. Neutron Activation Analysis] results from Mevorakh, that separate sources for Cypro-Phoenician and Black-on-Red wares are very unlikely. It seems that the basic chronologies of many sites in one culture or the other are off by at least a century. The preponderance of the evidence supplied by Birmingham and Van Beek demonstrates that the dates from Palestine are to be preferred.[56]

However, Birmingham's and Van Beek's systems were artificial devices, and cannot be used to solve a problem of such dimensions. Instead we propose that the two schools of chronology – the low Cypriot and the high Palestinian – are both partly correct, despite the radically different results they have produced. While the dates of the Cypro-Geometric must not be far removed (i.e. back in time) from the established historical Greek Archaic period, by the same token they cannot be separated from the archaeological Late Bronze Age. To pull the Early Iron Age in one direction or the other merely creates a Dark Age, higher or lower in the time-scale.

It could be said that Gjerstad came to (almost) the right result by the wrong means, whereas Van Beek arrived at the wrong result by the right means. There seems to be only one valid solution: to lower the date for the end of the Cypro-Geometric to match the Tyrian evidence, and to reduce its length to the two centuries the quantity of archaeological remains known from the period would suggest. This would in turn push down by some 150 years the absolute date for the end of the Late Bronze Age in Cyprus, currently set at c. 1050 BC. This would produce a far more reasonable picture, in which the cities of Cyprus abandoned at this time were resettled after only a few generations; the renaissance of literacy may have been equally rapid.

In the following chapter the archaeology of Palestine itself will be examined. Was Gjerstad justified in rejecting its high chronology, which conflicts so flagrantly with that of Cyprus?

CHAPTER 8

Biblical Archaeology Without Egypt

Few academic fields have spawned such intense controversy as the archaeology of the thin strip of coastal territory known today as Syria, Lebanon and Palestine. For three world religions (Judaism, Christianity and Islam) this is the 'Holy Land', and the sacred traditions attached to it inject an extra dimension of controversy into the perennial debates over dating.

The problem shows itself in two ways, reflecting the polarized extremes of biblical archaeology. First, the field has always attracted a devout breed of archaeologist happy to dig with a trowel in one hand and a Bible in the other. For example, if an excavator believes from the scriptures that an ancient mound must contain buildings from Solomon's reign, it is almost certain that sooner or later he will find structures which can fit the bill. The spurious air of biblical authority given to such a discovery can then make the identification stick, despite any evidence to the contrary. In the meantime a small tourist industry may even have grown up around this 'confirmation' of the Bible.

The other extreme concerns those whose scepticism can be as blind as faith itself, completely rejecting the value of the biblical record as a whole. This stance has been possible from the time of the Darwinian revolution in the 1860s, when the literal interpretation of the Creation was successfully challenged. Since then biblical texts have been subjected to the most painstaking scrutiny and dissection using the tools of literary criticism.[1] The dates the Old Testament gives, even those for historical periods which are potentially useful to archaeology, have been altered, mangled or rejected in an arbitrary fashion. It seems that the Bible has suffered from this kind of hypercritical treatment simply because it is the Bible. A similar approach would never have been taken with the sacred literature of other ancient Near Eastern societies.[2] Yet, as eager sceptics stress, has not archaeology repeatedly shown that the biblical narrative is untrue?

'The walls came tumblin' down'

The story of the Israelite capture of Jericho is a case in point.

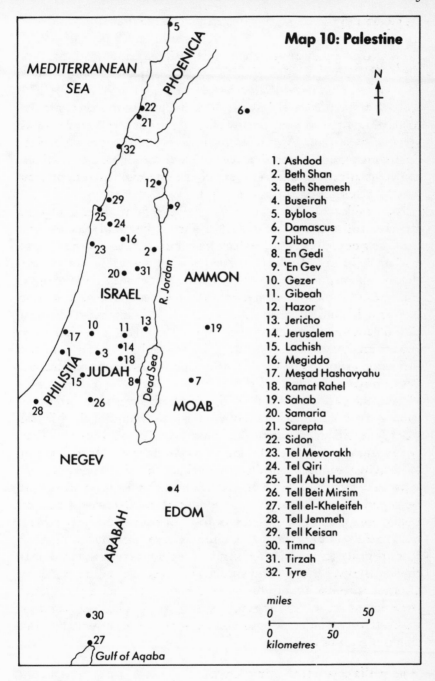

Map 10: Palestine

N

MEDITERRANEAN
SEA

PHOENICIA

1. Ashdod
2. Beth Shan
3. Beth Shemesh
4. Buseirah
5. Byblos
6. Damascus
7. Dibon
8. En Gedi
9. 'En Gev
10. Gezer
11. Gibeah
12. Hazor
13. Jericho
14. Jerusalem
15. Lachish
16. Megiddo
17. Meşad Hashavyahu
18. Ramat Rahel
19. Sahab
20. Samaria
21. Sarepta
22. Sidon
23. Tel Mevorakh
24. Tel Qiri
25. Tell Abu Hawam
26. Tell Beit Mirsim
27. Tell el-Kheleifeh
28. Tell Jemmeh
29. Tell Keisan
30. Timna
31. Tirzah
32. Tyre

ISRAEL

AMMON

R. Jordan

JUDAH

PHILISTIA

Dead Sea

MOAB

NEGEV

ARABAH

EDOM

Gulf of Aqaba

miles
0   50

0   50
kilometres

According to the Old Testament, this was the first city conquered by the Israelites after their long trek from bondage out of Egypt. Led by Joshua they approached the 'Promised Land' from the east, their God Yahweh assisting them by drying up the River Jordan so that they could cross in safety. Then, the mighty walls of Jericho collapsed spontaneously as the Israelite priests marched around them blowing trumpets; the invaders moved in and sacked the city (Joshua 5:13–6:27). According to the accepted chronology, it was Late Bronze Age Jericho, c. 1200 BC, which fell to the Israelites. However, the excavations of Jericho have shown no trace of these events at this period. Even the famous walls are missing.[3]

As an alternative, recent work by the biblical scholar John Bimson has tried to identify the Israelite Conquest of Canaan with the much earlier series of destructions which terminated the strongly walled cities of Middle Bronze Age Palestine.[4] Objections to this theory on chronological grounds have sometimes gone hand in hand with the presumption that the biblical narrative is discredited by its miraculous elements.[5] A more informed view must allow for the fact that Jericho lies on a major geological fault-line prone to sudden and violent earthquakes. In ten out of thirty recorded incidents, including one in 1927, the mud-slides caused blocked the River Jordan and stopped it flowing for one to two days.[6] This knowledge could throw a different light on the Jericho story: the fall of its walls and the damming of the Jordan may both have resulted from a disturbance along the fault-line.

It is easy enough, from the comfort of a departmental office chair, to dismiss the biblical narrative as unbelievable. Such an approach, however, reflects a poor methodology. Hundreds of the most important historical documents from the ancient world contain miraculous elements. For example, an inscription of Pharaoh Ramesses II states that the god Seth turned winter into summer so that his bride-to-be, a Hittite princess, could travel through Palestine untroubled by rain and snow.[7] Yet no one would use this to question the reality of this well-documented marriage alliance between the Hittites and Egyptians (see p. 307). The historian must first carefully weigh such accounts in the scales of reasonableness, using every possible control afforded by other disciplines, from geology to archaeology.

Rejection of the entire Old Testament record as a piece of impressive fiction is simply too glib. The early stories in Genesis, concerning Adam, Noah and so on, are of course the province of specialists in anthropology and mythology rather than ancient history. But the overtly mythological content in the narrative then steadily decreases, and by the time of the Israelite enslavement in Egypt we are on firmer ground. The tradition is credible, as Egyptian records from several periods describe sizeable 'Asiatic' slave populations.[8] After this comes the Exodus from Egypt and the long wanderings before the arrival in Canaan (Palestine), the land promised to the Israelites, as they believed, by their God. There is little that is intrinsically implausible in the biblical story of the Conquest as an armed invasion. Despite some inconsistencies, it gives a feasible picture of the strategy and tactics required by a relatively small force of invaders to capture well-defended cities.[9] The Conquest is followed by the vague period of the 'Judges', the local leaders of the Israelites during their fight to maintain and expand their hold on Palestine. The narrative seems to be a pastiche of traditions concerning the struggles of separate tribes in different areas, awkwardly arranged in a single sequence as a 'national' history. The last of the Judges was the famous prophet Samuel, who anointed Saul as the first king of a united Israel. Saul was followed by David and Solomon, the greatest of the Israelite rulers.

For the period of the Monarchy there is little reason to doubt the essential integrity of the biblical account. After the division of Israel into northern and southern kingdoms (Israel and Judah respectively) around 930 BC, its history begins to be keyed in firmly with that of neighbouring lands. The records of the Assyrians who invaded the Levant in the mid-9th century BC have confirmed not only the existence of kings such as Ahab and Jehu, but also their dates and the general political situation reflected in the Bible (see Table 8:1; see also Chapter 11). Later texts from Assyria and Babylonia corroborate the biblical narrative down to the end of the Israelite monarchy in 587 BC.

The Bible according to Egypt

Despite the generally agreed value of the biblical record from the beginning of the Monarchy to its downfall, linking it with the archaeological evidence raises a major difficulty. This is the 'mute' nature of Palestinian archaeology in one essential respect – no

Table 8:1

United Monarchy

Saul	Early 10th century BC
David	Early 10th century BC
Solomon	*c.* 950–930 BC

Israel	Judah	Mesopotamian synchronisms
Jeroboam I	Rehoboam	
930–909 BC	930–913 BC	
Omri		
885–874 BC		
Ahab		
874–853 BC		**853 BC** Shalmaneser III ~ *Ahab at the battle*
Jehu		*of Karkar*
841–814 BC		**841 BC** Shalmaneser III ~ *Jehu pays tribute*
Jehoash		**796? BC** Adad-nirari III ~ *Jehoash pays*
798–782 BC		*tribute*
Jeroboam II	Azariah	**742? BC** Tiglath-pileser III ~ *Menahem*
793–753 BC	792–740 BC	*pays tribute*
Menahem		**738 BC** Tiglath-pileser III ~ *Menahem pays*
752–737? BC		*tribute* (Cf. 2 Kgs. 15:19–20)
	Ahaz	**734 BC** Tiglath-pileser III ~ *Ahaz pays*
	735–715 BC	*tribute* (Cf. 2 Kgs. 16:7–9)
Pekah		**733 BC** Tiglath-pileser III ~ *Assyrian*
735?–732 BC		*conquest of Galilee* (Cf. 2 Kgs. 15:29; reign
		of Pekah)
Hoshea		**732 BC** Tiglath-pileser III ~ *Hoshea succeeds*
732–722 BC		*Pekah*
		731 BC Tiglath-pileser III ~ *Hoshea pays*
		tribute
		724–722 BC Shalmaneser V ~ *Siege and*
		capture of Samaria; end of Israelite monarchy
		(Cf. 2 Kgs. 17:4–6; reign of Hoshea)
		720 BC Sargon II ~ *Deportation of Israelites*
	Hezekiah	**712 BC** Sargon II ~ *Capture of Ashdod* (Cf.
	715–686 BC	Isaiah 20:1–2; reign of Hezekiah)
		701 BC Sennacherib ~ *Hezekiah attacked by*
		Assyrians; capture of Lachish (Cf. 2 Kgs.
		18:13)
	Manasseh	**post-677 BC** Esarhaddon ~ *Manasseh*
	696–642 BC	*supplies materials for building work at*
		Nineveh

Josiah 640–609 BC	**609 BC** Nabopolassar ~ *Egyptians support* *Assyrians at Harran* (Cf. 2 Kgs. 23:29; death of Josiah)
Jehoiakim 609–598 BC	**605 BC** Nabopolassar ~ *Battle of* *Carchemish* (Cf. Jer. 46:1–2; reign of Jehoiakim)
Jehoiachin 598–597 BC	**597 BC** Nebuchadrezzar ~ *Babylonian* *nominee appointed to Judaean throne* (Cf. 2 Kgs. 24: 10–17; Jehoiachin deported and
Zedekiah 597–586 BC	replaced by Zedekiah) **post-595 BC** Nebuchadrezzar ~ *Jehoiachin* *exiled in Babylon* (Cf. 2 Kgs. 25:27–30) **587/6 BC** Nebuchadrezzar ~ *Destruction of* *Jerusalem and blinding of Zedekiah* (only recorded in biblical texts, e.g. 2 Kgs. 24) **538 BC** Cyrus the Great ~ *Captures* *Babylon and allows deportees to return to their* *homelands* (Cf. Ezra 1; 6:3–5; Jews released by Cyrus) **515 BC** Darius I ~ *6th year, Temple in* *Jerusalem rebuilt* (only recorded in biblical texts, e.g. Ezra 6:13–18) **445 BC** Artaxerxes I ~ *20th year, Nehemiah* *appointed governor of Judah* (only recorded in biblical texts, Neh. 2:1)

The principal kings of Israel and Judah, together with the known synchronisms from the records of Assyrian, Babylonian and Persian rulers. Except where specified, the instances noted are recorded in Mesopotamian sources. These confirm the overall veracity of the biblical record over a period of four centuries. Many variant chronologies are current for the Judaean and Israelite kings but they differ at most by about five years. While it has become increasingly clear that Thiele's dates (1983) need some revision, they are, with minor adjustments, followed in this table and throughout the book.

inscriptions mention the major prophets, or even Israel's greatest kings, David and Solomon.

The first document from Palestine unequivocally referring to a biblical character is the stela of King Mesha of Moab found in Jordan. It relates events which can be certainly dated to the reigns of Omri and Ahab in Israel in the mid-9th century BC.[10] Unfortunately, since it was not found during a proper excavation, it is of no direct value in dating Palestinian archaeology. Towards the end of the Monarchy there are increasing finds of seals and ostraca (writings on pot-sherds); but while they name many private individuals,[11] the king, when mentioned, is generally referred to anonymously. A few seals and seal impressions have been discovered which may name Israelite or Judaean kings, but most of these were found out of context or unclearly stratified.[12] Only one well-stratified group of sealings seems to give the name of an Israelite monarch – the penultimate king of Judah, Jehoiachin, who reigned for six months in 597 BC. But even these remain controversial; the pottery they were found with has recently been redated to before 700 BC (see below).

FIG. 8:1   Seal of 'Shema the servant of Jeroboam' from Megiddo. Jeroboam is almost certainly the second Israelite king of that name (793–753 BC), making this one of the few native inscriptions mentioning a Hebrew monarch (*after ANEP*).

Given the absence of local inscriptions which can firmly link the archaeological record to biblical history, Palestinian sites have generally been dated by finds of imported material, principally Egyptian objects bearing the cartouches of particular pharaohs. Literally hundreds of scarabs have been found in Late Bronze Age strata. Following the conventional chronology for the 18th–20th Dynasties, these have to be dated between c. 1550 and 1175 BC. Despite the fact that Egyptian finds become less common during the Iron Age, its starting point, and hence the overall framework, still depends on these connections with New Kingdom Egypt.

The archaeological picture resulting from this reliance on Egypt has produced a curious and unsatisfying mismatch with the Old Testament account. For example, the end of the Late Bronze Age in Palestine is conventionally associated with the Israelite Conquest. Yet, as Bimson has stressed, the archaeological record at this point provides a very poor match, Jericho being the most conspicuous example.[13] While the first Iron Age levels are usually attributed to the Israelite conquerors, nothing has been found which definitely shows the presence of new settlers at that time. The early part of Iron Age II is thought to represent the 'Golden Age' of the 10th-century kings David and Solomon – yet its material culture is of a surprisingly low level. After Solomon's death his 'empire' split into two parts and the northern kingdom, Israel, gradually came under the domination of the Aramaeans from Syria – but neither of these important developments can presently be traced in the archaeology of Iron Age II. Invasions from Assyria, Babylonia and Persia followed in the 8th–6th centuries, and various destruction levels are supposed to be associated with them. However, at Lachish, the very 'type site' of the southern Kingdom of Judah, it has never really been resolved whether Level III was burnt by the Assyrian king Sennacherib in 701 BC or the Babylonian king Nebuchadrezzar in 597 BC.

The problems in linking the biblical and archaeological records have naturally had a serious effect on attitudes towards the Old Testament, apparently swinging the weight of evidence in favour of the sceptics. The case of Jericho has certainly shaken credibility in the story of the Israelite Conquest, and played a major part in the development of models which do not involve a military invasion.[14] Likewise on archaeological grounds the commercial and political ascendancy ascribed to Solomon has also been dismissed as a fantasy, an empire which existed only 'on papyrus'.[15] The existence of such discrepancies is particularly odd, as the Old Testament offers the only surviving consecutive history from any area of the ancient Near East. By comparison, the histories of Egypt and Mesopotamia had to be reconstructed by modern scholars. Moreover, the approach of the biblical authors, from raging prophets to pious chroniclers, is more even-handed than that of Egyptian and Assyrian scribes, whose main concern was the glorification of their kings' achievements. The prophets of Israel seemed to delight in recording the failure of their kings, harping on their military defeats more than their successes.

Dame Kathleen Kenyon, in her time the leading British archaeologist in the Holy Land, faced the matter squarely:

> From the tenth century BC . . . there is a record of events which should be reflected in archaeological evidence, without any of the ambiguities that make it so tempting to suggest variant theories concerning the earlier periods . . .[16]

As an exercise, we re-examined the archaeological record of Palestine *without* the input of Egyptian chronology. There were strong enough grounds for temporarily setting aside the Egyptian dates, given the problems their involvement has produced else-where in the Mediterranean. Instead, we evaluated the archaeo-logical record with the aid of non-Egyptian historical sources – biblical, Persian, Babylonian, Assyrian and Phoenician – together with the archaeological synchronisms provided by Cyprus, Greece and other countries. The method adopted was to work backwards, linking archaeology and history, step by step, from the known times of the Late Persian period to the 'unknown' of the Late Bronze Age. The results of this fresh look at biblical archaeology were quite extraordinary.

The Return from Babylon

The basis of rabbinic Judaism was laid after the return of the Jews from their Exile in Babylon, where they had been taken as captives by Nebuchadrezzar in 587 BC. Soon after he conquered Babylonia in 539 BC, the Persian King Cyrus granted the Jews their liberty. Among the returnees who trickled home over the next century were many who had acquired both wealth and influence in the land of their captivity. They resettled the land, rebuilt the Temple and refortified Jerusalem. In the mid-5th century, the governor Nehe-miah reformed Judah into a national state within the Persian Empire, while Ezra 'the Scribe' oversaw a return to strict adherence to the ancient Mosaic laws and customs.

Yet despite these activities, the archaeological record for the Persian occupation of Palestine (539–332 BC) is notoriously meagre. At many sites, the very definition of Persian strata has been difficult, while the period as a whole has few architectural remains.[17] Those levels that can be assigned to it are generally confined to the second part (after c. 450 BC). The earlier phase of the Persian domination is almost completely unrepresented. In his definitive survey Stern lamented that: 'Although the Persian period is a relatively late one from the archaeological standpoint, it is one of the most obscure eras in Palestine.'[18]

For the preceding period, that of the Jewish Exile in Babylon (587–539 BC), the situation is even worse. Albright claimed that 'archaeologically speaking, the country was a *tabula rasa*', arguing that Nebuchadrezzar had reduced the population of Judah to a mere 20,000 or so.[19] From a historical perspective, Albright's character-ization seems greatly exaggerated. While an impoverished material culture in Judah is only to be expected after the depredations of the Babylonians, life still went on. The biblical evidence suggests that outside of Jerusalem itself, only a relatively small proportion of the population (mainly the nobility and some craftsmen) was actually removed.[20]

A list given by Nehemiah (11:25–36) around 440 BC includes a number of important towns in the Shephelah (west) and the Negev (south) as inhabited by the 'residue of Israel' – suggesting that the Babylonian deportations seriously affected only the central hill country of Judah.[21] Lachish in the Shephelah is one of these remnant towns mentioned by Nehemiah. Yet, according to present archaeological dating, the site lay largely uninhabited between its destruction by the Babylonians in 587 BC and its resettlement in the mid-5th century BC.[22] Remains of the Babylonian and Early Persian periods are likewise missing at many other Judaean sites.

Thus well over a century of biblical history is only sparsely reflected in the archaeological record. Are we to assume, then, that there was a 'Dark Age' in Palestine between 587 BC and c. 450 BC? Archaeologists of the early 20th century held a different view, frequently dating material now placed *before* the Exile to the blank period which presently exists. This situation was altered radically during the 1930s, as Albright explained:

> Macalister and Watzinger, followed by many others, dated most of the characteristic pre-exilic pottery from southern Palestine in the Persian and Hellenistic periods. When this pottery was transferred to its proper date before 587 B.C. it left something of a void behind.[23]

Albright and others have tried to fill the lacuna left by this redating, but with no great success. The question arises: on what grounds was a redating of such consequence decided in the first place? The dates given by early fieldworkers were, admittedly, often based on slender evidence. But were they replaced by anything more solid?

The 'Lachish Letters'

A firm chronological peg is believed to have been found at Lachish, whose stratigraphy provides the key to Judaean archaeology. Here a settlement of the late Persian period, Level I, was founded around the mid-5th century BC – to judge from the imported Greek pottery. Immediately beneath this was Level II, a fortified settlement destroyed by fire. Excavation of its burnt gatehouse between 1935 and 1938 uncovered some extraordinary writings on pot-sherds (ostraca). This famous group of letters, sent by a Jewish commander named Hoshaiah to his superior Yaosh – apparently just before the city fell to an enemy attack – is the oldest known in the Hebrew script.

Before discovering these texts, the excavator of Lachish, J. L. Starkey, had already surmised that the destruction of Level II was the handiwork of the Babylonian invaders of 587 BC. He passed on the Lachish Letters for examination to the Hebrew specialist Harry Torczyner, who compared the personal names they contained with those in the Bible. He concluded that the ostraca belonged to the time of Jeremiah, the leading prophet of Judah during the Babylonian invasions of 597 and 587 BC.[24] As he worked on his translation, Torczyner began to identify individual events with those in the Book of Jeremiah. In Letter IV the mention of Lachish and Azeqah together, in a context suggesting that they were under military threat, invited comparison with Jeremiah's reference to these two cities as the last to withstand Nebuchadrezzar's final attack (Jer. 34:7).

Letter III refers to a mission to Egypt led by a commander named 'Yikhbaryahu son of Elnathan', and also, obliquely, to 'a prophet'. Torczyner claimed to find numerous references to this figure throughout the Letters, and even his name, 'Uriah'.[25] He connected these allusions to the biblical account of the extradition of the troublesome prophet Uriah in the reign of Jehoiakim (609–598 BC):

> . . . the king sent men into Egypt, namely Elnathan the son of Achbor, and certain men with him into Egypt. And they fetched forth Uriah out of Egypt, and brought him unto Jehoiakim the king; who slew him with the sword, and cast his dead body into the graves of the common people. (Jer. 26:22–3)

The obvious problem is that while the Letter mentions 'Yikhbaryahu son of Elnathan' as commander, Jeremiah talks of one 'Elnathan son of Achbor'. Nevertheless, Torczyner was sure that the two events were identical.

The Letters naturally attracted the attention of the finest Semitic scholars of the day, who re-examined the ostraca and in a series of articles published over the next decade completely eroded Torczyner's case. Names were reread and events reinterpreted; indeed, many readings were shown to be merely products of his fertile imagination. For example, Torczyner's 'Yikhbaryahu' was corrected to 'Coniah'.[26] Where he read the name of a prophet as 'Uriah', only the last three characters are actually visible: '-iah'. It could just as easily be any one of the dozens of other Hebrew names with this ending.[27]

With the benefit of hindsight it can be seen that Torczyner's detailed argument was built on sand. The only role played by a prophet in the Letters was the minor one of messenger.[28] As closely neighbouring cities, Lachish and Azeqah must have been endangered by common threats on many occasions. Nor can much be learnt from the fact that a Judaean general was sent on a mission to Egypt; again, this is something which could have happened numerous times.

The dissection of Torczyner's work took many years. Yet by the time it was all over no one seems to have noticed what had really happened. Almost without exception, the very scholars who had systematically pulled his case to pieces still accepted his date for the Letters. Albright, amongst others, took it on trust that the onomastic (name) evidence presented by Torczyner proved that they belonged to the time of Jeremiah.[29] However, our examination of the names known from the ostraca shows that Torczyner's conclusions were completely misleading. According to his analysis, 68.1 per cent of these names are known from the period of Jeremiah and only 40.9 per cent from afterwards. The true situation is that while 50 per cent match Jeremiah's time, 55 per cent reflect the period after the return from Babylon. Thus, contrary to Torcyzner's claim, this method of analysis favours a date after the time of Jeremiah, in the Persian period.[30]

Moreover, particular individuals in the Lachish Letters appear to be identifiable in the sources covering the mid-5th century BC.[31] One case is outstanding. Letter III concludes with the following passage:

And as for the letter of Tobiah servant of the king, which came to Shallum son of Jaddua through [via] the prophet, saying, 'Beware!', thy servant hath sent it to my lord.[32]

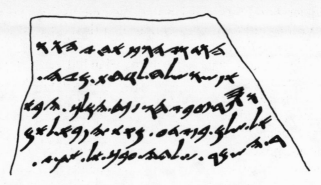

FIG. 8:2   Letter III from Lachish (*from Torcyzner et al. 1938*).

An extraordinary parallel to the letter-writer described here is found in the Bible. The principal enemy of governor Nehemiah was the half-Jew Tobiah, governor of Ammon (across the Jordan), whose status is reflected in his title 'the servant', universally agreed to be an abbreviation of 'servant of the king'.[33] Just as the Tobiah of the ostraca wrote to a Judaean nobleman conveying the warning message: 'Beware!', so the following is recorded by Nehemiah (6:17–19) of his enemy:

> Moreover in those days the nobles of Judah sent many letters unto Tobiah, and the letters of Tobiah came unto them . . . Also they reported his good deeds before me, and uttered my words to him. And Tobiah sent letters to put me in fear.

As for the anonymous prophet described as Tobiah's messenger in the ostracon, the biblical Tobiah likewise employed prophets – notably Shemaiah (Neh. 6:10), who was sent to terrorize Nehemiah with stories of plots against his life. Thus the Lachish Letters describe a prophet in the service of a powerful writer of threatening letters called Tobiah, with the particular title 'servant of the king' – a detailed complex of circumstances exactly paralleled in the Old Testament account.[34]

Further confirmation that the ostraca date to the time of Nehemiah comes from Letter VI. Despite some uncertain phrases, the main elements of this communication are clear.[35] Some letters from unnamed princes, and one by the King, had come into the hands of Hoshaiah, the writer of the Lachish ostraca. Reporting to his superior Yaosh, he described the words of the princes as being 'not good', expressing harmful intent ('to weaken our hands') regarding some undertaking by Hoshaiah's people in Jerusalem. He pleaded with Yaosh to intercede and remind the princes that their actions were contrary to the King's policy.

Again these circumstances are mirrored in Judaean history of the mid-5th century BC. Nehemiah had the blessing of the Persian King Artaxerxes to rebuild the wall of Jerusalem; all the Jews of the area participated, including one Hoshaiah, the first-mentioned of the 'princes of Judah' (Neh. 12:31–2). Other, more powerful, princes – i.e. Tobiah, governor of Ammon, the King of the Arabs and the governor of Samaria – fiercely opposed the project. They spread rumours that the rebuilding was an act of rebellion against the King (Neh. 2:19) and tried to intimidate the Jews by sending an open letter to Jerusalem accusing them of plotting rebellion. Its aim was, as Nehemiah (6:9) records, to ensure that 'Their [the Jews'] hands shall be weakened from the work, that it be not done.'[36]

Despite the limited information provided by the ostraca, the pattern of similarities is striking. It stands in stark contrast to that offered by the early 6th-century placement of the Lachish Letters. No parallel of equal substance, or even the identification of a single individual, has yet been found in the rich biblical literature concerning the time of Jeremiah, even after fifty years of research.

Following the lead given by our new interpretation of the Letters, Lachish II would have been destroyed, not in 587 BC by the Babylonians, but c. 440 BC under the Persians. The troubles during the governorship of Nehemiah,[37] as described by the eminent biblical historian John Bright, provide a feasible context for a violent assault on Lachish:

> Nehemiah had enemies on all sides . . . they incited – surely unofficially and while pretending ignorance of the whole thing – bands of Arabs, Moabites and Philistines to make raids on Judah. Jerusalem was harassed and outlying towns were terrorized; according to Josephus not a few Jews lost their lives.[38]

An incursion from nearby Philistia seems the most likely explanation for the destruction of Lachish II, as the material culture of the succeeding settlement (Lachish I) includes new pottery forms, altars and figurines known principally from coastal sites. Lowering the date for the end of Lachish II would also eliminate the long gap interposed by the conventional chronology before the beginning of Lachish I in the mid-5th century BC.[39]

Lachish III: Sennacherib or Nebuchadrezzar?

Despite this coherent picture, and the tempting evidence provided by the Lachish Letters, can the dating of such a key site really be lowered by as much as 150 years? This drastic shift for Lachish II seems less strange within the context of the long-standing argument surrounding the dating of the earlier strata. Almost since the first excavation of the site, academic opinion has been sharply divided between a 'low' and a 'high' chronology for Lachish III involving a difference of over a century. It has posed, in the words of the present excavator of the site, David Ussishkin, 'one of the most serious and central dating problems in Palestinian archaeology'.[40]

Both sides in the debate accept that Lachish II was destroyed by Nebuchadrezzar in 587 BC – unfortunately on the basis of Torczyner's slipshod scholarship. All estimates of the dates for earlier strata have been calculated from this baseline. Starkey discerned little change in the pottery of Lachish III to II and argued that the former had been destroyed by an earlier Babylonian invasion in 597 BC. He was followed by Albright, Kenyon and others.[41] The other school of thought, represented initially by Starkey's assistant Olga Tufnell and later by the prestigious Israeli archaeologist Yohanan Aharoni, opted for a far earlier dating. They highlighted the differences between the pottery of Levels III and II, suggesting a long passage of time;[42] further, there was no evidence of a Babylonian campaign in Palestine in 597 BC of sufficient duration to take in the siege and capture of a major city such as Lachish.[43] Instead they drew attention to the famous reliefs left by King Sennacherib of Assyria depicting in some detail his siege of Lachish in 701 BC.[44] The high chronologists attributed the destruction of Level III to this Assyrian conquest.

During the 1970s the idea was widely promulgated that the new excavations by Ussishkin had solved the problem once and for all.[45] Yet close examination shows his case was not based on any new evidence *per se*. His main conclusion, after intensive work at the site, was actually based on a negative argument – the elimination of the other possible candidates for the city supposedly laid waste and burnt by Sennacherib. Level II was ruled out by its conventional dating to the campaign of Nebuchadrezzar in 587 BC. Level IV, while it also came to 'a sudden end', showed few signs of burning,

FIG. 8:3 Portion of the Lachish reliefs of Sennacherib, showing the Assyrian attack on the city gate (*after Tufnell 1953*).

so its demise was tentatively attributed to an earthquake.[46] This left only Level III, which was ended by a massive conflagration.

The fatal flaw in this reasoning was, in a way, admitted by Ussishkin himself: 'the burning and destruction of Lachish are not specifically recorded in Sennacherib's annals'.[47] Indeed, it would be quite atypical for the Assyrians, who normally delighted in recording the burning and devastation of enemy cities, to omit such details with respect to Lachish. Sennacherib does record such actions for his campaigns in almost every other region except Judah.[48] In fact there may have been good strategic reasons why the strongholds of Judah, once taken, were not systematically demolished. Sennacherib states that the Judaean cities he captured were granted to the loyal kings of Philistia. In the very year that Sennacherib took Lachish he also had to fend off an incursion from Egypt.[49] It is therefore probable that the cities were turned over to Assyria's vassals in a relatively intact state.

Thus the fulcrum of Ussishkin's argument is illusory. The Assyrian records do *not* argue for a complete burning or devastation of the city. The deeper Level IV, which also seems to have met a violent end, actually provides a perfectly good match with the city besieged and captured by Sennacherib in 701 BC. The destruction of Lachish III would then logically belong to the well-attested attack on Lachish by Nebuchadrezzar in 587 BC (Jer. 34:7).

The last kings of Judah

The Lachish controversy is central to the understanding of the royal stamps impressed on the handles of storage jars found at numerous Judaean sites of the later Iron Age. Bearing the inscription *lmlk* ('belonging to the king'), these fall into two major classes, depicting either a four-winged scarab beetle or a two-winged sun disc.[50] Most likely the stamps, often accompanied by place-names, are marks identifying the royal vineyards where the contents of the jars were produced.[51]

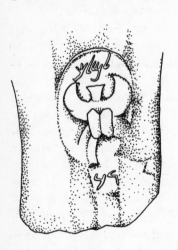
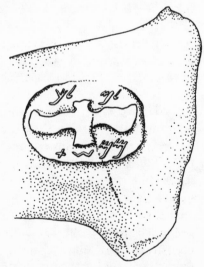

FIG. 8:4   Jar handles from Judah bearing the inscription *lmlk* ('belonging to the king') and royal symbols: (left) four-winged type with a stylised Egyptian scarab; (right) two-winged, resembling the symbol of royal aura known from Assyria (*after Naveh 1982*).

Before Ussishkin's excavations, the consensus was that the two-winged stamps were introduced by King Josiah (640–609 BC), the last ruler of Judah with any real power, during his administrative reorganization of the kingdom. The four-winged class was generally placed shortly before Josiah, though a few argued a date as early as the reign of Hezekiah (715–686 BC), the king who faced the invasion of Sennacherib.[52] Soon after the renewal of work at Lachish, Ussishkin discovered jars bearing both classes of stamp together in sealed deposits of Lachish III. Once it was felt that a date of 701 BC for the destruction of this level had been demonstrated beyond all doubt, the royal stamps as a whole had to be backdated to the late 8th century BC.

This redating of the stamps went hand-in-hand with a large-scale revision of Palestinian archaeology, one which had in fact already been advocated by Aharoni.[53] Sites whose destruction was once dated to 597 BC were thrust into the late 8th century. The last days of the Judaean kingdom were effectively robbed not only of their prime palaeographic material – the stamps – but also of many cities. It had to be assumed that numerous Judaean sites were laid waste and remained abandoned for the last century or so of the kingdom's history.[54] A wave of destructions now had to be attributed to the Assyrians, who actually claimed no such thing.

Alternatively, if – as we have argued here – Lachish III was actually burnt by the Babylonians in 587 BC, then the introduction of the royal stamps can again be attributed to the time of Josiah. Indeed, their distribution fits better with the historical circumstances of the late 7th century than with those during Hezekiah's reign.[55] Likewise, their disappearance can be seen as a natural consequence of the demise of the Judaean monarchy. Moreover, the horizon of destructions containing royal stamps can be restored to their logical context – during the campaign of Nebuchadrezzar which left Judah's cities in smoking ruins and brought the kingdom to an end.[56]

A final argument comes from another group of jar-handle impressions, giving the names of non-royal individuals. The most controversial of these 'private stamps' are those of 'Eliakim, steward of Yawkin'. Impressions were found at Tell Beit Mirsim, Beth Shemesh and Ramat Rahel,[57] in levels originally dated to the early 6th century BC. Albright therefore argued that the stamps belonged to an official of Jehoiachin, the penultimate king of Judah,

who ruled for six months in 597 BC before being deported by
Nebuchadrezzar. As he noted, Babylonian tablets mentioning this
king in exile show that his name was vocalized 'Yawkin', like that
on the Judaean stamps.[58] This attractive identification, once widely
accepted, had to be summarily rejected when the '597 BC' destruction levels were redated to 701 BC.

FIG. 8:5   Seal impression bearing the
inscription 'Eliakim na'ar [steward of]
Yawkin' (*after ANEP*).

After careful examination of the 'Eliakim' stamps and their
find-spots, Ussishkin showed beyond reasonable doubt that they
came from storage jars which also bore the familiar royal stamps on
other handles. Since he dates the royal stamps to before 701 BC,
Ussishkin saw this as conclusive proof that Albright was wrong.[59]
But the real significance of his discovery seems to have eluded
Ussishkin. As the Eliakim stamps were on jars also impressed by
seals marking them as crown property, it seems logical that he was a
royal official. This being the case, the Yawkin whom Eliakim
served was most likely a king. This raises an immense problem for
Ussishkin's dating, which places the Yawkin stamps a full century
before a ruler of this name took the throne. On the other hand, if
Lachish III and related sites were destroyed in 587 BC, the Judaean
king Jehoiachin can be restored to the palaeographical and
archaeological record.

The Assyrian conquest

The only remaining argument raised against a late date for the royal
stamps comes from the site of Ramat Rahel, a Judaean palace
complex near Jerusalem. Here nearly 150 stamps were found
beneath a layer containing pottery generally described as 'Assyrian
Palace Ware' of the 7th century BC. This was thought to provide
proof that the stamps were pre-Assyrian, agreeing with the case for
placing them before 701 BC at Lachish.[60] The argument depends, of

course, on the identification of this pottery as a product of the Assyrian Empire. Petrie was the first to identify it, during his excavations of Tell Jemmeh in southern Palestine. As it was clearly alien to the Palestinian repertoire, Petrie decided that he had uncovered the 'dinner service' of an Assyrian governor.[61] Now known from a scatter of sites in both Israel and Judah, its distinctive style has come to be accepted as a diagnostic feature of the Assyrian domination (c. 733–630 BC).[62]

However, it was pointed out more than ten years ago that the so-called Assyrian Palace Ware, judged by the evidence of Mesopotamian stratigraphy, must largely *postdate* the fall of the Empire, c. 610 BC. At the Assyrian capital of Nimrud it appears in the very latest levels and continues in the 'squatter' occupation of the 6th century BC.[63] The Palestinian archaeologist John Holladay drew attention to these finds and concluded that 'the floruit of the ware . . . should be placed in *and following* the last days of the Assyrian empire'.[64] The pottery could therefore reflect, not Assyrian influence, but Neo-Babylonian, at least in terms of its date.

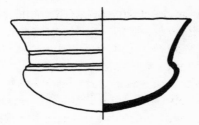

FIG. 8:6   Example of 'Assyrian Palace Ware' from Samaria, Period VII (*after Crowfoot et al. 1957*).

Applying these results to Palestine, Holladay suggested that Petrie's 'Assyrian' Fort and Residency at Tell Jemmeh were the work of Nebuchadrezzar, who may have established a garrison in the deep south of Palestine after his defeat of the Egyptians in 605–604 BC. An even later date, around 570 BC, when Nebuchadrezzar invaded Egypt, would be equally plausible.

Far from upholding the high chronology for Palestine, the presence of Assyrian Palace Ware actually places a considerable strain on the dating of strata currently assigned to the late 8th–7th centuries BC. All available evidence suggests that these levels really belong to the end of the Judaean kingdom and the period of the

Neo-Babylonian Empire. Recent work by Francis and Vickers on the chronology of the Archaic Greek pottery finds from southern Palestine is producing results broadly in step with the revision suggested here.[65]

Accordingly, the Assyrian period must be sought deeper in the stratigraphic record, in levels conventionally dated to the 9th century BC. The idea that the successive cultural phases of Palestinian archaeology have been mislabelled to such a serious degree may seem surprising, but the truth is that the chronology of early Iron Age Palestine is extraordinarily fluid. For example, the latest excavator of Tell Abu Hawam, a key site in southern Phoenicia, has lowered the date for the destruction of Stratum III, once associated with an Egyptian invasion around 925 BC, to as late as the 8th century, and possibly to the time of Sennacherib's conquest c. 700 BC (see Chapter 5).

In a period of history documented by both Mesopotamian and biblical records one might expect more straightforward answers – from, say, the discovery of items of unquestionable Assyrian origin, such as texts on clay tablets or stone, in specific strata. Unfortunately, most Assyrian inscriptions from Palestine are stray finds,[66] while the few known from excavations pose considerable problems. At Gezer in Israel a cuneiform tablet bearing the precise date 651 BC was found by its early 20th-century excavator in a stratum he dated to the 10th century BC.[67] Discovery of another 7th-century Assyrian tablet at Tell Keisan in southern Phoenicia caused pandemonium – the excavator had to revise drastically his already published interpretation of the stratigraphy and was accused by one of his site supervisors, in no uncertain terms, of manipulating the evidence.[68]

There are also many finds of Assyrian-style pottery in contexts conventionally dated as much as two centuries earlier than the initial invasion of Israel by Tiglath-pileser III in 733 BC.[69] A similar anomaly is presented by Black-on-Red Ware, dated by Cypriot archaeologists to the period 850–700 BC, but found repeatedly in '11th to 10th-century' contexts in Palestine (see Chapter 7). Indeed, it would seem, had not the beginning of the Iron Age been set by links with Egyptian chronology, that the cumulative weight of biblical, Persian, Neo-Babylonian, Assyrian, Greek and Cypriot evidence would have forced an overall lowering of Palestinian Iron Age dates.

FIG. 8:7 Almost identical 'Proto-Aeolic' (or 'Proto-Ionic') capitals from Megiddo (above), conventionally dated to the 10th/9th centuries BC, and from Salamis (below), belonging to the 8th–7th centuries BC. The tension between the Palestinian and Cypriot Iron Age chronologies, apparent from the pottery evidence, can also be seen in such architectural features (*after Shiloh 1979*).

The Samaria conundrum

A prime test of such a large-scale revision is provided by Samaria, the key site for the Iron Age archaeology of the northern kingdom, and often hailed as a case of perfect agreement between the archaeological and biblical records. Samaria was founded by King Omri of Israel (father of Ahab); after noting that he spent six of his twelve years' reign at his capital in Tirzah, the Bible relates the following:

> And he bought the hill Samaria from Shemer for two talents of silver, and built on the hill, and called the name of the city which he built, after the name of Shemer, owner of the hill, Samaria . . . Omri slept with his fathers, and was buried in Samaria: and Ahab his son reigned in his stead. (1 Kgs. 16:23–8)

Thereafter Samaria remained the capital of Israel. The generally accepted interpretation of its archaeology in the light of this passage is reasonable: the first evidence of major building activity should date from the reign of Omri (885–873 BC). This ground rule was followed by both the American and British teams who worked at the site. Uncovering the remains of a series of palaces, they attributed the first (Building Period I) to Omri. (See Table 8:2.)

Although it was generally accepted that the city was founded in the early 9th century BC, a conspicuous problem was raised by the pottery associated with the buildings. According to standard classification, the pottery found under the Samaria I floor belonged to the 10th century.[70] The British excavator, Kenyon, believed that the closest date for an architectural phase is provided by the latest pottery discovered in the rubble used to create a base for its construction. In this case, convinced that she was dealing with a

9th-century building, Kenyon had to argue that the generally accepted ceramic chronology was too high. In her opinion the pottery dated to the early 9th century BC.[71]

This was the starting point of a major dispute. Other archaeologists, largely Israeli and American, could not accept Kenyon's interpretation. In their view the pottery found on top of a given floor gives a closer date. But at Samaria the problem was not so simple. Not only was '10th-century' pottery found *under* the 9th-century floors; it was also found *above* them, in the levelling material and casemate (hollow) walls of Building Period II.

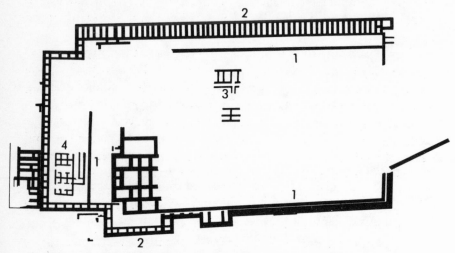

FIG. 8:8   Plan of the Israelite palace complex on the acropolis of Samaria: 1. Inner enclosure wall, Building Period I; 2. Casemate walls, Building Period II; 3. 'Ivory House', findspot of the largest collection of ivories; 4. 'Ostraca House' where the Samaria ostraca were discovered. The plan is partially reconstructed, following Crowfoot *et al.* 1942.

How could this be? Kenyon's opponents did not challenge the idea that Samaria I was built by Omri. Instead, they argued that her understanding of the archaeology was at fault and that the considerable amount of 10th-century pottery found underneath the 9th-century palace could be plausibly explained as the residue of an earlier settlement. Kenyon's main critic, G. Ernest Wright, suggested that 'Omri purchased not a bare hill, but a hill with a village on it.'[72] This hypothetical village curiously left no building remains, with the possible exception of two walls.[73] More awkward were the attempts to explain why the same ware found underneath

Samaria I also occurred above it. Wright believed that the pottery got there in debris from the pre-Omrid 'village' used to build the foundations of Samaria II. His argument breaks down under close examination. The ware in question was described by Kenyon as 'entirely uniform'.[74] This is surprising if it was introduced as levelling material. Underneath the floors of Samaria I it was frequently mixed with Early Bronze Age pottery from a long-abandoned prehistoric settlement.[75] It seems incredible that the builders of Samaria II selected the rubbish of only one period to use in their construction work. Wright himself noted that such a deposit 'would be expected to contain pottery from all earlier occupation levels on the site'.[76] According to the excavator it did not.

Kenyon stuck to her guns and redefined the '10th-century' pottery horizon as belonging to the early 9th. Then, using Samaria as an 'index site', she compared its pottery to that of neighbouring Israelite cities, such as Megiddo and Hazor, and reduced their dates accordingly. Kenyon's low chronology, however, never caught on. Taken to its logical extreme, it would have created a void between 9th-century levels and those from the earliest Iron Age, firmly placed by Egyptian evidence in the early 12th century BC. There seemed to be no way out of the dilemma, other than to reject the golden opportunity which Samaria offered of a fixed historical point for Palestinian ceramic chronology.

Both sides in the dispute tended to minimize the discrepancy between the dates for the building phases and the pottery. While Wright referred to the anomalous pottery as '10th-century B.C.', his own observations, as well as Kenyon's, reveal that many forms were actually characteristic of the 11th century BC.[77] At the same time Kenyon kept her pottery dates as high as the historical evidence would allow. She believed that the entire palace complex of Period I was built by Omri in his last six years, attributing Period II to Ahab (873–853 BC). This meant, in her view, that the controversial pottery could be dated no later than c. 870 BC.[78] As Wright pointed out, it seems excessive to allocate both kings a separate building phase, especially given Omri's short reign. More likely Omri began Samaria I and it was completed by his son.[79] If one were to take Wright's estimate of the time taken to build Samaria I together with Kenyon's understanding of the pottery, some of the '10th'-century ceramics would postdate the reign of Ahab. The palace of Samaria I, after Ahab finished it, could have been used for another two generations or so, which would mean that pottery styles conventionally dated around 1000 BC might actually have been used as late as *c*. 800 BC.

Examination of the later strata suggests that a reduction of this order does need to be made for the pottery of Samaria I–II. Beginning with the higher levels, VIII contains 5th- and 6th-century Greek pottery, and is thus reasonably securely dated; VII contains 'Assyrian Palace Ware', and is presently believed to represent Samaria under Assyrian rule, despite the fact that nothing found in this phase reflects the large-scale reconstruction which the Assyrian King Sargon II (721–705 BC) claimed to have carried out:

> [The town I] re[built] better than (it was) before and [settled] therein people from countries which [I] myself [had con]quered. I placed an officer of mine as governor over them and imposed upon them tribute as (is customary) for Assyrian cities.[80]

Following the dating of 'Assyrian Palace Ware' discussed above, VII would largely be a Babylonian level. This being the case, the Building Period termed Samaria V/VI would not be the last Israelite level before Sargon's conquest, but rather the final Assyrian, before their withdrawal *c*. 630 BC. This reduction is in step with the revised dates of 701–587 BC for Lachish III, the pottery of which is contemporary with that of Samaria V/VI.[81]

The work of Sargon of Assyria may then be reflected in Samaria Period IV. This included new constructions, repairs and alterations to the old casemate walls and buildings; most significantly, it was linked with 'the most important break' in the pottery sequence[82] – a change that could reflect the Assyrian deportation of the Israelites and resettlement of the site with foreigners from Syria and Babylonia. The famous Samaria ostraca, dated by the years of an anonymous ruler, belong to this level, judging from the type of sherds on which they were written.[83] It seems that they do not relate to any of the Israelite kings previously suggested, ranging from Ahab in the 9th century BC to Pekah in the mid-8th, but in fact to an Assyrian ruler, most likely Sargon or Sennacherib.

This would make Samaria III the final Israelite level, possibly built under Hoshea, last King of Israel (732–722 BC). The extensive work undertaken during Building Period II would then belong to a powerful king such as Jeroboam II (793–753 BC).[84] The bulk of the

Table 8:2

Period	Wright B	Wright P	Kenyon B	Kenyon P	Revision B	Revision P
Early Bronze Age	–	+	–	+	–	+
'11th–10th' century BC	–	1 & 2	–	–	–	–*
Omri (885–873 BC)	} I		I	1	}	
Ahab (873–853 BC)	} 3		II	2	} I	1
Jehu (841–813 BC)	II		III	3		
Jeroboam II (793–753 BC)	III	4	IV	4	II	2
Last Israelite (753–722 BC)	IV–VI	5 & 6	V–VI	5 & 6	III	3
Early Assyrian (722–c. 700 BC)					IV	4
Final Assyrian (c. 700–c. 630 BC)	} VII	7	} VII	7	V–VI	5 & 6
Post Assyrian and Neo-Babylonian					VII	7
Persian	VIII	8	VIII	8	VIII	8
Hellenistic	IX	9	IX	9	IX	9

The variant correlations (suggested by Wright, Kenyon and the present writers) between the Building and Pottery phases (B & P) of Samaria and historical periods. Our revision follows Kenyon's understanding that the latest pottery found under the floors of a given Building phase coincides with or slightly predates the time of its construction.

*Minor building activity (two walls) and possibly some pits for olive and wine pressing (see Stager 1990) may reflect a small settlement already in existence when Omri bought the site. This would have produced the very earliest pottery of phase 1 (Iron Age I), dated on our model to c. 900 BC.

beautiful ivories found at the site have generally been attributed to this phase and the time of Ahab (although they were actually found in disturbed or later contexts).[85] However, an 8th-century date seems more likely. As specialists in ancient ivory-working have repeatedly stated, they are extremely close stylistically to the ivories collected by Sargon II in his palace at Khorsabad.[86] Indeed, the Assyrian group includes many pieces probably manufactured in Israel. The prophet Amos (3:9–15), a contemporary of Jeroboam II, railed against the luxury exhibited by the Israelite royalty, who dwelt in 'houses of ivory'.

Thus a number of lines of evidence suggest that even the low dates of Kenyon were, overall, too high. While her starting point of *c.* 880 BC for Building Period I seems to be correct, her dating of Samaria II to *c.* 870 BC cannot be upheld. An early 8th-century date seems more likely. The fallout of the Samaria case-study, which would lower Early Iron Age pottery chronology by as much as 200 years, can be fully appreciated only by re-examining the archaeology presently ascribed to the Golden Age of King Solomon in the 10th century BC.

The Dark Age of Palestine

The wealth of King Solomon is described in such graphic detail in the Bible that his name is still a byword for opulence. His reign marked the zenith of ancient Israel's wealth, power and territorial extent. To the north and east, kings of Syria and Transjordan paid him homage, while Hiram I, ruler of the great Phoenician city-state of Tyre, was his ally, both politically and commercially. Solomon's marriage to a daughter of an unnamed Egyptian pharaoh gave him security to the south and unprecedented prestige for a Levantine king.

Solomon's reign, which ended *c.* 930 BC, is described in the Bible as forty years of almost uninterrupted peace, stabilized by a system of diplomatic alliances, strategically placed fortresses and a newly developed chariotry. Trade generated wealth: 'all the kings of Arabia' paid Solomon duties on the spice traffic passing through his domains. Ezion-geber at the head of the Gulf of Aqaba was developed as a port, and his navy, with the help of Phoenician maritime expertise, undertook commercial expeditions to distant lands, 'bringing gold and silver, ivory, and apes and peacocks' (1 Kgs. 10:22).

The riches gathered by Solomon were spent principally on a massive building programme. His primary achievement was the magnificent Temple, an inspiration to architects and mystics through the ages. Near the Temple he built a new palace for himself and another for his Egyptian queen, and extended the fortifications begun by his father David. He rebuilt the cities of Hazor, Megiddo and Gezer, and founded Tadmor (Palmyra), a trading centre deep in the Syrian desert (1 Kgs. 5; 7:1–12; 9:15–19).

What has archaeology revealed of these magnificent achievements? Unfortunately, it seems that little will ever be recovered of

Solomon's crowning glory, the Temple. In 587 BC it was razed to the ground by Nebuchadrezzar. Subsequent rebuildings of the Temple under the Persians and Herod the Great have completely obscured any remains. Nonetheless, Solomon's other extensive building projects should not all have escaped the spade, while the reported prosperity of his reign must have also have left some mark on the archaeological record.

Within the Egyptian-based framework for Palestinian stratigraphy, Solomonic remains have been sought in the period known as Iron Age IIA, dated c. 1000–900 BC, and particularly at Hazor, Megiddo and Gezer. The first remains to be confidently labelled 'Solomonic' were the palace and stables at Megiddo, protected by a substantial gateway and walls. Following this, Yigael Yadin, the late head of the Hebrew Institute of Archaeology, discovered another Iron IIA gateway at Hazor:

> . . . the gate's plan – comprising six chambers and two towers – as well as its dimensions were identical to those of the gate discovered earlier at Megiddo and ascribed by its excavators to the city of Solomon. Excitement in our camp intensified. This was real proof! Not only were our deductions in ascribing this stratum to Solomon correct, but the gate was also confirmation of the authenticity of the Biblical verse describing Solomon's activity in these two cities.[87]

Yadin followed this success with some 'excavations in a book', as he termed it. Searching through the site reports of Gezer, he discovered the plan of a gateway and walls 'exactly like those found in Megiddo and Hazor'.[88] Renewed work at Gezer showed the gate to be of Iron Age IIA date and the excavator William Dever wrote exultantly: 'The sealed pottery from the floors and the makeup below were characteristic red-burnished ware of the late tenth century BC. Solomon did indeed rebuild Gezer!'[89]

For Yadin, and nearly all biblical archaeologists, this pattern of evidence is completely satisfying. The Bible states that Solomon built at Hazor, Megiddo and Gezer; at each place walls and gateways of identical construction and similar dimensions were discovered, all associated with the Iron Age IIA pottery thought to have been used in Solomon's time. The attractive idea of the 'Solomonic cities' has now firmly entrenched itself, not only in the minds of scholars, but in the imagination of the public. Certainly

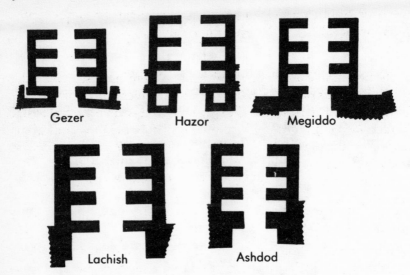

FIG. 8:9   Supposed 'Solomonic' gateways. They have all been dated by their excavators to the 10th century, with the exception of Lachish which Ussishkin dates to the 9th century (*after Soggin 1989*).

the gateways of Hazor, Megiddo and Gezer could have been made by the same builders. But were they really the servants of Solomon? Further gateways with the same plan have now been found at Lachish, not recorded as a centre of Solomonic activity, and Ashdod in Philistia.[90] The Bible is clear that Solomon's direct rule did not extend over the Philistines, making the occurrence of 'Solomonic' buildings in Ashdod rather surprising.

Moreover, the level of material culture associated with these Iron IIA structures is hardly reminiscent of the glories of Solomon's reign. In the words of the American biblical archaeologist James Pritchard:

These 'cities', even by ancient Near Eastern standards . . . were far from what one might call urban centres; they were more like villages. Within the walls of roughly cut stones there were floors of beaten earth or plaster. Artefacts of bone, stone, clay, an occasional metal tool or weapon, suggest a cultural level which was apparently lacking in both artistic sophistication and wealth. As yet no evidence has been found for the use of chariotry or for the metal trappings for the harnesses of horses. As for gold and other precious metals, its occurrence is limited to an occasional earring or other article of personal adornment. From the tenth-century level . . . at Megiddo not a single gold item is recorded by the excavators.[91]

The Solomonic problem becomes most acute in the search for the artistic products of his 'Golden Age'. The conventional chronology for the Palestinian Iron Age allows a long time-span for Iron I to IIA (*c.* 1200–900 BC), during which time probably the most ambitious artistic product was the so-called 'Philistine Ware' produced at coastal sites in the south, outside of Israel.[92] The problem of the Levantine ivories, invoked by Greek archaeologists for this period, but which are actually non-existent, has already been noted (see Chapter 4). Sculpture is completely lacking, as is monumental architecture.

'Was the Age of Solomon Without Monumental Art?', the title of a paper written by Albright in 1958, typifies the dilemma produced by situating Solomon in such a cultural Dark Age.[93] This problem was the focal point of the heated and wide-ranging debate between Frankfort and Albright (see Chapter 6), which polarized into two distinct schools of thought. Frankfort's dating of the artistic remains from Late Bronze and Iron Age Syria and Palestine was logical, but produced a result which distressed biblical archaeologists:

Once it is realised that the whole of North Syrian art of the first millennium B.C. represents a fresh start, made more or less simultaneously – and with varying resources of local talent – in a number of places, the attempts to fill the gap between 1200 and 850 B.C. with transitional work can be abandoned.[94]

While respecting Frankfort as 'the foremost comparative art-historian of the ancient East', Albright accused him of unwittingly conducting 'what amounts to a systematic campaign to discredit the entire Solomonic building tradition by the simple expedient of denying the existence of art or architecture in Greater Syria between ca. 1200 and 850 B.C.'.[95] Albright mustered a mass of objects, inscriptions and buildings which could arguably belong to the Solomonic Dark Age, sometimes by stretching the dates of material which fell on either side of the gap. But his attempt to defend the integrity of the biblical record failed. Much of his evidence, such as the 'Solomonic' strata from Megiddo, Hazor and Gezer, only serves to underline the low level of material culture in Palestine during the Iron IIA period.

A similar situation prevails in Phoenicia, where the reported wealth and building feats of the great Hiramic age, contemporary with those of Solomon in Israel, have not been matched on the ground. For example, at Byblos archaeologists have long lamented the 'curious fact' of the general 'absence of stratified levels from the Iron Age'.[96] This has usually been blamed on the lack of excavation at the main ancient towns, which continue to be inhabited, as well as the current political situation. Nevertheless, the recent, albeit very small-scale, work at Tyre and Sarepta confirm the poor picture of early Iron Age Phoenician archaeology. The 10th-century finds from Tyre are meagre,[97] while the evidence recovered from Sarepta is very limited and the possibility of 'a considerable abandonment' from the 11th to the 9th century BC has been discussed.[48] The uncomfortable conclusion, for those who adhere to both the conventional chronology and the biblical account, was spelt out by James Muhly:

> This is really quite remarkable. The great age of Phoenician mercantile activity, the time of Hiram I, of Solomon and the biblical accounts relating to Ezion-geber, the Tarshish fleet and three-year voyages to the Land of Ophir, is simply not documented in the archaeological record from Tyre and Sarepta.[99]

Israelite settlement or divided monarchy?

The problem of Solomonic and Hiramic archaeology requires urgent reconsideration against the background of the wider chronological problems reviewed earlier. Have the wonders of Solomon's reign simply been sought in the wrong strata?

It has already been noted how Kenyon tried to lower the 10th-century BC date of the pottery found at Megiddo, Samaria and other sites. But rather than deprive Solomon of his buildings at Megiddo, Hazor and Gezer and thrust him into an even worse Dark Age, biblical archaeologists elected to keep a high chronology. In the long run, this merely passed problems further down the line, creating a second 'Dark Age' in the Neo-Babylonian and Early Persian periods. Our re-examination of Samaria suggests a redating of the pottery styles conventionally placed c. 1000 BC to the late 9th century, making Iron II levels much later than Solomon.

Could Solomon then belong earlier in the Iron Age? This seems unlikely, as the Iron I period (1200–1000 BC) reveals an even lower cultural level than Iron II. At the major cities, such as Lachish and Megiddo, there are conspicuous gaps in the Iron I sequence.[100] Many other sites are short-lived villages or farmsteads, where the pottery evidence is so ambiguous that dates suggested for them range between the 14th and 11th centuries BC.[101] Indeed, some of the settlements attributed to Iron I may actually belong to the Late Bronze Age. The overall picture is so patchy that, were it not for the Egyptian synchronisms which set its beginning, the period as a whole could be considerably telescoped.

On the standard scheme the earliest Iron Age levels are thought to reflect the arrival of the Israelites in the Promised Land. This understanding, once an axiom of biblical archaeology, has been subjected to intense criticism in recent years. The Egyptian King Merneptah refers to 'Israel' in a text conventionally dated to c. 1220 BC.[102] Because of this, Albright and other biblical archaeologists placed the destructions which occurred in Palestine at the end of the Late Bronze Age to around 1230 BC.[103] New archaeological evidence, relatively dated by Egyptian finds, has steadily eroded the concept of a distinct horizon of destructions around this time. It now appears that they were staggered, occurring at three periods roughly dated to 1225, 1200 and 1175 BC. Any resemblance to the biblical account of the Conquest under Joshua has been completely spoilt.[104]

The transition from the Late Bronze Age to the Iron Age can now be seen as a more gradual process. There is also increasing doubt as to whether the archaeological record reflects the influx of a new population; indeed, there are no 'breaks in continuity worth noting'.[105] Traditionally the arrival of the Israelites has been thought to be indicated by five new elements in the material record: large storage jars with collared rims; a new kind of cooking pot; plastered cisterns to store water; small houses with a ground plan of four or so rooms and rows of supporting pillars; and terraced fields.[106] These features are most common in the rugged area of the central hill country, where much early Israelite settlement concentrated – a coincidence which encourages many archaeologists to see them as diagnostic of the earliest Israelite settlers.

A recent study by Gloria London, an ethnoarchaeologist specializing in the use of pottery by modern agricultural societies in Cyprus and the Levant, throws an entirely different perspective on these supposedly 'Israelite' features. She shows convincingly that they need not reflect the arrival of a new ethnic element in the hill country, but simply differences between the material culture of country folk and town dwellers. For example, large storage jars are more useful to isolated, self-supporting communities; families in cities, with access to markets, had neither room nor need for large, individually owned jars. [107]

The Israelites entered Canaan from the south, after a long sojourn in Egypt and many years of wandering in the desert. If they were truly responsible for the new elements which appear in the early Iron Age, we would expect these to betray southern influences. The opposite is true. A 15th-century BC prototype for 'four-roomed' houses is known from the Euphrates region. The particular style of building with pillars can be seen in Late Bronze Age Syria, notably at Ugarit. [108] Collared rim jars have now been found from a much wider area than that originally claimed by the Israelites. For example, at the Jordanian site of Sahab, within the ancient Kingdom of Moab, storage jars of the same design were found with Syrian motifs stamped on their rims. [109] The evidence for new cultural influence on Palestine in the early Iron Age clearly favours an origin in the north rather than the south.

If the Iron Age did not herald the arrival of the Israelites, a major pillar supporting the conventional understanding of Palestinian archaeology topples. On the non-Egyptian chronological model presented here, the changes seen at the beginning of the Iron Age would not reflect Israel's settlement in the early 12th century, but the breakup of its United Monarchy in the late 10th century BC – perhaps the most surprising consequence of our revision.

Even before Solomon's death (c. 930 BC), his empire was beset by severe political difficulties. With the connivance of Egypt, Edom in the south rebelled and became an independent kingdom. Damascus

---

A comparison of the conventional and alternative dates for the archaeological phases of Late Bronze Age to Iron Age Palestine. The conventional dates are based on synchronisms with the generally accepted historical chronology of Egypt. The alternative dates are consistent with the biblical record and other non-Egyptian evidence and are in step with the compression of Egyptian historical chronology argued in Chapter 10.

Table 8:3

CONVENTIONAL DATES

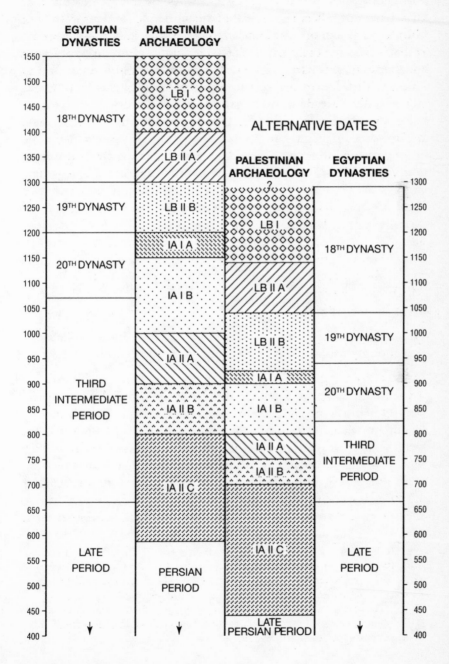

in Syria was liberated by a military adventurer, founder of an Aramaean dynasty which was to put constant pressure on Israel's northern border. Meanwhile disruptive forces were at work in the heart of the kingdom. It seems that the burden of local taxation was borne largely by the northern tribes of Israel, Judah in the south perhaps even being exempt.[110] This favouritism bred resentment, and one of Solomon's own officials, Jeroboam, rebelled. When Solomon died Jeroboam returned from exile in Egypt and raised the flag of independence in the north. The shaky unity of the twelve tribes was shattered, and the two halves of the Divided Kingdom became preoccupied by internecine strife. The Egyptians moved in to take advantage of these troubles and restore their own authority in the area. The fortresses built by Solomon's heir Rehoboam were seized, and Pharaoh 'Shishak' had to be bought off with the treasures of the Temple. Bright assessed the inevitable results of these developments:

> The empire of David and Solomon was gone. We may assume that the economic consequences of this were serious. Tribute ceased to flow in. With the trade routes along the coast no longer Israelite monopolies, and with internal strife making the free passage of trade difficult if not at times impossible, most of the lucrative adventures undertaken by Solomon collapsed. Although we lack direct evidence of it, the economy of Israel must have been damaged severely.[111]

On the model suggested here, direct evidence of such an economic recession is provided by the material culture of Iron Age I, which shows a marked decline in prosperity from the last LBA levels. The increase in rural settlements is also understandable. The Solomonic experiment, in which Israel struggled to be a major economic power with a cosmopolitan culture, had failed. When the system collapsed and trade no longer generated wealth, a shift back to the land would have been a natural response. The northern origin of the 'new' elements in the early Iron Age can also be logically explained: not by the Hebrews arriving from the south, but as a reflection of the increasing domination of Israel by the Aramaeans from Syria. Likewise, the destruction of many cities during the transition from the Late Bronze to Iron Age could reflect the wars which disintegrated Solomon's Empire, including the invasion of Shishak c. 925 BC and the earliest incursions of the Aramaeans.

Solomon in all his glory

The conclusion that the Solomonic era is to be found at the end of the Late Bronze Age is one of the most significant fallouts of our experimental chronology. Despite the fact that some 250 years are presently placed between the Bronze Age and the reign of Solomon, archaeologists have always tacitly accepted that the detailed biblical description of his Temple falls within the tradition of Late Bronze Age architecture. Only two identifiable temples are known from the Iron Age; both are small, and their plans bear little resemblance to that of the Temple. On the other hand, comparisons are repeatedly made between Solomon's work and the temples of the Late Bronze Age, particularly that from Hazor.[112]

King Hiram of Tyre, himself a noted builder,[113] played a major role in the building of the Temple. He supplied the timber needed for the project, masons to prepare the stone (1 Kgs. 5:7–18) and a master craftsman to cast the bronze furnishings.[114] The method of

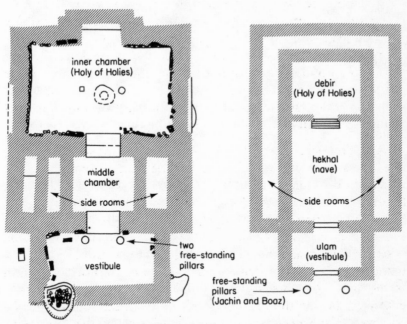

FIG. 8:10   (Left) The last Late Bronze Age Temple at Hazor; the excavator Yadin (1972, 97) remarked that: 'The main interest of the plan . . . is its basic resemblance to that of Solomon's temple, built about 300 years later.' (Right) A reconstruction of Solomon's Temple following the Old Testament account (drawing by Rosemary Burnard).

stoneworking used is significant: the Temple, Solomon's palace and the house he constructed for his Egyptian queen were all built of 'costly stones . . . sawed with saws, within and without' (1 Kgs. 7:9). Building with ashlar masonry – i.e. large blocks of stone squared with saws – was a specialized technique known from only a few periods in ancient Palestine. Ashlar masonry is indeed known from the '10th-century' levels, such as that at Megiddo traditionally ascribed to Solomon.[115] But the period of ashlar *par excellence* was the Late Bronze Age, when it seems to have been a technique especially favoured by the Canaanites of the coast. Unfortunately, the LBA levels of Tyre itself have barely been touched. The magnificence of its palace was, however, compared in an El-Amarna letter[116] to that of Ugarit on the Syrian coast, where excavation has revealed a truly monumental palace complex of the '14th–13th centuries' BC incorporating some of the finest ashlar masonry known.[117] Other prime examples come from early '12th-century' Kition in Cyprus, a city which may have been under the sway of Hiram of Tyre (see Chapter 7).

Regarding the elaborate metal furnishings which Solomon commissioned for the Temple, a telling comment was recently made by P. Moorey:

> The Levant is rich in academic anomalies for students of Iron Age metalworking: to make best sense of the unique (and still understudied) description of the bronze equipment made for Solomon's Temple (1 Kings 7:13–51) resort is commonly made to Cyprus or to Canaanite sites of the Late Bronze Age.[118]

Perhaps the most interesting of these items are the ten elaborate four-wheeled stands or trolleys built to hold ritual basins. Their side-panels and upper ledges were decorated with scenes including animals and trees (1 Kgs. 7:27–37). Except for their generous dimensions, the biblical text gives a blueprint for a series of intricate four-wheeled stands known from late 13th–early 12th-century Cyprus (see Plate 12). As Catling stated, although their resemblance to the examples made for Solomon's Temple 'raises a chronological difficulty, the relationship can hardly be denied'.[119]

The 'chronological difficulty' arises because of Catling's conclusion, based on an exhaustive study, that production of such complex stands ceased during the 12th century BC (see Chapter 4). Most of the stands have been found in Cyprus, and to judge from the

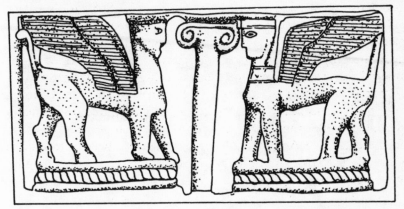

FIG. 8:11   Panel from a Cypriot four-sided stand, currently dated to the 12th century BC, showing sphinxes flanking a stylised palm tree (*after Shiloh 1979*). The construction and decoration of such distinctive stands are described in minute detail in the biblical account of the furniture commissioned by Solomon for his Temple (mid-10th century BC); 'on the plates of the ledges thereof, and on the borders thereof, he graved cherubim, lions and palm trees' (1 Kgs. 7:36). As Albright demonstrated, biblical 'cherubim' were actually sphinxes.

discovery of a stone mould apparently used for casting the decorative panels, Enkomi was a centre of production.[120] The Old Testament credits Solomon's wheeled stands to the Phoenician craftsman lent him by King Hiram. Given Hiram's probable involvement in Cyprus, we can see the stands, in a revised chronology, as the product of joint Cypro-Phoenician workshops – flourishing around not 1200 BC but 950 BC.

Much is known of the liturgy of the first Hebrew Temple from the Book of Psalms. Traditionally the bulk of these hymns, once set to music, were written in the time of Solomon's father, King David (early 10th century), who made the initial preparations for the building of the Temple. The striking resemblance between Psalm 104 and an Egyptian Hymn to the Sun-Disc, presently dated to the 14th century BC, has already been noted (see Chapter 1). The massive archive from the Late Bronze Age palace of Ugarit includes a wealth of sacred and poetical texts written in 'Canaanite', essentially the same language as Hebrew; the close parallels which they provide to the themes, grammar, syntax, vocabulary and subtleties of poetical expression in the Psalms have been the subject of innumerable studies.[121] Indeed, it has even been suggested that some of the Psalms and related literature may have really been

composed in the 2nd millennium BC,[122] long before the reign of
King David. On our new model, David would have been working
within a Late Bronze Age tradition of poetry and song; the question
of literary 'throwbacks' does not arise.

The material culture of Palestine at the end of the Late Bronze
Age is best seen at Megiddo. Here the Bible (1 Kgs. 9:15) suggests
that Solomon built a 'monumental palace compound'. Such a
structure was found in Stratum VIIA, the last LBA level at Megiddo. Although badly preserved, the palace found in this stratum 'was
an imposing edifice, decorated with wall paintings'.[123] Unlike the
'10th-century' Stratum IV ascribed to Solomon, which is devoid of
luxury items or imports, the remains of Stratum VIIA reflect the
rich material culture expected from the biblical description. Finds of
imported Mycenaean and Cypriot wares attest to the thriving trade
of the city at this time.

But the most exciting discovery was the subterranean treasury
attached to the palace, containing the largest cache of ivories known
from the ancient Levant (see Plate 17).[124] It includes panels for
decorating furniture, pen-cases, trinket-boxes, stands, and
figurines, superbly carved and showing a wide variety of influences, including both Hittite and Egyptian. One is reminded of
the biblical verse (1 Kgs. 10:29) describing Solomon's trade with
both Egypt and the 'kings of the Hittites'. One ivory, a plaque
showing a monarch holding court, is of particular interest. He is
seated on a throne decorated with sphinxes. If it was intended to
represent a specific rather than an idealized ruler, would it be too
much to imagine that in this ivory we actually have a depiction of
the Egyptianized King Solomon?

FIG. 8:12   Ivory from Late Bronze Age Megiddo showing a king holding court
(*after ANEP*).

The 'lost mines' of Solomon

The question of how Solomon could afford his luxuries has pro-
voked one of the most heated controversies of biblical archaeology.
Though tribute and commerce must have played their part, these
alone may not be enough to account for the short-lived economic
miracle of his reign. Popular legend has even granted him access to
fantastic mineral resources overseas, such as 'secret' or 'lost' mines
in Africa or even Spain (see Chapter 2).

More realistically, it has long been suspected that Solomon had a
source of wealth much closer to hand. Israel is poor in all mineral
resources except for one – the rich copper of the Arabah desert
south of Judah, mined intermittently at Timna from prehistoric to
Roman times. Since Solomon developed the port of Ezion-geber on
the Gulf of Aqaba, at the extreme end of the Arabah, it seems logical
that he took full advantage of the mining area just to the north. This
was the conclusion reached by Nelson Glueck after his intensive
exploration of the area in the 1930s. On the basis of historical
probability and the pottery he found, Glueck decided that the
Timna copper mines had been exploited from the time of Solomon
onwards, down to the 6th century BC.[125]

Glueck's case for the dating of the pottery came largely from his
excavations of Tell el-Kheleifeh, near the Gulf of Aqaba. 'Period
IV' could be reasonably dated to the 7th to 6th century BC by the
many vessels it contained imitating Mesopotamian forms.[126] The
local ware of this phase also included painted pottery known as
'Edomite Ware'. Having a firm footing for Period IV, Glueck dated
preceding levels from the 8th to 10th centuries BC. Likewise he
placed the pottery of the Arabah in general between the 6th and 10th
centuries, allowing the possibility that the Timna copper had been
worked by Solomon.

Yohanan Aharoni, together with Benno Rothenberg (once
Glueck's assistant), took great exception to these conclusions; they
insisted that the pottery from Timna belonged to Iron Age I and
could therefore be dated no later than the 11th century BC.[127]
Glueck, supported by the heavyweight authority of Albright,
vigorously defended his original dating in 1969.[128] Yet in the very
same year Rothenberg's excavations at Timna uncovered a temple
replete with Egyptian material of the 19th–20th Dynasties together
with the Early Iron Age pottery. Aharoni and Rothenberg appeared

to be completely vindicated. Mining activity at the site was sharply redated to *c.* 1300–1150 BC, after which time it was supposedly abandoned until Roman times.[129]

This seemed to scotch any possibility of the Timna copper having been mined during the reign of Solomon. In the preface to Rothenberg's publication of the site, Sir Mortimer Wheeler remarked on the strange result:

> In spite of traditional associations of King Solomon with the mines and the landscape, the great king is probably the most eminent absentee from the archaeological sequence.[130]

Were Glueck and Albright simply misguided in their conviction that Solomon must have exploited the Arabah mineral resources? Perhaps not. For one thing, much uncertainty still surrounds the redating of the pottery. It is clear that Glueck had not distinguished properly between the 8th–6th century 'Edomite Ware' found at Tell el-Kheleifeh and the pottery from Timna, now known as 'Midianite' and placed in the 13th–12th centuries BC: he wrongly treated them as much the same. Nevertheless, there is apparent continuity between the two styles. It has been admitted that the present centuries-long gap in the tradition of painted pottery in this area of north-western Arabia makes little sense.[131] Numerous similarities between the Midianite and Edomite wares actually make 'some degree of chronological overlap perfectly plausible'.[132] Further, Glueck ascribed several examples of what is now known as Midianite Ware to Periods III–IV at Tell el-Kheleifeh (8th–6th centuries BC);[133] if he were correct, then the currency of Midianite Ware would be extended over a surprisingly long period. As in so many other areas, the introduction of Egyptian synchronisms has resulted in either an implausible gap in the local sequence, or an equally unlikely stretching of the material.

Moreover, Glueck's original conclusion that the Timna mines were in use during the 10th century BC is now supported by a number of radiocarbon dates on material associated with mining activity.[134] Thus exploitation of the Arabah copper may still have been a major contributory factor to the economic strength displayed by Solomon. The only real stumbling block for the radiocarbon dates and the circumstantial case provided by history, economics, and, indeed, the tensions inherent in dating the local pottery sequence, is the glaring evidence of the Egyptian material at Timna.

FIG. 8:13   Egyptian rock relief from Timna in southern Palestine depicting Ramesses III making offerings to the goddess Hathor (*after Rothenberg 1988*). Such remains show that Egyptian control of the area was re-established during the 20th Dynasty. Evidence of the last rulers of the 19th Egyptian Dynasty is lacking. This recession in the Egyptian Empire would coincide, on our chronology, with the rise of Solomon's Empire, which must have included the mining area of Timna. Ramesses III would then be the 'King Shishak' who invaded southern Palestine *c.* 925 BC (see Chapter 10).

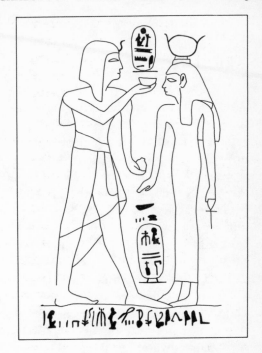

However, the results of our experimental analysis suggest that Egyptian chronology may be wrong by some 250 years and that a completely new picture of biblical archaeology can be developed which at last restores harmony between the historical and strati-graphical records. With respect to the copper at Timna it seems that King Solomon's mines were not 'lost' so much as stolen – by the constraints of the conventional Egyptian chronology.

CHAPTER 9

The Empty Years of Nubian History

The Nile flows northward through the swamp and savanna lands of the Sudan into the harsh Nubian desert until, after crossing several cataracts, it reaches the ancient border of Egypt at Aswan. Nubia, now part in Egypt and part in Sudan, spans this inhospitable region, from the First Cataract (Aswan) to the Fourth. The northern part (Lower Nubia), between the First and the Second Cataracts, lies beneath the waters of Lake Nasser, created by the building of the new Aswan Dam. In the 1960s UNESCO organized an extensive campaign to save monuments and to survey and excavate other sites throughout Lower Nubia.[1] This was the third archaeological survey of Nubia this century: the first (1907–11) and second (1929–34) were both made necessary by the enlargement of the old Aswan Dam.[2] Consequently, the archaeological coverage of this northern region is extensive, but it has always been interpreted from an Egyptian chronological perspective. In contrast, excavation in Upper Nubia, south of the Second Cataract, and the more southerly Butana region, between the Nile and Atbara, has focused almost exclusively on royal cemeteries or temple sites.

The political state which flourished in Nubia and the central Sudan (Butana) from the 8th century BC until the 4th century AD is given various names – Kush, Napata or Meroe – and covered most of the area from Aswan to Khartoum.[3] The earliest Kushite kings were buried in pyramid tombs at el-Kurru, near the northern 'capital', Napata. In the later years of the 8th century BC these Kurru kings expanded their power northward into Egypt and ruled there as the 25th Dynasty until the mid-7th century BC. Nuri, opposite Napata, became the burial place of the successors of the 25th Dynasty until the 4th century BC, when a new royal cemetery was established at the southern residence city of Meroe. The Meroitic period lasted until the 4th century AD, when the state disintegrated into smaller kingdoms.

The chronology of Nubia before the 25th Dynasty (c. 700 BC) is entirely dependent upon that of Egypt. All Nubia's connections with the Mediterranean were through Egypt (principally the Nile route, but perhaps also via the oases of the Libyan desert); it is

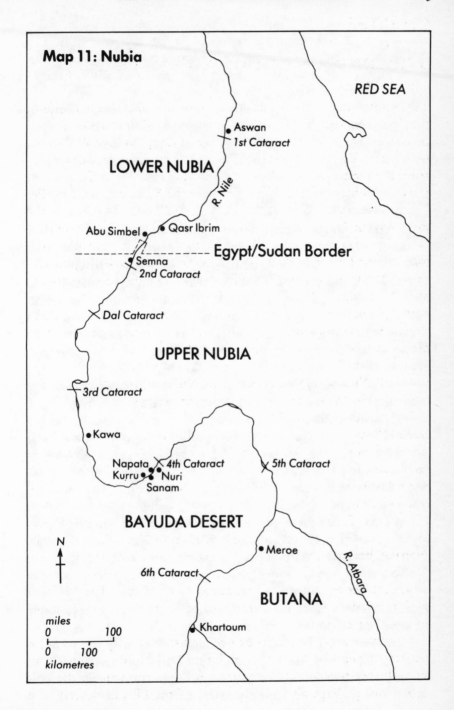

Map 11: Nubia

therefore impossible to establish relative chronologies between Nubia and the Near East which do not rely on Egyptian links. No chronological checks against other regions of North-east Africa can be made because almost nothing is known of the cultures there. Nubia's internal chronology is likewise dictated by Egypt's, because although relative chronologies can be established between sites and cultures within Nubia their 'absolute' historical position is, at present, determined from Egyptian-derived artefacts or associations.

From colony to kingdom: *Exeunt omnes*

During the Egyptian New Kingdom (conventionally the 16th–12th centuries BC, the equivalent of the Late Bronze Age of the Near East) Nubia became an Egyptian dependency, controlled by a viceregal administration.[4] The extensive building works of the New Kingdom pharaohs, such as the temples of Abu Simbel, and the 'Egyptianization' of the Nubian elites led earlier scholars to suggest a dissolution of local culture and even the 'disappearance' of much of the indigenous population during the 18th Dynasty (conventionally the 16th–14th centuries BC).[5]

All discussions of Nubian history in the late New Kingdom and the period following have been concerned with one of two major issues: either the collapse of the viceregal administration, or the rise of the Kingdom of Kurru, its conquest of Egypt and rule there as the 25th Dynasty. These have nearly always been considered as separate and unrelated phenomena.[6] Indeed, all the writing on this period has been Egyptocentric, obsessed by those problems directly related to Egypt, and using only Egyptian-type evidence. Thus in any period where there are no large stone monuments or hieroglyphic texts historians can only envisage a hiatus, or 'Dark Age'. At best the region is said to have 'regressed' to a 'tribal level'.[7]

The period between the end of the viceregal administration during the last years of the 20th Dynasty (*c.* 1070 BC) and the first datable inscriptions of the 25th Dynasty in the 8th century BC has become one of the most significant gaps in Nubian history.[8] The apparent lack of archaeological material in this Dark Age is balanced by a corresponding increase in the use of colourful language. The American archaeologist William Adams, one of the leaders of the UNESCO campaign, characterizes the period as follows:

FIG. 9:1 The great temple of Abu Simbel in its original setting. The colossal figures on each side of the entrance represent its builder, Ramesses II of the 19th Dynasty (*from Maspero 1896*).

Nubia vanished entirely from history. Its erstwhile Egyptian conquerors had returned to their native soil, and the indigenous population had retreated somewhere into the wilderness of Upper Nubia, whence they were to emerge with a vengeance three centuries later.[9]

Archaeologists working in Nubia have always thought that the evidence from the excavated cemeteries showed a decline in population throughout the New Kingdom. They proposed that an extended dry period, causing low floods of the Nile, resulted in a diminishing agricultural production and an eventual exodus of the population; the Egyptian settlers and administrators, Egyptianized Nubians, local princes and some of their retainers to Egypt, and the rest of the indigenous population to Upper Nubia.[10]

The idea that there was a massive depopulation of Nubia, and the removal of the viceregal elite, raises many questions which have never been considered in Nubian studies. To dismantle a 500-year-old bureaucracy is no overnight matter: records of land tenure, endowments, taxation assessments, viceregal correspondence, orders and details of building works all have to be disposed of, or transferred elsewhere. Were the temples closed down? If so, what happened to their administrative records, furniture and fittings, libraries, and, most significant, cult images? How was the Nubian nobility accommodated in Egypt at a time when the Egyptian noble families were exerting ever stronger claims to hereditary office and the land that provided their incomes?

'A land shadowing with wings beyond the rivers of Kush'

Having created a Dark Age in Nubia, it is not surprising that historians have treated the appearance of the Egyptianized 'Kingdom of Kurru' in the mid-9th century BC as a new beginning, largely unrelated to the end of the Viceregal period. So firmly entrenched has this idea become that Adams was forced to make the bizarre comment that it 'took some time for the lesson of the pharaohs to sink in'.[11]

Indeed, few writers considering the end of the viceregal administration and the rise of the Kingdom of Kurru discuss the Dark Age itself; most restrict themselves to a passing comment on the lack of evidence from this period. Accordingly, the sudden expansion of Kurru power in the second half of the 8th century BC has baffled Nubian archaeologists. As rulers of Egypt the Kushite kings became involved in the politics of the Near East, and their conflict with Assyria for the mastery of Palestine and Phoenicia ensured them a place in the biblical record.

Within Egypt the chronology of the later 25th Dynasty kings is fairly securely established through their connections with the succeeding 26th Dynasty and with the Assyrian emperors.[12] Shabaqo reigned for fifteen years[13] and his successor, Shebitqo, for ten or twelve.[14] Taharqo's active reign of twenty-six years is well attested from buildings, inscriptions and documents from both Egypt and Nubia.[15] The later years of the reign were disrupted by Assyrian invasions led by Esarhaddon (in 674 and 671 BC) and by Assurbanipal (in 667/666 BC). Tanwetamani inherited his uncle's throne, and political problems, in 664 BC. A final Assyrian invasion (664/663 BC) brought about the collapse of Kushite rule in Egypt, although Tanwetamani continued to be acknowledged in Thebes until 656 BC. In that year Thebes finally submitted to Psamtik I of Sais, and Egypt was reunited under the rule of the 26th Dynasty.

Isaiah (36:6) proclaimed reliance upon Egypt under Kushite dominance to be leaning upon a broken reed,[16] but the collapse of that rule in the wake of the Assyrian invasions became the focus of Hebrew prophecies. The power of Kush, Isaiah's 'land shadowing with wings' (18:1), was destroyed with the Assyrian sack of Thebes in 663 BC. This catastrophe resounded throughout the ancient world, and was later invoked as a dire warning by the prophet Nahum (3:8–9) for the Assyrian capital of Nineveh itself.

The abundant inscriptional material for the 25th Dynasty has been arranged into a generally accepted historical sequence and chronology:[17]

Piye (or Piankhy)	747–716 BC (conquest of Egypt c. 728 BC)
Shabaqo	716–702 BC
Shebitqo	702–690 BC
Taharqo	690–664 BC
Tanwetamani	664–656 BC (recognized only in Upper Egypt)

Scholars can say that with the 25th Dynasty Egyptian history is once again on firm ground after the problems of interpreting the evidence for the preceding dynasties (21–24) of Libyan rule. But this confidence is relatively new. Earlier Egyptologists, notably Petrie, had profoundly different understandings of what was essentially the same evidence. The classical tradition has it that the Kushite king who conquered Egypt was Shabaqo, and, indeed, he is acknowledged as first ruler of the Dynasty in the King List of Manetho (see Chapter 10). However, because the massive Invasion Stela of Piye (or Piankhy)[18] unearthed by Auguste Mariette records *his* conquest of Egypt and the submission of the Delta dynasts, Piye is now accredited with the foundation of the power of the 25th Dynasty and it is assumed that Shabaqo's invasion was later, and simply consolidated Kushite power. Still, as Sir Alan Gardiner observed:[19]

It is strange . . . that Manetho makes no mention of the great Sudanese or Cushite warrior Pi'ankhy who about 730 B.C. suddenly altered the entire complexion of Egyptian affairs.

A number of factors in the inscriptions of Piye, and the building activities in the Sudan which carry his name, created such difficulties that scholars, including Petrie and the brilliant German Egyptologist Richard Lepsius, thought that there were as many as three kings of this name; the earliest the conqueror of Egypt, and the others ruling after the 25th Dynasty withdrawal from Egypt.[20] Although Egyptology is doubtless correct to accept the existence of only one Piye, the material still presents a number of problems and focuses attention on a further question – the origins of the 25th Dynasty in Nubia.

The traditional interpretation of the evidence for the 25th Dynasty does, indeed, make it burst from the historical void in quite extraordinary fashion. But can this be right? Where did these rulers come from and how did they establish their power?

Rulers over a deserted land

The abundant material from the royal cemeteries and monuments records many of the 25th Dynasty royalty, and also sheds some light on their predecessors. A reconstructed genealogy proposed by Dows Dunham and Laming Macadam in 1949 is widely accepted.[21] However, they made two key assumptions which are not confirmed by the evidence. They proposed that Piye and Shabaqo were brothers, and that their immediate predecessors Kashta and Alara were also brothers. Since Shabaqo was certainly a son of Kashta, the throne could be seen to pass from brother to brother in each generation. This tidying up of the genealogy provided overly simple solutions to some complex historical problems.

The only genealogy preserved for the Kushite royalty (other than straightforward parentage) gives the ancestry of King Aspelta (c. 593–568 BC) and is recorded on that ruler's accession stela.[22] Aspelta is stated to have been the brother of one king and the son of another, while his mother, Queen Nasalsa, was descended from six generations of ladies called 'King's Sister'. All the names of Aspelta's relatives were erased in ancient times, but some can be restored with certainty (see Table 9:1). Placed beside the firm genealogical evidence derived from the burials and inscriptions (see Table 9:2), Aspelta's ancestry extends back two generations before that of Kashta and Alara (i.e. to c. 800 BC), the earliest rulers of this family whose names are known from monuments.

Alara, the chieftain to whom the expansion of the family's power was later attributed, did not adopt Egyptian royal titles.[23] His successor, Kashta, assumed a throne name (prenomen), but it was not until the reigns of Piye and Shabaqo that the full royal style, of

Table 9:1

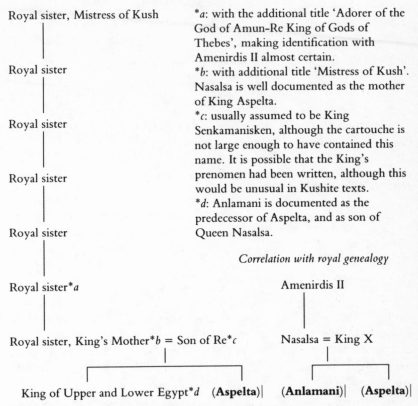

Royal sister, Mistress of Kush

Royal sister

Royal sister

Royal sister

Royal sister

Royal sister*a

Royal sister, King's Mother*b = Son of Re*c

King of Upper and Lower Egypt*d (**Aspelta**)|

*a: with the additional title 'Adorer of the God of Amun-Re King of Gods of Thebes', making identification with Amenirdis II almost certain.

*b: with additional title 'Mistress of Kush'. Nasalsa is well documented as the mother of King Aspelta.

*c: usually assumed to be King Senkamanisken, although the cartouche is not large enough to have contained this name. It is possible that the King's prenomen had been written, although this would be unusual in Kushite texts.

*d: Anlamani is documented as the predecessor of Aspelta, and as son of Queen Nasalsa.

Correlation with royal genealogy

Amenirdis II

Nasalsa = King X

(**Anlamani**)| (**Aspelta**)|

The genealogy of Aspelta, the longest known from the 25th Dynasty. Unfortunately, all the names were erased in ancient times, but some can be restored from other sources (see right). Such genealogical information for the rulers of Nubia extends only as far back as the late 9th century BC, before which we are supposedly confronted with a lengthy gap in documentation until the end of Egyptian viceregal administration during the 20th Dynasty.

five names, was used.[24] Yet inscriptional material agrees with the Aspelta genealogy that there were important rulers before Alara and Kashta. Queen Pebatma, known to have been a wife of Kashta, is called a 'King's Daughter' on her contemporary monuments. The fact that this title is not used by the other royal women of the very early 25th Dynasty suggests it is no meaningless honorific and that there was an as yet unidentified Nubian king in the previous generation.

The evidence from the burials of the Kushite royalty in the

Table 9:2

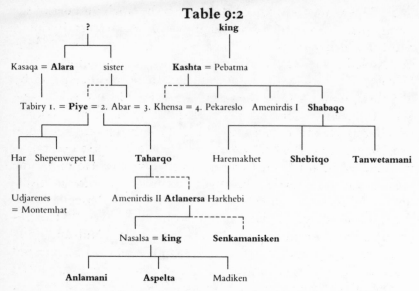

A reconstructed genealogy of the 25th Dynasty derived from various sources. The generally accepted genealogy proposed by Macadam (1949) made all the persons members of one family, a reconstruction which fitted the ideas he proposed for matrilinear succession in Kush. Macadam assumed various relationships (e.g. that Kashta and Alara and that Piye and Shabaqo were brothers), for which there is no supporting evidence from the monuments. These are omitted in the reconstruction here, which allows for the possibility of three different families closely connected by marriage.

cemetery of el-Kurru appeared to resolve some of the questions about the origins of the 25th Dynasty, but re-examination of the material has raised even more difficult ones.

The Kurru cemetery was excavated by George Reisner, the founder of Nubian archaeology, on behalf of Harvard University and the Boston Museum of Fine Arts in 1918 and 1919.[25] The latest burials were of those kings well-known from inscriptional evidence as the founders of Kushite power, Kashta and Piye (Piankhy), and as rulers over Egypt, Shabaqo, Shebitqo and Tanwetamani.[26] The prime position in the site was dominated by a sequence of burials which Reisner attributed to five ancestral 'generations' ending with Alara. Allowing twenty years per generation and a base date for Alara of *c.* 760 BC, Reisner calculated the date of the commencement of the el-Kurru cemetery at about 860 BC.

Reisner based his interpretation on the developmental nature of the graves in the cemetery, moving from simple tumuli to pyramids. This sequence is logical, and given the small number of the tombs there seems to be no good reason to increase Reisner's number of generations.[27] However, some of the artefacts from the earliest of the 'ancestral' burials have recently been identified as 20th Dynasty (i.e. 12th–11th century BC) in date.[28] This material is, by its nature, unlikely to be 'heirloom' or acquired from rifled New Kingdom tombs. Some of the most significant is painted pottery which was clearly manufactured for the funeral ceremony and ritually broken at that time.[29] It seems that this first generation must indeed be attributed to the later 20th Dynasty. However, the radiocarbon tests carried out on the material, admittedly insufficient and so far unpublished, would seem to fit Reisner's calculated 9th-century BC date for the earliest graves.[30] The re-examination of the material from el-Kurru presents Nubian studies with a serious problem: either Reisner's chronology (internal and exact) is correct, or the cemetery comprises two or more groups of graves, of different periods, having no relationship to each other. It is impossible to have a compromise solution which spreads the ancestral burials over the 300 or so years from the late 20th Dynasty to the mid–8th century, because of the limited number of graves.[31] If Reisner's interpretation is correct, then the 20th Dynasty finds were deposited in the 9th rather than the 11th century BC.

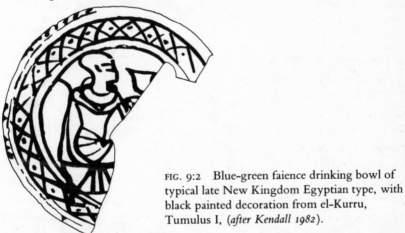

FIG. 9:2   Blue-green faience drinking bowl of typical late New Kingdom Egyptian type, with black painted decoration from el-Kurru, Tumulus I, (*after Kendall 1982*).

Such a radical compression of the length of time from the end of the 20th Dynasty until the beginning of the 25th, whilst flying in the face of conventional Egyptology, removes the Nubian Dark Age at a single stroke. The chieftains buried at el-Kurru would, in this new

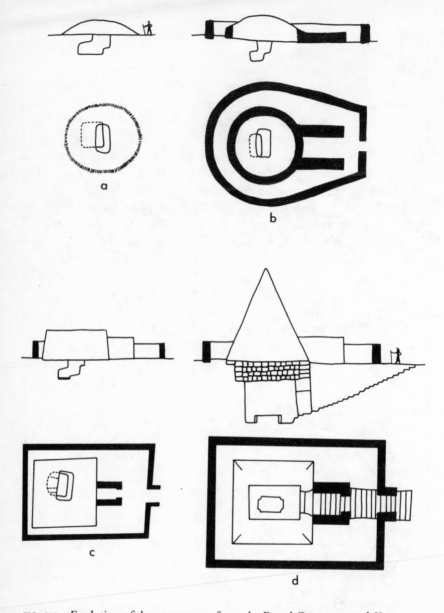

FIG. 9:3   Evolution of the grave types from the Royal Cemetery at el-Kurru, with dates following Kendall (1982):
a. Kurru Tumulus 1 (*c.* 1100–1000 BC)
b. Kurru Tumulus 6 (*c.* 1000–900 BC)
c. Kurru 10 (*c.* 850–800 BC)
d. Kurru 17 – tomb of Piye (*c.* 747–716 BC)

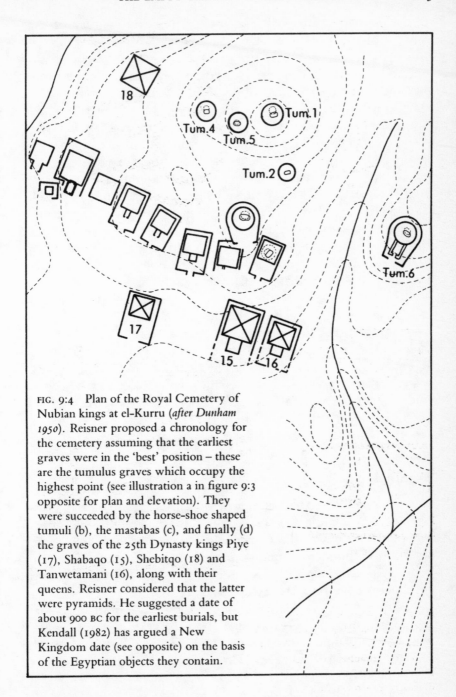

FIG. 9:4   Plan of the Royal Cemetery of
Nubian kings at el-Kurru (*after Dunham
1950*). Reisner proposed a chronology for
the cemetery assuming that the earliest
graves were in the 'best' position – these
are the tumulus graves which occupy the
highest point (see illustration a in figure 9:3
opposite for plan and elevation). They
were succeeded by the horse-shoe shaped
tumuli (b), the mastabas (c), and finally (d)
the graves of the 25th Dynasty kings Piye
(17), Shabaqo (15), Shebitqo (18) and
Tanwetamani (16), along with their
queens. Reisner considered that the latter
were pyramids. He suggested a date of
about 900 BC for the earliest burials, but
Kendall (1982) has argued a New
Kingdom date (see opposite) on the basis
of the Egyptian objects they contain.

model, be powerful local rulers who, within a century of the collapse of viceregal rule, extended their authority over much of Nubia and then assumed the pharaonic titles. In the light of this reappraisal a whole new view of post-pharaonic Nubia becomes possible, which conforms more closely to parallel situations in many other post-imperial societies.

Other radiocarbon dates seem to confirm this picture. Samples from the site of Qasr Ibrim, in that region of Nubia thought to be totally depopulated during the 10th–8th centuries, have given dates of 920–800 BC and 1040–850 BC associated with the earliest known building work there.[32] The tests were on camel dung, in itself startling, since camels were believed not to have been introduced into Nubia until considerably later. Of course, the presence of one stronghold does not mean that there was a large population in Lower Nubia, but it does show that the political situation was rather different from that usually drawn.

More striking still are the radiocarbon results from the site of Kerma, at the northern end of the Dongola Reach. This, one of the most important settlement and cemetery sites to have been exca-vated in Nubia, was the centre of a powerful state from the Egyptian Middle until the early New Kingdoms. Archaeological material there is securely datable to the Hyksos rulers of the Second Intermediate Period (see Table 10:1), and to the early 18th Dynasty, yet radiocarbon tests on early to mid-18th Dynasty graves yielded absolute dates some 200 years later than expected.[33]

Lightening a Dark Age

A more convincing historical scheme can be proposed for post-pharaonic Nubia than the Dark Age scenario advocated by most scholars. Of course, the evidence for such a scheme is hard to produce, without challenging our preconceptions about Egyptian history in the late New Kingdom and the following Third Intermediate Period (21st–25th Dynasties).

It is quite conceivable that upon the withdrawal of the viceregal administration, or its secession, in the closing years of Ramesses XI, the power vacuum was filled by local princes who assumed the Egyptian royal style.[34] Hans Goedicke[35] suggested that such a situation is perhaps revealed by reliefs from Kawa and Gebel Barkal bearing cartouches of a King Menmaetre-setepen-Amun. These are usually ascribed to the late Napatan or early Meroitic period (4th–2nd centuries BC), but the name emulates the Ramessides of the 20th Dynasty, like those of their successors in Egypt. The idea that these reliefs might belong to the immediate post-Ramesside period has received scant consideration, although there is much in its favour. Another king usually attributed to the 4th century BC may actually better belong in this epoch. Ary-mery-Amun adopted the same throne-names as Shoshenq III of the 22nd Dynasty, which might give some idea of his *floruit*.[36]

Both of these Nubian kings have been dated to the 4th century BC, but a number of factors suggest that they were contemporary with the Libyan rulers of Egypt in the post-Ramesside period. The form of their titles and the style of the few relief fragments attributable to them have caused them to be designated 'neo-Ramesside'. But this 'neo-Ramesside' phase is strikingly anachronistic. If it does belong to the 4th century BC there is nothing in the period preceding it in Nubia, nor in contemporary Egypt, with which it can be paralleled. Its 'neo-Ramesside' nature is more logically explained as an immediately post-Ramesside phenomenon, and as such directly comparable with the Libyan period in Egypt. Many kings of the 21st–23rd Dynasties used titularies modelled upon those of their Ramesside predecessors, while the art of the period likewise continues their traditions.

The only generally accepted post-Ramesside monument in Nubia, an important relief carved in the temple of Thutmose III at Semna, has been largely ignored by Nubian studies.[37] Belonging to a Queen Karimala, the absolute dating of its very difficult text is uncertain, but all scholars who have discussed it have attributed it to the Third Intermediate Period.[38] On stylistic grounds, a later date is impossible. The text itself seems to refer to military conflicts, and may well reflect a period of internal strife in Nubia during the post-Ramesside period.

Whether such kings constituted a dynasty, or whether they were rival rulers is impossible to tell. Equally obscure is whether Karimala was the wife of one of these kings, or whether she reigned in her own right. What is clear, though, is that the rise of the Kurru kingdom in the late 9th and 8th centuries BC can be considered within a different context: it need no longer be claimed to emerge from a historical vacuum, but can be seen as the most successful chiefdom of perhaps a number vying for supremacy in Nubia.

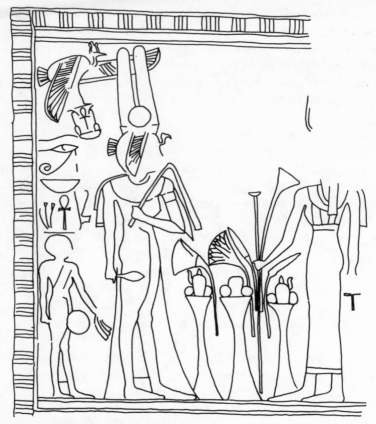

FIG. 9:5   Relief of Queen Karimala from Semna, carved on the facade of the
18th Dynasty temple. The scene shows the Queen, accompanied by a young
girl, in front of the goddess Isis. Karimala wears the vulture headdress and two
falcon-plumes with sun-disk, while she is protected by the hovering image of
the vulture-goddess Nekhbet. The texts (omitted here) give her titles as King's
Chief Wife, King's Daughter and apparently King of Upper and Lower Egypt
(*after Grapow 1940, and Dunham & Janssen 1960*).

From these points alone it can be seen that any changes in the
interpretation of Nubian history and chronology would have a
major impact on the study of Egypt. However, the Nubian evidence, whatever it suggests internally, is usually made to conform
to the accepted Egyptian chronology. If the end of the 20th Dynasty
were to be lowered to somewhere around 850 BC, thereby according with the Kurru material, the Third Intermediate Period would
be drastically reduced. This presents no problem for the interpreta-

tion of the Nubian evidence. Indeed, the advantages of such a lowering are considerable, leaving a period of a little over a century for the Neo-Ramesside rulers and for the establishment of the authority of the Kurru Dynasty by Alara and Kashta.

The implications of such a revision for Egyptian chronology are, of course, profound.

CHAPTER 10

Egypt: The Centre of the Problem

The trail of Dark Age questions eventually brings us to Egypt. Apparently fixed by a number of astronomical observations, Egyptian chronology has the reputation of being scientifically sound. Therefore it has been used as the yardstick for dating the prehistoric and early historic cultures of North Africa, the Near East, the Mediterranean, and large areas of Europe. Yet, as has been seen time and again, the broad application of Egyptian dates to these areas has produced innumerable conflicts in the interpretation of local stratigraphy and dating. The most common effect has been the insertion of elusive Dark Ages into the history of these cultures.

Egypt is almost encircled by countries in which its chronology has raised immense difficulties. Even on Egypt's doorstep, the archaeology of Nubia presents a disturbingly familiar pattern, with a Dark Age lasting from the collapse of Egyptian government (c. 1070 BC) down to the re-emergence of Nubia under the Kurru kingdom in the mid-8th century BC. This prompts the restatement of a question raised by Torr[1] at the end of the last century: is the chronology of Egypt really as firm as it is claimed to be? Indeed, could a substantial shortening of Egyptian chronology resolve many of the furious dating arguments that have bedevilled Old World archaeology over the last hundred years?

A wide range of evidence suggests that the solution to the enigmas of the Dark Age lies in drastically reducing the date for the end of the Late Bronze Age. Abundant archaeological evidence makes it certain that the transition from the Late Bronze to Early Iron Age in the Eastern Mediterranean was contemporary with the late 19th and early 20th Dynasties of Egypt.[2] Consequently, a lowering of Late Bronze Age chronology would also necessitate a reduction in the dates for the Egyptian New Kingdom (18th–20th Dynasties). This could be achieved only by a compression of the period immediately after the New Kingdom. By the time of the 26th Dynasty (664–525 BC) we are well within the era of solidly dated history, where large-scale adjustments can be ruled out by a wealth of interlocking evidence from Greek, biblical, Assyrian and Babylonian sources, as well as Egyptian. Between these two bench-

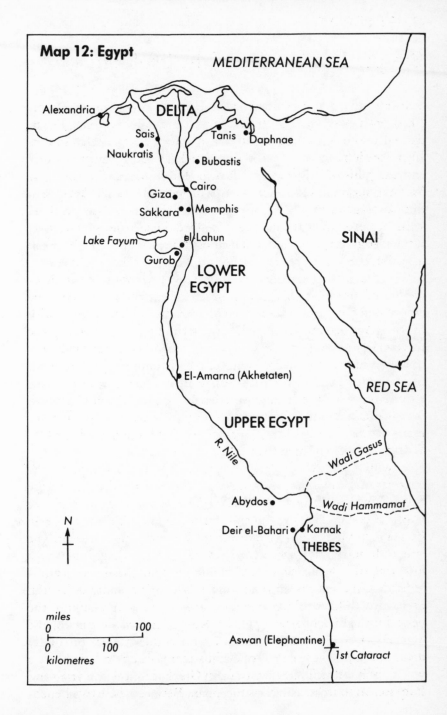

Map 12: Egypt

marks, the end of the 20th Dynasty and the beginning of the 26th, lies the so-called Third Intermediate Period (TIP). The dates of this somewhat obscure epoch (c. 1070–664 BC) curiously parallel those of the Dark Ages reviewed above.

Material culture during the Third Intermediate Period (TIP) was in some ways impoverished compared to that of the New Kingdom.[3] Nevertheless, it was not a Dark Age in the sense that this term has been applied to Greece, Anatolia, Nubia and other areas. Evidence of all types is abundant, indeed extremely rich, in comparison with Egypt's two earlier Intermediate Periods. The problem with the TIP is not one of a dearth of evidence (as is often the case elsewhere), but rather one of the huge quantity of data which needs to be ordered into a coherent historical picture. Detailed studies of its history and chronology have been undertaken in recent years by Kenneth Kitchen and others.[4] (Kitchen's work is followed here for conventional TIP dates.) Yet despite the thoroughness, indeed brilliance, of much of this work, it must be remembered that it has all been undertaken within the framework of a high chronology – with the underlying, tacit assumption that the overall Egyptian dating is basically sound. The length of the TIP has not been determined by careful reconstruction working back from the firm dates of 26th Dynasty Egypt but, curiously, by a reverse process. Its starting point depends on the accepted date for the end of the New Kingdom (c. 1070 BC), derived from astronomical dates. Consequently, a length of time has first been created, and the TIP then used to fill it.

Egyptian chronology in perspective

> What is proudly advertised as Egyptian history is merely a collection of rags and tatters.[5]

So wrote Sir Alan Gardiner, one of this century's foremost Egyptologists, in his self-styled swansong, *Egypt of the Pharaohs*. In the preface to this work Gardiner expressed his regret that 'what is euphemistically called Egyptian history' still had to rely on the dynastic system described by an Egyptian priest, Manetho, who wrote under one of the Ptolemaic kings of the 3rd century BC.

Manetho's history of Egypt, the *Aegyptiaca*, is now lost, but summaries and ostensible extracts survive in a number of much later works, notably those of Josephus (1st century AD), Julius Africanus (3rd century AD), Eusebius (4th century AD) and Syncellus (*c.* 800 AD).[6] These preserve, in different and often contradictory versions, an *Epitome*, giving the names and reign-lengths of the Egyptian pharaohs, arranged into a system of thirty Dynasties or ruling houses. The sequence begins with the unification of Egypt by King Menes, founder of the 1st Dynasty, and ends with Nectanebo II, the last native pharaoh (360–343 BC) before the Persian emperors reconquered Egypt, to rule it briefly until their defeat by Alexander in 332 BC. As Gardiner tartly observed:

> . . . no Egyptologist has been able to free himself from the shackles imposed by the native annalist's thirty Dynasties and these are likely always to remain the essential framework of our modern expositions.

Reluctantly, he admitted that there was little chance of its ever being abandoned.[7]

Egyptologists have divided Manetho's dynastic system into four major epochs preceded by an 'Archaic' and separated by 'Intermediate' periods (the approximate dates follow the conventional scheme:

Table 10:1

Early Dynastic (Archaic)	1st and 2nd Dynasties (2920–2650 BC)
Old Kingdom	3rd to 8th Dynasties (2650–2135 BC)
1st Intermediate Period	9th to early-11th Dynasties (2135–2040 BC)
Middle Kingdom	late-11th to 12th Dynasties (2040–1785 BC)
2nd Intermediate Period	13th to 17th Dynasties (1785–1550 BC)
New Kingdom	18th to 20th Dynasties (1550–1070 BC)
3rd Intermediate Period	21st to 25th Dynasties (1070–665 BC)
Late Period	26th to 30th Dynasties (665–343 BC)

This historical framework has been given an absolute chronology on the basis of astronomical calculations. The theory of 'Sothic' dating (discussed below) gives fixed points of 1872 BC for Senusret III (year 7) of the 12th Dynasty, and 1540 BC for Amenhotep I (year 9) of the 18th Dynasty. Falling roughly in the middle of the entire scheme, these dates are used as the starting point for the calculation, both backwards and forwards in time, of Old, Middle and New Kingdom chronology.

Flesh is added to this dynastic skeleton by using the detailed

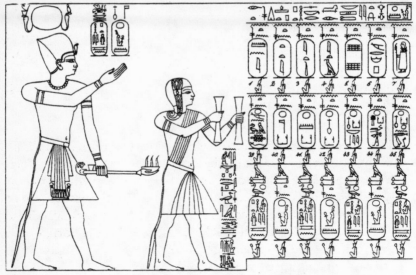

FIG. 10:1   Portion of the king list from the Temple at Abydos. Seti I and his
son, the future Ramesses II, are depicted making offerings to 76 'ancestors',
represented by cartouches containing their names and beginning with Menes,
traditional founder of the 1st Dynasty. The value of the list as a historical tool
is reduced by its omission of kings whose reign was no longer regarded as
legitimate – such as the Hyksos Dynasties and Akhenaten and his immediate
successors in the late 18th Dynasty, including Tutankhamun (from Lepsius
1864).

evidence from the monuments, notably the few surviving official
king lists preserved in temples or on papyrus. Unfortunately, none
of these sources, invaluable as they are, is later than the reign of
Ramesses II of the 19th Dynasty. For subsequent periods, to
establish the succession and reign-lengths of the kings, varied
evidence must be used, the most important of which are monuments dated by regnal years, but also private texts recording the
careers and genealogies of officials. If contemporary material is
lacking, the figures given by Manetho are still adhered to, although
it is generally admitted that these should not be given too much
weight.

    Such, then, is the nature of the system upon which so much of
Old World history and archaeology depends. The assumptions
which lie behind it need thorough re-examination to answer the
question: have archaeologists been relying on a scheme which has a
genuine scientific basis?

The setting of Sirius

The fundamental axiom of Egyptian chronology until recently was the validity of Sothic dating. While the related calendrical problems are extremely complex (involving the assumption that the Egyptians had two lunar calendars for religious purposes, as well as a civil one), the basic theory is relatively straightforward. I. E. S. Edwards gives a succinct explanation:

> The 12 months were divided into 3 seasons bearing names which are generally rendered Inundation, Winter and Summer, each season consisting of four months. The year began in the season of Inundation, and in the ideal year the first day of the first month of the season of Inundation coincided with the first day on which the dog-star Sirius [Sothis] should be seen on the eastern horizon just before the rising of the sun (i.e. roughly about 19 or 20 July in the Julian calendar). Since the dynastic Egyptians never introduced a leap year into their civil calendar, New Year's Day advanced by one whole day in relation to the natural year in every period of four years. As a result of this displacement New Year's Day and the day on which Sirius rose heliacally actually coincided for no more than four years in every period of approximately 1460 years (i.e. 365 × 4), the so-called Sothic cycle.[8]

Thus, according to the theory, the heliacal rising of Sirius (Sothis), together with the seasons, gradually revolved around the civil calendar. After 730 years they would have completely reversed with respect to the solar year, returning to their original position only after a period of some 1460 years:

> Dates in Egyptian records were generally set out according to a fixed formula: . . . If in addition to this formula, a document tells us that Sirius rose heliacally on that day it is only necessary to count the number of days which had elapsed since the first day of the year given in the formula and multiply the total by four to obtain the number of years since the beginning of the particular Sothic cycle.[9]

References to the rising of the star Sirius can therefore be used to calculate absolute dates, using the sliding-scale of the wandering civil calendar. An anchor point for the retrocalculation of the Sothic cycle is provided by the Roman writer Censorinus, who stated that in the year 139 AD the heliacal rising of Sirius coincided with New

Year's Day. The previous cycle would therefore have begun around 1460 years earlier,[10] c. 1321 BC. This date also seems to be referred to, as the beginning of the 'era of Menophres', in a medieval marginal gloss to a manuscript of the 4th-century AD Alexandrian astronomer Theon. It is from this point in time, 1321 BC, that the Sothic dates for the Middle and New Kingdoms are calculated.[11]

FIG. 10:2   Isis as the goddess of the star Sirius – from the tomb of Montemhat, Mayor of Thebes during the reign of Taharqo of the 25th Dynasty and the early years of Psamtik I of the 26th Dynasty (after Parker 1950).

The key Sothic date for the Middle Kingdom is provided by two papyrus fragments found at el-Lahun, dated to year 7 of an un-named pharaoh, but reasonably attributed to Senusret III on palaeographic grounds.[12] This document does not give the beginning of a Sothic cycle, but a calendar date for the rising of Sirius, which can be retrocalculated as 1872 BC if the sighting of Sirius was made in the Memphis-Lahun region. If, however, the sighting was made at the lower latitude of Elephantine, as Rolf Krauss has recently advocated, the date would be reduced to 1830 BC. For the early New Kingdom a Sothic date is provided by the Ebers Papyrus for year 9 of Amenhotep I. If the observation were made at Thebes, where the document was found, the date produced would be 1517 BC; Krauss favours Elephantine, which would lower the date to 1506 BC.[13]

The rough parameters allowed by these two fixed Sothic points have been refined by dates drawn from comparing modern retro-calculations of past lunar cycles with Egyptian records of the moon's phases known from the reigns of some pharaohs. But because the lunar cycle repeats itself within a short time-span variant dates are possible. Those canvassed for the accession of Thutmose III are 1504, 1490 or 1479 BC, and those for Ramesses II, 1304, 1290 or 1279 BC. The lowest alternatives for both kings are those presently preferred by most Egyptologists.[14]

Prima facie, the theory of Sothic dating may look watertight. Closer examination, however, reveals a web of interlocking assumptions, each of which requires intensive re-examination. Work is still needed to confirm the original astronomical and calendrical calculations (made at the turn of this century) with the aid of contemporary techniques. In 1969 M. F. Ingham, at the request of ancient historians, did perform a check on the length of the Sothic cycles. Unfortunately, rather than working from the known end of the scale (i.e. modern retrocalculation linked with the report of Censorinus), he took as the starting point an assumed date of 4227 BC for the beginning of the first relevant Sothic cycle![15] More recently, Archie Roy, Professor of Astronomy at Glasgow University, has described the 'meagre grounds' on which 'astronomy was brought in to fix the absolute dating of the pharaoh list of Egypt', concluding that 'the classical astronomical chronology rests on very weak ground and that there is a need for very much more careful examination of texts referring to calendars, festivals . . . ' etc.[16]

There are good reasons for rejecting the whole concept of Sothic dating as it was applied by the earlier Egyptologists, simply on the grounds that it did not make allowance for any calendrical adjust-ments. It is assumed that the Egyptians allowed the civil calendar and the seasonal cycle, to which the lunar-religious calendar was tied, to progress further and further out of alignment. Richard Parker, the respected authority on the matter, even proposed that there were three calendars running concurrently: the civil, a parallel lunar and the natural lunar.[17] Yet not one document appears to be dated by more than one system.

Indeed, a glance at the much better documented (calendrically speaking) Hellenistic and Roman periods shows that several major reforms were put into effect within the space of only three centuries. The Ptolemies were particularly fond of dabbling with the calendar, but never arrived at a satisfactory solution.[18] Continuing difficulties with the Egyptian calendar inspired Julius Caesar, while he was in Alexandria, to devise his own system. He attempted to impose his new Julian calendar on the Roman world in 46 BC.[19]

With respect to earlier periods, we simply do not know what kind of reforms may have been put into effect, or when, but the strong suspicion that adjustments were made should be enough to throw into the gravest doubt any calculations involving the assumption that the calendar was not tampered with throughout the whole of the Middle Kingdom, New Kingdom, Third Intermediate and Late Periods. *If a single calendrical adjustment was made in the period before the Ptolemies, it would completely invalidate the Sothic calculations for any prior period.*[20]

The waxing of the moon

Wolfgang Helck has recently stressed a long-standing problem concerning the reliability of the Sothic reference in the Ebers Papyrus. While the 'emergence of Sothis' is referred to in this text, no day is specified.[21] It is now increasingly considered to be 'highly doubtful and should not be used any more in the chronological calculations'.[22]

This rejection of the Ebers fixed point leaves the absolute chronology ultimately dependent on the single Sothic reference from el-Lahun. Yet this sole Sothic date from the Middle Kingdom can hardly be used to support the conventional chronology for the New Kingdom, since between the two periods lies the Second Intermediate Period, the length of which is still completely uncertain.[23]

Because of these problems Egyptologists are turning increasingly to lunar records for an astronomical dating of the New Kingdom. While many of these can be made to fit with the dates originally calculated from the Sothic theory, they are based on only one observation and are of no value to absolute chronology since new moons will occur on the same civil date at twenty-five-year intervals.[24] Thus single lunar dates can really be used only to fine-tune an already established absolute chronology.

Of far greater significance than isolated lunar references is the information in another papyrus from el-Lahun,[25] giving sufficient data to determine the length of lunar months over an entire year. John Read calculated that the observations recorded in the papyrus match perfectly with the pattern of lunar conditions in the year 1549 BC. Therefore, in Read's opinion, this 'placement of the Illahun [el-Lahun] calendar with an apparent 12 for 12 fit has to constitute one of the greatest chronological anchor points in ancient recorded history'.[26]

Despite Read's confidence in this absolute date, an immediate problem arose from the fact that it falls, in the conventional chronology, early in the 18th Dynasty. Yet the el-Lahun papyrus has always been assigned a date in the Middle Kingdom, some two and a half centuries earlier. Consequently Read had to argue for a redating of the text (in the relative sense) to the 18th Dynasty. Parker demonstrated that this was impossible on historical grounds: the papyrus certainly dates to the late 12th Dynasty. He rejected Read's interpretation in favour of his own, which, even after emending one of the entries on the papyrus, still allows for a match of only ten of the twelve recorded dates with modern retrocalculations for the year 1813–1812 BC.[27] Parker's method had already been resolutely dismissed by Read:

> This type of chronology, where one claims the historical record is wrong rather than his own analysis, is no chronology at all.[28]

A logical solution would be to combine Read's absolute date of 1549 BC for the lunar sequence with Parker's relative date in the 12th Dynasty for the papyrus. However, the possibility of such a late dating for the Middle Kingdom was never raised in the debate, since both parties involved accepted the present framework of Sothic chronology as fundamentally sound. For those who still believe that Egyptian chronology is firmly established by astronomical fixes, the el-Lahun lunar data remain a glaring anomaly. Taking these at their face value would demand an automatic reduction of Egyptian chronology by some 250 years.

Shishak and Shoshenq

The accepted, Sothic-linked, framework for TIP chronology is thought to be bolstered by a major synchronism with biblical history. In year 5 of Rehoboam, the Kingdom of Judah was invaded

by 'Shishak king of Egypt' (1 Kgs. 14:25–6). The Egyptians seized
Rehoboam's fortified city, marched on Jerusalem and forced its
submission, the furnishings of Solomon's Temple and palace being
handed over as tribute. On the basis of biblical chronology, which
for this period is sound (see Chapter 8), the event can be confidently
dated near the year 925 BC.[29] Since the decipherment of hieroglyphics in the 1820s, Shishak has been identified with Pharaoh
Shoshenq I, founder of the Libyan 22nd Dynasty. First suggested
by Jean-François Champollion himself, the identification has become an axiom for both Egyptologists and biblical scholars alike
and is the only generally accepted synchronism with Western Asia
between the 13th and 8th centuries BC.

The link between the two kings was suggested by the obvious,
though perhaps superficial, resemblance of their names. While
there were several pharaohs during the Libyan period with the
name Shoshenq, only one, the founder of the 22nd Dynasty, is
known to have campaigned in Palestine. On the monumental
gateway he constructed at Karnak in year 21 of his reign Shoshenq I
left a record of an expedition to Palestine, believed to reflect the
actual invasion of Rehoboam's kingdom by Shishak. On the
assumption that Shoshenq probably campaigned at the start of his
reign, the link is used to date the beginning of the 22nd Dynasty
(and the Libyan domination) to 945 BC, described by Peter van der
Meer as 'the first Egyptian date fixed on real facts'.[30] It also agrees
with the broad estimates for the date of this dynasty calculated from
the Sothic chronology for the New Kingdom.

The identification, however, remains extremely problematic.
Inscriptional evidence from Byblos suggests that the date for
Shoshenq I should be reduced from the late 10th century to c. 800 BC
(see below, p. 251), a possibility which would immediately rule out
any connection with Shishak. Chronological problems aside, the
identification seems to fall down on the geographical evidence.
Jerusalem, the focal point of Shishak's campaign according to the
Bible, is not named at all in the list of Palestinian towns recorded by
Shoshenq I.[31] Rehoboam prepared fifteen towns against Egyptian
attack, 'fortified cities' which were taken by Shishak before he
approached Jerusalem.[32] But only one of them, Aijalon, appears in
the list of Shoshenq I. Indeed, his inscription includes very few
Judaean towns at all; as Aharoni remarked in his standard work on
biblical geography:

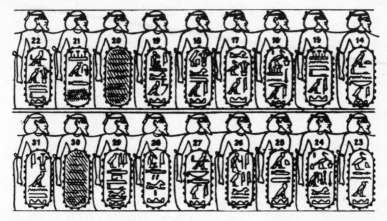

FIG. 10:3   Section of the list of Palestinian placenames left by Shoshenq I on the 'Bubastite Portal', Karnak. The names, surmounted by icons of Asiatic prisoners, are arranged in geographically related strings, this section concentrating mainly on the Jezreel/Esdraelon Valley area of central Israel (*see Kitchen 1986*).

It is clear from the Egyptian text that the main objectives of the expedition were not the towns of Judah and Jerusalem, but rather the kingdom of Israel on the one hand and the Negeb of Judah on the other.[33]

Yet the Old Testament records an Egyptian attack only on Judah, at the same time making it abundantly clear that Jeroboam, King of Israel, was an ally rather than an enemy of Egypt.[34]

Given the almost complete disagreement of geopolitical factors between the campaigns of Shishak and Shoshenq I, there remains only the similarity of the two names to support the identification. The case for this synchronism, equivocal at best, should hardly prevent a reworking of TIP chronology if other, more convincing evidence demands it.

The length of the Third Intermediate Period

Abandoning the shackles imposed by Sothic dating and the synchronism between Shoshenq I and Rehoboam of Judah, we are free to question the presently accepted estimates for the length of the TIP. It is true to say that the monumental and inscriptional evidence for various kings, priests and officials has been arranged within an already predetermined time-span. A close look at the available data reveals little to inspire confidence in the idea that we are dealing with a soundly constructed period of history.

Many TIP kings, on close examination, are mere ciphers, names on lists, with little or no evidence for the lengthy reigns attributed to them in modern reconstructions. For example Takeloth 'I' is known *only* from one genealogy and has no attested monuments,[35] yet he is assigned a reign of fifteen years (889–874 BC) in the generally accepted chronology. Similarly, Osorkon I is attributed thirty-five years (924–889 BC) on the most equivocal evidence.[36] Equally suspect is the twenty-six years of sole rule accorded to Smendes (1069–1043 BC), whose reign is thought to have bridged the transition between the 20th and 21st Dynasties. There are only two 'monuments' and no year-dates definitely attributable to him;[37] the figure is simply taken from Manetho.

What has not been fully appreciated is that *for every doubtful year of Egyptian history granted to the Third Intermediate Period, another year is added to the Dark Ages of the Eastern and Central Mediterranean, the Near East and Africa.* It is therefore a question of the utmost importance that the TIP chronology is clearly demonstrable. Even the three examples given above (Smendes, Osorkon I, Takeloth I) show that it may be inflated by several decades.

Greater flexibility in the chronology is possible if due consideration is given to the fragmented condition of Egypt after the New Kingdom. The period was characterized by a breakdown of centralized authority. Under the 18th and 19th Dynasties the pharaoh was the unquestioned, sole ruler of the land. After the reign of Akhenaten, and even more so in the later 19th and 20th Dynasties, noble families exerted their hereditary claims to particular offices and there was considerably less emphasis on the role of the king as the source of all authority. This situation crystallized in the TIP, when Egypt became almost 'feudal'.

A further factor of great significance in Late New Kingdom Egypt is the Libyan question. Merneptah and Ramesses III both faced large-scale Libyan incursions into the Delta. In the latter years of the 20th Dynasty Upper Egypt was also affected. These were not simply military raids, but major population movements apparently necessitated by severe famine in the Libyan homelands.[38] Whilst the Egyptians initially tried to repel these waves, the later solution was to settle thousands of captured Libyans within Egypt, where their fighting ability was needed to enhance the power of the kings (now usually resident in the Delta) and to strengthen the eastern Delta.[39]

Whilst the Libyans were in many ways acculturated, they clearly retained many features of their original socio-political structure. The growing power of Libyan nobles in Egypt contributed significantly to the breakdown of the kingdom into a patchwork of feudal states. By the time of the Assyrian invasion of Assurbanipal in 666 BC Egypt was ruled, according to the Assyrians, by no fewer than '20 kings'.[40] The writings of Greek historians reflect this situation in the tradition of a 'dodecarchy', the coalition of twelve kings who ruled before Psamtik I (664–610 BC) of the 26th Dynasty reunited the country.[41]

It is generally agreed that several of the later TIP dynasties ruled concurrently, for example that the earliest kings of the 26th Dynasty were contemporary with the later rulers of the Kushite 25th (c. 715–664 BC). Likewise it is also agreed that the early 25th overlapped with the later 22nd *and* 23rd Dynasties. Thus Manetho's scheme of dynasties for this period is not treated as strictly successive. Whether Manetho understood *his* sources as meaning that a given dynasty began only after its predecessor had finished will probably never be known, as his original work is lost.[42] The Church Father Eusebius, who transmitted one of the major recensions of Manetho's work, certainly had a different understanding:

> It seems . . . that different kings held sway in different regions, and that each dynasty was confined to its own nome [province]; thus it was not a succession of kings occupying the throne one after the other, but several kings reigning at the same time in different regions.[43]

The moot point, therefore, concerns exactly how much the different dynasties overlapped. The generally accepted arrangement of the dynasties – as canonized in Kitchen's work on *The Third Intermediate Period in Egypt* – involves three major assumptions:

1   That the 20th, 21st and 22nd Dynasties were successive, with no overlaps, and that their kings were the sole monarchs of Egypt (with the exception of the priestly line which adopted pharaonic titles at Thebes during the 21st Dynasty).
2   That the fragmentation of Egypt into several kingdoms began

with the establishment of the independent 23rd Dynasty under Pedubast I, quite late in the 22nd Dynasty (Kitchen: 818 BC).

3 That central authority was restored by Psamtik I of the 26th Dynasty, who during his first ten years of reign (664–654 BC) rapidly eliminated all the other claimants to kingship.[44]

A number of recent studies have challenged some of Kitchen's interpretations, notably with respect to the nature of the 23rd Dynasty. Indeed, Donald Redford has pointed out that the Dynasty has served as a 'catch-all' for otherwise difficult to place kings.[45] The Theban, rather than Delta, origin of the Dynasty has been emphasized by several writers.[46] One of these, David Aston, has suggested the effective removal of Takeloth II from the 22nd Dynasty, reassigning him to the Theban 23rd. This in itself should reduce TIP chronology by at least twenty years, but because he still accepts the overall parameters of the period as set by Kitchen, Aston chose merely to add an equivalent number of years to the reign of an earlier king to compensate.

Moreover, numerous 'anomalies' in the accepted version of TIP history and archaeology tend to throw the basic assumptions underlying the whole framework into doubt. Taken together, they suggest that there were far greater overlaps between the 20th–26th Dynasties than the conventional chronology allows.

Timeless art and monuments?

The art of the TIP has received relatively little attention, but it is clear that during a period conventionally lasting 350 years there are several phases without stone statuary and with little monumental architecture. At the same time, Ramesside traditions in painting and other arts continued. The pottery of this entire period is notoriously difficult to date, that from the end of the New Kingdom being indistinguishable from that of the early 25th Dynasty.[47] A standard work on Egyptian art, by Irmgard Woldering, devotes only one page to the 'Libyan Period' and that mainly to historical narrative, with the summary: 'The few works of art to have survived from the Libyan Period maintain the style of the Ramessid Era.'[48]

It should be noted that the badly ruined nature of the Delta cities, notably Tanis and Bubastis, makes it difficult to examine post-Ramesside work in detail, and it is these sites that played a major role in the TIP. However, the Temple of Amun at Karnak continued to be a major sanctuary, and royal attention is demonstrated by the Nile-level texts recorded on the quay there and the installation of members of the Delta royal families as priests and votaresses. Despite this attention, Stevenson Smith's major history of art and architecture notes that, with the exception of the colonnades and gateway built by Shoshenq I:

> Little else of architectural importance is known for a period of some three hundred and fifty years, until a new stimulus came from the south with the invasion of the Kushite king [Piye] . . .[49]

It was not architecture alone that suffered neglect. In his important genealogical study of the TIP, Morris Bierbrier observed that during the 21st Dynasty information for Theban families is limited, because the main source, stone statues of private persons dedicated in the temples, 'would seem to disappear almost totally'[50] – a bizarre absence not encountered in other periods of Egyptian history. Yet with the advent of the 22nd Dynasty 'a wealth of data on the priests and officials of Thebes' is known, the primary evidence being 'the large collection of votive statuary' from Karnak.[51]

One of the major depositories of royal objects from the TIP, and fundamental to any assessment of artistic development during the period, is the royal necropolis of Tanis (see below). Yet the objects from these burials present a number of stylistic problems. The gold mask of King Psusennes I of the 21st Dynasty (Kitchen: 1039–991 BC) is 'conventionally reminiscent' of the New Kingdom. Likewise, a silver bowl from the same tomb is described as continuing a type of Ramesside bowl dated to the 13th century BC. Yet such vessels as this are also seen as a source of inspiration for the Egyptianizing metal bowls produced by the Phoenicians in the 8th century.[52] The jewellery from this tomb belongs to a stylistic group regarded as the model for the Egyptian motifs of Phoenician and Syrian ivory-working from the same century.[53] An Egyptian-style alabaster vessel has been found at Assur in Iraq, bearing an inscription of the wife of the famous Assyrian King Sennacherib (701–681 BC). Surprisingly, it has been observed that it is 'exactly similar' to a jar-stand from the tomb of Psusennes, presently dated 300 years earlier.[54]

Thus the finds from the tomb of Psusennes provide a double

mystery, inviting comparisons with both Egyptian material placed by Sothic dating in the 13th–12th centuries BC and Near Eastern material dated by local chronology to the 8th.

Just as votive statuary is supposed to have disappeared almost completely during the 21st Dynasty, so examples of painting are rare throughout the TIP, except for the decoration of coffins. Yet despite this paucity of surviving examples, the Ramesside style is supposed to have continued. Perhaps most startling is the description of the so-called Saite Oracle Papyrus, now in Brooklyn Museum, which dates from year 14 of Psamtik I (651 BC):

> Quite as remarkable as the beauty of the drawing is the persistence of the Ramesside style here, particularly in the long shaven skulls of the priests . . .

In this case the continuation of a tradition of painting, other examples of which are noted by Stevenson Smith, lasts for more than 400 years,[55] uninfluenced by the changes which appear in the 25th Dynasty.

The Apis bulls

The burials of Apis bulls at Sakkara are potentially one of the most important sources of chronological information for the TIP. The Apis bull was one of the patron cults of the city of Memphis, and had its origin in the earliest period of Egyptian history. Regarded as the manifestation of the god Ptah, during its lifetime the Apis resided in the precinct of his temple, and upon its death it was mummified and buried in the Memphite necropolis at Sakkara. Immediately following its death a search was made throughout Egypt for a replacement bull, which custom required should be black with a number of distinguishing markings.

Burials of Apis bulls from the late 18th Dynasty onwards have been recovered. The earliest so far known (from the reign of Amenhotep III until the early years of Ramesses II) were made in individual graves, but later bulls were interred in the vast subterranean catacomb known as the Serapeum. The first burial there was made in year 30 of Ramesses II, in what is known as the Lesser Vault, a gallery containing seventeen chambers. The Greater Vault was used from the 26th Dynasty until the Roman period.

Beginning with the 26th Dynasty, the burial of an Apis bull was

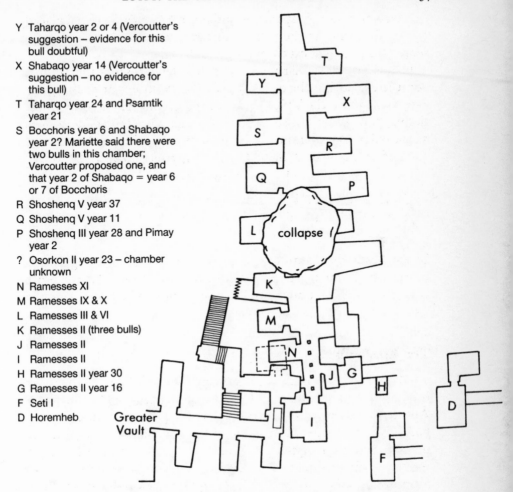

Y Taharqo year 2 or 4 (Vercoutter's suggestion – evidence for this bull doubtful)

X Shabaqo year 14 (Vercoutter's suggestion – no evidence for this bull)

T Taharqo year 24 and Psamtik year 21

S Bocchoris year 6 and Shabaqo year 2? Mariette said there were two bulls in this chamber; Vercoutter proposed one, and that year 2 of Shabaqo = year 6 or 7 of Bocchoris

R Shoshenq V year 37

Q Shoshenq V year 11

P Shoshenq III year 28 and Pimay year 2

? Osorkon II year 23 – chamber unknown

N Ramesses XI

M Ramesses IX & X

L Ramesses III & VI

K Ramesses II (three bulls)

J Ramesses II

I Ramesses II

H Ramesses II year 30

G Ramesses II year 16

F Seti I

D Horemheb

FIG. 10:4 Plan of the Lesser Vaults of the Serapeum at Sakkara. There are a number of problems in the attribution of the chambers to particular reigns. In the Greater Vault, begun by Psamtik I, the bulls were buried in massive stone sarcophagi, each in its own chamber which was walled up after the burial ceremony. In the Lesser Vaults the bulls appear to have been mummified and laid in the chambers in their coffins without sarcophagi. Some chambers are supposed to have had more than one burial in them (*after Malinine et al. 1968*).

marked by an official stela recording its age and dates of installation and death, but during the TIP this information must usually be derived from the many private dedications by priests and nobles.

The excavation of the Serapeum complex was made by Mariette in 1851, but hurriedly and unscientifically – doubtless much valuable information was lost. All the available Serapeum inscriptions have been re-examined and published[56] but there is still no agreement in the attribution of some stelae without royal names to particular kings.

The sequence of burials in the Lesser Vault which begins in year 30 of Ramesses II continues through his reign, and to the end of the 20th Dynasty. However, the next attested burial is year 23 of Osorkon II, followed by year 28 of Shoshenq III, and bulls of Pimay, Shoshenq V and Bocchoris of the 22nd and 24th Dynasties. An inscription of year 2 of Shabaqo supposedly found in the chamber of the Bocchoris bull is believed to record the Kushite conquest of Egypt. The next certain Apis is that buried in year 24 of Taharqo. Another gap occurs in the reign of Psamtik I. Here a bull buried in year 21 is stated to be the successor to that buried in year 24 of Taharqo, but no burials are known from the rest of this long reign. A stela of Necho II commences the Late Period sequence, and states that the bull was installed in year 53 of Psamtik I.

The most striking gap in this sequence is for the 21st and early 22nd Dynasties, so far totally unattested. On the conventional dating this period was some 210 years, during which time there should have been about twelve Apis burials, based on an average life expectancy of eighteen years, as calculated by Jean Vercoutter.[57] An 'embalming table' with the name of Shoshenq I suggests that there may have been one 22nd Dynasty burial which has not been recovered, but the complete lack of any records for the 21st Dynasty is still extraordinary.

Genealogical records

It is often stated that the genealogies of high officials provide 'confirmation of the basic soundness' of the conventional chronology for the TIP.[58] Yet, describing the source material available on TIP genealogies, Bierbrier drew attention to an extraordinary gap in the record:

> With the advent of Dynasty XXI the copious sources of information which were available in the previous two dynasties vanish. Administrative papyri and ostraca prove practically non-existent. Votive statuary would seem to disappear almost totally. Graffiti and inscriptions decline to a few badly preserved exam-

ples . . . because of this dearth of material, it is not possible as in Dynasty XIX and Dynasty XX to present a coherent outline of the descent of various families and their interrelations.[59]

From the next dynasty we again have plentiful source materials in the form of votive statues, administrative documents and private and royal inscriptions, which provide a wealth of genealogical data on the priests and officials of Thebes.[60] Although not as rich as the Theban evidence, there are similar records from elsewhere in Egypt. A prime example is the genealogy of Pasenhor recording a family of Memphite officials for the whole span of the 22nd Dynasty (see Table 10:2). The paucity of information during the 21st Dynasty and its subsequent re-emergence in the 22nd Dynasty provides a curious parallel to the lacuna in the Apis burial record.

According to Bierbrier there appear to be only two genealogies which span the period from the 19th/20th to the 22nd Dynasties: that is, ones in which ancestors are recorded as holding office in specific reigns. These are the Genealogy of Ankhefenkhons from Thebes,[61] and the so-called 'Memphite Genealogy' (in the Bode Museum, Berlin).[62]

The Genealogy of Ankhefenkhons, who was a contemporary of Osorkon I (22nd Dynasty), reaches back through nine generations to one Ipuy, who was a priest of the mortuary cult of Merneptah, and thus lived in the reign of that king or his immediate successor.[63] The conventional interval between Merneptah and Osorkon I is about 300 years. Bierbrier normally allows an average of twenty-five years per generation, which for nine generations would give a result of 225 years, very short of the figure one should expect from the accepted dates. Because of this, Bierbrier assumes that there must be three or four generations missing from the Genealogy.[64] It is equally likely that the Genealogy is correct and that the period between the two kings has been over-extended.

The Memphite Genealogy, dating from the reign of Shoshenq V, gives a continuous succession of high priests of Ptah of Memphis, going back to the beginning of the Middle Kingdom.[65] The last eight generations can be corroborated from other sources, and the Genealogy realistically gives four generations for the long reign of Ramesses II (father of Merneptah).[66] However, there are serious problems in the recording of the 20th and 21st Dynasties; only one generation is given between Ramesses II and the reign of

[. . .] **(R.II)**

Ptahemakhet B HPM

Asha-khet A HPM

Pipi A HPM

Harsiese J HPM

Pipi B HPM

Asha-khet B HPM

Ankhefensekhmet A HPM

Shedsunefertem HPM **(Sh. I)**

Pahemnetjer

Iufoenptah

Pahemnetjer

Sasekhmet

Pahemnetjer

Pashersekhmet

Pahemnetjer

Ankhefensekhmet
(Sh. V)
'Memphite Genealogy'

Table 10:2

Composite genealogy of royal and elite families from the
Third Intermediate Period. Only two genealogies having
definite links with both New Kingdom and TIP rulers
(names shown in bold) have been identified – those for the
Memphite priests and the family of Ankhefenkhons.
These confirm each other regarding the overall number of
generations involved. The composite shows that the
number of generations allowed by the conventional
chronology between the later kings of the TIP and the
early 26th Dynasty (Psamtik I) is too great, as is the
distance of time back to Ramesses II. Names of kings in
the royal genealogy are enclosed in cartouches.

Royal Genealogy

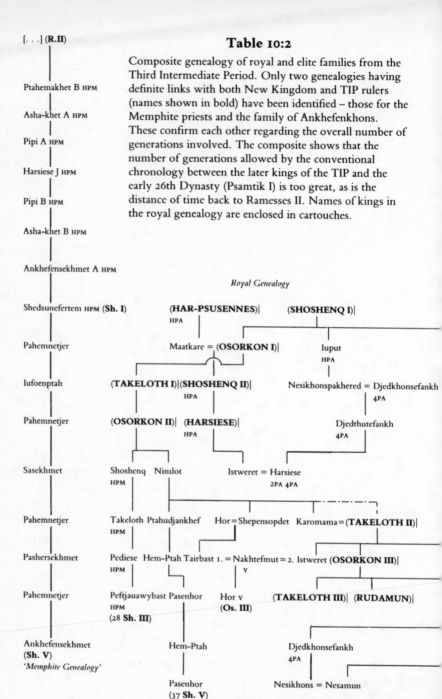

Namenkhpre
(30 **Psamtik I**)

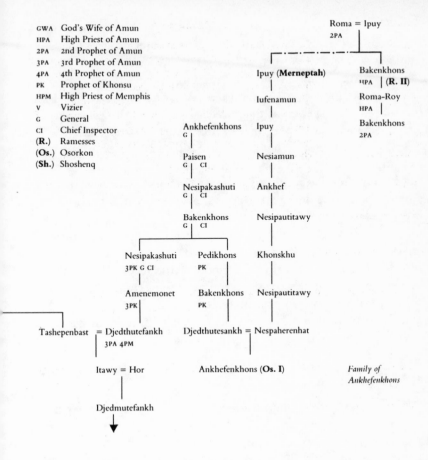

GWA   God's Wife of Amun
HPA   High Priest of Amun
2PA   2nd Prophet of Amun
3PA   3rd Prophet of Amun
4PA   4th Prophet of Amun
PK   Prophet of Khonsu
HPM   High Priest of Memphis
V   Vizier
G   General
CI   Chief Inspector
(R.)   Ramesses
(Os.)   Osorkon
(Sh.)   Shoshenq

Roma = Ipuy
2PA

Ipuy (**Merneptah**)   Bakenkhons
               HPA   (**R. II**)

Iufenamun   Roma-Roy
               HPA

Ankhefenkhons   Ipuy   Bakenkhons
G   2PA

Paisen   Nesiamun
G   CI

Nesipakashuti   Ankhef
G   CI

Bakenkhons   Nesipautitawy
G   CI

Nesipakashuti   Pedikhons   Khonskhu
3PK G CI   PK

Amenemonet   Bakenkhons   Nesipautitawy
3PK   PK

Tashepenbast = Djedthutefankh   Djedthutesankh = Nespaherenhat
             3PA 4PM

Itawy = Hor   Ankhefenkhons (**Os. I**)   *Family of*
                                             Ankhefenkhons

Djedmutefankh

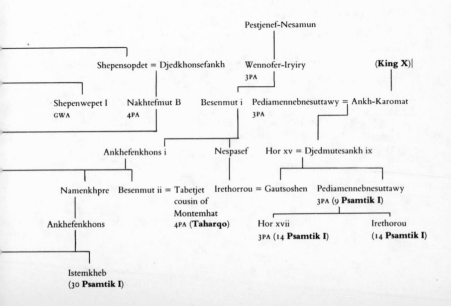

Pestjenef-Nesamun

Shepensopdet = Djedkhonsefankh   Wennofer-Iryiry   (**King X**)
                                     3PA

Shepenwepet I   Nakhtefmut B   Besenmut i   Pediamennebnesuttawy = Ankh-Karomat
GWA   4PA   3PA

Ankhefenkhons i   Nespasef   Hor xv = Djedmutesankh ix

Namenkhpre   Besenmut ii = Tabetjet   Irethorrou = Gautsoshen   Pediamennebnesuttawy
                       cousin of   3PA (9 **Psamtik I**)
Ankhefenkhons   Montemhat
                       4PA (**Taharqo**)   Hor xvii   Irethorou
                                         3PA (14 **Psamtik I**)   (14 **Psamtik I**)

Istemkheb
(30 **Psamtik I**)

Amenemnisu of Dynasty 21, and there is confusion in its record of the other kings of this Dynasty. Kitchen has suggested that six or seven entries were simply omitted from the list by a copyist.[67] But whilst it is virtually impossible that one family held the office in unbroken succession from the Middle Kingdom to the late TIP (approximately 1250 years by the standard reckoning), this document, at least in its later part, may well accurately represent the number of generations.[68] What is striking is that the number given in the Memphite Genealogy for the period between Ramesses II and Shoshenq I matches that implied by the Ankhefenkhons genealogy. This independent agreement strongly suggests that the data should not be dismissed lightly.

The work of Kitchen and Bierbrier on genealogies has been immensely important and influential, but has argued for lacunae in the records when these appear to conflict with the accepted chronology. Lieblein, one of the earliest scholars to make an extensive examination of the genealogical material (see Chapter 1), worked rather differently, taking the evidence at face value and arguing for a large overlap between the 21st and 22nd Dynasties.[69]

The Inhapi cache

During the 21st Dynasty the problem of pillaging in the Theban royal necropolis became so acute that the high priests of Amun made 'a last frantic effort to put an end to such sacrilege', by preparing a secret cache of royal mummies in a rock-cut tomb originally prepared for Queen Inhapi near Deir el-Bahari. The bodies of many of the most powerful pharaohs of the 18th and 19th Dynasties (including Thutmose III and Seti I) were reinterred here, coffins, mummies and other funerary furniture being piled up in an apparently hasty fashion. This inconspicuous hiding place was sealed in year 10 of Pharaoh Siamun, penultimate ruler of the 21st Dynasty.[70]

The discovery in this cache of a 22nd Dynasty mummy, that of one Djedptahefankh, who held the offices of 2nd and 3rd Prophet of Amun, is therefore puzzling. Djedptahefankh was buried in year 11 of Shoshenq I or soon after,[71] conventionally some thirty-four years after the final deposits in the tomb by Siamun. It thus has to be assumed that the secret cache was 'reopened once more in the reign of King Shoshenk I' to inter Djedptahefankh,[72] the only evidence for its disturbance between year 10 of Siamun and the discovery of the cache in the 1870s.[73] Is it plausible that this secret hiding place should have been reopened after thirty-four years for the burial of a single priest?

Further, it was reported by Gaston Maspero, who cleared the tomb in 1881, that the coffin of Djedptahefankh was found deep within the mountainside, and not at the entrance of the crowded tomb as one would expect for a later, intrusive, burial. Elizabeth Thomas notes that the evidence for the placement of the burial depends on the extremely unsatisfactory reports made of the tomb clearance and suggests that Djedptahefankh's coffin may instead have been found in the entrance corridor. Yet Thomas's supposition seems to have been made largely on the (chronological) assumption that Djedptahefankh was a 'late arrival'.[74] Whatever the case regarding the coffin's precise position, a straightforward reading of the evidence indicates that Djedptahefankh was buried in the cache before its closure in year 10 of Siamun. This would clearly conflict with the present chronology, which places Shoshenq I after Siamun and which allows no overlap between the 21st and 22nd Dynasties.

Royal tombs at Tanis

Striking evidence that something is amiss with the conventional placement of the 21st and 22nd Dynasties comes from the royal tomb complex at Tanis, discovered in 1929 by Pierre Montet. In the south-western corner of the main temple enclosure he uncovered the underground burials of Psusennes I and Amenemope of the 21st Dynasty, Osorkon II and Shoshenq III of the 22nd Dynasty, as well as three unattributed tombs.[75]

Montet and his architect Lézine were clearly puzzled by the relationship between Tomb I, belonging to Osorkon II, and Tomb III, containing the burials of Psusennes I, Amenemope and others. After careful examination they reluctantly concluded that Tomb I had been constructed *before* Tomb III – this in spite of the usual understanding that Osorkon died more than a century *later* than the reign of Psusennes. Tomb I abuts Tomb III on the western side. That Tomb I already existed at the time when Tomb III was constructed is indicated by the awkward arrangement of the side and entrance chambers in the latter, something that can only be

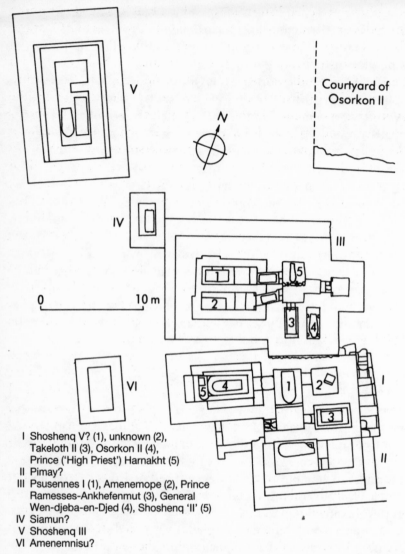

FIG. 10:5   Plan of the Royal Burials at Tanis (*after Montet 1947, and Dodson 1988*).

explained by a shortage of ground space. Further, it was, clear that the northern outer wall-face of Tomb I had actually been cut into in order to accommodate the antechambers of Tomb III.

Lézine and Montet were forced to conclude that Osorkon II had taken over a tomb built for a much earlier individual,[76] a view still generally adhered to: 'it seems clear that the tomb's original owner must have preceded Psusennes I, and if a king can only have been Smendes or Amenemnisu'.[77] It also has to be assumed that Osorkon found Tomb I in an undecorated condition, since there is no trace of a previous occupant, a strange state of affairs if this was a royal burial. If the tomb was undecorated, or unoccupied, it is hard to understand why Psusennes went to the trouble of building the awkwardly positioned Tomb III, and, indeed, why Tomb I shows no trace of occupation in the two centuries which are thought to have elapsed between an unnamed predecessor of Psusennes I and Osorkon II. Further, Psusennes would have been required to construct Tomb III so close to Tomb I and to chip away parts of its façade only if there were another structure already existing to the north. Within a few feet of the northern outer face of Tomb III lies the south-west corner of one of the temple's great courtyards, the foundation deposit of which shows that it was built by Osorkon II.[78] Thus structures of Osorkon are to be found on *both* sides of Tomb III, and they seem to have been the constraining factor in its placement. The overall picture of evidence certainly points to the 21st Dynasty Psusennes I having constructed his tomb after the building work of the 22nd Dynasty Osorkon II.

Note should also be made of the grave-goods found with the burial of Osorkon's young son Harnakht. The child was buried in his father's burial chamber and his limited grave-goods contained objects with the cartouche of the 21st Dynasty King Amenemope, assumed to be the successor of Psusennes I.[79] Why should the son of Osorkon II have been buried with material bearing the name of an obscure predecessor? The interval in time between Amenemope and Osorkon II, according to the conventional chronology, is 110 years. While the rifling and reuse of material from the neighbouring burial of Amenemope is of course possible, the complex of evidence from Tanis as a whole suggests a far more intimate relationship between Psusennes I and Amenemope of the 21st Dynasty and the kings of the mid-22nd Dynasty than has hitherto been realized.

Offices at Thebes

Kitchen's thorough survey of the vast quantity of material available has created a basic structure for the history of the most important offices at Thebes.[80] It is striking that although the major genealogical problems commented upon by Bierbrier belong to the early TIP (i.e. Dynasty 21), Kitchen also has gaps in his lists of many office-holders for the *later* TIP, the very period in which the genealogical information is richest. Given the clearly hereditary nature of the offices, it is perplexing why these lacunae should occur. Kitchen himself, discussing the high priests (or 1st Prophet) of Amun, was compelled to suggest that the position had fallen into abeyance for perhaps thirty to fifty years (between 754/734 and 704 BC).[81] This is extraordinary, since for all of the 22nd Dynasty this major Theban benefice was held by royal princes acting as representatives of the Tanite throne.

Similar gaps occur throughout the 22nd Dynasty in Kitchen's lists for the 2nd Prophets (between *c.* 960/945–935 BC, 910–855 BC and 820–740 BC), 3rd Prophets (*c.* 920–875 BC) and a shorter one for the 4th Prophets (705–680 BC).[82] In the case of the last the situation clearly reveals that the position was taken away from the Nakhtef-mut family, which had held it for six generations.[83] (A parallel situation occurs with the offices of High Priest of Amun and God's Wife of Amun – see below.) That a lowering of the pontificates of the Nakhtefmut family is actually possible is indicated by their relationship with the family of Montemhat, which has posed a major problem for Bierbrier.[84]

Whilst an occasional priest *may* be unattested because of loss of monuments, large omissions would seem to be unlikely given the quantity of the material. It is therefore unaccountable why the worst gaps in the record occur in the most important by far of the Theban benefices, that of the God's Wives of Amun.

In the New Kingdom the office of God's Wife was held by the King's Chief Wife, and this persisted until the time of Ramesses VI, who installed his daughter Isis. It is assumed that from this time onwards the God's Wife was a sort of vestal virgin who presided over a college of priestesses drawn from the daughters of the nobility and the Libyan dynasts.[85]

Towards the close of the TIP and in the 26th Dynasty the office became a political instrument of the Delta and Kushite monarchs.[86] The God's Wives of Amun did not use their own regnal year numbers, and the exact date of the accession of each is known only for the later holders. The succession was by adoption and estab-lishes links between the 23rd, 25th and 26th Dynasties. These later officiants are abundantly documented and their sequence recon-structed as follows:[87]

23rd Dynasty	Shepenwepet I
25th Dynasty	Amenirdis I
	Shepenwepet II
	Amenirdis II
26th Dynasty	Nitocris
	Ankhnasneferibre

For the earlier part of the TIP the evidence is much patchier. Kitchen commented that 'the institution of God's Wife of Amun continued throughout the Libyan epoch, although few incumbents are known before its end'.[88] A recent study by Jean Yoyotte has reconsidered all the evidence for the office during the 21st and 22nd Dynasties. For the 21st Dynasty, only two God's Wives are known. Maatkare was probably the daughter of Pinudjem I. She was buried in the Inhapi cache along with a mummified pet monkey, thought by the excavators to be her baby, and made the subject of some wildly romantic theories about a vestal's fall from virtue.[89] Probably from the later 21st Dynasty is a Henttawy, known only from *ushabti* burial figures.[90]

Mehytenweskhet was probably the earliest 22nd Dynasty votaress.[91] Karomama was contemporary with Osorkon II and is depicted with Takeloth II in a Karnak chapel.[92] Before the well-attested sequence of votaresses beginning with the 23rd Dynasty princess, Shepenwepet I, there is evidence for one other incumbent named Kedemerut. The similarity of her *ushabti* figures to those of both Karomama and the 25th Dynasty kings suggests that all should be placed fairly close in time. Kedemerut may thus have been the only God's Wife between Karomama (Kitchen: 870–840 BC) and Shepenwepet I of the late 8th century.[93]

Libyan Dynasty finds outside Egypt

The discovery of Egyptian objects in the Late Bronze Age levels of other cultures regularly decides their chronology. The situation begins to change in the early Iron Age, when, with the decline of the New Kingdom Empire, finds bearing the name of datable pharaohs become much rarer, even in the Levant. The last significant remains of the 20th Dynasty in Palestine, including a statue base from Megiddo, are from the reign of Ramesses VI. Only a few scarabs are known from the remaining Ramessides,[94] and there is nothing which is certainly attributable to the 21st Dynasty.[95] While the situation can be quite easily attributed to a period of weak pharaonic power, it is interesting that it parallels the gaps in the records of the Apis bulls, God's Wives and genealogies as well as Egyptian statuary and other art forms.

With the Libyan period of the 22nd and 23rd Dynasties material with royal cartouches begins to be found again outside Egypt. This is the time of the developed Iron Age, and in almost every case there is some other means of dating the contexts in which the objects were found. Each instance is different, but the surprising result is that the local dating evidence always conflicts with the Egyptian.

Two certain objects of Shoshenq I, founder of the 22nd Dynasty (Kitchen: 945–924 BC), are known from Palestine. One, a monumental stela at Megiddo, is valuable historically in that it confirms his claim of an Asiatic campaign, but was unfortunately unstratified.[96] The second, a statue fragment discovered in the Phoenician city of Byblos at the turn of the century, was also found out of context. Nevertheless, a clue to its date is given by a worn inscription in the Phoenician alphabet which a Byblite king has proudly added around the royal cartouche of Shoshenq on the piece. This states that Abibaal, King of Byblos, had the statue brought from Egypt, and dedicated it to the goddess Baalath-Gebaal ('Lady of Byblos').[97]

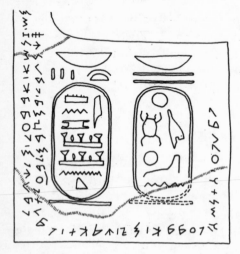

FIG. 10:6 Statue fragment of Shoshenq I found at Byblos. Around the cartouches of this Pharaoh a Phoenician inscription was added by the local king Abibaal (*after Montet 1928*).

A similar dedicatory inscription was found on another chance find, this time a bust of Shoshenq's son Osorkon I (see Plate 16).

The author of the Phoenician text was King Elibaal of Byblos, son of King Yehimilk. The script was identical to that used in Abibaal's inscription on the Shoshenq statue,[98] showing that the two Byblite kings were close in time, perhaps successors, like the pair Shoshenq I and Osorkon I. This strongly suggests that the Phoenician texts were added soon after the manufacture of the statues as it is hard to believe that two Byblite kings of the same period would, by chance, have chosen to reinscribe statues of two long-dead Egyptian monarchs who were also contemporaries. Most likely, the sculptures were diplomatic gifts sent by these pharaohs to the kings of Byblos, perhaps as part of a package in return for a shipment of the much-prized pine and cedar of the Lebanon; the Byblite kings probably inscribed them upon arrival. If the statues were specially commissioned by the pharaohs as gifts for the two kings, the respective claims of Abibaal that he 'brought' his statue from Egypt, and Elibaal that he 'made' his, then make reasonable sense.

Thus the evidence of the statues provides an extremely valuable synchronism, not only between two pairs of Egyptian and Byblite rulers, but between Egyptian chronology and a stage in the development of the Phoenician alphabet. The importance of the two inscriptions lies in their being part of a group from Byblos which forms the earliest corpus of Phoenician texts. Building inscriptions are known from two more kings, Yehimilk and Shipitbaal – the latter calls himself son of Elibaal, son of Yehimilk, providing a clear sequence of kings. It is assumed that Abibaal was another son of Yehimilk and the predecessor of Elibaal. Two other rulers are known from inscriptions in the same script – Ahiram and his son Ithobaal, who are generally placed before the Yehimilk family. The result is the following sequence of Byblite kings:[99]

Ahiram		
Ithobaal (son of Ahiram)		
Yehimilk		
Abibaal	————————	Shoshenq I
Elibaal (son of Yehimilk)	————————	Osorkon I
Shipitbaal (son of Elibaal)		

The date of these kings has been the subject of long-standing controversy. When the inscriptions were first published, many scholars saw no great differences between the form of the letters and those of the early Hebrew script on the stela of King Mesha of

Moab, firmly datable to about 840 BC (see p. 167). Benjamin Mazar placed the series between 950 and 750 BC. The terminal date he based on the fact that Tiglath-pileser III of Assyria records that a Byblite king called Shipitbaal paid him tribute around 740 BC. [100] Albright preferred a much higher chronology, partly based on his stylistic dating of the coffin of Ahiram, the first in the sequence, to the 12th century BC. Eventually he opted for a 10th-century date for the whole group, to satisfy the evidence of the synchronism between Abibaal and Elibaal and the early 22nd Dynasty. Naturally he had to reject Mazar's synchronism between this Shipitbaal and the one mentioned in 8th-century BC Assyrian annals. [101]

Albright's 10th-century BC date for the Byblite inscriptions became universally accepted, and indeed provides the backbone for dating the evolution of the Phoenician script. For example, it provides the basis for dating the 'Proto-Canaanite' group of inscriptions, with slightly less developed forms, to the 11th century BC – an extremely confusing result since the characters used in these inscriptions bear a great resemblance to the Greek alphabet of the 8th century BC (see Chapter 4). This has placed classical archaeologists in a considerable dilemma. Its cause is the canonical dates for the Byblite inscriptions, which are almost entirely dependent on the conventional dates from Shoshenq I, themselves dependent on his identification with the biblical Shishak (see above, pp. 229–31). This, as noted above, is a highly dubious link. Moreover, there are now independent, palaeographic, grounds for questioning the date of the inscriptions.

Mazar, forty years after his original paper and now a grand old man of biblical archaeology, resurrected his suggestion that the Shipitbaal of Byblos reigned c. 740 rather than c. 900 BC. Comparing the shapes of the Byblite letters to later Phoenician forms, he toyed with the idea of lowering the entire sequence, but in the event he felt obliged to leave them where they are because of the accepted dates for the 22nd Dynasty. [102]

The controversy was reopened recently by palaeographer Ronald Wallenfels. Beginning with the inscribed sarcophagus of Ahiram, he presented both stylistic and archaeological evidence suggesting that it was considerably younger than the 10th century BC. For example, the shaft of the burial contained a mass of Cypriot pottery from the Cypro-Geometric III Period (850–700 BC). [103] Certain Phoenician and Syrian inscriptions exist which are definitely datable, from their historical contents, to the early and mid-8th century. By a minute comparison of their letter forms and grammar with the Byblite inscriptions, Wallenfels argued that there was no reason to place the latter 200 years earlier. Such differences as there are, he shows, can be explained simply in terms of a Byblite dialect. Wallenfels thus redated the '10th-century' sequence to the late 9th to early 7th centuries, and was confident enough of his case to challenge the conventional date for Shoshenq I.[104]

The new palaeographic dating presented by Wallenfels matches the Assyrian reference to a Shipitbaal in c. 740 BC. Abibaal, two reigns before Shipitbaal, must then have reigned not much before 800 BC. Thus, together, the palaeographic and Assyrian evidence would date his contemporary Shoshenq I 125 years later than his usual placement.

Other evidence for a lowering of 22nd Dynasty dates comes from the find of a relief chalice fragment at Buseirah in Edom, southern Palestine. The distinctive style of the piece means that it must belong to the early 22nd Dynasty, conventionally the 10th to early 9th centuries BC. However, the date of its context is some 200 years later. The major occupation at Buseirah is currently dated to the 8th to early 7th centuries BC, agreeing with the fact that the earliest biblical references to Bozrah (Buseirah) were made by the mid-8th-century prophets Amos (1:12) and Micah (2:12). The archaeological dates may have to be lowered by our revision of Palestinian stratigraphy discussed in Chapter 8. In any event, the excavator Crystal Bennett was certainly correct to state that 'there is still no evidence to support a sedentary occupation of Buseirah before the beginning of the 8th century B.C.'.[105] Angela Milward, a specialist in Egyptian chalices invited by Bennett to comment, could only assume that the find was part of an 'heirloom'. Nevertheless, since Buseirah was of so little importance before the 8th century, she had to add that:

> . . . it is rather remarkable that an Egyptian chalice, which would have been a rare and costly item even then, should have found its way to Buseirah at such an early date, possibly the tenth or ninth century.[106]

Moving later into the 22nd Dynasty, a scarab of Osorkon I or II was found in a tomb at Salamis, Cyprus, the other contents of which were dated by Karageorghis to around 700 BC. It is assumed to be another heirloom.[107] At Samaria, the conventional dates for Osorkon II (Kitchen: 874–850 BC) have been used to support a 9th-century BC date for the famous ivories (to the time of Ahab) through an associated find of an imported alabaster vase bearing the name of this pharaoh. However, specialists in ivory-working have long noted the close resemblance of the Samaria examples to 8th-century BC ivories from Phoenicia, Syria and Assyria (see pp. 186–7). A similar date should be given to the Samarian material. If the ivories are allowed to date the alabaster, rather than the converse, then the Egyptian vase would belong to the mid-8th rather than the mid-9th century BC.[108]

Finds of Libyan material with more direct Assyrian links confirm this pattern of 'late' contexts. At Assur an alabaster vase was found with an inscription of a Libyan prince called Takeloth,[109] whose titles suggest that he was the son either of Shoshenq III (825–773 BC) or of Osorkon III (787–759 BC).[110] But the vase also bore a secondary inscription of the Assyrian King Esarhaddon (681–669 BC), stating that it was looted from the palace of the King of Sidon, a city which he sacked in 677 BC. On the analogy of the Byblite statues, we can assume that the vase arrived at Sidon as a gift, probably in the early 7th century BC. Similar alabaster vases are known from Nimrud, also from a 7th-century BC context, linked with Esarhaddon, which may also have been looted during Esarhaddon's attack on Sidon, or perhaps his conquest of Egypt in 671 BC.[111]

Further alabaster vases bearing the cartouches of Osorkon II (874–850 BC), Takeloth II (850–825 BC) and Shoshenq III (825–773 BC) come from Spain. They occur as cinerary urns in the graves at Laurita (Cerro de San Cristobal near Almuñécar) associated with Greek and Phoenician pottery datable to c. 700 BC. For example, the burial with the Shoshenq vessel was accompanied by two Early Protocorinthian vases which cannot date any earlier than the first quarter of the 7th century BC.[112] A scarab of Pedubast I (818–793 BC) comes from a similarly dated Spanish grave at Baixo Alentejo.[113]

A comparable date is suggested by the discovery of an alabaster vase fragment with the name of 'Pashedenbast son of [King] Shoshenq' from the royal cemetery at Nuri in Sudan, in which the earliest burials are from the reign of Taharqo (690–664 BC).[114] Whilst much of the other TIP material from Nubia can be associated with the 25th Dynasty conquest of Egypt,[115] there are some earlier small objects including scarabs of Shoshenq I and III from the cemetery of Sanam, which is supposed to have begun with the reign of Piye, and a scarab of Shoshenq I from Gebel Moya.[116]

At Carthage a number of Libyan period scarabs were found in tombs, along with pottery from the earliest days of the city. The scarabs carry the names of Pedubast I (eight tombs), Pimay son of Shoshenq III (one tomb) and Osorkon III (one tomb).[117] Cintas attempted to use these finds to date the tombs to the early 8th century BC, supplying the evidence needed to take the history of Carthage back to its traditional foundation date of 814 BC. Unfortunately for Cintas, the Greek and Phoenician pottery also excavated from the lowest levels shows that they can be no earlier than about 720 BC (see p. 54), which would leave the scarabs, now rarely mentioned, as another collection of ostensible 'heirlooms'.

Individually, these finds of 22nd–23rd Dynasty material in 'late' contexts (Byblos, Buseirah, Salamis, Samaria, Assur, Nimrud, Almuñécar, Baixo Alentejo, Nuri, Sanam and Carthage) can conceivably be explained as valued objects treasured for many years after their manufacture. However, taken together there seems to be a disturbing number of such finds. There also seems to be a pattern in the 'late' contexts running from c. 800 BC for the founder of the

Table 10:3

Shoshenq I (945–924 BC) – c. 800 BC (Byblos)

Osorkon I (924–889 BC) – early 8th century BC (Byblos)

Early 22nd Dynasty chalices (c. 950–850 BC) – mid-8th century BC (Buseirah)

Osorkon II (874–850 BC) – mid-8th century BC (Samaria); c. 700 BC (Spain)

Takeloth II (850–825 BC) – c. 700 BC (Spain)

Shoshenq III (825–773 BC) – c. 720 BC (Carthage); c. 700 BC (Spain)

Pedubast I (818–793 BC) – c. 720 BC (Carthage); c. 700 BC (Spain)

Prince Takeloth (c. 800 or 765 BC) – early 7th century BC (Sidon/Assur)

Pimay (773–767 BC) – c. 720 BC (Carthage)

Osorkon III (789–759 BC) – c. 720 BC (Carthage); c. 700 BC (Spain)

List of principal 22nd and 23rd Dynasty finds outside of Egypt which have independently datable contexts. The dates given are the earliest allowed by the local archaeological evidence; those for the Byblos statues follow Wallenfels (1983).

22nd Dynasty through the mid-8th century to a late-22nd Dynasty group around 700 BC (see Table 10:3).

Towards a new Egyptian chronology

With the demise of Sothic dating and the apparent untenability of the equation of Shoshenq I with the biblical Shishak, the entire basis for the conventional length for the Third Intermediate Period collapses. A throng of evidence from almost every area of the Mediterranean, and from Nubia on the very doorstep of Egypt, calls for a lowering of the Egyptian dates and a radical shortening of the TIP. Indeed, our review of the internal evidence from Egypt itself suggests the same.

It is too early to offer a complete revised scheme, with every king slotted neatly into place. The sheer bulk of the material to be assessed requires lengthy re-examination. But without giving precise dates for each pharaoh, broad lines of a new construction already emerge from the evidence.

The starting point for a revised chronology must be the later 25th Dynasty, whose last kings can be fixed exactly in time by links with the 26th Dynasty and the Assyrian kings. Whilst there is still some doubt, the date of the Kushite invasion of Egypt by Shabaqo is most likely to fall within the parameters established by Kitchen and Redford, i.e. 716–711 BC.[118] The important question for the early 25th Dynasty is whether Piye invaded Egypt before or after Shabaqo (see Chapter 9).

The Piye Stela is one of the most valuable sources for the history of the later TIP, as it lists the Libyan dynasts he confronted in Egypt. As well as Piye's main opponent Tefnakht, 'Great Chief of the Libu' and ruler of Sais, there were numerous 'Chiefs of the Ma' and other local dignitaries, and four rulers classed as Pharaohs: Osorkon, Iuput, Peftjauawybast and Nimlot. The identification of these kings has posed a major problem. Objects of Nimlot and Peftjauawybast confirm their status as kings, but the identity of both remains obscure, although it is assumed that they were scions of the 22nd or 23rd Dynasty. Iuput is even more puzzling: there are a few royal monuments bearing this name, but it is a moot point whether to attribute them to the Iuput ('II') of Piye's time or to an earlier king of this name, Iuput 'I'.[119]

Osorkon, whilst evidently the most respected of the pharaohs

listed by Piye, remains an enigma. Kitchen makes him 'Osorkon
IV', a ruler attested only by the slender evidence of one small
object.[120] Earlier Egyptologists assumed that Piye's Osorkon was
to be identified with the well-documented Osorkon III.[121] That he
must be close in time to the early 25th Dynasty is manifest from the
adoption of Shabaqo's sister by Osorkon III's daughter as a God's
Wife. An inscription of the two God's Wives in the Wadi Gasus is
dated to years 19 and 12 of two respective kings.[122] It is most likely
that these are the two rulers who are elsewhere associated with these
votaresses: Osorkon III and Shabaqo.[123] This would mean a substantial reduction in the dates given by Kitchen for Osorkon III
(787–759 BC). Following Kitchen's date of 716 for the accession of
Shabaqo, the Wadi Gasus inscription would belong to 705 BC,
placing the beginning of Osorkon III's reign in 723 BC. There are
important repercussions from this:

1 Osorkon III would be the King Osorkon ('Shilkanni') reigning
   in 716 BC referred to by Assyrian records.[124]

2 He can also be equated with the like-named king of the Piye
   Stela, obviating the need for the creation of a fourth King
   Osorkon.

3 Likewise, there is no need for two kings Iuput when only one is
   monumentally attested.

4 Peftjauawybast can be identified with the High Priest of Memphis of that name, who was of the senior line of the Tanite royal
   house.[125]

5 A general lowering of Libyan period dates can be effected,
   which would suit the evidence from private genealogies showing a much shorter time between the contemporaries of Osorkon III and individuals of the late 25th/early 26th Dynasties.[126]

6 The genealogical and related evidence establishing that Osorkon II and III were separated by no more than two
   generations[127] means that the dates for the mid-22nd Dynasty as
   a whole should be considerably lowered.

Fitting with the above, there is evidence that the length of the
22nd Dynasty has been greatly overstretched. The chronicle of
Prince Osorkon lists the offerings he made as High Priest of Amun
at Thebes between year 11 of his father, Takeloth II, and year 28 of

Shoshenq III.[128] There is nothing recorded after year 24 of Takeloth or before year 22 of Shoshenq III. Unless we assume a gap of twenty years in his career as High Priest, there must have been a considerable overlap between these two reigns. Such an overlap is supported by the Apis data, where there are no known bulls between year 23 of Osorkon II and year 28 of Shoshenq III. A compression of the chronology at this point would also remove the only obstacle to the otherwise attractive identification of Osorkon the High Priest of Amun with the future Osorkon III, assumed by earlier Egyptologists[129] but incompatible with Kitchen's long chronology. To have served under both pharaohs (without any overlap of reigns) his pontificate would have had to have lasted for fifty-five years, and if twenty years old when appointed, Osorkon would have been seventy-five years old at his accession and, after twenty-eight years of reign, about 103 at his death.[130]

If Osorkon III's first regnal year (c. 723 BC) immediately followed his last attestation as High Priest of Amun in year 39 of Shoshenq III, then the latter's accession can be placed around 761 BC. An overlap of some twenty years between Shoshenq III and Takeloth II brings Takeloth's first year to c. 765 BC. The reign of Osorkon II must also overlap with the early reigns of Takeloth II and Shoshenq III to satisfy the Apis evidence. Taking nineteen years as the average life-span of an Apis bull, and assuming that the bull buried in year 23 of Osorkon II was the predecessor of that buried in year 28 of Shoshenq III, the reign of Osorkon II would have begun in c. 775 BC. There is no evidence for an independent reign of a 'Takeloth I' before Osorkon II.[131] Osorkon I, who reigned for fifteen years, may be taken as his immediate predecessor, beginning his reign c. 790 BC. The twenty-one years of his father, Shoshenq I, brings the foundation of the 22nd Dynasty to c. 810 BC.[132]

For the 21st Dynasty the major anomalies reviewed above – the lack of Apis burials, statuary and genealogies and objects outside of Egypt – strongly recommend a return to the solution proposed by Lieblein at the turn of the century, which was to treat the 21st and 22nd Dynasties as largely contemporary. This would resolve some of the archaeological mysteries connected with the 21st Dynasty, notably the problems of the Inhapi cache and the royal tombs at Tanis. The evidence of the latter, taken at face value, suggests that Psusennes 'I' of the 21st Dynasty was buried after Osorkon II of the 22nd.[133]

The surprising conclusion reached is that the 20th Dynasty, rather than ending in 1069 BC, may have ended shortly before the accession of Shoshenq I, here dated to c. 810 BC. The 21st Dynasty may have ruled independently for only one generation. Allowing twenty-five years for this period and 115 years for the 20th Dynasty would place its founder, Sethnakht, c. 950 BC. The period of time between the accession of Sethnakht and year 30 of Ramesses II is some sixty years, bringing us to c. 1010 BC for the year in which the first Apis bull under Ramesses was buried in the Lesser Vault. Between 1010 BC and 644 BC (year 21 of Psamtik I) are 366 years. Seventeen bulls are known from the Serapeum to fill this period. If we assume no gaps in the Apis bull evidence (bar, say, one), then we arrive at a very plausible average age for the life of the intervening bulls of between twenty and twenty-one years, agreeing well with previous estimates of the average life of these bulls.

Application of this experimental chronology to other areas produces some remarkable results. It agrees with the external datings for the Libyan Dynasty finds outside Egypt. Now only a few of the objects need to be considered as heirlooms; most would have been deposited in contexts shortly after their manufacture. The new accession date for Shoshenq I of c. 810 BC agrees perfectly with the late 9th-century date for contemporary material at Byblos. Thus Shoshenq I cannot be the biblical Shishak.[134]

Who, then, was the king of Egypt who brought about the downfall of Solomon's empire, and looted the Temple of its treasures c. 925 BC? On the dates suggested here, the king in Egypt at this time would have been Ramesses III, who is known to have re-established Egyptian control in Palestine. The biblical name 'Shishak' could well be a corruption of the Egyptian 'Sessi', the common abbreviation of the name Ramesses.[135]

Our compression of Third Intermediate Period chronology results in an overall lowering of the dates for the New Kingdom (18th–20th Dynasties) by some 250 years. Arguments against such a reduction could cite radiocarbon evidence, some of which apparently supports the conventional chronology. Other results, however, accord with the reduced dates advocated here.[136] There is also a suspicion that the publication of dates is far from unprejudiced.[137] The currently available radiocarbon results can best be described as equivocal, and far more need to be available to test out both accepted and revised chronologies. The stubborn –

Table 10:4

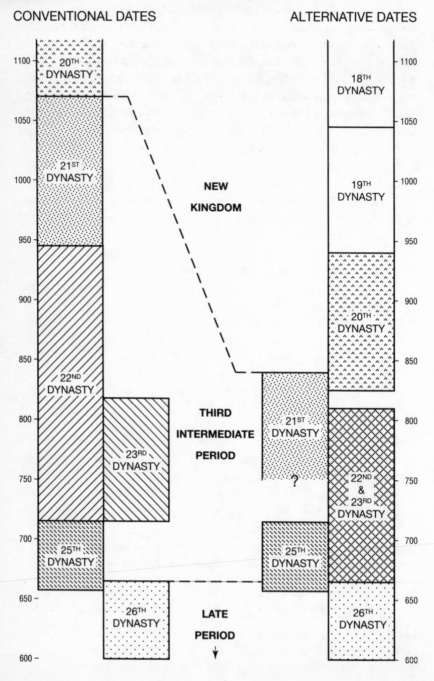

CONVENTIONAL DATES

ALTERNATIVE DATES

indeed arrogant – refusal of modern Egyptologists to consider a reduction of dates, and their insistence on the 'correctness' of the standard Egyptian chronology, still provides the mainspring of the interminable Dark Age arguments afflicting the archaeology of Nubia, the Near East and the Mediterranean. Early Egyptologists were usually more tentative about their chronology, continually revising their opinions in the light of fresh evidence. Sadly, the study of Egyptian chronology seems to have become so ossified that it cannot question its fundamental assumptions, accepted more for familiarity than for any basis in fact.

A comparison of the conventional dates for the Third Intermediate Period with the provisional alternative scheme. A substantial compression in the overall chronology can be achieved by allowing greater overlaps between the TIP dynasties (particularly the 21st and 22nd), and by strict adherence to the reign-lengths actually given by the contemporary Egyptian monuments, rather than those provided by Manetho. The result is a substantial lowering in time of the New Kingdom and with it the Late Bronze Age of the Eastern Mediterranean (cf. Table 8:3). NB: The 24th Dynasty, which lasted thirteen years at most, is not shown here; on the conventional dating, it reigned in the western Delta concurrently with the last years of the 22nd and 23rd dynasties, and is of little chronological significance in either scheme.

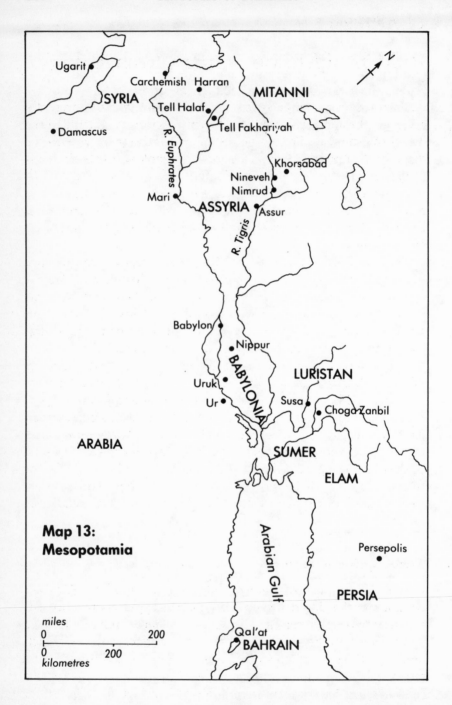

Map 13:
Mesopotamia

Riddles of Mesopotamian Archaeology

An extraordinary range of evidence suggests that the presently accepted chronology for ancient Egypt is seriously at fault. If the Third Intermediate Period were shortened substantially, then the dates for the Egyptian New Kingdom as a whole would be dramatically lowered. Similar reductions could then be made in the chronology for the Late Bronze Age of the entire Mediterranean. As a result, the troublesome dark periods that infest the Iron Age cultures of the Old World would be shortened or, in some cases, even eliminated.

The case for such a reduction seems persuasive, even compelling, but – a sceptic might argue – not conclusive. Fortunately, there is another area in which we can test our revision of chronology. This is ancient Mesopotamia, whose twin civilizations of Assyria and Babylonia (in, respectively, the north and south of modern Iraq) have already played an important role in our investigations.

The Assyrians, in particular, figure prominently in the histories of many Mediterranean peoples, including the Syrian Hittites, Aramaeans, Phoenicians, Cypriots, Israelites, Edomites and Egyptians. Their lands were incorporated, by degrees, into the Assyrian Empire during the 9th to 7th centuries BC. By unifying these diverse areas, reorganized into imperial provinces and stamped with the mark of a single authority, the Assyrians paved the way for the 'world empires' that followed – those of the Neo-Babylonians, the Persians and, ultimately, the Macedonians under Alexander the Great.

The Assyrian adventure

It was the promise of finding the rich palaces of the Assyrian conquerors that lured the first antiquarian explorers to northern Iraq during the 19th century. The existence of the Assyrian Empire had always been known from biblical and classical sources, which described the power and splendour of its kings in almost fabulous terms. There seemed every likelihood, then, that the huge *tells* (mounds) of Assyria concealed ruins of considerable interest. In

1843 a French diplomat named Paul Emile Botta undertook the first major archaeological excavation in Iraq. Khorsabad, where he dug, proved to be a treasure trove of sculptures, metalwork, ivory carvings and other *objets d'art*. He had discovered the palace of Sargon II, the 8th-century BC king who deported the 'Ten Tribes of Israel' and carried Assyrian arms as far as the marches of Egypt.

Only two years later, the great British explorer Sir Austen Henry Layard followed up Botta's success with the excavation of Nimrud and Nineveh.[1] The Bible-educated Western world was entranced by his discoveries. At Nimrud he found the 'Black Obelisk', showing Jehu, King of Israel, kissing the feet of the Assyrian King Shalmaneser III. From the dust of Nineveh he unearthed a series of reliefs (now in the British Museum) depicting the Assyrian King Sennacherib seated on a throne as he directs the siege of the Judaean city of Lachish (see p. 176). More graphic confirmation of the Old Testament narrative could hardly be wished for: these scenes provided some of the first concrete links between biblical history and archaeology. At the same time, the majestically bizarre style of Assyrian sculpture had an appeal in its own right. The effect of the monstrous guardian figures found by Layard at Nimrud was described by Mallowan:

> the world at large was startled by these great stone phantoms, resurrected nightmares which the people of ancient Israel must have seen in their dreams when they were beset by the cruel might of Assyria.[2]

Public interest supported the call for further excavations. Further surprises were in store, many particularly welcome in an age when faith in the authority of the Bible was being tested to its limits by the challenge of Darwin's followers. Amongst the tablets of the enormous library of the 7th-century BC King Assurbanipal at Nineveh, a diligent British Museum worker named George Smith came across some fragments of the Babylonian equivalent of the biblical Flood story. Immediately after announcing his discovery in 1872, Smith was approached by a representative of the *Daily Telegraph*, who offered him funds for a new expedition to recover more of the Flood text. Miraculously, Smith found another fragment after only five days' work at Nineveh. His luck ran out on his third expedition: he fell fatally ill with dysentery, aggravated by the punishing heat of a Mesopotamian summer.[3]

FIG. 11:1   Gypsum winged bull from Nimrud, carved for the palace of king Assurnasirpal II (883–859 BC) and first exhibited at the British Museum in October 1850. The creature has five legs, in order for two to be seen from the front and four from the side (*Illustrated London News*).

This adventurous scramble for historical treasures eventually gave way to systematic, larger scale projects. By the turn of the century excavation of the capitals of Babylonia and Assyria was underway, with German teams starting work at Babylon in 1899 and Assur in 1903.[4] Scientific archaeology in Mesopotamia had begun. Cultures far older than those of the Assyrian Empire known from the Bible were now being uncovered in the deeper strata of the mounds. Those in southern Iraq were proving to be classic examples of the *tell* as a layer-cake of history. The remains of 'Late', 'Middle' and 'Old' phases of Assyrian and Babylonian civilization were recognized. Beneath those again were the levels of the Sumerians and their forebears, the originators of Mesopotamian civilization, reaching back to an almost unimaginable antiquity.

But perhaps the most important breakthrough in Mesopotamian archaeology had already taken place, not in Iraq, but in Europe. Here a trio of scholars (Sir Henry Rawlinson, Edward Hincks and Jules Oppert) had been tirelessly working towards the decipherment of the cuneiform script of ancient Mesopotamia. As early as

1847 provisional readings of cuneiform tablets could be made, one immediate discovery being that the same language (Akkadian) had been spoken by both the Assyrians and the Babylonians. The way was now open to address the next task in hand: how to date the immense amount of material being uncovered from the mounds of Iraq.

The resurrection of Mesopotamian history

Memories of Assyrian and Babylonian history have always been part of our received knowledge, from the classical writings of the ancient world. For the scholars who began the task of reconstructing ancient chronology this proved to be something of a mixed blessing. 'Histories' of Assyria were well known in Roman times – we can learn, for instance, from St Augustine of Hippo's *City of God* (written *c*. 420 AD) the names of the kings who supposedly ruled at the time of Abraham's birth or of the Exodus of the Israelites from Egypt. But in common with other Graeco-Roman writers, Augustine worked with a 'king list' consisting of a stream of outlandish names, barely any of which are recognizably Assyrian.

Pseudo-histories of Assyria enjoyed wide popularity in the classical world, not so much for their chronological content as for their preoccupation with fantastic characters, such as the transvestite King Sardanapalus, said to have been spinning wool as he was burnt alive in his palace. An even more lurid cycle of tales surrounded the warrior-queen Semiramis. She was supposed to have murdered her husband in order to gain the favour, then the hand in marriage, of King Ninus; together they conquered the whole of Asia except India, before her ambitions led her to kill Ninus as well; she founded Babylon, built its famous Hanging Gardens and was in her turn murdered by her son – also lover – Ninyas.[5] The life of the historical Assyrian Queen Sammuramat, whose name was borrowed for the legend, was a much tamer affair.[6]

Such yarns were merely a useless distraction for 19th-century scholars struggling to glean serious information about Mesopotamian history. Fortunately, among the clutter of garbled traditions, there was a vein of genuine, and quite invaluable, historical knowledge. Some extraordinary fragments have survived from the work of a Babylonian priest called Berossus (3rd century BC; see Chapter

12). Like his contemporary, the Egyptian Manetho (see Chapter 10), Berossus prepared for a Greek-speaking audience a lengthy history of his country, from 'before the Flood' to the time of Alexander. Sadly, very little survives, but what does is enough to show that scholars of the Hellenistic world still had access to cuneiform historical records.[7] As known from tablets written under the Seleucid kings of Babylonia (3rd to 1st centuries BC), there were still many scribes conversant with Akkadian cuneiform, even in an age when it had long been superseded by Aramaic and Greek as the language of commerce and government.[8]

The historical thread between the classical and ancient Babylonian worlds was thinly stretched, but not broken. Indeed, a Greek astronomical treatise from as late as the 2nd century AD contains one of the most valuable chronological sources ever discovered, known as the 'Canon of Ptolemy'. Claudius Ptolemy, the famous Greek mathematician and geographer, recorded for posterity the names and reign-lengths of the kings of Babylon from Alexander the Great, who died there in 323 BC, back to Nabonassar, who ascended the throne in 747 BC.[9] How Ptolemy came across documents containing such information is uncertain, but his interest in them lay mainly in their astronomical content. The sources available to him, now lost, provided detailed records of lunar eclipses observed by the ancient Babylonians, which Ptolemy dated according to an era beginning with the accession of King Nabonassar.

Ptolemy's King List enabled 19th-century scholars to take their first confident step back into the past of Mesopotamia. Following the decipherment of cuneiform the skeleton of history after 747 BC could be fleshed out from the records of the Babylonians themselves. Most important, the next stage of reconstruction could also be achieved – to give precise dates to Assyrian history by linking it with that of Babylonia. Since some of the Assyrian kings, such as Sennacherib and his son Esarhaddon, were included in Ptolemy's Canon for the periods when they also ruled Babylonia, synchronisms could easily be drawn between the two countries. The discovery of other sources, such as the *Babylonian Chronicle* published in 1887, provided further details.[10]

Before the 8th century BC, however, Babylonian records become very patchy. To go back beyond this point, Assyrian texts had to be used. As a means of reckoning, the Assyrians delegated different officers of state, beginning with the king himself, to be the 'eponym' (name-giver) for each year. Thus, if an event was dated to the year of governor X of city Y, a scribe could determine when it happened by referring to a list of such 'eponyms'. In 1862 Sir Henry Rawlinson was fortunate enough to discover a major Eponym List, giving every incumbent from 911 BC down to 660 BC.[11] The information from the 'two Canons' (those of Ptolemy and the eponyms) could then be combined, with a result proudly described by Sir Henry's nephew, George Rawlinson:

> These two documents, which harmonise admirably, carry up an *exact* Assyrian chronology almost from the close of the Empire to the tenth century before our era.[12]

With only minor adjustments, the system devised by the Rawlinsons is still accepted today, although in the late 19th century it met strong opposition from some biblical scholars. The archaeological discoveries at Nimrud and Nineveh provided vivid links between the histories of Assyria and Israel; not only from reliefs, but also from cuneiform records of Assyrian military campaigns in Palestine. Shalmaneser III encountered two Israelite kings, Ahab and Jehu, in 853 and 841 BC respectively, according to the canonical system. Yet counting the reigns of Israelite monarchs recorded in the Bible back from the end of the Kingdom in 722 BC (also fixed by Assyrian records), one arrives at dates for Ahab and Jehu some 45 years earlier than those given by Shalmaneser's annals.

FIG. 11:2   A pictorial synchronism from Assyria, depicted on the 'Black Obelisk' from Nimrud. Shalmaneser III (858–824 BC) receives tribute from Jehu, king of Israel, who kneels before him (*from Breasted 1916*).

For a while it seemed there was a genuine conflict between the Bible and canonical Assyrian chronology. It was even suggested that there was a hidden 'gap' in the Eponym Canon, masking a collapse of the Assyrian Empire during the early 8th century BC, a theory which fitted some of the misleading chronological information in the pseudo-histories of classical times.[13] The idea eventually lost its currency, however, when it became clear that there were no mistakes in either set of data, but only in our understanding of the biblical evidence. Closer study of the internal chronology of the Israelite kings showed that some had reigned for a number of years jointly with their fathers and/or sons. The Bible records the overall total of their regnal years, including such co-regencies. Thus it was Hebrew chronology, not Assyrian, which needed adjustment, by a downdating of half a century.[14]

More recently, however, a serious attack was launched on the veracity of Ptolemy himself. In 1978 a study by the American astronomer Robert Newton, entitled *The Crime of Claudius Ptolemy*, accused him of having perpetrated a massive scientific fraud, 'a betrayal of the ethics and integrity of his profession that has forever deprived mankind of fundamental information about an important area of astronomy and history'. According to Newton, all Ptolemy's claimed astronomical observations were fabricated; even worse, he had fudged, or even faked, Babylonian lunar eclipse data in order to match his own shaky calculations.[15] One reviewer of Newton's work even suggested that 'Ptolemy's forgery may have extended to inventing the lengths of reigns of Babylonian kings'.[16]

Even so, Newton's strongly worded attack has done little to tarnish Ptolemy's reputation as one of the first great astronomers. As more reasonable historians of science have shown, the standards Newton applied to Ptolemy's work were far too exacting. Ptolemy may have selected from, thereby 'smoothing out', the observational data available to him, but this is a very different matter from Newton's charge of outright forgery.[17]

But what of Ptolemy's Canon, by which 19th-century historians had set so much store? Was Newton right to claim that 'studies of Babylonian chronology need to be reviewed in order to remove any dependence upon Ptolemy's king-list'?[18] On this question Mesopotamian archaeology can now fully repay its debt to the old astronomer. Though Newton glossed over the fact, Ptolemy's

figures for the regnal years of Babylonian kings have been completely vindicated by a wealth of cuneiform texts, including chronicles, short king lists and dated business documents. The dates
derived from Ptolemy's Canon can also be checked using the
information from cuneiform 'astronomical diaries'. The Babylonians, originators of western astrology, were, as Ptolemy knew,
meticulous observers of the night sky. Their records of the posi-
tions of planets and stars, committed to clay by people who
believed that these had a vital influence on earthly matters, are
extremely detailed – so much so that the observations given in
various tablets from the 7th to 5th centuries BC can be precisely
dated to a year, month and even day by modern astronomers.[19]

Final confirmation of the whole canonical system comes from
another astronomically fixed point, this time provided by Assyrian
records. A solar eclipse is clearly referred to in the Eponym List for
the month of Simanu in a year which must, according to the links
with Ptolemy's Canon, have been 763 BC. The fundamental importance of this observation for ancient chronology was stressed by
van der Meer:

> This eclipse of the sun has been astronomically fixed, on grounds
> that have never been questioned, as having taken place on June
> 15th 763 B.C., according to modern reckoning. This year is
> therefore used as a base reckoning for the Assyrian calendar. It is
> the sheet-anchor upon which depends not only the Assyrian
> chronology but also that of the whole of Western Asia.[20]

A step in the dark

The solar eclipse of 763 BC brings us full circle, through Assyrian
chronology and its links with Babylonia, to the lunar eclipse
records of Ptolemy. The resulting picture, with checks and cross-
checks provided by every source from modern astronomy to the
Old Testament, is as watertight as one could ask for any period of
ancient history. Assyrian history is firmly datable, with a margin of
error no greater than a year, as far back as 911 BC, when the
continuous Eponym List began; Babylonian history is equally
certain at least as far back as 747 BC, when Nabonassar took the
throne.

Before these dates historians tread on uncertain ground. The

custom of naming years after eponyms began in the Middle Assyrian period, but the lists covering periods prior to 911 BC are so
fragmentary that they cannot serve as a guide for reconstructing
Mesopotamian history. Other dating strategies had to be adopted
by the Rawlinsons and their contemporaries.

Two tempting clues were provided by Late Assyrian records. An
inscription of Sennacherib claims that on his capture of Babylon he
recovered a royal seal seized 600 years ago by an earlier conqueror
Tukulti-Ninurta I, which had somehow returned to Babylonia. As
Sennacherib sacked Babylon in 702 and again in 689 BC, Tukulti-
Ninurta I would have been reigning by 1289 BC at the latest.
Another record of Sennacherib, this time clearly relating to his
second conquest of Babylon, says that he recaptured the idols stolen
by the Babylonians from Assyria at the time of Tiglath-pileser I,
418 years before. Tiglath-pileser's reign would therefore have
begun by 1107 BC.[21]

Nineteenth-century archaeologists took these dates at face value
and developed around them a framework for Assyrian history
stretching back to 1300 BC. Babylonian kings were shuffled into
place alongside their contemporaries, following the information
given in a cuneiform chronicle known as the *Synchronistic History*.
On the surface all seemed plausible – except that the framework
adopted left a conspicuous gap in Mesopotamian history. Assyriologists had not found a single king, record or monument which
could be dated with certainty to the period between Tiglath-pileser
I's son, Assur-bel-kala, who died *c.* 1060 BC, and a second Tiglath-
pileser who reigned *c.* 950 BC, shortly before the period covered by
the continuous Eponym Canon.[22] A similar blank at approximately
the same time was reluctantly accepted for Babylonian history.[23]

Strangely, the possibility never seems to have been considered
that something had gone seriously awry and that the dates calculated for Assyria were too high. By this stage, links with Egyptian
chronology had been established via the El-Amarna letters (see
Appendix 4) and Mesopotamian archaeologists had little alternative
but to accept the idea that the history of Assyria and Babylonia was
interrupted by a yawning void during the 11th to 10th centuries BC.

Yet the whole problem of a gap seemed to dissolve when tablets
giving an extensive list of Assyrian kings were found in 1927. They
contained a King List drawn up by the Assyrians themselves in the
8th century BC. Three versions of this document have now been

FIG. 11:3   Assurbanipal (668–627 BC), last of the great Assyrian Emperors,
portrayed in a relief from Nineveh (British Museum). The scene shows the king
hunting, but he also prided himself on his literacy. His scribes recopied
thousands of ancient documents, and Assurbanipal's enormous library,
excavated earlier this century, provided some of the most important documents
for the reconstruction of earlier Mesopotamian history (drawing by Rosemary
Burnard).

discovered, agreeing in all essentials on the reign-lengths and
genealogies of the kings from the 8th century BC back to the
semi-legendary founders of the monarchy, 'who ruled in tents',
perhaps to be dated as early as the 3rd millennium BC.

For Assyriologists the discovery was like a gift from the gods.
The King List not only extended Assyrian history to a previously
unimagined antiquity; it also conveniently provided the names of a
sequence of kings to fill the irksome void in 1st-millennium history.
The monuments and inscriptions of Assyrian monarchs over a
period of more than a thousand years could now be arranged in
sequence and dated, with seeming confidence, according to their
position in the list.

The meaning of this extraordinary document will be investigated
in the next chapter. For the moment the focus will be on the picture

of Mesopotamian archaeology and history which has resulted from accepting the dates given by the King List. Does the evidence from Mesopotamia, as is sometimes argued, support a high Egyptian chronology? Or does it confirm our suspicion that the 'dark centuries' in the histories of so many cultures are the by-product of an incorrect chronology? We begin our examination with Assyria.

The gap in Assyrian archaeology

While it has been claimed that 'Assyria was the one power in western Asia that survived the upheavals at the end of the Bronze Age',[24] it is also agreed that it underwent a serious cultural and political recession at this time. Indeed, the period between 1200 and 900 BC has been aptly described as the 'Dark Age of Mesopotamia'.[25] Exactly how long this period of decline lasted is, of course, a moot point.

At the time of the thriving Late Bronze Age civilizations of Mycenae, Cyprus, Anatolia and Egypt, Assyria was a small but vigorous kingdom. Its language, religion and culture owed much to the older civilization of Babylonia, but it had already developed its own, distinctly militaristic, ethos. The chief god Assur was a warrior deity *par excellence*, who gave his 'viceroys', the Assyrian kings, a divine mandate to mete out savage justice to those who failed to acknowledge him. During the 2nd millennium BC the rulers of Assyria shook off the dominance of the Mitannian Empire to the north and assumed the status of 'Great King', dealing on an equal footing with the long established monarchies of Babylon, Hatti and Egypt.

Assyrian armies extended the kingdom northward and westward and then, under King Tukulti-Ninurta I (dated by the king list to the late 13th century BC), they undertook their most audacious venture. Tukulti-Ninurta led his troops south and crushed the Babylonians. The walls of Babylon were thrown down and the idol of the great god Marduk was carried off to Assyria as a captive, together with its dethroned king. To many Assyrians this deed must have seemed sacrilegious, for they too venerated Babylon as a holy city. Indeed, one of the repercussions of the campaign seems to have been internal strife within Assyria itself: Tukulti-Ninurta's son led a rebellion, and the conqueror of Babylon was murdered in his own palace.[26] No Assyrian king dared assault the city of

Babylon again until Sennacherib, who sacked it in 689 BC; he paid the same price as Tukulti-Ninurta, being slaughtered by his own sons as he 'worshipped in the house of Nisroch his god' (2 Kgs. 19:37).

Exactly what happened after the death of Tukulti-Ninurta is difficult to know, but his sons seem to have fallen out in a dispute over the succession. Subsequently, for a period estimated as fifty years, few records survive.[27] Then there is a respite from the confusion: after the sons of Assur-dan I, three kings (Assur-resh-ishi, his son Tiglath-pileser I and his son Assur-bel-kala) ruled in succession, leaving enough texts for us to reconstruct a history of their time. Tiglath-pileser's records are particularly extensive: he was a skilled general, leading Assyrian troops as far as the Mediterranean Sea, where he undertook a marine hunting expedition.[28]

Following this line of kings (presently dated to 1132–1056 BC), available documents dry up again for another 120 years – at the time of the mysterious gap which confronted 19th-century Assyriologists. The King List provided the names and reign-lengths of a sequence of monarchs to fill the lacuna, yet the discovery made little practical difference. The kings of this blank period appear to have left few, if any, records of their campaigns, decrees, building work or other efforts. Some are completely unattested in contemporary monuments or inscriptions (see Chapter 12). It is difficult not to draw a comparison with the Third Intermediate Period in Egypt, where many kings allowed generous reigns are actually mere ciphers. Only by the reign of Assur-dan II (934–912 BC) is there enough information to feel that we are again dealing with a real period of Assyrian history.[29]

Thus for over 250 years, from the death of Tukulti-Ninurta I in 1208 BC to the renaissance at the end of the 10th century BC, Assyrian history is an almost complete blank – apart from the interlude around the time of Tiglath-pileser I. The gap in documentation extends to all kinds of literature. Assyriologist Simo Parpola recently drew attention to the fact that:

. . . with the exception of a few scattered royal inscriptions, virtually no contemporary texts such as letters, administrative records, or legal documents are extant from the early part (1200–1150) or the crucial second half of the period (1050–900).[30]

The absence of datable literary and religious texts from these times make it impossible to detect trends – indeed, no changes appear to have occurred.[31]

Developments in art are also difficult to trace. Not only is there a dearth of material, but styles on either side of the gulf between the 12th and 10th centuries BC are curiously similar. One scholar noted that the forms and decoration of the intricately carved Assyrian seals of the 12th century are 'clearly late', as they 'point the way to the ornate figures which line the walls of the Neo-Assyrian palace of Assurnasirpal [mid-9th century BC]'.[32] The sculptors employed by this king, in the words of another expert on Assyrian art, 'worked within a tradition which went back to the thirteenth century BC'.[33] Not surprisingly, then, the dating of the few sculptures which might belong to this grey period has been hotly debated.[34]

Assyrian archaeology has produced little, in terms of building or occupation phases, to bridge this gap. Unfortunately, most of the major excavations at the prime sites were carried out 'before the principle of stratigraphy was recognized',[35] and in many cases evidence for continuity or discontinuity across the gap may have been destroyed by the brutal techniques of early excavators. Nevertheless, even where better archaeological investigations have been carried out, the published reports are still disconcertingly silent about material remains from the Dark Age. The temple built by Tiglath-pileser I at Assur is a striking exception.[36]

Assyrian recession: Aramaean expansion

There is one process, however, which can be detected in Assyrian history in the years following Tukulti-Ninurta I's death. The records of the Late Assyrian kings show that they had to recover a considerable amount of territory in north-western Mesopotamia from a people known as the Aramaeans. The Aramaeans, as we know from these records and the Old Testament, were fierce tribesmen from the Syrian desert. In the time of David and Solomon (late 11th–10th centuries BC) their 'empire', a loosely knit confederation of kingdoms, stretched from the northern reaches of Israel to the Euphrates. Damascus became the most important Aramaean kingdom in Syria, while their main power centre in Mesopotamia was the city-state of Bit-Bahiani, modern Tell Halaf.

Since the Aramaeans dominated much of western Assyria during its period of recession, it might be thought that the remains of sites like Tell Halaf would help to fill the blank in Assyrian archaeology between the 12th and 9th centuries BC. As it happened, the excavation of Tell Halaf merely provided fuel for further chronological contention. Its most important building was 'the palace of Kapara', as cuneiform inscriptions in 'barbaric Assyrian' show. Yet the impressive reliefs (see Plate 19) which decorated the palace and its gateway posed a considerable problem. The original excavator, Baron Max von Oppenheim, ascribed them to the 3rd millennium BC, because of apparent Sumerian influences.[37] His extremely high dates are universally regarded as unacceptable: the inscriptions, including one in the Aramaean alphabet, could not possibly have been this early, and he had to argue them away as much later additions. A somewhat more reasonable scheme was offered by A. Goetze, who saw in the reliefs motifs from Mitannian art, best known from its seals, which are indirectly dated by Egyptian chronology. He placed the sculptures in the 19th and 14th centuries BC, and the inscriptions in the 12th century.[38]

Anton Moortgat, the next excavator of the site, took a very different view, arguing that there was no good reason to dissociate the inscriptions from the buildings. Further, the Late Assyrian influence evident in the reliefs led him to place the whole series in the 1st millennium BC. His scheme allowed two building phases for the palace complex: the first around 900 BC, followed by the 'Kapara period' ending in 808 BC, by which time the Assyrians finally recovered the area from the Aramaeans and absorbed it into their empire as the province of Guzan.[39]

These conclusions did not stop Tell Halaf becoming embroiled in the long-running battle between Frankfort and Albright over the dating of ancient Near Eastern art (see Chapter 8). Frankfort agreed with Moortgat's 9th-century BC dating, but felt obliged to explain the conspicuous Late Bronze Age motifs on the reliefs in terms of a revival of Mitannian styles.[40] Yet his idea that they had been preserved through the medium of Assyrian sculpture failed to take into account the almost complete lack of intermediate examples from Assyria itself during the Dark Age. Albright saw local continuity as the answer and backdated the reliefs to the 10th century BC,[41] thereby hoping to help alleviate the gap in monumental art that the standard chronology imposes.

The small finds associated with the palace of Kapara were published some years later.[42] As many objects bore comparison to 9th-century Assyrian material, Moortgat's dating seemed to be vindicated; it was now also supported by studies comparing the Tell Halaf reliefs with those of the Neo-Hittite states of northern Syria.[43] At this point one might have thought that the matter was closed; unfortunately, Moortgat's dating still left unresolved the enigma of the Bronze Age elements in the sculpture, which continue to bother art historians.[44] For example, the Tell Halaf sculptures reflect influences not only from the Mitannian Empire of northern Mesopotamia, but also from as far away as Mycenaean Greece. As a disciple of Frankfort, Helene Kantor accepted the late dating for the reliefs, but remarked with surprise that:

> Unlikely though it may seem to find in local and clumsy Syrian reliefs of the ninth century the continuation of features of Mycenaean sculpture, centuries older and now quite extinct, this is yet the case.[45]

A direct challenge to the consensus view has been made by Jeanny Canby, who objected with regard to the evidence of the small finds that 'there is far too little comparative material yet available for the eleventh and tenth century in Assyria to date such items precisely'.[46] Canby argued that a 9th-century date was far too low, given the number of parallels which could be drawn between the sculpture of Tell Halaf and that from Late Bronze Age Hazor in Palestine. These include a particular kind of undecorated stela sharing a 'striking physical resemblance', while 'the strong stylistic resemblance between the seated figures from Halaf and those from Hazor suggests that the stone carvers were working within a single tradition'.[47] Accordingly, Canby revived the possibility of a 2nd millennium date for Tell Halaf.

Within the conventional chronology, the Tell Halaf sculptures remain a mystery. While there are sound reasons for dating the construction of Kapara's palace to the 9th, or at the earliest the 10th, century BC, its sculptures have to be treated as 'archaizing' works, reflecting the art and iconography of long vanished civilizations. On the other hand, if Egyptian chronology is radically lowered, then the terminal date for the Late Bronze Age civilizations of Mitanni, Mycenae and Hazor would come down to as late as *c.* 950, rather than *c.* 1200 BC. The influence of their art on that of the 1st millennium Aramaeans can then be seen as quite natural.

FIG. 11:4 (Above) Sculpture of lion from Tell Halaf (northern Iraq), 9th century BC. As Kantor demonstrated, such crude figures preserved many of the motifs from the Late Bronze Age art of the Mycenaeans. The way in which the lion's musculature is depicted follows closely the style used on Mycenaean ivories, such as one of the collection found on Delos (below). Note in particular the flame pattern on the rear legs in both examples (*after Kantor 1956*).

Another conundrum with wide-ranging ramifications is presented by a discovery made in 1979 at the Aramaean site of Tell Fakhariyah, only 2 kilometres from Tell Halaf. Near the edge of the ruined city, a farmer unearthed a life-size stone statue of an Assyrian official, bearing a bilingual inscription in Assyrian cuneiform and the Aramaean alphabet.[48] The texts announce its dedicator to be one Adad-it'i, son of Shamash-nuri; in the Assyrian text they are described as governors of Guzan (the Assyrian province which centred on Tell Halaf), while the Aramaean inscription simply refers to them as 'king'. Circumstantial evidence leaves little doubt that this Shamash-nuri was the same official as that given in the Assyrian Eponym List for the year 866 BC.[49]

The inscribed statue, accordingly, was made some time in the mid-9th century BC. So far, so good. However, the Aramaean text on the same statue raises an enormous problem. In the opinion of the eminent palaeographer Joseph Naveh,[50] the Tell Fakhariyah script belongs to the 11th-century 'Proto-Canaanite group', as dated by the standard Egyptian chronology. Alan Millard, one of the team responsible for the publication of the Tell Fakhariyah statue, naturally took a different view. While he agreed that the script has a 'very archaic appearance' he pointed to some features which might suggest a date later than the 11th century BC – including the extraordinary resemblance of the Tell Fakhariyah letters to those of the 8th-century BC Greek alphabet.[51]

Naveh, however, argues an 11th-century BC origin for the Greek alphabet – and thus the contentious statue has now taken centre stage in the unsolved controversy over the dating of the earliest Greek alphabet (see Chapters 4 and 10). Despite the apparent 9th-century BC fix provided by the Assyrian text, Naveh (supported by Cross) is adamant that the Tell Fakhariyah script belongs to the 11th century BC. Stephen Kaufman, in a balanced review of the problem, neatly summarized the paradox it presents:

> Given the weight of the evidence pointing toward, if not demanding, a ninth century date for the Fakhariyah statue, how is one to accommodate such a dating to the apparent eleventh century character of the script of the inscription? What has to 'give'?[52]

Kaufman provided no real answer to the problem.[53] Unknown to him, the factor which can 'give' is the Egyptian chronology, which through the dates it provides for Semitic palaeography comes into direct conflict with Assyrian chronology at Tell Fakhariyah. Like the problem of Tell Halaf, the apparent paradox of the Tell Fakhariyah inscription disappears once we revise Egyptian chronology.[54]

Babylonia the illiterate?

Babylonian archaeology has never produced an equivalent of the grand Assyrian King List. Partial lists have been discovered, but in contrast to the Assyrian practice of arranging monarchs in a single line, the Babylonians structured their history into dynasties, named after the ruling family or their place of origin (like the British Houses of Stuart or Hanover). As collated by modern historians, they form a sequence which runs from the Persian Empire, back through the 8th-century BC Nabonassar (of Ptolemy's Canon), through various short dynasties, then, via the Kassite kings of the Late Bronze Age, to the famous law-giver Hammurabi of the 1st Dynasty of Babylon.

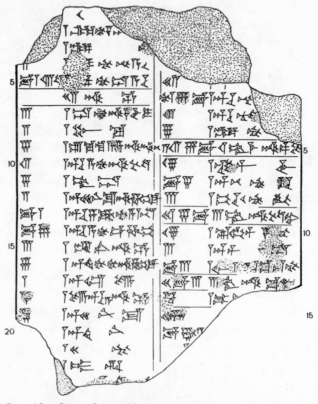

FIG. 11:5   One side of cuneiform tablet (CT 33332) giving the text known as 'Babylonian King List A'. Each column gives the name of a king, preceded by the number of years which he reigned. The horizontal lines mark summaries where the total length of each dynasty is given. The left-hand column lists the kings of Babylon from the mid-8th to early 7th centuries, including the Assyrian conquerors Sargon, Sennacherib and Esarhaddon. The right-hand column and the other side of the tablet give fragmentary sequences from earlier dynasties (*courtesy of British Museum*).

The dynastic sequence by itself, however, cannot provide an absolute chronology. The reign-lengths of many kings are unknown, while the two available lists covering the Kassite period are extremely fragmentary. Further, like the Third Intermediate Period in Egypt, evidence is often lacking about the exact relationships between the dynasties; some may have overlapped, ruling simultaneously from different power centres, such as the great cities of Babylon and Isin or the 'Sealand' region of the Arabian Gulf.

In Egypt, archaeologists turned to Sothic dating to provide an absolute framework. Similar attempts have repeatedly been made to date the 1st Dynasty of Babylon by using astronomical data to provide a 'fixed' point. Yet none of these efforts can truthfully be described as successful (see Appendix 3). During the 2nd and early 1st millennia it is the connections with Egyptian and Assyrian history which really provide the absolute dates for Babylonia (see Appendix 4). For example, it is known that Kashtiliash, one of the last kings of the Kassite Dynasty, was removed from the throne by Tukulti-Ninurta's conquest of Babylon, presently dated to 1235 BC. Other links are given by Assyrian records and the *Synchronistic History*, a digest of Assyro-Babylonian relations over several centuries.[55]

Thus the conventional dates for Babylonia before the 8th century BC are actually a product of the Assyrian King-List chronology and the Egyptian Sothic-based chronology. The result is a suspiciously familiar scenario, described as follows by John Brinkman, the leading authority on the 'Post-Kassite' period:

> Babylonian history during the first quarter of the first millennium B.C. may be characterized as a period of obscurity or 'dark age', with the land frequently overrun by foreign invaders and with the central government often unable to assert its jurisdiction in many areas. Little source material has survived from these turbulent times, and this little is sometimes quite difficult to date.[56]

The term 'Dark Age' seems like an understatement when the archaeological remains from Babylonia usually dated between c. 1050 and 750 BC are examined. Even the most important cities show little trace of activity over this long period. After flourishing under the Kassite kings of the 15th to 14th centuries BC, the great city of Ur waned a little in importance, but there is enough evidence, both written and archaeological, to trace its history down to the mid-11th century BC. The last remains from this period consist of some inscribed bricks of King Adad-apla-iddina (1068–1047 BC). Then the documentary record becomes a complete blank over a period of something like 350 years; archaeological remains are equally elusive.[57] Ur returns to well-documented history and archaeology only at the end of the 8th century BC. Similarly, at Uruk, which survived as a major religious centre from Sumerian to Hellenistic times, there is nothing to fill the gulf between the 12th-century BC Kassites and the renaissance of the city under the 8th-century BC Chaldaean domination.[58]

An equally bleak picture is related by Brinkman for the whole country:

> Archaeological sources are . . . meagre. Architectural remains which may belong to this time are usually minor repairs on older structures, with no inscription left to record the identity of the repairer. (In fact, no buildings have yet been excavated in Babylonia which can be dated with certainty to the time of any ruler between 1046 and 722 B.C.)[59]

Over the last forty years several regions of Babylonia have been surveyed to determine how settlement patterns changed throughout its history.[60] The major technique used has been the systematic collection of pottery sherds available from the surface. Such sampling, once put through the mill of statistical analysis, can reveal a broad profile of settlement, including areas away from the major urban centres. For most periods of Babylonian history the results have been very productive; for the Post-Kassite period, however, the work ran into difficulty. The problem confronting the archaeologists was that it was almost impossible to identify any pottery styles characteristic of the Dark Age. The little material which might belong to it was hard to distinguish from Kassite wares.[61] With such scanty data the conclusion was inevitable that this was 'the low point of urban settlement in Babylonia during historical times'.[62] The sheer exasperation which the search for remains of Post-Kassite times produced can be judged from the following comment by the leading fieldworker Robert Adams:

> . . . [it] remains a little-known intercalary period, with attitudes towards its limited cultural attainments aptly summarized by casual reference to it among fieldworkers as the 'V.D.' (Various Dynasties) period.[63]

The later Babylonian lists enumerating the 'various dynasties' of this period provide little consolation. For many kings there is no contemporary evidence even to substantiate their existence:

For the ancient historian, who traditionally relies on written sources for the main outlines of his presentation, this period offers a disappointing dearth of material. To date, fewer than sixty texts are known which originated in Babylonia during these two and half centuries [*c.* 1000–750 BC]. Of these, more than thirty are very short inscriptions on 'Luristan bronzes', which usually bear one or two lines of text giving the name of the king or the private person and sometimes his title or genealogy; two thirds of these jejune inscriptions duplicate one another.[64]

Brinkman's figure of sixty documents from the Babylonian Dark Age is reduced to an abysmally small number when one considers that the Luristan bronzes, representing more than half the texts, were apparently found outside Babylonia itself, in the Zagros mountains to the east (in modern Iran). This poverty of written material is remarkable: cuneiform texts from other periods of Babylonian history are usually numbered by the thousand. No fewer than 12,000 texts are known from the preceding Kassite period (thought to have lasted about 500 years).[65]

Are we really to believe that the Babylonians wrote almost nothing for some 250 years? Or have the records from this time simply perished? This possibility can be discounted completely. By its very nature cuneiform was never written on perishable materials such as parchment or papyrus. Clay is the only really suitable medium for the script, written by impressing a series of wedge shapes into wet clay with a stylus. Baked tablets can last almost indefinitely. Stone and metal, often used for precious objects or official inscriptions, are, of course, even more durable.

The equally remote possibility of deliberate destruction has to be considered, because of a curious legend recorded by the Hellenistic chronicler Berossus in the 3rd century BC:

> Nabonasaros collected together and destroyed the records of the kings before him in order that the list of the Chaldaean kings might begin with him.[66]

Even if Nabonassar (747–734 BC) had attempted to erase the evidence of his predecessors, it is inconceivable that he could have destroyed not only their royal inscriptions, but also every economic and private document mentioning them from the whole of Babylonia. This unlikely story may instead reflect a real problem encoun-

tered by Berossus and his contemporaries.[67] Like modern historians
they may have searched vainly for records from the long period
thought to lie between the Kassite Dynasty and the time of
Nabonassar. The legend of this king's purge may be the ancient
Babylonian attempt to explain an apparent gap in their history.[68]

The scarcity of documents from the Post-Kassite period poses yet
another riddle. Given the tiny number of surviving texts, how
could literacy have been preserved at all? Babylonia, from the 8th
century BC onwards, was widely respected by its contemporaries
(including the Assyrians, Hebrews and Greeks) as a centre of
literature, possessing an immense corpus of written knowledge
from mathematics and astronomy to medicine and philosophy.
Writing, introduced by the Sumerians as long ago as 4000 BC,
formed the very basis of the carefully ordered Babylonian society,
dependent on its day-to-day records of business transactions, sales
of land, wills, loans of money etc. How the complex Babylonian
administrative or commercial systems could have survived for so
long with so few written documents is simply unfathomable.

An 'occupational enigma' in the Arabian Gulf

The mystery of the Post-Kassite Dark Age extends southwards
from Babylonia to the Arabian Gulf. Here, the coasts and islands of
north-eastern Arabia were home to a civilization almost as old as the
Sumerians themselves.[69] Myths referring to the area of Bahrain as
the 'pure', 'holy' land of Dilmun, the equivalent, or even prototype, of the biblical Garden of Eden,[70] might suggest an ancestral
connection between the Sumerians and the Gulf. Another tradition,
recorded by the Greek historian Herodotus, that the Phoenician
traders of the Lebanon were ancient colonists from the Gulf, has
been recently reconsidered in the light of archaeological finds
suggesting contact between the two regions during the Early
Bronze Age.[71]

From the 4th millennium BC onwards there is evidence from the
Gulf for rich communities of seafaring merchants thriving on the
trade routes between Mesopotamia, Africa and India. During the
Late Bronze Age, Bahrain, in particular, continued to prosper.
Activity from this period is represented by numerous burials,
surface finds and Level III at Qal'at, the island's main archaeological
site.[72] The settlement here spread over a large area, producing texts

with Kassite royal names and pottery closely resembling Kassite-
Babylonian ware. Together with the evidence of letters and inscrip-
tions mentioning Kassite governors of Dilmun, the finds show that
Bahrain was under Kassite control during the 15th to 13th centuries
BC.[73]

Then, in the late 12th century BC, the region vanishes from
history, reappearing again only in Late Assyrian times.[74] Given the
scarcity of Babylonian texts from this period, it is hardly surprising
that references to Dilmun cease, but documentation of all kinds also
disappears in the Gulf region itself. Between Kassite-period Qal'at
III and the 8th century BC there is supposedly a long lacuna at the
site, aptly described by the current excavators as 'an occupational
enigma'.[75]

Evidence of an intermediate phase between Qal'at III and the
renewed settlement of the late 8th century BC has been discovered
recently, but the finds are puzzling. They occur above the remains
of the Kassite period, after traces of abandonment, and immediately
below those of Qal'at V, with 8th to 7th-century Assyrian connections. It might have been deduced from this that the new intermediate phase (labelled Qal'at IV) belonged to the 9th or early 8th

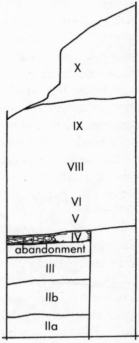

FIG. 11:6   Section from Qal'at, Bahrain. In
descending order the levels represent the
Islamic (X), Sassanian (IX), and Parthian to
Seleucid (VIII) periods. VI is the Neo-
Babylonian level and V the Neo-Assyrian (8th
century). Immediately below this is the
recently identified phase IV, separated from the
Kassite levels of the 13th century and before (III
and II) by a brief period of abandonment (*after
Kervran et al. 1987*).

centuries BC. Yet the pottery, alongside new forms showing Arabian influence, includes ware which directly continues the Kassite repertoire, showing that the Level IV material belongs to the beginning of the occupational gap. Comparison with other Mesopotamian ceramics also suggests a 12th to 11th-century date.[76] These chronological conclusions leave a paradox: where the pottery shows continuity (between Qal'at III and IV) the stratigraphic evidence suggests a short interruption; but where there is supposed to be a long period of abandonment (between IV and V) no sterile layer can be traced.

Archaeology in the Arabian Gulf is admittedly still in its infancy. Yet the evidence available so far falls, almost predictably for an area ultimately dependent on Assyria and Egypt for its chronology, into a classic Dark Age pattern.

The fractured past of early Iran

The dependence on an Assyrian-based chronology also extends eastward, to Iran. Here, centuries of contact with Babylonia resulted in the crystallization of a quasi-Mesopotamian state in the foothills of the Zagros mountain range, with cities using cuneiform writing, ziggurats, cylinder seals and other familiar trappings of Babylonian culture. Nonetheless, Elam, as this kingdom was known by the 2nd millennium BC, remained a distinctive and vigorously independent civilization, the most important eastern rival to the imperial ambitions of Babylonia and Assyria throughout the Late Bronze and Iron Ages.

After the crushing blows dealt by Assyrian and Babylonian invasions in 646 BC and 596/595 BC, Elam was eventually absorbed by a hitherto unimportant people called the Parsua (Persians). Susa, once the capital of the Elamite kings, became the administrative centre of Persia. As a result Elam played a small but significant role in the transformation of Persia from a tiny Iranian state to an empire of almost global scope. Elam's integration into the kingdom of the Persians meant that they were familiar with Mesopotamian-style culture, including the use of cuneiform script, perhaps even before their conquest of Babylon in 539 BC. Elamite was still a primary language for the state inscriptions of the Achaemenid kings in the 5th century BC, when the Empire stretched from the Balkans to India.[77]

From both native records and Assyro-Babylonian sources, a history of Elam has been reconstructed, for the Bronze Age up to the invasion of Nebuchadrezzar I of Babylon around 1105 BC, and for the later Iron Age after c. 800 BC. Yet between these two periods '300 years of silence' are supposed to have descended on Elam.[78] René Labat, in the Cambridge Ancient History, describes the extraordinary picture of Elamite history imposed by its dependence on the accepted Mesopotamian chronology:

> . . as a political power Elam was finished. This period was followed by a dark age of three centuries, during which there are no native texts nor are there allusions to Elam in the Mesopotamian sources. Undoubtedly broken up internally, Elam was not to be mentioned again until 821 BC when Elamite, Chaldaean and Aramaean troops were defeated by the Assyrian king Shamshi-Adad V.[79]

Explanations of this curious state of affairs vary considerably. The historian Elizabeth Carter rejected Labat's understanding that Elam was 'broken up internally'. Since the 'Neo-Elamite' civilization of the 8th century BC onwards was clearly a continuation from the Late Bronze Age 'Middle Elamite', Carter felt unable to accept that the country 'underwent sudden and utter collapse'. Yet she was at a loss to provide an alternative explanation:

> . . . the historical realities behind the documentary eclipse, as well as the chronological and circumstantial connections between the end of the Middle Elamite monarchy and first-millennium population changes in Iran, have yet to be ascertained.[80]

Attempts to fill this historical lacuna by reference to the archaeological record have met with little success. The Middle Elamite period of powerful Late Bronze Age dynasties, down to c. 1100 BC, is well represented by material remains, as is the Neo-Elamite civilization of the 8th–7th centuries BC. But the dating of the intervening period, labelled Neo-Elamite I, is fraught with chronological problems. The original scheme proposed by leading specialist Pierre de Miroschedji actually left an ugly gap of 100 years in the sequence – between the end of Middle and the beginning of Neo-Elamite I culture. To avoid this he tried to rationalize the chronology by extending the Middle Elamite period down to 1000 BC – a modification unsupported by textual evidence – in order to meet his dates for Neo-Elamite I (1000–725/700 BC).[81]

Even with de Miroschedji's revision the accepted scheme faces serious difficulties. Excavations at the important Ville Royale II site at Susa uncovered a series of levels spanning the latter 2nd and early 1st millennia BC. Level 11 contained numerous examples of 'Elamite goblets', a ware characteristic of the Middle Elamite period. In the succeeding Level 10, these vessels continue to be found, though in smaller amounts, while their shape became very elongated and the fabric much coarser. As Level 10 followed 11 without interruption, de Miroschedji assigned it to the last phase of his Middle Elamite, c. 1100–1000 BC.[82] Yet similar elongated goblets were found at the nearby site of Choga Zanbil, in a destruction level dated by its excavator R. Ghirshman to the Assyrian invasion of Elam in 647/646 BC[83] – a context several hundred years later than that suggested by the Susa finds. De Miroschedji was forced to reject Ghirshman's dating in order to follow the evidence linking the pottery to a much earlier period.

The high dates for the end of Middle Elamite civilization followed by de Miroschedji and most other scholars require the intermediary Neo-Elamite I phase to cover up to 300 years. In the excavations at Ville Royale II this long period is represented only by 'fragmentary surfaces and rooms'. Indeed, 'the archaeological evidence for the Neo-Elamite period in Susa is scant. Even less is known of the surrounding countryside.'[84] Identifying the characteristic pottery of Neo-Elamite I has evidently caused great difficulty; it 'has only recently been described and very few finds datable to c. 1000–725/700 B.C. are known'.[85] Other material remains are equally elusive:

> No stratified seals or sealings of the Neo-Elamite I period exist and even unstratified finds that can be reasonably assigned to that period on stylistic grounds are few and far between.[86]

The region of Luristan, which lies to the north of Elam in the Zagros mountains, has been poorly explored archaeologically. Even so it has provided, mainly through the unofficial 'excavations' of its highland tribesmen, one of the richest collections of metallurgical finds from the entire ancient Near East. The pieces include daggers, axes, hammers, belts, human and animal figurines, horse brasses, bracelets, pendants and other jewellery – often intricately decorated with mythological scenes or fantastic creatures, and all of superb craftsmanship. Since most of these pieces became available for study only after trickling through the hands of local antiquities dealers, it has to be taken on trust that they all come from sites in Luristan. All the same, enough of the bronzes form a group stylistically homogeneous enough to justify the term 'Luristan Bronzes'. But the lack of archaeological context means that they pose a particularly difficult problem for specialists in the development and typology of ancient metalwork. While a number of examples belonging to the group have now been excavated from a few sites, largely cemeteries, these have proved to be almost as difficult to date as the bronzes themselves.[87]

FIG. 11:7 Fantastic figures depicted on a bronze quiver from Luristan. Like all the enigmatic bronzes from this region its dating is uncertain; dates suggested for this object range from 1100 to 500 BC (*after Muscarella 1988c*).

Some of the bronzes, principally daggers, bear the names of Babylonian kings (fourteen in all) who are dated by the conventional Mesopotamian chronology to between 1132 and 944 BC.[88] Yet the texts were incised on the weapons subsequent to their manufacture, leaving the possibility that they may have been added much later. Indeed, because of the Kassite influence apparent in their decoration, the French chronologist Claude Schaeffer ascribed the bulk of the Luristan Bronzes to 1500–1200 BC, leaving only a few pieces with Assyrianizing designs for the Early Iron Age.[89] Strikingly different dates for the collection as a whole have been offered by other scholars. Ghirshman, concentrating on the parallels offered by Late Assyrian art, dated them to the 8th century BC, while Kantor placed some pieces in the 7th century BC and others even as late as the Persian period (6th century BC onwards).[90] Such low estimates contrast strangely with the 12th to 10th-century dates presently assigned to the Babylonian kings whose names appear on some of the weapons.

No consensus has ever been reached regarding the date of the collection, many archaeologists accepting the unhappy comprom-ise that the bronzes were manufactured over a period of a thousand years or so.[91] The Luristan conundrum, while it may present special problems of its own, thus seems to typify the general difficulty in dating archaeological remains from the Post-Kassite period, in both Iran and Mesopotamia.

Climate and chronology

The Dark Ages of 1st-millennium Mesopotamia and its dependent regions, once neglected as something of a 'non'-period, are now receiving increasing attention. Brinkman's extensive studies of Kassite and Post-Kassite Babylonia prepared the ground by assembling the complete range of literary evidence available; at the same time, they have revealed the full implications which the conventional chronology holds for our understanding of Babylo-nian history. Field archaeologists have made repeated efforts to identify remains from this period, but with frustrating results. New excavations in the Arabian Gulf have found evidence which goes some way to filling the archaeological hiatus there, but the finds are almost impossible to interpret within the confines of the traditional chronology.

Most recently an attempt has been made to explain the existence of the Mesopotamian Dark Age in terms of a climatic catastrophe. A joint study by meteorologist J. Neumann and Assyriologist S. Parpola developed the theory that the decline of both Assyria and Babylonia in the early 1st millennium was due to a protracted drought. Their primary evidence is literary – from the meagre records dated between 1200 and 900 BC and later texts referring to this period. The documents contain several references to bad har-vests, high grain prices, and famines – according to a late chronicle, the Assyrians were even driven to cannibalism during the reign of Tiglath-pileser I. As a contrast, they have assembled numerous Assyrian texts of the 8th–7th centuries BC which describe heavy rainfall, snow, swollen rivers and floods.[92]

Physical traces of this climatic upheaval were sought by Neumann and Parpola in palaeoclimatic studies, which suggest a widespread period of drought towards the beginning of the 1st millennium BC. In most cases, however, it is difficult, if not impossible, to correlate the data with the historical record. The most certain evidence comes from Ugarit on the north Syrian coast, where the latest Bronze Age buildings were embedded in a layer of pale, powdery soil, contrasting with darker, richer layers both above and below it.[93]

Modern rainfall records suggest that north Syria and Mesopotamia share very similar weather patterns. Assuming that the same conditions prevailed in the past, it is reasonable to link the Ugaritic evidence with the (albeit patchy) literary record from Mesopotamia. The sharp drop in rainfall which Neumann and Parpola envisage could have destabilized the urban states of Mesopotamia and, at the same time, encouraged the incursion of Aramaeans and other semi-nomadic peoples from the desert fringe into the 'Land of the Two Rivers'. Their conclusion is that: 'the dramatic political, military, and socio-economic setbacks of Assyria and Babylonia during these "dark centuries" were ultimately due to an adverse change in climate'.[94]

The overall case for a period of drought in several areas of the Eastern Mediterranean and Near East at the beginning of the Early Iron Age cannot be ignored: a climatic upheaval may well have played a role in the collapse of the Late Bronze Age civilizations in this region (see Chapter 13). All the same, it is difficult to escape the impression that the real ailment affecting Mesopotamian history and archaeology is one of chronology. Drought cannot explain why the 9th-century BC Aramaeans used Late Bronze Age motifs in their sculpture and an alphabet which was two centuries out of date; why there are no discernible developments in Assyrian art, religion and literature between the 12th and 10th centuries BC and why there is so little datable material from these centuries; how the Babylonians maintained a literate society through a period of 300 years which has only sixty texts to offer; or how a similar feat was achieved in Elam where no texts at all have been recovered for the same span of time; and, indeed, how and why there was overall cultural continuity in areas such as southern Mesopotamia and the Arabian Gulf from around 1100 to 800 BC, when there are barely any settlement remains.

A strong whiff of unreality pervades the accepted scheme of Mesopotamian history during the Dark Age. A shorter time-scale, as is shown by every other region examined, would seem to be the only solution capable of restoring a realistic focus on the evidence. At this stage, the one remaining obstacle to constructing a rational chronology for the ancient world would appear to be the monolithic King List recorded by the ancient Assyrians, backbone of the accepted Mesopotamian dating system.

CHAPTER 12

The Exaggeration of Antiquity

In the 1st century AD the Jewish historian Josephus composed a lengthy rejoinder to the anti-Semitic diatribes penned by contemporary Greek writers.[1] Surprisingly, Josephus's primary aim was not to answer claims that the Jews were decadent or corrupt, but the accusation that they were a 'young' people, only recently arrived on the stage of Mediterranean history. Josephus demonstrated, through a skilful use of the Egyptian, Babylonian, Phoenician and other sources available to him, that the Jews could claim a far longer history, documented by written records, than the Greeks. Honour, to the best of our knowledge, was then satisfied.

One of the most extraordinary stories recorded by the Greek 'Father of History' Herodotus (c. 440 BC) concerns a bizarre anthropological experiment conducted by King Psamtik of Egypt (664–610 BC). He arranged for two newly born babies to be confined in a remote location, isolated from any contact with the outside world except for a shepherd, who was commanded to feed them but never to utter a word in their presence. The theory was that the first words spoken by the children would provide objective evidence of the natural language of mankind. It would show which tongue, and therefore which people, was the 'oldest'.[2] The outcome, that after two years one child bleated the Phrygian word for bread, *bekos*, is of no consequence. What is of interest is that, according to Herodotus, there was a competition taking place in the 7th century BC between the Egyptians and their neighbours over which was the senior nation.

These two cases highlight a factor frequently overlooked in modern studies of ancient historiography[3] – the desire to claim and demonstrate a venerable antiquity. This oversight is odd, given that the urge is no stranger to the 20th century. Not long ago German historians were diligently falsifying and inventing history in order to prove the seniority of an ancestral, and imaginary, master race. Elizabethan scholars not only promulgated the idea that the Tudor monarchy descended directly from King Arthur, but also that he had subdued Greenland, so providing a 'legitimate' counterweight to the claims of Spain and Portugal to the New World as a whole.[4]

The motives behind such efforts are best expressed by the old adage 'first come, first served', whether the desired goal is control over economic resources, precedence over territorial rights, or power in any other shape or form.

A dynastic race?

A desire to claim seniority over neighbouring races can be seen in the inflated estimates given by many ancient peoples for their national histories. When the Greek politician Solon visited Egypt in the 6th century BC he was chided by a priest of Sais when he tried to recount the history of his country: 'Oh Solon, you Greeks are all children, and there's no such thing as an old Greek!' The priest explained that while Greece had no written records except for the most recent events, Egyptian archives spanned 8000 years, from the time when their institutions were first created.[5] In the following century Herodotus visited the country and was told that the Egyptians had a recorded history stretching over 382 generations back to the first king of Egypt – he calculated from this that their history began no less than 11,340 years before his time.[6]

Equally exaggerated figures are found in the works of the later chroniclers who played a major role in shaping our understanding of Near Eastern and Egyptian chronology. The history written by the Babylonian priest Berossus in the 3rd century BC includes claims of the most fantastic antiquity. After the time of the Flood, according to Berossus, a dynasty of eighty-six kings ruled for no less than 33,091 years.[7] His contemporary, the Egyptian priest Manetho, produced an epoch of similar length for the earliest, divine, rulers of Egypt. Professor W. G. Waddell, compiler of the standard edition of Manetho, suggested that:

> The works of Manetho and Berossus may be interpreted as an expression of the rivalry of the two kings, Ptolemy and Antiochus, each seeking to proclaim the great antiquity of his land.[8]

Since the original writings of Manetho are lost, as are those of Berossus, it is impossible to see how far the desire to exaggerate may have affected his work. Nevertheless, it is clear that his system of dynasties was used subsequently by Graeco-Roman scholars to produce a misleadingly long Egyptian history. It was easy to overestimate its duration by assuming that the dynasties Manetho listed all reigned consecutively. While some overlaps between them have had to be accepted by modern scholarship, reluctance to abandon the original sequence has been a major contributory factor to the inflated length given to the Third Intermediate Period (see Chapter 10).

The Assyrian view of the past

While the exaggerations of the Hellenistic chroniclers are generally admitted, a more trusting attitude is generally adopted towards chronological source material which has been excavated – such as the cuneiform tablets which give the Assyrian King List on which the modern chronology for Mesopotamia depends. Of the three surviving versions, the principal one, from Khorsabad, can be dated exactly to 738 BC. The copy housed by the Seventh Day Adventist Seminary must be somewhat later, as it finishes with Shalmaneser V (726–722 BC). The third, or 'Nassouhi List', ends with the reign of Tiglath-pileser II (966–935 BC); it has therefore been dated two centuries earlier than the other copies, though this is only an assumption.[9] Thus all are relatively late texts, the products of an attempt by Assyrian scholars to give some structure to their country's past – reason enough in itself to take their chronological statements for much earlier periods with a pinch of salt.

There is ample evidence to show that the 'dates' given by the ancient Mesopotamians for their own history were often wide of the mark. An inscription of the 6th-century Babylonian King Nabonidus states that the famous King Hammurabi reigned 700 years before Burnaburiash, while modern reckoning separates them by some 300 years. Nabonidus also claimed that 3200 years elapsed between his own time and that of King Naram-Sin of the Akkad Dynasty.[10] This would place Naram-Sin c. 3750 BC, a full 1500 years older than any modern estimate! Albright argued that Nabonidus's calculation for the date of the Akkad Dynasty agreed with, and was probably borrowed from, that of the scholars employed at the court of the 8th-century Assyrian King Sargon II.[11]

It is hard to discern the exact reasoning behind such estimates, although a significant factor seems to have been calculations based on astrological cycles.[12] It is fair to say that there is no evidence that the Assyrians and Babylonians had any use for, or indeed concept of, historiography in the modern sense of the impartial recording of history. Even the laconic and dry jottings of the late Babylonian chronicles may have been written in the service of astrology, which needed dated records of events in order to calculate when similar happenings would recur.[13] As J. Lewy noted, the Assyrians shared this world view, in which cycles played a paramount role:

> The Assyrians' interest in history . . . was prompted by the belief in the periodic recurrence of historical events. This belief, in turn, was based to all appearances on the assumption of an interconnexion of events on earth and the motion of the stars: since, owing to the large planetary periods, certain heavenly constellations recur at periodic intervals, events on earth were expected to repeat themselves periodically.[14]

The auspicious time for rebuilding an Assyrian temple was therefore when the 'correct' number of years was believed, or claimed, to have elapsed since its last restoration. The determination of such periods of time was certainly one of the motives behind the Assyrian interest in chronology.

Whatever the case, it is also important to note that there were variant chronological systems available to the Assyrians. An informative comparison can be made between the figures given by two Assyrian monarchs, Shalmaneser I (conventionally 13th century BC) and Esarhaddon (7th century BC), for the history of the Temple of Assur. This was founded by the early king Ushpia, then successively restored over the centuries by kings Erishu, Shamshi-Adad I, Shalmaneser I and Esarhaddon.[15] The two documents are in accord with respect to the first period mentioned (Ushpia to Erishu), in that no figure is given. Otherwise they disagree. For the second interval (Erishu to Shamshi-Adad) there are contrasting figures of 126 (Esarhaddon) and 159 (Shalmaneser) years. For the third period (Shamshi-Adad to Shalmaneser), Esarhaddon gave 434 years, while Shalmaneser himself recorded 580 years.[16] It is interesting to note that Esarhaddon's final figure, for the time that had elapsed between himself and Shalmaneser, is also 580 years, again raising the suspicion that a numerological interest was involved in such estimates.

Nevertheless, many of the periods of time given by the Assyrians have been accepted as factual by modern historians.[17] For example, considerable weight has been given to Sennacherib's claim that an event 418 years before his conquest of Babylon took place in the

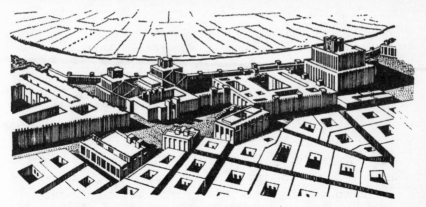

FIG. 12:1   Reconstruction of the northern part of the city of Assur by Walter Andrae (*after Frankfort 1969*).

reign of Tiglath-pileser I (see Chapter 11). The figure agrees perfectly with the conventional Assyrian chronology, yet this is hardly surprising. It shows only that the ancient scholars who made this calculation were using the same figures as those in the surviving Assyrian King List.[18] The date given by Sennacherib for Tukulti-Ninurta I is, on the other hand, some sixty years higher than that provided by the King List,[19] showing again the existence of variant chronologies. Clearly, none of these ancient 'dates' can be used as a genuine check on the extant King List.

The purpose of the Assyrian King List

Because the Kinglist preserves a detailed series of Assyrian rulers, their genealogies, and their lengths of reign which is supposed to be complete for more than a millennium preceding 722 B.C. and because it is the only text which provides such a skeleton essential to all historical work, there has been an understandable tendency on the part of historians to utilize this evidence gratefully, sometimes with little critical examination.[20]

Thus wrote Brinkman, the leading authority on Mesopotamian chronology. The chronology provided by the Assyrian King List is convenient, but an important question is too often overlooked by those who, somewhat naïvely, take its testimony at face value: why did the Assyrians, who clearly did not share the modern view of history, compile their King List?

A recent paper by David Henige introduced a wide range of anthropological and ethnographic data to the study of ancient Near Eastern king lists, concluding as follows: 'The chronological recollection and reconstruction of the past can be approached on at least four levels: as myth, symbol, charter, and calendar.'[21] Henige's challenging study recommends a comparative, as well as a far more critical, approach to chronological traditions such as the Assyrian King List. Understanding the function it held for the society which created it is a prerequisite to a study of its chronological information.

One cannot impute to the Assyrians a straightforward desire to exaggerate simply for its own sake. While there may well have been a degree of rivalry with other kingdoms (such as Babylonia) over which held seniority, this was never explicitly stated. However, very similar motives emerge from a closer study of the historical value of the Assyrian King List.

The list begins with '17 kings living in tents', the first twelve names of which correspond to those beginning the Babylonian 'Genealogy of the Hammurabi Dynasty';[22] eight of the royal names included are actually those of tribes or geographical areas. Consequently, the earliest section is generally accepted as being an 'artificial construct', the purpose of which was to 'provide the founder of Assur's independence with a genealogy linking him to the Amorite tribes that swept all over Mesopotamia upon the fall of Ur'.[23] The next part of the document gives a genealogy of ten royal Assyrian ancestors for Shamshi-Adad I. William Hallo assessed its value:

> As it stands, the section is a patent fiction: Shamshi-Adad was not a descendant of Ushpia as stated in it, nor a native Assyrian who ruled a great empire with Assur as its capital . . .[24]

The next section begins the King List proper, giving the royal succession through the attested Dynasty of Puzur-Assur I to the successors of Shamshi-Adad I, including a fictional genealogical link which makes Naram-Sin the son of Puzur-Assur II.[25] According to Hallo, this 'patriarchal age' of Assyrian history (down to c. 1700 BC), when reconstructed 'as objectively as possible from contemporaneous documents . . . bears only a minimal resemblance to the historiographical reconstruction of the later Assyrian scribes'.[26] Thus the King List tradition for the earlier period is of

FIG. 12:2   Stela showing Hammurabi, the
great law-giver of the 1st Dynasty of
Babylon, receiving his laws from the Sun-
god. The names of his forebears, as given
by Babylonian traditions, were grafted on
to the beginning of the King List of
Assyrian monarchs in order to give them a
more respectable ancestry (*from Breasted
1916*).

great interest but of little chronological value.

It is really only after *c.* 1700 BC (beginning with the dynasty of
Adasi) that the King List is regarded as a serious historical source,
one which constitutes 'the chronological corner-stone of later
Assyrian historiography and enjoys to this day a high, if not
altogether deserved reputation among Assyriologists'.[27] Present
analyses thus tend to divide the King List into two halves: an early
ahistorical portion distinguishable (although the dividing line is
blurred) from the later, 'trustworthy' section which provides the
backbone of Near Eastern chronology down to the 8th century BC.

Apart from synchronisms with Egypt (see below), controls on
the validity of the later King List tradition are limited. Even so, the
available material, including contemporary royal inscriptions and
the internal evidence of the lists and their variants, provides certain
evidence that the surviving version of the King List has been
deliberately 'smoothed out' to give the impression of an unbroken
royal succession down to the 8th century BC. For example, the
names of several rulers are known who were for some reason
considered illegitimate by later kings and omitted from the canonical list.[28] The most significant example is Ili-hadda, attested as a king
of Assyria by a letter from the Babylonian ruler Adad-shuma-usur,
who wrote to the 'kings of Assyria' Assur-nirari and Ili-hadda.
Ili-hadda is agreed to have been a contemporary of Assur-nirari III
(1202–1197 BC).[29] He was known to the compilers of the King List,
but is mentioned only as the father of Ninurta-apil-Ekur
(1191–1179 BC) and not as a king in his own right. It seems highly
probable that there were other rulers whose inscriptional evidence
(if any) has been lost or was deliberately destroyed by subsequent
kings.

Other strategies were adopted by the compilers of the King List to give the impression of untroubled continuity. One was to imply ancestry by adjusting genealogical relationships. B. Landsberger has provided a valuable critique of the royal ancestries given in the later portions of the list. Arguing from inherent chronological improbabilities regarding the number of generations given between kings 48 and 71 (conventionally 17th and early 14th centuries), he concluded that the tradition incorrectly describes no fewer than eleven rulers as 'son' of their predecessors when they were actually brothers.[30] Brinkman agrees that:

> . . . half the genealogical attributions of this section of the Assyrian Kinglist are likely to be erroneous. For these reasons, it is probably unsafe to accept genealogical statements of the Assyrian Kinglist as true without supporting evidence . . . Especially for kings in the second millennium.[31]

Brinkman notes seven kings of the later 2nd and 1st millennia BC whose parentage is given differently in contemporary royal inscriptions or in the three versions of the King List.[32] A cluster of such anomalies occurs in the period shortly before Assuruballit I (1365–1330 BC): three of his royal predecessors are given an incorrect parentage. Thus one can reconstruct two quite different genealogies for Assuruballit's family from the evidence of the monuments and the King List.[33] Another case occurs as late as the mid-8th century BC: Tiglath-pileser III is given as the son of his predecessor Assur-nirari V when one of his own inscriptions shows he was actually the son of Adad-nirari III.[34] This 'error' is remarkable, as the King List recording this is thought to have been written in the reign of his successor. Surely the compilers must have known that the parentage they gave for Tiglath-pileser III was false. Brinkman highlights other problems which cast doubt on the accuracy of the list: there are discrepancies regarding the reign-lengths of four kings, while one version omits Shalmaneser II (1030–1019 BC) altogether.[35]

In the light of such evidence for manipulation within the Assyrian King List tradition, its main purpose can be clearly defined. Hallo had this to say:

> Summing up a thousand years of Assyrian historiography as represented chiefly by King Lists and royal inscriptions, we may

say that its purpose was to stress the antiquity and continuity of Assyrian institutions: independence, seat and seed of kingship, and worship of the god Assur at the city named for him.[36]

Co-regencies and parallel dynasties

The compilers of the canonical Assyrian King List undoubtedly excluded certain rulers and invented genealogical links to present an illusion of continuity. From the point of view of chronology, what is needed is knowledge of other imperfections in the 'unbroken seed of kingship' which may have been masked by smoothing out the data. Some possibilities which would have major effects on the overall chronology of Mesopotamia merit close examination.

The practice of co-regencies between kings and their heirs, to ensure the succession and the stability of the state, seems to have been common in the ancient Near East. In some periods of Egyptian history (such as the Third Intermediate Period; see Chapter 10), it may have been the rule rather than the exception. The discovery of frequent co-regencies in Israel and Judah revealed the very principle enabling the development of a consistent chronology for the ancient Hebrew kings.[37]

In Mesopotamia no certain instances of co-regency have yet been identified, but there is some suggestive evidence. The curious double-datings known for some Kassite Babylonian kings[38] might lend themselves to such an interpretation. In Assyria, two possible co-regencies are indicated by a peculiarity contained in the mid-12th century section of the King List. After Assur-dan I (1178–1133 BC), his sons Ninurta-tukulti-Assur and Mutakkil-Nusku are mentioned as kings, but accorded no regnal years. Instead they are said to have 'ruled/held the throne *tuppisu*', an enigmatic phrase which is usually translated as an indeterminate period, or a short space of time less than a full year.[39] It is possible that they were assigned no regnal years because they ruled jointly with their father Assur-dan I, but died before they could succeed him.

A further co-regency, this time between Assur-dan I and his father, Ninurta-apil-Ekur (1191–1179 BC), is suggested by the discrepant reign-lengths given for these two rulers in different copies of the list. One gives Ninurta-apil-Ekur's reign as three years and another as thirteen, while Assur-dan I's reign is given as forty-six or thirty-six years. The current chronology favours the higher figures given for both kings, though Brinkman has allowed the possibility of following the lower figure given for Ninurta-apil-Ekur. The result would be a reduction in Assyrian chronology by ten years.[40] Brinkman did not, however, consider the obvious possibility of a ten-year co-regency as the explanation for the scribal variants. Conceivably, there were other such cases which have left no trace at all in the King List, given its tendency to present reigns as a series of consecutive and independent quantities.

Another possibility, which would have had even more acute effects on absolute chronology, is that the arrangement of the King List may mask the existence of more than one dynasty ruling in Assyria at the same time. The institution of dual monarchy is well attested in anthropological literature. In some cases two royal lines fulfil different functions (e.g. religious versus military), while in others it is more obvious geopolitical factors that bring about a division.[41] The custom of dual kingship merits considerable study and may have been a much more common phenomenon in the ancient world than is currently appreciated. Henige recommends testing two models within the Near East, one with two groups of rulers holding office simultaneously, the other with kingship being shared between more than one group by an 'alternating or rotational system'.[42]

In the King List the existence of parallel dynasties would have been disguised by presenting them as successive; historical or genealogical links between such dynasties may even have been added to give the succession verisimilitude. Indeed, such practices seem to have been standard tools of ancient Mesopotamian historiography. The Sumerian King List records the dynasties of Sumer from the earliest times to the 1st Dynasty of Isin, conventionally c. 2000–1800 BC. Named after different cities, they are listed consecutively: each entry ends with the formula '(dynasty) X was defeated (in battle), and its kingship was carried off to Y', while the document continues with the first ruler of the 'next' dynasty.[43] Yet controlling evidence has shown that most of the dynasties, 'if not all, were contemporaneous to a greater or lesser extent'.[44] The Sumerian King List by itself is actually worse than useless as a chronological source. Leo Oppenheim explained the political purpose of the document, composed in the reign of Utu-hegal of Uruk, as follows: 'To demonstrate that his country had always been united under one king – though these kings were ruling successively in different capitals . . . '[45]

The composition of the Sumerian and Assyrian king lists are separated by more than a millennium, as well as belonging to different cultural milieux, but the comparison may be instructive. Similar instances of the development of parallel reigns and dynasties into artificial sequences are known from other documents much closer in time to the period when the surviving copies of the King List were prepared. The *Babylonian Chronicle* describes Assyro-Babylonian relations from 747 to 668 BC.[46] It also contains notices of the accessions, deaths and lengths of reign of contemporary Elamite rulers, presented as a single series in chronological succession. However, as E. Carter and M. W. Stolper argue:

> There is reason to believe that this arrangement is procrustean; that early in the Neo-Elamite period, as was certainly true later, competing local rulers claimed the royal title in Elam simultaneously; that some kings listed in the Chronicle had longer local reigns than the Chronicle acknowledges.[47]

The so-called *Synchronistic Chronicle*, composed in Neo-Assyrian times, comprises two columns of names presenting the kings of Assyria and Babylonia, paired by lines drawn after their names to indicate that they were contemporary.[48] Arno Poebel recognized that the compiler must have drawn on an earlier version with more than two columns to accommodate periods when there were multiple Babylonian dynasties ruling at the same time.[49] The attempt to merge the Babylonian dynasties into a single sequence resulted in numerous problems, including the placement of Shamshi-Adad I's name next to no fewer than eight Babylonian kings! One can only agree with the view expressed by M. B. Rowton, 'that fundamentally what mattered in Mesopotamian chronology was the sequence of events, not the magnitude of the interval between them'.[50]

For Assyrian history itself, Poebel long ago drew attention to an interesting possibility which is particularly worthy of further investigation, as it falls in the period contemporary with the Eastern Mediterranean Dark Ages and the Egyptian Third Intermediate Period. He argued that on the death of Tukulti-Ninurta I (c. 1205 BC) Assyria may have fragmented into four separate kingdoms: under Assur-nadin-apli, Assurnasirpal and Enlil-kudurusur (all named as kings and sons of Tukulti-Ninurta in various sources) and Ili-hadda.[51] Assur-nadin-apli bore the rare title 'king of kings', which may indicate that he held 'some kind of suzerainty over the other principalities'. That there were still two separate Assyrian kingdoms during the reign of Assur-nadin-apli's son Assur-nirari (III) is shown by the extraordinary letter from the King of Babylonia addressed to both Assur-nirari and Ili-hadda as 'kings of Assyria'.

Apart from a grudging acceptance that Ili-hadda bore the title of king (in some form) alongside Assur-nirari III, Assyriology has not pursued Poebel's conclusion further. Accepting the version of history given by the King List, it is assumed that a single monarchy was restored after the death of Assur-nirari III, under Ili-hadda's son Ninurta-apil-Ekur. The King List states that Ninurta-apil-Ekur and Ili-hadda were descendants of the much earlier King Eriba-Adad (I), so presumably they sprang from a cadet branch of the Assyrian royal stock. It is assumed that the kingship now passed to this family, the line of Tukulti-Ninurta's descendants having died out. After this the King List presents a continuous royal line down to the 8th century BC. The genealogical links it gives can be confirmed from contemporary texts down to the sons of Tiglath-pileser I in the mid-11th century BC. After this point, however, independent confirmation is lacking and a difficult section of the King List has to be crossed before arriving at the safe ground provided by the reign of Adad-nirari II (911–891 BC) and the continuous eponym sequence.

This notoriously problematic part of the King List overlaps with the dark period of Assyrian archaeology during the 12th to 10th centuries BC (see Chapter 11). For more than a century documentation is extremely patchy. Two of the kings, whose reigns together amount to forty-seven years, left no inscriptions at all; they are known only from later material, principally the Assyrian King List.[52] Shalmaneser II (1030–1019 BC) and Tiglath-pileser II (966–935 BC) each have only a single stela,[53] and indeed Shalmaneser II is actually omitted from one version of the King List.[54] Other information is highly suspect, such as the list of eponyms for Assur-nirari IV (1018–1013 BC), a king who is otherwise known only from his mention in the King List. His entry in the eponym list reads: 'Assur-nirari, One after Assur-nirari, Second (after Assur-nirari)' and so on, with a summary 'Six years'.[55] During this period not a single piece of information regarding relations with Babylonia is known. As Brinkman notes, the 10th century 'is the longest stretch of time between 1350 and 610 B.C. for which no direct contacts between the two countries are recorded'.[56]

Indeed, there is nothing, apart from the testimony of the King List itself, to reassure us that the sequence after the sons of Tiglath-pileser I represents a line of kings holding sole rule over Assyria. It is tempting to suggest that this part of the list incorporates some obscure predecessors of Adad-nirari II, who reigned as a secondary line in the shadow of the more powerful Ili-hadda Dynasty; both lines may have been established in the confused period after Tukulti-Ninurta I's death. If the two were considered as overlapping dynasties, the result would be to shorten Assyrian chronology by some 110 years. The reign of Tiglath-pileser I, currently dated to 1115–1077 BC, would be redated to roughly 1010–970 BC. Significantly, this would bring him into line with our suggested revision of Hittite and Egyptian history. Tiglath-pileser I refers to a Hittite king, Ini-Teshub, who falls on the present chronology in the 'blank' period at Carchemish. On the evidence of Hittite genealogies we have redated Ini-Teshub, King of Carchemish, to the early years of the 10th century BC (see Chapter 6), and the synchronism between the two rulers can now be realized.

The following statement by Henige, while specifically directed at other materials, would seem to apply particularly well to the composition of the Assyrian King List:

> Manetho and the compiler(s) of the Sumerian King List did not devise their structures primarily with chronological aims in mind, but – as did the compilers and processors of many king-lists – from a desire to demonstrate exemplary social and political unity, genealogical legitimacy, and incidentally an incomparable antiquity. The idea of contemporaneous rulers and competing centers of power undermines each of these premises and would be regarded as anathema by those interested in legitimation. And what greater legitimators than those who compile genealogies and kinglists?[57]

Social and political unity and genealogical legitimacy were certainly paramount considerations of those who drew up the Assyrian King List. The concocted genealogy of Shamshi-Adad I (and even his insertion in the list), the exclusion of many uncanonical rulers

and the invention of numerous genealogical links between kings as
late as the 8th century BC all served this end. There is therefore a
strong case for suspecting that 'contemporaneous rulers and competing centers of power' in the form of parallel dynastic lines may
have also been eliminated. If they were disguised by presenting
them as successive, and dressed for the part by the inclusion of
genealogical links, the subterfuge would be almost undetectable in
the King List which resulted.

Synchronisms or circular arguments?

The search for the fault behind the flawed chronologies of ancient
Europe and the Central Mediterranean has brought us a long way.
Step by step, we have traced the cause, via the Greek-based
chronologies of Europe, to Egypt. In Anatolia and Palestine we
found independent evidence suggesting that Sothic chronology has
to be wrong. Mesopotamia is an area whose chronology is generally thought to be independent of Egypt's. Yet examination of its
history and archaeology reveals problems quite as acute as those in
the classic Dark Ages of the Eastern Mediterranean.

Strangely enough, Mesopotamian history is generally believed to
support the validity of the conventional Egyptian chronology. For
the 2nd millennium BC, sources such as the correspondence which
passed between the 'Great Kings' have enabled the development of
a pattern of synchronisms between Mesopotamia and Egypt which
would seem to provide a cross-check confirming the absolute
chronologies of both. (Table 12:1 illustrates the royal synchronisms
generally referred to in the literature.)

For the 1st millennium BC, the earliest synchronism between the
two areas comes from an Assyrian text of Sargon II, dated to
716 BC, which refers to an Egyptian ruler Shilkanni, an Assyrian
rendering of the name Osorkon. On the conventional Egyptian
chronology this reference required the creation of a fourth King
Osorkon; instead, our model suggests that the pharaoh in question
was the well-attested Osorkon III (see Chapter 10).

Before the 8th century BC the only other direct link between
Egypt and Assyria comes from the El-Amarna letters, conventionally dated to the 14th century BC. One of these is addressed to
Akhenaten by Assuruballit, King of Assyria. A straightforward
reckoning based on the figures given in the Assyrian King List
places an Assuruballit (I) in the mid-14th century, the date arrived at

Table 12:1

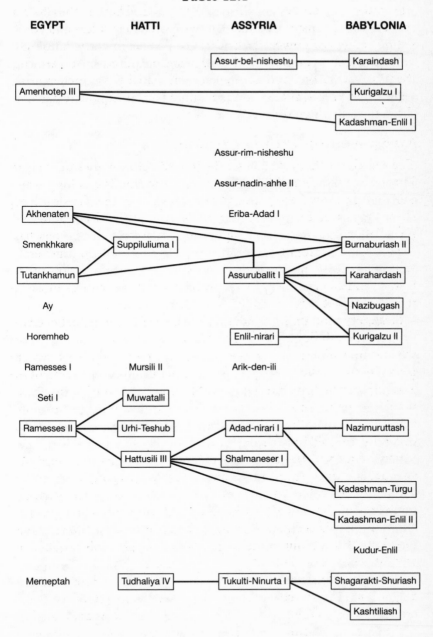

Table showing the generally accepted royal synchronisms between Egypt and Western Asia during the 15th and 13th centuries BC

for Akhenaten within the Sothic framework of Egyptian chronology. Nevertheless, the synchronism is not entirely satisfactory, because of a conspicuous discrepancy regarding the name of Assuruballit's father, given differently in the El-Amarna letter and the King List (see Appendix 4). Indeed, Assuruballit occurs, as noted above, at a point in the list where the information it gives on the order and genealogies of rulers is highly suspect.

Aside from this direct link between Egyptian history and the Assyrian King List, there are also indirect connections via Hatti (the Hittites) and Babylonia. As Late Bronze Hittite chronology was founded on the basis of links with New Kingdom Egypt (see Chapter 6), it will have to change in step with any adjustments made to that of Egypt. Hatti also plays an important role as an intermediary between Egypt and Mesopotamia, as the Hittite kings corresponded with those of Assyria and Babylonia. The imperial archive found at Boghazköy has been held to establish the following links with the kings of Assyria:

Urhi-Teshub – Adad-nirari I
 Hattusili III – Adad-nirari I and Shalmaneser I
Tudhaliya IV – Tukulti-Ninurta I

This pattern of synchronisms seems to provide strong support for dating Ramesses II, the undoubted contemporary of Urhi-Teshub and Hattusili, to the mid-13th century BC, where the Assyrian King List places a succession of rulers by the names of Adad-nirari–Shalmaneser–Tukulti-Ninurta. Nevertheless, examination of the texts shows that most of these 'synchronisms' are dubious. Some of the letters cited as evidence actually give the name of only one correspondent; in other cases the crucial names are fragmentary and have to be restored (see Appendix 4). In fact, there seems to be only one reasonably certain link between the Hittite and Assyrian kings. Two letters suggest the contemporaneity of King Tudhaliya IV and a Tukulti-Ninurta in Assyria, but there is no certainty that this was the Tukulti-Ninurta I known from the Assyrian King List.

The second 'go-between' area is Babylonia, which provides good synchronisms with Hatti and also most of the 2nd-millennium BC links between Mesopotamia and Egypt. The El-Amarna correspondence gives the names of four Kassite kings of Babylonia. Karaindash is referred to as an ancestor who had dealings with

FIG. 12:3 Egyptian relief commemorating the marriage of Ramesses II (seated between two gods) and a Hittite princess. She approaches from the right, followed by her father, Hattusili III (*from Maspero 1896*).

Egypt, while the other three (Kurigalzu, Kadashman-Enlil and Burnaburiash) were clearly contemporary with Amenhotep III, Akhenaten and Tutankhamun. A few generations later the Hittite King Hattusili III (the contemporary of Ramesses II) wrote to another Kadashman-Enlil, King of Babylonia; the letter also mentions that Hattusili had previously corresponded with his father, Kadashman-Turgu (see Appendix 4).

As these five Kassite rulers are dated to the 14th and 13th centuries BC, the synchronisms would seem to provide an impressive array of evidence supporting the conventional Egyptian dates. Closer analysis reveals, however, that the placement of Kassite kings of these names in the accepted Babylonian chronology actually depends principally on the Egyptian and Hittite evidence rather than on native documentation. None of these '14th to 13th century' Kassite rulers is given in any Babylonian king list or chronicle, with the exception of a problematic reference to a Burnaburiash (see Appendix 4). Otherwise, the very existence of a king by this name in the mid-14th century BC is, as Brinkman notes, only inferred, from an admittedly equivocal genealogical link, and 'from the fact he is known to have been . . . the approximate contemporary of Assur-uballit I of Assyria . . . They both wrote Amarna letters to Akhnaton.'[58] Thus any attempt to maintain the status quo in Egyptian chronology by reference to Kassite Babylonian synchronisms would be merely an exercise in circular reasoning.

Summarizing the evidence for synchronisms between Egypt and Mesopotamia during the 2nd millennium BC, there seem to be only two points at which Assyrian or Babylonian history independently places a ruler of the correct name contemporary with one known from Egyptian or Hittite sources. These instances are an Assurubal-lit (contemporary with Akhenaten) and a Tukulti-Ninurta (contemporary with King Tudhaliya IV). The coincidence of these two sets of names can hardly be held to provide adequate confirmation of the accepted Egyptian chronology. Their ultimate value obviously depends on the questionable reliability of the King List as a chronological source. Our revision of Egyptian and Hittite history has already provided two new synchronisms, linking Osorkon III and Sargon II, and Ini-Teshub of Carchemish with Tiglath-pileser I. The second falls into place with Assyrian history if we assume that there were two dynasties ruling concurrently after the time of Tukulti-Ninurta I. The possibility exists, given the problems in the genealogy of Assuruballit I, whose family seems to have been awkwardly grafted into the King List, that a second 'tuck' should be made in earlier Assyrian history and that the synchronism of an Assuruballit and Akhenaten can be maintained within a revised scheme, placing them both at the end of the 12th century BC rather than in the mid-14th.[59]

In short, the generally accepted dates for Egypt cannot be substantiated simply by reference to the conventional chronology of Mesopotamia derived from the Assyrian King List.

FIG. 12:4 Pharaoh Akhenaten, conventionally dated to the 14th century BC. The large archive of diplomatic correspondence (written in cuneiform script) discovered at his capital of Akhetaten (El-Amarna) provides some of the main evidence for synchronisms between Egypt, Assyria, Babylonia and the Hittites during the Late Bronze Age.

The 'broken reed' of Egypt

The prophet Isaiah (36:6), warning the Jews not to depend on Egyptian military aid against the Assyrians, described Egypt's authority as a 'broken reed'. The same has proved to be true in chronological matters, although in this case it is Assyria which sometimes leans on Egypt for support. The Assyrian King List is deemed to be sound from the 14th century BC onwards because of the El-Amarna letters. Hence M. B. Rowton's remark:

> The earliest point at which verification becomes possible is the accession of Assur-uballit I, in or about 1365. Measured against the Egyptian and Hittite evidence this date is found to be closely correct.[60]

Likewise Babylonian chronology for the mid-2nd millennium BC has been largely reconstructed with the help of Egyptian and Hittite records. Indeed, the two pillars of Old World chronology – the Egyptian and the Assyrian – were developed together by modern scholars at the turn of the century. It is not surprising, then, that they appear to support each other. What is ironic is that as Egyptologists grow steadily less confident in their own chronology, Mesopotamian history is now increasingly used to fine-tune Egyptian dating. The recent acceptance of an eleven-year reduction for Ramesses II went hand-in-hand with a similar lowering allowed by the Mesopotamian evidence.[61] The possibility of much larger scale reductions in both the Egyptian and Mesopotamian systems has, however, never been fully explored.

The real significance of the relationship between Mesopotamian and Egyptian chronologies was admirably expressed by the American scholar George Hanfmann some forty years ago. Apart from the introduction of new scientific dating techniques, which still have to be fully integrated with the traditional methods, little has changed since he wrote. Indeed, his general warning is still valid today for archaeologists working on the Late Bronze Age of the Near East and Eastern Mediterranean:

> Finally, a word of caution must be added regarding the so-called 'absolute' dates . . . it is well to remind ourselves from time to time that the two great pillars of the chronology of the Bronze Age, the Egyptian and the Mesopotamian, are not two stout towers resting on immovable foundations. They may rather be

likened to two buoys linked by a chain and anchored, to be sure, yet raised or lowered by the waves of the sea. Both chronologies include problems which cannot as yet be solved except by reasonable guesses – the specific years to which observed astronomic data should be assigned, the estimates for the lengths of obscure periods, and the evaluation of possible gaps, duplications, and exaggerations in Royal lists and building inscriptions.[62]

Hanfmann's words were almost prophetic. The case for accepting the astronomical dates for Egyptian history is now so riddled with doubts that the whole structure can be seen to be creaking at the seams. As it totters, it is no longer acceptable merely to prop it up, with generous 'lengths for obscure periods'. The gaps in the evidence were, and remain, on the whole, quite real. The 'royal lists' of the ancient world did indeed exaggerate, and modern scholars are no longer obliged to accept their inflated estimates. The cumulative results of 100 years of archaeological research give them the lie.

CHAPTER 13

The End of the Dark Ages?

There can be no real doubt that in many parts of the Old World there was a dramatic collapse of civilization at the end of the Late Bronze Age. The centralized economies controlled from the palaces disintegrated, the old trading markets broke up, diplomatic contacts were lost and major settlements were abandoned. However, the cause or causes behind these momentous changes are unclear.

Numerous universal theories have been offered to explain why the great empires and powerful states of the past have crumbled away. The division of theories used here broadly follows that of American archaeologist Joseph Tainter in his recent world survey *The Collapse of Complex Societies*.[1] Within the general explanations he has considered, ten separate interpretations of the events at the end of the Late Bronze Age can be discerned. The solutions proposed fall within, or combine factors drawn from, the following categories:

1   The notion of cultural decadence has always been a favourite of moralists. Arnold Toynbee's cyclical theory of history is perhaps the best-known version. He suggested that the collapse of the Hittite Empire was due to an excess of 'sadistic extravagance', while the Egyptian New Kingdom was an enfeebled old wreck, drained by a corrupt bureaucracy and the 'wanton adventure' of imperial ambitions in the Levant.[2] Of course, sweeping claims of this ilk scarcely count as explanations, given that decadence is invariably in the eye of the beholder.

2   Invasions by outside barbarians – notably the so-called Sea Peoples in Anatolia, Cyprus, the Levant and Egypt, the Dorians in Greece, the Phrygians in Anatolia, the Aramaeans in Mesopotamia and the Israelites in Palestine – are frequently invoked as a destructive mechanism. Such 'external' causes are rarely convincing because they cannot in themselves show why the civilized society was unable to cope. After all, the flood-plain empires of Mesopotamia were continually harassed by nomadic tribes, but in other periods usually got the

better of them. Also, in the case of the Dorians their very
existence is a matter of some doubt, while there is good reason
to believe that the prominent role assigned to the Sea Peoples is
an exaggeration.[3] Population movements are usually a symp-
tom, rather than a cause, of the decline of centralized states.

3   A variant on this theme, but involving technological change,
     was argued by Gordon Childe, the great Marxist prehistorian.
     He suggested that the introduction of iron meant that 'peasants
     and barbarian tribes' were able to manufacture weapons which
     allowed them to challenge the armies of the Mycenaean and
     Hittite states.[4] Attractive as this may be to those seeking
     evidence for the class struggle in history, archaeological re-
     search shows that iron was not available in significant amounts
     even after the inception of the 'Iron Age', least of all to peasants
     and barbarians.[5]

4   Internal conflicts have been suggested for Egypt, which began
     to fragment into a series of small kingdoms after the end of the
     20th Dynasty. Similar developments have been detected in the
     breakup of the Hittite Empire.[6]

5   The close links between the various 'Great Kings' of the Late
     Bronze Age (Egypt, Hatti, Assyria, Babylonia and Ahhi-
     yawa)[7] suggest that a 'domino theory' may form part of the
     explanation for the collapse. If the different empires had be-
     come partly interdependent then the disappearance of one
     would severely weaken the others.

6   Over-centralization of authority has been proposed by Colin
     Renfrew for Mycenaean Greece.[8] Ever-increasing amounts of
     energy were expended on maintaining the palace-based elite,
     until its demands became too great for the economy; when this
     happened the central authority simply disappeared.

7   Most explanations involve some kind of economic collapse. A
     simple one of food shortages caused by mismanagement is
     generally felt to be insufficient, as it relates too specifically to
     the abilities of the ruling class concerned. One version of this
     theory attributes the sharp rise in the price of grain at the end of
     the 20th Egyptian Dynasty to the corruption of officials.[9]
     More complex explanations propose that the ruling class was
     somehow distracted by other concerns, to the detriment of the
     basic economic well-being of the state. In this vein, Tainter
     argues that the Mycenaean cities became locked into a com-

petitive spiral in which they had to devote ever greater resources to military strength and administration. Against this,
the archaeological record shows no evidence of increasing
warfare or bureaucracy over the Mycenaean period. Similarly,
he suggests that the Hittite Empire over-extended itself
through expansion and thereby neglected the economy.[10] It is
difficult, however, to see how the Hittites' strenuous efforts to
maintain control over Syria, with its important trade routes,
can be considered as disadvantageous to their economy.

8   The ultimate result of economic decline would be famine. If
populations were on the point of starvation then social breakdown would eventually occur, leading to large-scale looting
and eventually revolution. Such a series of events has been
proposed for the end of the Hittite Empire.[11] One explanation
often given for a state of famine is a change in the climate to
very dry conditions at the end of the Late Bronze Age. This has
been applied to Mesopotamia, Syria, Anatolia and Greece.
Much drier weather would have made it impossible to culti-
vate large parts of these areas.[12]

The idea of a widespread drought is, however, difficult to
substantiate. Although modern weather conditions can be
used to produce models of climate patterns which would, if
they persisted, have led to very dry and hot conditions in
Greece, these would not have had such drastic effects on
Anatolia.[13] Equally, simulations of drought in Anatolia do not
match the supposed dry spell in Greece. Further, the textual
evidence presented to bolster the case for a Mesopotamian
famine amounts to only a dozen examples in the entire 300-
year Dark Age.[14] One final point which is not yet satisfactorily
resolved is the question of the appropriate weather patterns to
use. If it is felt that pan-European effects should be expected,
then drought theorists must deal with the fact that there are
many radiocarbon-dated records of pollen from Central and
Northern Europe which show the existence of a wet climate at
this time.[15]

9   A variant on the theme of climatic disaster is the recent
suggestion that an eruption of the volcano at Hekla in Iceland
took place in 1159 BC. This appears to show up in Irish
tree-rings as a period of two decades of low sunshine and high
rainfall.[16] However, it is not really clear how this would relate

to the supposed drought in the Near East. Indeed, it could even counteract it.

10 Widespread earthquakes have also been put forward as the cause for the destruction of many Late Bronze Age cities. In the 1940s Claude Schaeffer developed a model involving periods of intense seismic activity to explain the general collapse of Near Eastern civilization at the end of both the Early and Middle Bronze Ages, which he later extended to the end of the Late Bronze Age on the basis of his excavations at Ugarit.[17] Similarly, archaeologists working in Cyprus and Greece have often seen earthquakes as the elemental force which destroyed many major centres.[18] The effects of earthquakes, however, can usually be overcome – Schaeffer himself had to invoke a climatic change at Ugarit to explain its subsequent desertion.

None of these universal causes for the collapse at the end of the Late Bronze Age has proved satisfactory. They cannot take into account the different social contexts provided by each area, which are bound to have modified the response to military, political, economic or natural difficulties.

Moreover, one must remember that gaps and recessions are not limited to the great kingdoms alone, but are also postulated for the cultural sequences of surrounding areas – in the Central and Western Mediterranean, the Balkans, Nubia, the Arabian Gulf and eastern Iran. Explanations relating to over-centralization, mismanagement or internal strife are clearly not applicable to the less complex societies they supported. Invasions are often proposed for Italy, but their reality is doubtful and their impact uncertain. Climatic changes have been mooted for Nubia but not elsewhere. One could argue that local aristocracies dependent on controlling access to outside goods would have vanished when foreign traders ceased to operate in these areas. But this may only apply in particular cases, such as the idea that Nubian gold dried up with the secession of Nubia from Egypt at the end of the 20th Dynasty.[19] Yet this hardly accounts for the depopulation of Nubia for some 300 years. The existence of a Dark Age covering the whole of the area surveyed in this book still lacks any convincing explanation despite the best efforts of archaeologists and ancient historians over the last 100 years.

Why centuries of darkness?

Even where a collapse of civilization is evident, one must also ask why the subsequent recession lasted so long and was so widespread. It is sometimes suggested that the depth of the breakdown in political structures meant that they took centuries to build up again.[20] Such assertions need to be carefully examined in each case, for there can be no general rules concerning the tempo of social development. If the conditions are right, states and even empires can be built within a single lifetime. Invasion theories have again been used here, the assumption being that 'simple' barbarians took no interest in such matters.[21] In reality, it is more usual for barbarian invaders to adopt imperial trappings in order to claim a degree of legitimacy in the eyes of the conquered population. One has only to think of the speed with which the Mongol warlord Kublai Khan, after his conquest of China, assumed traditional titles and ruled as a Chinese Emperor. Others have argued that newcomers such as the Phrygians, sometimes thought to have precipitated the fall of the Hittite Empire, opted for a nomadic lifestyle in the region they had conquered.[22] Against this interpretation is the fact that it is based merely on silence – the lack of any settlement remains for hundreds of years.

One supposedly long-lasting factor is the claimed drought, which continued until 900 BC and the end of the Dark Age, at least in some areas, according to its proponents. The evidence for the drought happening at all is equivocal, and that it was a centuries-long affair is even less likely. Pollen diagrams from Jordan, Syria, Turkey, Iran and Greece, dated independently of the archaeological chronology, do not show a long-term dry spell between 1200 and 900 BC.[23]

A more persuasive reconstruction of events has been suggested by Anthony Snodgrass with respect to Greece. Tying together literary, excavation, seed and animal-bone evidence, he argues that in the Early Iron Age there was a shift towards a more pastoral economy, with the Protogeometric period being dominated by cattle-raising.[24] However, Snodgrass does not take into account the pollen data given by cores of sediments drilled from the Osmanaga Lagoon near Pylos in Messenia and Lake Voulkaria in western Greece.[25] The calibrated radiocarbon dates from these cores show that olive cultivation became important around 1500 BC, and continued to be so for several hundred years. This would agree with the conventional chronology, as the Linear B tablets, particularly those from Pylos, show that the Mycenaeans produced olive oil on a massive scale. But the Osmanaga core also shows that olive cultivation continued well after 1200 BC, indeed peaking around 950 BC – in the middle of the supposed Dark Age! Olive cropping and pressing require large quantities of manual labour.[26] This hardly fits Snodgrass's picture. Instead, if the collapse of Mycenae occurred in the late 10th century instead of the 12th, then the swift decline of olive cultivation would provide a perfect match with his post-palatial pastoral society.

Revivals, perishables and heirlooms

At this general level of analysis, attempts to deal with the Dark Ages have been unimpressive. Equally, in most of the specific Dark Age problems reviewed earlier the proposed explanations are unconvincing, and become steadily less so the more times they are repeated. Many of the arts and crafts supposedly lost during this time, but reappearing afterwards little changed, are said to have been preserved elsewhere. One of the most striking examples of this supposed process is the skill of ivory-working, thought to be forgotten in Greece but maintained in the Levant. However, the conventional chronology also creates a hiatus in the Levantine ivory-working tradition at the very same time. To explain this, the interpretation has to be extended to one in which craftsmen transferred their skills from ivory to perishable materials such as textiles and wood.

Theories involving the use of perishable items have always been popular explanations for the obvious gaps in the evidence for several other skills, including writing and painting on pottery. The textiles and carved wooden objects to which the craftsmen supposedly transferred their attention have not been discovered. Such occasional finds as may be made eventually would represent only a tiny proportion of the original examples. It will, therefore, always be possible to claim that the 'missing links' of craft production remain to be found. However, it is difficult to believe that this transference between materials was anywhere near so widespread a phenomenon as current interpretations would require. The wider this theory is applied, the harder it is to accept, and the more it looks instead like a convenient excuse for the lack of evidence.

A more reasonable explanation at the level of individual finds is the heirlooms theory; after all, the preservation of objects is a practice familiar enough from both ancient and modern times. An instructive case from the Late Bronze Age concerns exports from Egypt to Greece. Four plaques made of faience bearing the name of Amenhotep III have been unearthed at Mycenae. The only complete example was found in the destruction level of a house dated to the end of Late Helladic IIIB. Yet Amenhotep III died over 150 years before this on any chronology, when the previous pottery style, LHIIIA, was current. In contrast to this treatment of the faience plaques, scarabs of Amenhotep III occur in Crete with contemporary burials.[27] The conclusion must be that, while rare and exotic pieces were sometimes kept as valuable souvenirs, more ordinary items were more likely to be deposited not long after their manufacture.

This is a clear contrast to the situation which supposedly applies to the Egyptian 22nd and 23rd Dynasties, where all their objects found outside Egypt have to be interpreted as heirlooms, even down to the most humble scarab. The elaborate bronze tripods and stands from Late Bronze Age Cyprus might well have been treasured, but that all of them (in Sardinia, Sicily and Greece) were kept for centuries seems much less likely. Even more difficult to believe are cases involving pottery – both less rare and more liable to breakage than bronzework. The presence of Late New Kingdom Egyptian pots decorated with funerary scenes in mid-9th century tombs at el-Kurru in Nubia might be dealt with by arguing that they were heirlooms. This would be remarkable, since the Nubians are supposed to have packed their bags and left Nubia in the 12th century BC, leading a nomadic lifestyle until their return. Like ideas of revivals and perishables, the closer the heirloom theory is examined the less believable it becomes.

The new picture

In the course of our investigation we have encountered many interminable dating controversies: Torr versus Petrie over the dating of Mycenaean civilization; Gjerstad and Gierow versus Müller-Karpe and Peroni on the earliest remains at Rome; West Semitic palaeographers versus classical archaeologists on the introduction of the alphabet; Francis and Vickers versus the traditionalists on the chronology of the Greek Archaic; Albright and Akurgal versus Frankfort and his school over the dating of Syrian art; Palestinian versus Cypriot archaeologists on the Black-on-Red Ware question; Kenyon versus Wright over the pottery of Samaria; Rothenberg and Aharoni versus Glueck and Albright on the Timna mines; Naveh and Cross versus Millard over the dating of the Tell Fakhariyah inscription; de Miroschedji versus Ghirshman on Elamite pottery.

All these disputes can now be seen in a fresh light. The irony is that both sides in most of these cases were to some extent correct. It was the overall framework within which they were arguing that was wrong.

With the lower chronology proposed here, in which the Late Bronze Age in the Eastern Mediterranean ends around 950 rather than 1200 BC, the problems are solved and an entirely new understanding emerges.

Beginning with Egypt, the theory of Sothic dating should no longer be used to calculate the chronology of the New Kingdom. If the Third Intermediate Period is not stretched to an unreasonable length by Sothic dates, then the 22nd and 23rd Dynasty pharaohs whose finds are so often out of place abroad will have reigned much later. This in turn means that the objects bearing their names become contemporary with the deposits in which they occur.

Outside Egypt, a lowering of New Kingdom dates would remove any need to postulate the desertion of Nubia. The long-ignored evidence for rulers during the supposed Dark Age instead shows that after less than a century the place of the Egyptian viceroys had been taken by local kings.

By redating the beginning of the Iron Age in Palestine from the early 12th century BC to the late 10th, a completely new interpretation of the archaeology of Israel can be offered: one which is in perfect harmony with the biblical record. The search for the riches of Solomon's reign can be brought to an end – they have already been found, but simply not recognized, in the material remains of the Late Bronze Age. By shortening the early Iron Age a cultural hiatus in Palestine can be closed. A reduction in the dates for the later Iron Age, as argued by the evidence of the Lachish Letters, removes a second Dark Age in the Babylonian and early Persian period.

With respect to the important question of ivory-working, one of the latest objects from the LBA cache at Megiddo belongs to the reign of Ramesses III, who on our provisional redating of Egyptian history invaded Palestine around 925 BC. The closure of the deposit might then fall around 900 BC, only two generations before the next datable ivories, c. 850 BC. In short, there was no real interruption between the Late Bronze Age and Iron Age ivory-carving traditions of the Eastern Mediterranean.

New finds demonstrate that the Neo-Hittite kings of Syria can finally be linked with the last Hittite emperors, a connection supported by the evidence from archaeology, radiocarbon dating and sculptural comparison. The Hittite Empire did not die out c. 1200 BC but instead gradually broke up during the 10th century BC, leaving local rulers to claim authority over their own lands in the same fashion as the Nubian chiefs.

By removing the ghost dynasties of Assyrian history, continuity can be restored between the art of the Middle and Late Assyrian periods. In step with this, the extended period of 'illiteracy' in Babylonia and Elam during post-Kassite times is transformed into a much shorter phase in which texts were scarce but not wholly absent. Likewise, the 'occupational enigma' in the Persian Gulf can be resolved and the hiatus in settlement evidence closed.

The disappearance of writing in Cyprus and Greece and its reappearance 300 years or more later loses its status as one of the great mysteries of ancient times. Redating the Byblite inscriptions means that the supposedly 11th-century Levantine alphabet copied by the Greeks properly belongs to the 9th century BC (confirmed by the Assyrian date for Tell Fakhariyah inscription); its arrival in Greece during the 8th century is therefore no longer a surprise. Equally, the massive gap in the use of the Cypriot script shrinks dramatically. The long-standing Black-on-Red Ware problem is resolved by harmonizing Palestinian and Cypriot stratigraphy.

The emergence of Archaic Greek city-states in the 8th century BC has presented many puzzles, with the signs of continuity from the Mycenaean palace centres ignored because of the impossibility of their influence persisting for so long. The Mycenaean world did collapse, but in the mid-10th century BC, with civilization reviving soon after to flourish even more vigorously.

In the Balkans, the ties between the Balkan pottery complex and the Mycenaeans at one end and Geometric material at the other do not have to be seen as incompatible alternatives. In the revised chronology presented here, the Balkan Complex neatly bridges the period between the two, rather than being stretched out over four centuries. At Troy the mysterious gap in occupation for some two and a half centuries can be largely closed. The famous War of the Greeks against the city (if we follow the usual association with the destruction of Troy VIIA) would have taken place in the mid-10th rather than early 12th century.

The Phoenician colonization of the Mediterranean does not provide a conflict between the historical sources and the archaeology, once it is realized that ancient historians exaggerated the age of the settlements. Further, the archaeological evidence from Palestine does not clash with that from Carthage and Spain once the chronology of the former has been corrected.

An overlap between the supposedly separate Proto-Villanovan and Sub-Apennine cultures in central Italy makes good sense of the archaeological evidence. In the new dating scheme this interpretation becomes perfectly feasible, as is a lower date for the earliest remains at Rome.

In Sicily there is no need to develop unlikely hypotheses involving the abandonment of the coast on two separate occasions. The traditional chronology has been spread out to fill the gap between the Mycenaeans and Greek colonists. If the Late Bronze Age is lowered in date, then the unnecessary phases in the Sicilian Iron Age, represented only by burials, can be dispensed with.

Over the last century chronology has provided the focus of some of the most protracted and troublesome debates in a wide variety of fields, from European prehistory to biblical archaeology. All these can now be seen as the product of a common cause – a misplaced faith in the immutability of the established framework. The resulting Dark Ages and all their ramifications really amount to a gigantic academic blunder, perpetuated by the convenience of a seemingly reliable time-scale, as well as the sheer complexity of the issues involved. Our investigation shows that these controversies have been largely unnecessary. With the lower chronology proposed here, many simply disappear, along with the illusory Centuries of Darkness.

APPENDIX I
Dendrochronology and Radiocarbon Dating

The beginnings of dendrochronology, or tree-ring dating, go back to Leonardo da Vinci. He was apparently the first to note that the yearly growth of trees in spring-time produces a sequence of annual tree-rings in the wood. The regularity of this process means that the age of a tree at the time it was felled can be worked out simply by counting up the rings on the stump.

A tree's annual rings vary in width and density according to the climate in that particular year – for example, thicker rings are added in good years. Trees growing in the same area at the same time will therefore produce similar successions of ring widths. Thus if a newly felled tree some 200–300 years in age is examined, the rings from its early life can be matched with their counterparts in the later rings of a tree long since dead. The rings in this older tree can then be matched with those from even older ones, and so on, extending the sequence back in time as far as possible.[1] Absolute dates can then be assigned to the timbers in the succession, the only source of inaccuracy being the need to allow for the growing time represented by the sapwood (the soft outer part of the tree which has not yet formed proper rings) on the timber.

However, trees of different species vary greatly in their sensitivity to the weather, so that effective sequences have to be built up using a single species. Even trees of the same species from the same locality will react slightly differently to growing conditions – the absolute widths of the rings they form in a given year will not be the same, and what has to be compared is the succession of narrow and wide rings.

Dendrochronology is therefore a statistical method: an absolute requirement is that sequences are of sufficient length to provide statistically significant comparisons between different sets of tree-rings.

Since dendrochronology is relatively straightforward, why is it not the dominant method of archaeological dating? The reasons for this are practical

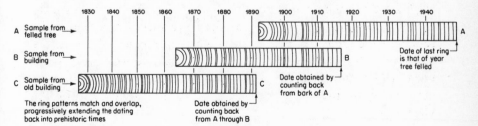

FIG. Appendix 1:1   How a dendrochronological sequence is built up by matching patterns of rings of varying thickness from different trees (drawing by Rosemary Burnard).

rather than technical. First, tree-ring sequences may simply not be available. In a few countries such as Egypt trees are so scarce that local dendro-chronologies could never be built up. Furthermore, in large parts of the globe long sequences are still being developed – for example, the Eastern Mediter-ranean juniper succession so far stretches back only to 1073 AD.[2] Second, even when a sequence does exist, its application to archaeological dating can still be difficult, since there is a real lack of archaeologically significant timbers. Most excavations produce no wooden objects, because they have rotted away. Only at those sites in very dry or very wet conditions will wood survive. Bog finds are common, but they generally lack useful archaeological associations. For example, dendrochronology has shown that a trackway of oak timbers at Timahoe West in Ireland was built in 1483±9 BC, but this absolute date has no application beyond the site as no cultural finds came from the trackway.[3] Finally, where one or two timbers from a site are datable they may have been reused from older buildings without this being apparent.

Yet the potential for dendrochronology is great, as shipwrecks in the Mediterranean are being found in increasing numbers. Cases where the ship's hull survives are perfect for giving dates to large cargoes containing a wide variety of items from different countries. What is lacking at present is a continuous tree-ring sequence into which to slot these ship's timbers.

Because of these limitations, radiocarbon dating, discovered in 1949 by Professor Willard Libby of the University of Chicago, remains the main scientific method for chronology building.[4] Carbon has three naturally occur-ring isotopes – that is, atoms with the same chemical properties but different atomic weights. Two of these isotopes, ^{12}C and ^{13}C, are stable, while the third, ^{14}C, is radioactive. Carbon-14 (or radiocarbon) is formed continuously in the Earth's upper atmosphere by the action of cosmic rays on nitrogen. Carbon is an essential constituent of living tissue, absorbed by all plants and animals, passing back into the atmosphere as they decompose after death. Because Carbon-14 is an unstable radioactive isotope, it constantly changes back into nitrogen by the emission of an electron. The rate of this decay back to nitrogen is usually expressed in terms of a 'half-life' of about 5730 years. This means that half of the Carbon-14 in a block of carbon will revert to nitrogen in 5730 years, half of the remaining portion in another 5730 years to leave a quarter of the original, and so on. The older the sample the more difficult it is to measure the shrinking Carbon-14 content accurately, with a practical limit of around 40,000 BC. This means that the method, which in ideal conditions can differentiate between the Carbon-14 content of ancient samples only 100 years apart in age, is particularly suitable for archaeological dating.[5]

However, it is not possible in practice to give precise radiocarbon dates because of uncertainties involved in the measurement of samples. Therefore Carbon-14 dates are always quoted with a 'Standard Deviation' which repres-ents their degree of accuracy. For example, a date of 1000 bp (before present) with a Standard Deviation of fifty years has a 68.3 per cent chance (one Standard Deviation) of lying between 950 and 1050 bp, a 95.3 per cent chance (two Standard Deviations) of lying between 900 and 1100 bp, and a 99.8 per cent chance (three Standard Deviations) of lying between 850 and 1150 bp.

Many problems have been encountered in applying radiocarbon dating to archaeology. First, in practice the vast majority of results have a Standard Deviation greater than fifty years, so that single dates for sites are of little value, particularly in resolving arguments such as those discussed in this book, where a century or two is often the scale of the debate. Accordingly, accepted practice today (on those sites where Carbon-14 samples are actually taken) is to produce a series of dates for each site. Second, in certain circumstances old carbon can be absorbed by living organisms and produce radiocarbon dates that are too old. For example, volcanoes often release old carbon before their eruption, something which may well be a contributory source of confusion in the debate over dating the explosion of Thera.[6] Further problems arise with the dating of both shellfish and reeds, which are affected by the presence of old carbon in seawater and freshwater respectively.[7] Ironically, reeds were at one time specially selected for radiocarbon tests in Egypt because of their use as bonding material in the brick walls of tombs and temples.[8]

There are also severe difficulties in assessing the closeness of the association between dated samples and the event for which a date is required. Charcoal has produced the vast majority of Carbon-14 dates because it is present in large amounts on most archaeological sites, and in acid soils may well be the only organic material to survive.

Unfortunately, there are two distinct problems related to the use of charcoal. One is that large wooden beams used for construction may well be fashioned from trees which had grown for several hundred years. If the building is then burnt down, the outer part of the timbers will be destroyed, leaving behind pieces from the centre of the beams. If these remaining sections of the original timbers are then sampled for radiocarbon dating they will give a falsely old reading. (Short-lived materials such as grain, nuts and seeds, and hide, are now much preferred, but such dates are still rare.) Of course, if the timbers were reused from older buildings the discrepancy would be even greater. A clear example of this has been noted by dendrochronologist Peter Kuniholm from a house in the Phrygian capital on the city mound at Gordion. While one group of timbers had been felled in the 7th century BC, 'three other

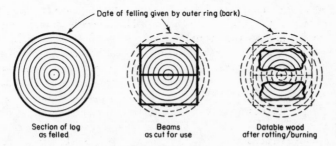

FIG. Appendix 1:2   An example of the 'old wood' problem. The core of a large squared timber left after the outer part has burnt away will give radiocarbon dates far earlier than the date at which the tree was felled (drawing by Rosemary Burnard).

pieces were cut about four centuries earlier. If only the latter had been collected the result would have been an entirely erroneous notion about the date of [the building].'[9]

The other problem with charcoal samples is that many Carbon-14 dates have been obtained by collecting together large amounts of fragmentary charcoal. This can easily be moved around sites by continuing activity and differs from bones in that the condition of the sample cannot indicate how quickly it was buried. The consequence of these two drawbacks is that it has been argued that the estimate of the potential age-lapse between a sample and the stratum in which it was found should be around 200 years in the case of charcoal from long-lived species of trees.[10]

An added complication for radiocarbon dating has been the growing realization that one of the assumptions underpinning the trustworthiness of the method was unsound. It was originally believed that the proportion of Carbon-14 to Carbon-12 was nearly constant through time. This has proved not to be the case. A mismatch between radiocarbon results and the conventional historical chronology of Egypt led to a re-examination of the Carbon-14 method. With the development of dendrochronological sequences, one way in which the validity of radiocarbon dates could be tested was against the

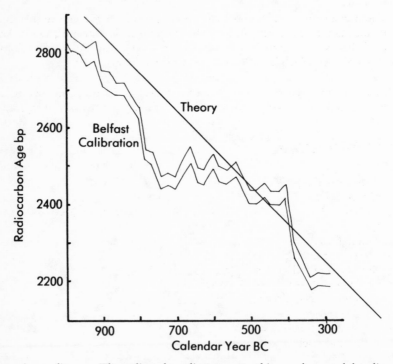

FIG. Appendix I:3   The radiocarbon disaster area: objects whose real date lies between 800 and 400 BC (in calendar years) will all produce radiocarbon dates between 2450 bp (500 bc) and 2550 bp (600 bc) (*after Baillie & Pilcher 1983*).

separately developed tree-ring chronologies of oaks from Ireland and Germany and bristlecone pines from California.[11] These comparisons showed that before about 500 BC radiocarbon dates are too young. The 'calibration' required to convert Carbon-14 results into calendar years rises to over a millennium for the Neolithic of Europe. This contributed significantly to the abandonment of traditional ideas of the spread of copper-working in the Old World (see Chapter 1). Uncalibrated dates are normally expressed as bc, and calibrated or calendar dates as BC.

Unfortunately, calibration is not a simple matter – the amount of Carbon-14 in the atmosphere fluctuated greatly in the past, at times falling and then rising again significantly within a single century. The calibration curve produced by comparing radiocarbon dates to the tree-ring chronology, rather than being a smooth progression, is full of short-term wiggles. At certain points a radiocarbon result can be calibrated to several alternative calendar dates, without any way of being sure which is the correct choice.

A notably complex period is the '1st-millennium BC radiocarbon disaster'. Between 400 and 800 BC the calibration curve is essentially flat, with calendar dates within that range all equivalent to a radiocarbon date of around 500 bc. As Michael Baillie, who developed the Irish oak dendrochronology, has said:

> The immediate conclusion is that it is impossible to sensibly resolve the radiocarbon dates of any samples whose true ages lie between 400 and 800 BC. This is a catastrophe for Late Bronze Age/Iron Age archaeology although one which has been predicted for some time.[12]

This means that for the latter part of the period discussed in this book radiocarbon dating can unfortunately never provide any answers.

Notes and references

1 Baillie 1982.
2 Kuniholm and Striker 1983, 1987.
3 Munro 1987.
4 For a readable account of the history of radiocarbon dating, see D. Wilson 1975.
5 Gillespie 1984.
6 Olsson 1987, 18–22.
7 Gillespie and Polach 1979; Yates 1986.
8 Fishman *et al.* 1977, 195; Weinstein 1980.
9 Kuniholm 1988, 8.
10 Warner 1985.
11 Pearson and Stuiver 1986; Stuiver *et al.* 1986.
12 Baillie and Pilcher 1983, 58.

Greek and Roman Theories on Ancient Chronology

The ancient Greeks had their own chronological traditions, continued by the Romans, which gave dates for key events in their past such as the Trojan War and the foundation of new cities. Modern historians have usually assumed that these were soundly based on reliable information. Indeed, the traditional estimates for Carthage, Rome and the western Greek colonies have been a major factor in determining the dates assigned by archaeologists to the earliest remains uncovered at these sites. In the case of Troy, the ancient dates for the war waged against it by the Greeks seem to agree, well enough, with those given by archaeologists to the destructions of levels VI and VIIa – the two candidates for the Troy of Homer's poems.

But do the traditional dates really provide credible support for the conventional archaeological chronology? The central questions are: how were these estimates arrived at, and what sources were available to the ancients?

The date of the Trojan War

The standard archaeological dates for the destructions of Troy VI and VIIa, based on finds of Mycenaean pottery, are roughly 1300 and 1200 BC respectively (see Chapter 3). Proponents of either city as the Homeric Troy of the Heroic Age have naturally sought to bolster their claims by reference to the classical dates for the Trojan War – all broadly in line with the conventional archaeological chronology.

Our earliest written source on the date of the Trojan War is the mid-5th-century historian Herodotus (II, 145), who placed it some 800 years before his own day, i.e. c. 1250 BC. His rough estimate was apparently based on a generation count, since he gives it in the context of a discussion on tracing back genealogies to the Greek gods. Herodotus (VII, 204; VIII, 131) recorded the ancestries of Leonidas and Leotychides, the two kings of Sparta who fought in the Persian Wars, taking them back fifteen and sixteen generations to the time of Aristodemus, who led the Return of the Heraclids to Laconia (VI, 52). Traditionally, there were two generations between the Trojan War and the invasion of the Heraclids (Pausanias IV, 3, 3). Also allowing for the three generations (including that of Leonidas and Leotychides) between the Persian Wars and Herodotus brings us to a grand total of twenty or twenty-one generations between his time and the Trojan War. An estimate of forty years for a generation may therefore have been used by Herodotus to calculate his date for the Trojan War – i.e. 20 × 40 years = 800 years before his time (but see below).

Differing estimates for the date of the Trojan War are given by (or deduced from) other classical sources:

The Locrians of Opus (late 4th century BC)	*c.* 1346 BC
Herodotus (*c.* 450 BC)	*c.* 1250 BC
Timaeus (*c.* 270 BC)	1234 BC
Cleitarchus (*c.* 270 BC)	1234 BC
The Parian Marble (264 BC)	1209 BC
Eratosthenes (late 3rd century BC)	1184 BC
Sosibius (*c.* 320 BC)	1172 BC
Ephorus (*c.* 340 BC)	1169 or 1149 BC
Phaenias of Eresus (*c.* 320 BC)	1129 BC
Callimachus (early 3rd century BC)	1127 BC[1]

The most influential of these calculations was that made by the great polymath Eratosthenes of Cyrene (*c.* 275–194 BC), who was royal tutor in the court of the Hellenistic King Ptolemy III Euergetes, as well as the head of the great Library of Alexandria from 234 BC. His *Chronographiae* was the first systematic attempt to produce a chronological framework for political and literary history. As well as using broader estimates based on generation counts, Eratosthenes successfully combined all the available chronological schemes available to him (King and Archon lists, Olympic records etc.) into a unified system. Because of his great authority as a scholar Eratosthenes' date of 1184 BC for the Trojan War was followed unanimously by subsequent writers, including the Church Fathers Clement of Alexandria (*c.* 150–215 AD) and Eusebius of Caesarea (*c.* 260–340 AD), and even today is often held in high respect. A surviving fragment summarizes his calculation:

> From the fall of Troy to the Return of the Heraclids is 80 years, from that time to the Ionian colonisation 60 years, an additional 159 years to the regency of Lycurgus, and 108 years to the year preceding the 1st Olympiad, from which there is an interval of 297 years to the expedition of Xerxes.[2]

Carthage and Rome

The next major chronological landmark in classical writings was the founding of Carthage in North Africa by the Phoenicians of Tyre. Roman writers were particularly interested in the date of its foundation, since until its destruction in 146 BC Carthage was the main rival to Roman power. Legends suggested that the origins of the two cities were intertwined. Flying from Troy after its fall, Aeneas, ancestor of the Roman kings, visited Queen Dido (or Elissa), the founder of Carthage. He loved her and left her, the first cause of grievance between the two great cities, sailing to Italy where he began the dynasty which was to rule Rome. So intimately were the histories of the two cities connected that some writers even claimed they were founded in the same year. The Sicilian historian Timaeus placed this event in 814 BC (thirty-eight years before the First Olympiad), while Apion set it in 752 BC.[3]

Others followed the traditions more literally, and since Aeneas was supposed to have visited an already existing Carthage, its founding was placed a suitable length of time (sixty or seventy years) before that of Rome. These calculations give variant dates (depending on that for Rome), but all fall in the late 9th century BC. Other calculations were based on estimates of the life of the city before its destruction, giving a wider range of dates, as different as 894 and 746 BC. Of all the dates offered, modern historians have tended to prefer those of Timaeus (814 BC) and Trogus Pompeius (825 BC).[4] A late 9th-century date also seems to agree with the information reported by Josephus from the Annals of Tyre (but see Chapter 2).

The age of Rome itself was in serious dispute in antiquity, as Cicero testifies. The various traditional estimates ranged in their fullest extent from 875 BC to 729 BC, while the majority agreed on a date between 759 and 748 BC. During the 1st century BC the choice was eventually narrowed down to one between 751 BC (offered by the Greek historian Polybius) and 753 BC (popularized by the Roman polymath Varro).[5] The list of consuls compiled in the time of Emperor Augustus indicates the year 752 BC, perhaps as a compromise.[6]

Any local records which might have been available for Carthage presumably vanished during the destruction of the city by the Romans in 146 BC, so it may never be known whether there was any firm basis for the dates offered for its foundation. In the case of Rome, the longest record available to its historians was the consular list beginning with the start of the Republic in 509 BC, but even this appears to be reliable only from c. 300 BC. It is clear that nothing existed by which Roman historians could have calculated an accurate date for the foundation of their city. In the absence of continuous local records, all the foundation dates given for Carthage and Rome depended on attempts to relate them in time to a major event of the past, such as the Trojan War, or to express them in terms of a chronological system, such as the Greek Olympiads.

The Era of the Olympiads

The most widely used system of dating in classical antiquity was that of the Olympic Games, which were regularly held in Greece every four years up until their abolition in AD 393 by the Emperor Theodosius. The period from one celebration to the next was known as an 'Olympiad', the first of which was traditionally reckoned as beginning in the year 776 BC.

The later Olympiads are frequently used by classical historians and can be fixed in time precisely from a number of lines of evidence.[7] For example, the death of Alexander the Great, unquestionably dated to the year 323 BC, is recorded as having taken place in the first year of the 114th Olympiad.[8] Counting back from this point, one easily arrives at 776 BC, the universally accepted date for the 1st Olympiad. But how did the ancients know that as many as 113 Olympic Games took place before this event?

The earliest evidence for the existence of a numbered system of Olympiads may appear in the work of a Sicilian writer, Philistus of Syracuse, active at the beginning of the 4th century BC.[9] But the fragment on which this is based derives from a much later source (Stephanus of Byzantium, c. AD 500), and the number itself, lacking from the original, is only a modern emendation.[10] Polybius (c. 200–115 BC), the historian of the rise of Rome, testifies that Timaeus (c. 270 BC) was the first to utilize the list of Olympic victors as a chronological tool.[11] The actual use of numbered Olympiads as a basis for dating is first found in the work of Eratosthenes at the end of the 3rd century BC.

Whenever it first occurred, the application of numbers or synchronisms to a cycle of games would have required a list of past Olympiads. Since it is almost certain that no such list was officially kept from when the games began, its retrospective drawing up would have required some clear documentary evidence, even if scattered. It seems that some inscriptions (or other written evidence) commemorating individual victors in different Olympiads were available. Perhaps also groups of victors, or short lists of winners in a specific competition in successive games, had been recorded. According to Plutarch (*c.* AD 50–120), it was Hippias of Elis, in the late 5th century BC, who first drew up a list, of what seem to be the victors in the *stadion* races, presumably working from such records. It was therefore only after Hippias that the Olympic Games could have become of general value for dating or chronography, and it was not until the Hellenistic period that the victors' list became completely settled.

Yet many questions remain. Exactly what kind and how extensive was the documentation available to Hippias? Did he really manage to assemble scattered evidence for victors of the same athletic competition from over ninety Olympiads, enabling him to create a complete list up to his own time? How critical by modern standards were his methods? Indeed, were the games held every four years right from the beginning? Strong doubts about the validity of the early Olympiads were expressed earlier this century by Beloch[14] and, already in antiquity, Plutarch himself was sceptical:

> However, it is hard to find out precise years, and especially those derived from the Olympic victors, the list of whom is said to have been published at a late period by Hippias of Elis, who began [his work] from nothing that can inspire confidence.[15]

Where does this leave us? One must be justified in being wary of the first ninety Olympiads, suspicious of the first fifty and extremely doubtful of the first twenty-five. Both E. Bickerman and A. E. Samuel, the leading experts on classical chronography, have warned against trusting too readily in the early part of the surviving list, the latter stating that:

> Plutarch's assignment to Hippias of Elis the distinction of first compiling a list of winners would suggest that we too should be very dubious about chronographic evidence from Olympiads much before the middle or beginning of the fifth century.[16]

In fact we simply do not know when the Olympic Games began, and the accepted date of 776 BC, upon which so many synchronisms of events have rested since antiquity, can hardly be used as a fixed chronological point. Hippias' list could have stretched the evidence considerably. A much lower date for the 1st Olympiad in the 7th or even 6th century BC would not be unrealistic. In any case there must be serious doubts about the value of early dates reckoned in Olympiads, as Burn has noted:

. . . the real weakness of early Greek dates expressed in terms of Olympiads is that even if there was an eighth- and seventh-century victor-list it certainly did not give synchronisms with historic events. Even if it is true that Chionis of Sparta won the furlong race for the third time in 656, still the thesis that the colony of Istrios [Histria] was founded in the same year remains, no less, simply a calculation by later scholars.[17]

Archons and Athenian chronology

A second chronological system available to ancient Greek historians depended on the list of archons, the chief magistrates of state in Athens. The Athenian archon list made its début as a historical tool with the publication of Hellanikos' *Attic History* at the end of the 5th century BC. The official list (as given on the Parian Marble of 264 BC) ran from 1068 BC, beginning with a group of archons appointed for life, followed by a number elected for a ten-year term, with the office eventually becoming annual in 683 BC.[18]

The earliest known fragment of an archon list was discovered in the Athenian Agora and is dated on palaeographic grounds to the 420s BC.[19] The names it gives are placed in the 590s BC in the official list, but this fragment clearly cannot be used as a check on the accuracy of the dates ascribed to these archons. There are good grounds to believe that this list was the first of its kind. Herodotus, writing at the time of its preparation, appears to be unaware of it – indeed, he mentions the name of an archon only once (VIII, 51).

Most classical historians dismiss the section before 683 BC, but tend to accept its subsequent record of annual officials. However, if the Agora fragment belonged to the first attempt to draw up an official record of archons, then this should make us wary of the archon list before the 5th century. Samuel concluded that although it has been 'assumed that an archon list was kept from earliest times, and, supplemented annually, provided a reliable guide for dating', 'the evidence does not make me confident of this assumption'.[20] Moreover, like the problem of dating by Olympiads, it has been stressed by Mosshammer that 'An archon's name can be a date to a historian only if events are regularly associated with archons' names.'[21]

Generating an ancient chronology

It is clear that most of the precise dates offered by classical writers for events in the remote past must have been based on highly artificial reconstructions and calculations: 'Fixed points which they used, such as the sack of Troy (traditionally 1184) and the first Olympiad (776), have an air of exactitude which is certainly deceptive.'[22]

Mosshammer says of the 5th- and 4th-century records on which the historians depended for their raw material:

The lists set in order the names of magistrates and priests, kings and victors who lived two hundred years or more earlier than the time these lists were published. The earlier portions of the lists must themselves be regarded as the product of reconstruction . . . no archival practice of state or temple that might have maintained earlier versions of the lists is demonstrable, despite the best efforts of modern scholars.[23]

As Solon was made aware during his trip to Egypt, the ancient Greeks possessed written records for a woefully short period of history (see Chapter 12). In the absence of sequential records the official lists seem to have been cobbled together from occasional documents, poems and folk memories.

Genealogies, some apparently stretching back to the Heroic Age, presented a ready framework for the enquiring ancient Greek historian. Any attempts to translate these into absolute dates relied, of course, on being able to assign a dependable average length to a generation. Unfortunately there is no reason to believe that the ancient Greeks themselves ever reached a consensus on this question. For example, while Herodotus may have used a forty-year generation to calculate the date of the Trojan War, it should be noted that the only length which he actually stipulated was 33.33 years (i.e. three generations per century; II, 142). Elsewhere he states that twenty-two generations of Lydian kings (descendants of Heracles) reigned for 505 years, giving an average generation length of only twenty-three years.[24]

Later chronographers used their own estimates for a generation, Eratosthenes for example apparently adopting forty years as his working figure.[25] Both this and the 33.33 years followed by many others (from Herodotus onwards), if used as the basis for chronological calculations over more than two or three generations, would result in a cumulative error. The further they went back, the greater the inflation of the time-span. The potentially enormous degree of inaccuracy involved is demonstrated by the fact that comparative data from the ancient to modern worlds suggest something between twenty-five and twenty-nine years as an acceptable estimate for a generation.[26] Adopting these more realistic parameters one could calculate a date-range for the Trojan War using Herodotus' genealogies for the Spartan kings (averaging 20.5 generations) between 1045 and 963 BC.

Further, as Sir Isaac Newton pointed out long ago, continuous father-to-son successions for the two Spartan royal lines over twenty-one generations is highly improbable on biological grounds. He suggested that the genealogies recorded by Herodotus and others must in fact have been a king list. From his own analysis of recorded dynasties he arrived at an average of eighteen to twenty years for a reign-length;[27] Burn, taking the English and French monarchies as a basis, produced a figure of 23.5 years.[28] Using the range provided by Newton and Burn gives a date for the Trojan War lying between 931 and 819 BC.

Thus, were it possible to treat the Spartan list as a reliable basis for calculating the date of the Trojan War, using realistic estimates would lead to a much lower date than those of Herodotus or Eratosthenes. With this in mind Burn, in 1935, attempted to reduce the date to around 1000 BC. Twenty-five years later he felt compelled to withdraw this now 'quaint suggestion', because, 'with the continued progress of archaeology', a date before 1200 BC seemed to be required.[29]

Burn was forced to change his mind by his faith in the modern archaeological dating of Mycenaean pottery. Had he been aware that the Egyptian chronology on which this is based is faulty, he might not have retreated from his original proposition that:

> the majority of dates, earlier than the period of the Persian Wars, which pass current in our Greek history text-books, are wrong and should be 'scaled down' by a certain proportion of their distance from 500 B.C.[30]

Burn's overall argument was sound. The high dates provided by ancient chronographers are often inconsistent with the synchronisms given by the earliest historical sources. For example, there is a well-known clash between the Olympiad date frequently cited by classical authors for Phaidon (the king of Argos who supposedly introduced coinage into Greece), and the information given by Herodotus. Whereas Pausanias (VI, 22) stated that Phaidon interfered with the administration of the 8th Olympic Games, i.e. in 748 BC, Herodotus (VI, 127) clearly linked him with other historical Greek figures of the early 6th century.[31] Herodotus himself provided little in terms of a chronology for Greek history before his own times, using neither archons nor Olympiads. In many cases his yardstick was the relationship between various Greek states (e.g. Samos, Corinth, Athens) and the long established Kingdom of Lydia, which dominated the Aegean coast of Anatolia inhabited by the Ionian Greeks, including Halicarnassus, home of Herodotus.

With Lydia we have a unique opportunity to check Herodotus' chronology against an absolutely dated external source. Herodotus gave precise reign-lengths for the Lydian dynasty, which began with the usurper Gyges and ended with the fabulously wealthy Croesus, overthrown by the Persians in 547 BC. Working back from this date using Herodotus' figures one arrives at 714–686 BC for the reign of Gyges. Fortunately, there is a cross-check here, provided by the records of Assurbanipal (668–627 BC), Emperor of Assyria, which mention 'Guggu king of Luddi'. As these describe Guggu's alliance with Psamtik of Egypt, who took the throne in 664 BC, Gyges was certainly still alive by that date. Further, analysis of the various texts referring to Guggu indicates that his death, at the hands of Cimmerian invaders from the north, must have fallen shortly after 650 BC.[32] Herodotus therefore placed Gyges at least twenty-five and very likely nearly forty years too early, and his Lydian chronology needs to be reduced.

Although it would be rash to try and scale down the traditional Greek dates uniformly, as Burn once suggested, it is conspicuous that where controls are available they seem to be exaggerated.[33] One way in which such errors inevitably crept into the calculations for events such as the Trojan War was through overestimating the length of a generation. Dynastic lines may also have been misinterpreted as genealogies, in line with the general tendency to exaggerate the length and purity of one's pedigree found throughout the ancient world (see Chapter 12). A combination of these factors set the age of the Heroes (the traditional equivalent of the Late Bronze Age) far too early in time. Once the high dates had been fixed everything else was drawn up to fit into the framework.

A flagrant example of the way the chronology could be extended to match prevailing notions comes from the Romans. Some of their earliest traditions put the Fall of Troy close in time to the founding of Rome – in one version Romulus (originally Rhomus) was the grandson of Aeneas the Trojan refugee.[34] A problem arose when this scheme was compared to the canonical Greek system:

> Greek researchers into chronology, notably Timaeus and then Eratosthenes of Cyrene . . . made the Romans aware that their myths were still much too thin upon the ground. For, once it was established that the Trojan War had taken place – that Aeneas and Ascanius had lived – at a date not far from 1100 B.C., and that Rome had not been founded until three hundred years later, there remained a subsequent yawning gap to be filled. And so the mythographers duly filled it – with a list of the kings of Alba Longa. A few traditions on this subject dated back to earlier times. But the king-list, as we have it, is made up by historians of the third, second and first centuries B.C.: or more particularly Cato, whose interests in such towns prompted him to attempt a circumstantial account.[35]

How far sheer invention played a part in the development of other detailed chronological schemes for Greek history is difficult to tell. But the Roman example clearly illustrates how the ancient system, once in existence, acquired its own momentum and could gather more 'evidence' to support it as time went on.

Notes and references

1 Clinton 1834, 123–40.
2 *FGrHist* 241 F 1a.
3 Cintas 1970, 99–244.
4 Cintas 1970, 219–44.
5 See Gjerstad 1962, 36–9.
6 Degrassi 1954.
7 For example, Eusebius (*c.* AD 260–340), the 'Father of Church History', in his work *Preparation for the Gospel* (X, 9), places the fourth year of the 201st Olympiad in the fifteenth year of the Emperor Tiberius, i.e. AD 28.
8 See e.g. Diodorus Siculus XVII, 113, 1.
9 *FGrHist* 556 F2.
10 Cf. Mosshammer 1979, 86–7.
11 *FGrHist* 566 T10.
12 Plutarch, *Life of Numa* I, 6.
13 Moretti 1957.
14 Beloch 1913, 148–54.
15 Plutarch, *Life of Numa* I, 4 (trans. N. Kokkinos).
16 Bickerman 1980, 75; Samuel 1972, 190.
17 Burn 1935, 144.
18 Bickerman 1980, 69.
19 Samuel 1972, 196.

20 Samuel 1972, 196.
21 Mosshammer 1979, 88.
22 Warmington 1969, 28.
23 Mosshammer 1979, 92–3.
24 Mosshammer 1979, 106.
25 Burn 1935, 130–1.
26 Henige 1981.
27 See Manuel 1963, 66.
28 Burn 1935, 131.
29 Burn 1960, 408; he did not, however, abandon his lower generation and reign-lengths (still placing the beginning of the Spartan list in the mid-10th century BC), but argued that the link between this and the Trojan War was fictional.
30 Burn 1935, 130.
31 According to Herodotus, Leocedes son of Phaidon was one of the suitors of the daughter of Cleisthenes, tyrant of Sicyon, active during the 570s BC according to the traditional dates.
32 Cogan and Tadmor 1977, 84.
33 For examples from the early 6th century BC, see Burn 1935, 141–2; 1960, 405.
34 Grant 1973, 108.
35 Grant 1973, 106.

APPENDIX 3

The 'Venus Tablets' of Ammizaduga and the dating of the 1st Dynasty of Babylon

One of the longest running debates in the field of ancient chronology concerns the dating of the 1st Dynasty of Babylon, which ruled southern Mesopotamia before the advent of the Kassites. The Dynasty reached its peak under Hammurabi, most famous for his reform and codification of Babylonian law. He was greatly revered by later Babylonian kings, including the 6th-century Nabonidus, who claimed in one inscription that Hammurabi had reigned 700 years before the Kassite ruler Burnaburiash (see Chapter 11). Letters from Burnaburiash were found among the El-Amarna correspondence in Egypt, dated by the conventional chronology to the 14th century BC. Following Nabonidus' figure, Hammurabi would have reigned before 2000 BC, a date widely accepted by historians early this century. Given the uncertain meaning of the Babylonian king lists,[1] there was no other way of determining the age of the 1st Dynasty, an essential step towards dating all earlier periods of Mesopotamian history and prehistory.

Then, in 1912, a new method for dating the 1st Dynasty was proposed. The great Jesuit astronomer Franz Xaver Kugler discovered a reference to year 8 of King Ammizaduga, penultimate ruler of the 1st Dynasty, in some fragmentary tablets recording the appearance and disappearance of a celestial body called 'Ninsianna'. Since this was a title of the great goddess Ishtar, who manifested herself in the planet Venus, Kugler assumed that this body was the subject of the observations. By retrocalculating the movements of Venus, he produced alternative dates of 2041, 1977 and 1857 BC for the first year of Ammizaduga within the range of time then considered historically feasible. On astronomical grounds he preferred 1977 BC. Since the internal chronology of the 1st Dynasty is well established, this gave dates for Hammurabi from 2124 to 2081 BC.[2] Thus Kugler's results agreed well enough with the figure given by Nabonidus.[3]

If the 1st Dynasty could be securely dated by astronomical means – as Kugler hoped – it would supply an invaluable clue to the dating of the Kassite Dynasty which followed, and hence to the chronology of 2nd- and 1st-millennium Mesopotamia as a whole. A fixed point would also be provided for early Anatolian chronology, as it is generally thought that the 1st Dynasty was terminated when the Hittite King Mursili I marched south and sacked Babylon, leaving the Kassites to take advantage of the ensuing political vacuum.[4]

Unfortunately, the 'Venus Tablets' have never provided the clear-cut answer they once promised. The choice between the various astronomical dates possible has been complicated by a number of factors. Foremost was the discovery, from a text found at Mari in northern Iraq, that Hammurabi was the contemporary of Shamshi-Adad I of Assyria.[5] With the publication of the Assyrian King List from Khorsabad[6] it became clear that, short of assuming vast gaps in the list, Shamshi-Adad could not possibly have reigned in the 3rd millennium BC – more likely, he lived no earlier than the 18th century BC. The historically feasible range for Hammurabi was accordingly reduced by three centuries and new calculations had to be made from the 'Venus Tablets'. The following were offered as candidates for Ammizaduga's year 1: 1702, 1646/1638 and 1582 BC.[7]

These dates formed the focus for the continuing discussion over whether a 'High', 'Middle' or 'Low' chronology should be adopted for Hammurabi and the 1st Dynasty. Various archaeological synchronisms with the Middle Bronze Age cultures of the Eastern Mediterranean meant that the ramifications of the problem spread far from Iraq, the uncertain chronologies of Anatolia, Syria, Palestine, Cyprus and Crete all becoming embroiled. Indirect links with 12th Dynasty Egypt established via the key site of Alalakh in northern Syria tended to rule out the High Chronology and favour the Middle solution – a case proposed by Sidney Smith, and taken to heart so much by Albright, an erstwhile High chronologist, that he eventually became an adherent of the Low scheme.[8] Initially Smith was so confident of his Middle chronology for the 1st Dynasty that he proudly announced it as confirming the precise dates for the Egyptian 12th Dynasty given by Sothic chronology.[9]

Yet to date, the controversy remains unresolved. In August 1987 a major conference was held at Göteborg, Sweden, to debate the issue, but with little agreement among the numerous participants.[10] Perhaps the most striking fact to emerge was that almost all the archaeologists present, from a wide range of fields, were still prepared to limit the range of their investigations to the traditional 'High', 'Middle' or 'Low' possibilities supposedly allowed by the 'Venus Tablets'. Only the expert on the notoriously complex stratigraphy of Alalakh, Marie-Henriette Gates, was prepared to dismiss the value of the astronomical dating of the 1st Dynasty.[11] At the same conference a frank admission was made by mathematician Peter Huber, currently the leading authority on the astronomical interpretation of the Tablets:

> The Venus Tablet data is of very poor quality. It is, in fact, the worst data set I have seen as a statistician. From the number of discrepancies between duplicate texts and internal inconsistencies between dates of disappearance and appearance of the planet, and the stated durations of invisibility, one may guess that 20% to 40% of the dates recorded in the text must be grossly wrong.[12]

Yet, staggeringly enough, Huber proceeded to filter out the observations which he considered to be trustworthy and to 'squeeze objective negative information out of the Venus data by using statistical approaches'. Thus, for example, having purged the texts of 'the corrupt last' section, Huber decided that the Low chronology could be rejected altogether. The Middle chronology could be dismissed as unlikely on similar grounds, leaving the High date of 1702 BC for Ammizaduga's Year 1 as the favoured figure.[13]

The problem with Huber's approach is that most of the 'inconsistencies' and 'discrepancies' which he sees spring from the fact that many of the observations do not appear to suit the observed behaviour of the planet Venus as it is known today. A very different approach was once taken by another scientist, John Weir, whose investigation made much greater efforts to treat the evidence, as a whole, as reliable. He experimented with the idea that the observations were made to the north of Babylon, and found a better fit with the data. He also allowed for bad weather conditions, which could have interfered with normal celestial observations; the abnormally long invisibility recorded for Venus in year 12 might, he thought, have been due to the dust clouds raised by the volcanic explosion of Thera in the Aegean (which happened at some time between the early and mid-2nd millennium BC).[14] Further, without rejecting a large percentage of the data, Weir showed that it describes a feasible planetary orbit, albeit not the one which is presently retrocalculated for Venus: 'it would appear that some modification in the shape of the Venus orbit has taken place since the time of Ammizaduga'. To explain this, he surmised that a large body may have passed through the Solar System, temporarily perturbing the orbits of Venus, the Moon and the Earth.[15] Reviewing Weir's extraordinary solution, Huber remarked that it was 'highly improbable, but not to be excluded'.[16] What seems to have escaped Weir himself is that if the orbit of Venus had actually changed in the way he described, then all the standard retrocalculations on which he based his work must be scrapped: while he plumped for the Middle Chronology of Smith, his own suggestions would invalidate its very basis.[17]

Whatever one makes of Weir's model, it does provide an instructive contrast to the standard interpretations such as Huber's, which by its own admission has to reject as much as 40 per cent of the data on the tablets in order to extract from it a standard Venerian orbit. Given this, and the fact that a more literal interpretation of the data can provide a feasible orbit, one wonders whether the body observed was really the planet Venus after all. Studies by British astronomers Victor Clube and Bill Napier of the orbits of meteor streams and asteroids have shown that there were sizeable cometary bodies in the Solar System during Bronze Age times which have since disintegrated.[18] Could Ninsianna itself, after all, have been a comet of the type they envisage? Weir himself has recently allowed this possibility.[19]

So exasperating are the problems involved in interpreting the Tablets that some have rejected their chronological value altogether. Otto Neugebauer, the leading historian of ancient science earlier this century, expressed the gravest scepticism; his lead was eventually followed by Sidney Smith himself, who, as Gates has stressed, went on record at the 1950 Rencontre Assyriologique as stating that the Venus observations were a 'factitious combination'. Reiner and Pingree, who have published an analysis of all the available Venus Tablet fragments, concluded that 'this text has undergone a considerable process of expansion and corruption prior to its being inscribed on the tablets available to us',[20] leaving serious doubts as to whether all of the data, or any, really belong to the reign of Ammizaduga. It should be remembered that none of the extant copies of this text – used to control the date of the 1st Dynasty of

Babylon – is actually any earlier than the 7th century BC. Citing such disclaimers, Gates proclaimed, rather optimistically, that the High, Middle and Low dates are 'now generally recognised as invalid', a claim unfortunately contradicted by the very theme of the 1987 conference in which she participated. As she noted: 'Certain ideas die hard, and a scheme as convenient as these Venus risings is difficult to dismiss once it has become, justly or unjustly, adopted.'[21]

A final overriding problem exists with all the standard interpretations of the Tablets. Even granted the assumptions that they do refer to Venus, that its orbit has not significantly altered, that one may legitimately 'massage' the data and that enough material was accurately transmitted from the reign of Ammizaduga over several hundred years, the scope of the astronomical investigations has always been constrained by what has been deemed to be a historically feasible range. This approach began with Kugler, who initially limited his calculations to a time period now conclusively demonstrated to be impossibly early. Rowton, writing the definitive chapter on New Eastern chronology in the *Cambridge Ancient History*, argued that 'a date for the end of Babylon I after 1500 B.C. is out of the question' – since according to the modern reconstruction, the first Kassite dynast to rule Babylon was ten reigns before the Burnaburiash of the El-Amarna period. Throwing this figure into the air, Rowton juggled it together with the possible astronomical dates and other clues from the standard chronologies for Hittite and Syrian archaeology and the conventional understanding of the Assyrian king list[22] – both ultimately dependent to some degree on the accepted Egyptian chronology. Rowton's five-ball act is impressively skilful, but serves only to underline the fact that the 'Venus Tablets' have never really been allowed to perform on their own, in the sense that they have not been used to provide a genuinely objective or independent astronomical dating.

With the reduction of dates for the 18th Dynasty, and with them the El-Amarna letters, by some 250 years, argued in this book, Rowton's parameters would be considerably widened. It should be noted that Huber's statistical analysis, while preferring 1702 BC as the best date for Ammizaduga's Year 1, admitted that 1518 BC was 'about equally good' and provided 'an astronomically feasible solution'.[23] Followed through, this could provide an 'Ultra-Low' chronology: Hammurabi's dates would be 1627–1584 BC, as opposed to the 1792–1750 of the currently favoured Middle Chronology, and the Hittite sack of Babylon would have taken place in 1466 rather than 1595 BC. One should not put too much weight on this possibility, however, given the dire problems involved in interpreting these texts.

Clearly the last words have yet to be written on the so-called Venus Tablets. At present all that needs to be said is that there is no astronomical proof of the date of the 1st Dynasty of Babylon – be it High, Middle or Low – and that the tablets provide no serious obstacle to the large-scale lowering of Babylonian history proposed here. Nor, as is sometimes imagined, can they in any way be conceived as providing indirect support for the accepted Sothic-based chronology for Egypt.

Notes and references

1 Babylonian King List A (see *ANET*, 272) summarizes the Kassite Dynasty as lasting 576 years and 9 months with 36 kings. This total is hard to verify, however, since half the royal names, in the central portion, are missing from the list (see Appendix 4). It is also unknown when the Kassite Dynasty actually took control of Babylon itself, as many of the earliest Kassite kings seem to have ruled over a different area of Babylonia.

2 For convenient summaries of the early attempts to date the Venus Tablets, see Weir 1972, 1–15; Huber 1987, 5–6.

3 Albright (1921, 83, 86, 94) still approved Nabonidus' date, claiming that Kugler's 'remarkable astronomical dating for the 1st Dynasty of Babylon' was 'practically certain'.

4 Rowton 1970, 207–8, 232.

5 S. Smith 1940, 2.

6 Poebel 1942, 1943.

7 Huber 1987, 6.

8 Albright 1965, 55–6. Albright eventually concluded that the low chronology was in agreement with the dates for Middle Bronze Palestine 'established on a solid basis by astronomically fixed Egyptian synchronisms'.

9 S. Smith 1940, 29.

10 Åström 1987, 1989.

11 Gates 1987, 76–7.

12 Huber 1987, 6.

13 Huber 1987, 7.

14 Weir 1972, 40–1, 29–31.

15 Weir 1972, 68, 78.

16 Huber 1974, 86.

17 In 1982 Weir completely revised his conclusions in the light of Huber's orbital retrocalculations, and now follows him in accepting the High Chronology. Nevertheless he still refers to 'a modification in the shape of the Venus orbit' to resolve certain discrepancies, which would throw out the basic assumption behind Huber's work.

18 Clube and Napier 1982.

19 Weir 1986. It should be noted that Dilbat, rather than Ninsianna, was the more usual name for the planet Venus in Babylonian astronomical texts, leaving the possibility that Ninsianna was a different body altogether.

20 Reiner and Pingree 1975, 25.

21 See Gates 1981, 37, n. 171.

22 Rowton 1970, 231–3.

23 Huber 1987, 12.

APPENDIX 4
Synchronisms between Egypt, Mesopotamia and the Hittites during the Late Bronze Age

The pattern of synchronisms between Egypt and Mesopotamia usually thought to support the conventional chronology was briefly discussed in Chapter 12; it is assessed here in more detail.

1. Assyria and Egypt (14th century BC)

The only synchronism between named kings of Egypt and Assyria during the Late Bronze Age is provided by two letters from the El-Amarna collection (EA 15,16). These were written by Assuruballit, King of Assyria,[1] one (EA 16) being addressed to Pharaoh *Naphuria*, the cuneiform version of Neferkheprure, prenomen of Akhenaten. Their author is assumed to be the Assuruballit known from the Assyrian King List and dated by its chronology to the 14th century BC.[2] Although universally accepted, the identification is not without problems. In EA 16 Assuruballit mentions that his father Assur-nadin-ahhe corresponded with Egypt; yet the King List and the available monuments agree in describing Assuruballit as the son of Eriba-Adad. In his introduction to the inscriptions of Assuruballit I, Luckenbill reviewed a possible explanation:

> The word 'father' may here have the meaning 'ancestor', as often in the Assyrian texts, but even so our difficulties are not all cleared up. In the texts given below Assur-uballit does not include Assur-nâdin-ahê among his ancestors, although he carries his line back six generations.[3]

While the El-Amarna letter may well reflect some other relationship (e.g. adoptive) other than direct filiation between Assuruballit I and an Assurnadin-ahhe, this is merely hypothetical, and the possibility remains that the El-Amarna correspondent was *not* the Assuruballit son of Eriba-Adad known from the monuments, but another, as yet unattested, ruler. Thus the much vaunted synchronism between Akhenaten and Assuruballit I, the main linchpin between Egyptian and Assyrian Late Bronze Age chronologies, is flawed and must be treated with caution.

2. Assyria and Hatti (13th century BC)

Regarding the links held to exist between the Assyrian and Hittite empires during the 13th century BC, these depend mainly on the royal correspondence found at Boghazköy, since neither the Hittite nor Assyrian kings name their opposite numbers in their annals – with the exception of the problematic reference to Ini–Teshub of Carchemish by Tiglath–pileser I (see Table 6:2; see also Chapter 12).

A major problem in attributing a name found in such correspondence to a given individual is that Hittite and Assyrian royal nomenclature was very repetitive. For example, five kings called Shalmaneser are given by the Assyrian King List for the period between the 13th and 8th centuries BC. Some of the Boghazköy letters do not include the names of either author or recipient, and have been ascribed to particular kings by guesswork; only those letters which do contain at least one name merit close consideration:

(a) KBo I 20 refers to a King Adad-nirari, although there is no mention of Assyria.[4] The letter is attributed to Hattusili III, but this is merely a deduction based on the presently accepted dates for Adad-nirari I. Little can be established from the evidence of this letter except that there was a King Adad-nirari ruling in Assyria (?) during the Hittite Imperial period.

(b) KUB XXIII 102 is a reply from a Hittite to an Assyrian king, neither party being mentioned by name. Rowton considers that 'the reference to Wasašatta identifies the addressee as Adad-nērari I', as the annals of that ruler describe his defeat of one Wasašatta, King of Hanigalbat (Mitanni).[5] However, the name (Waša-) on which Rowton places such weight is incomplete, and has been discounted by Gelb in his summary of Mitannian history: 'A reference to Waša[šatta] in a Hittite letter . . . is too doubtful to use.'[6]

(c) KUB XXIII 88 is apparently addressed to a king of Hatti (the expression 'My Brother', used between Great Kings, is present), but his name is lost. It may be from a King Shalmaneser ($\check{S}ul$-ma-nu-a-$\check{s}a$-ri-id), but the name has to be heavily restored, as only the characters a-$\check{s}a$-ri-$[i]d$ survive.[7] The letter is assumed to be addressed to Hattusili III, but again this is a deduction based on the accepted dates for Shalmaneser I. All this letter tells us is that there may have been a Shalmaneser ruling in Assyria during the time of the Boghazköy correspondence.

(d) KUB XXIII 99 has been held to synchronize Shalmaneser I with Tudhaliya IV. However, while the letter was written by a King Tudhaliya, the reading of the addressee's name as Shalmaneser is highly equivocal. Likewise, it is not absolutely certain that the letter was addressed to an Assyrian.[8]

(e) RS 34.165 (found at Ras Shamra/Ugarit) was apparently sent to the King of Ugarit (name unknown) by an Assyrian monarch. The body of the text refers to a Tudhuliya (sic), King of Hatti, while the beginning has the last element of a name which could be restored as Shalmaneser. The editor of the text was uncertain whether the sender was Shalmaneser I, or whether the letter refers to him as the father of Tukulti-Ninurta I.[9] Again, such fragmentary evidence can hardly provide a sound synchronism.

(f) KUB III 74 provides the best synchronism which can be derived from the Hittite-Assyrian correspondence. It was sent by a King Tudhaliya to a King Tukulti-Ninurta,[10] an Assyrian ruler if we combine the evidence from letter (g).

(g) KUB XXVI 70 was written by an unnamed correspondent to a Tukulti-

Ninurta, not addressed as a king but generally assumed to be the Tukulti-Ninurta who was the recipient of letter (*f*); it refers to the 'King of Assyria, your father', to whom Urhi-Teshub (an earlier Hittite king) had written.[11] The letter must come from one of the four kings who succeeded Urhi-Teshub before the end of the Hittite Empire; Tudhaliya IV is a candidate. Taken together the evidence of letters (*f*) and (*g*) would provide a synchronism between an Assyrian king named Tukulti-Ninurta and the Hittite King Tudhaliya IV.

3. Babylonia, Hatti and Egypt (15th to 13th centuries BC)

Most of the 2nd-millenium synchronisms between Egypt and Mesopotamia concern the Kassite kings of Babylonia. The El-Amarna correspondence (EA 1–11, 14) names four Kassite kings: Karaindash, Kurigalzu, Kadashman-Enlil and Burnaburiash. With the exception of the first, who is referred to as an ancestor who had dealings with Egypt in the past, these rulers can be synchronized with the Egyptian correspondents Amenhotep III, Akhenaten and Tutankhamun, conventionally dated to the 14th century BC. A few generations later the Hittite King Hattusili III, indisputable contemporary of Pharaoh Ramesses II, wrote to Kadashman-Enlil, King of Babylonia, the letter (KBo I 10) showing that Hattusili had also corresponded with Kadashman-Enlil's father Kadashman-Turgu.[12]

However, the existence of these synchronisms provides no support for the conventional Egyptian chronology, since the dating of the five Kassite kings is mainly dependent on Egyptian and Hittite evidence. None of the kings in question is mentioned in a contemporary Assyrian source. Nor are the names of the '14th to 13th century' sequence of Kassite rulers given in any king list. The most important source, Babylonian King List A, lists six early Kassite rulers down to one Tazzigurumash (obverse i), at which point the tablet breaks off. After several missing and damaged lines, regnal years for three kings are given, but their names are missing (obverse ii). Then (line 4) the name 'Ka-dash(?)[. . .]' occurs (regnal years missing), followed by Kudur-Enlil (restored), Shagarakti and Kashtil.[13] Since Kings Shagarakti-Shuriash and Kashtiliash are known from other sources to have been contemporary with Tukulti-Ninurta I of Assyria (conventionally 1243–1207 BC),[14] it is usually thought that the broken name 'Ka-dash(?)[. . .]' must be the Kadashman-Enlil (II) who corresponded with Hattusili III. However, since other royal Kassite names could be restored here[15] this is merely an assumption.

Another document with information spanning this period is the late compilation known as the *Synchronistic King List*, which arranges ostensibly contemporary rulers of Assyria and Babylonia in parallel columns.[16] Column i finishes with the name of Ulamburiash, an early Kassite ruler currently dated to *c.* 1500 BC. No names for the '15th' or '14th' centuries are preserved, while col. ii begins, after a gap of only one line (!), with the names of Tukulti-Ninurta of Assyria and Kashtiliash of Babylonia (the latter restored from other documents).

Thus the placement of the 14th- and 13th-century Kassite kings known from the El-Amarna and Boghazköy correspondence does not depend on the evidence of Babylonian king lists. As Brinkman clearly stated: 'this section of the dynasty is not preserved in any of the king lists'.[17]

Outside of the king lists, the chronicles are the next most valuable source of dynastic information for Babylonia. Two cover the relevant periods: the so-called *Synchronistic History* and the parallel version *Chronicle P*.[18] The correspondents of Hattusili III (Kadashman-Turgu and Kadashman-Enlil) do not appear in these texts. With regard to the earlier El-Amarna group, there is no reference to a Kadashman-Enlil or a Kurigalzu in the position required for them by the accepted chronology. There is a mention in the *Synchronistic History* of a Burnaburiash in a context describing the relations between Assuruballit and the Kassites; however, the version given by *Chronicle P* implies that he was an ancestor, rather than a contemporary of the events described.[19] Of the El-Amarna names this leaves Karaindash, referred to by Kadashman-Enlil as an ancestor in a letter to Amenhotep III (EA 10:8–10). As the *Synchronistic History* places a Karaindash alongside the Assyrian Assur-bel-nisheshu (conventionally 1417–1409 BC)[20] this is thought to agree with the El-Amarna evidence. Even so, as the reference to Karaindash in the letter is retrospective, with no information given on his Egyptian contemporaries, the synchronism is too vague to be of significant value.

In conclusion, any attempt to confirm the conventional Egyptian New Kingdom chronology by reference to Babylonia would involve dangerously circular reasoning, since the absolute dates for the Kassite rulers in question ultimately depend on Egyptian synchronisms. Further, Babylonian history and chronology during this period still remain extremely unsettled. For example, the evidence of a recently published Kassite legal text appears to upset the conventional sequence of '13th-century' rulers (including Kadashman-Turgu and Kadashman-Enlil) previously felt to be well established. As Brinkman concluded: 'we have not seen the last revision or reevaluation of Middle Babylonian chronology'.[21] Indeed, the evidence would certainly allow a major reconstruction of Kassite Babylonian history in line with the shortening of Assyrian chronology argued here.

Notes and references

1 Knudtzon 1907–15; Mercer 1939.
2 The only other attested ruler of this name being Assuruballit II, who reigned briefly towards the end of the Assyrian Empire (611–609 BC).
3 *ARAB* I, 21.
4 Otten 1959, 66.
5 Rowton 1959, 10 (n. 44).
6 Gelb 1944, 81 (n. 253).
7 Otten 1959, 66.
8 Otten 1959, 65.
9 See Singer 1985, 100–1 for discussion.
10 Otten 1959, 65.

11 Otten 1959, 67–8.
12 Rowton 1966, 243–8.
13 *ANET*, 272.
14 See Ch. 12, n. 19; Grayson 1975, 161.
15 The reading 'Ka-' is certain, '-dash-' less certain; Kadashman-Harbe, Kadashman-Turgu and Kadashman-Buriash would be equally plausible restorations.
16 *ANET*, 272–4.
17 Brinkman 1976, 14.
18 Grayson 1975, 157–77.
19 van der Meer 1947, 16.
20 Grayson (1975, 158) notes a 'serious chronological problem' at this point of the Chronicle, which places Assur-bel-nisheshu and Puzur-Assur (III) in the reverse order to that given by the Assyrian King List.
21 Brinkman 1983, 74.

Notes and References

Abbreviations

AAA	*Annals of Archaeology and Anthropology*
AJA	*American Journal of Archaeology*
ANEP	J. B. Pritchard (ed.), *The Ancient Near East in Pictures*, Princeton Univ. Press, 1954.
ANET	J. B. Pritchard (ed.), *Ancient Near Eastern Texts Relating to the Old Testament*, Princeton Univ. Press (3rd edn with supplement), 1969
AnSt	*Anatolian Studies*
ARAB	D. D. Luckenbill, *Ancient Records of Assyria and Babylonia*, Vols I & II, Univ. of Chicago Press, 1926 & 1927
AR	*Archaeological Reports*
BA	*Biblical Archaeologist*
BAR	*Biblical Archaeology Review*
BAR Int. Ser.	British Archaeological Reports, International Series
BASOR	*Bulletin of the American Schools of Oriental Research*
BAT	Proceedings of the International Congress on Biblical Archaeology, *Jerusalem April 1984*, Jerusalem: Israel Exploration Society, 1985
BCH	*Bulletin de Correspondence Hellénique*
BSA	*Annual of the British School at Athens*
CAH	*The Cambridge Ancient History*, Cambridge Univ. Press (current editions cited unless otherwise stated)
EAEHL	M. Avi-Yonah and E. Stern (eds), *Encyclopedia of Archaeological Excavations in the Holy Land*, Oxford Univ. Press, 1975–8
FGrHist	F. Jacoby (ed.), *Die Fragmente der Griechischen Historiker*
IEJ	*Israel Exploration Journal*
JARCE	*Journal of the American Research Center in Egypt*
JEA	*Journal of Egyptian Archaeology*
JFA	*Journal of Field Archaeology*
JHS	*Journal of Hellenic Studies*
JNES	*Journal of Near Eastern Studies*
OJA	*Oxford Journal of Archaeology*
PEQ	*Palestine Excavation Quarterly*
PPS	*Proceedings of the Prehistoric Society*
RDAC	*Report of the Department of Antiquities, Cyprus*
SAC	*Studies in Ancient Chronology*
SIMA	Studies in Mediterranean Archaeology

Notes

1 · *The Evolution of Old World Chronology*

1 Atkinson 1952, 236–7.
2 Piggott 1938; for the Wessex Culture and its supposed Mycenaean links, see Thorpe 1990.
3 Atkinson 1952, 237.
4 Atkinson 1956, 165.
5 Pitts 1982, 128–9.
6 Atkinson 1969.
7 Harding 1984, 264.
8 Piggott 1965, 73.
9 Renfrew 1973, Chapter 9.
10 Redford 1987, 27.
11 Freud 1939.
12 Wheeler 1954, 24.
13 Ussher 1650.
14 White 1896, 253.
15 Grafton 1975.
16 Grafton 1975, 176–7.
17 Newton 1728, 187.
18 Manuel 1963.
19 Hoare 1812, 7.
20 Cunnington 1974, 30.
21 Gräslund 1987, 3.
22 Thomsen 1848.
23 Daniel 1975, 28.
24 See, for example, Morgan 1877.
25 Briggs 1988, 351.
26 Montelius 1885.
27 See the definitive biography, Drower 1985, Chapter II.
28 See discussion in Chapter 10.
29 As early as 1648 Gravius Bainbridge experimented with the idea of a Sothic cycle. In 1758 Nicolas Fréret was the first astronomer to calculate a heliacal rising of Sirius on the first day of the New Year in 1322 BC. In the years following the decipherment of hieroglyphics in 1822, attempts, notably by the astronomer Jean-Baptiste Biot, began to be made to link the Sothic cycle with the monuments. However, before the 20th century there was little agreement among Egyptologists regarding the significance of the astronomical data – for example (see Torr 1896, ix), dates offered for the beginning of the 18th Dynasty ranged from 1703 BC (Mariette) to 1591 BC (Lepsius).
30 Meyer 1904; Petrie 1896, 29–34. An outstanding question was whether only one Sothic cycle elapsed between the 12th and 18th Dynasties. Petrie maintained that a second cycle intervened, thus producing dates for the Middle Kingdom a full 1460 years earlier than those followed by his

contemporaries, an idea which died with him in 1942 (see Drower 1985, 314–15).

31 Schliemann 1875 & 1881.
32 Schliemann 1878.
33 Dohl 1986; cf. Easton 1984.
34 See Hall 1901, 6.
35 Evans 1901/1902.
36 Cited in Drower 1985, 149.
37 Petrie 1890, 271.
38 Torr 1896, v; for a brief account of the Torr–Petrie debate, see conveniently Drower 1985, 185–6.
39 Lieblein 1873.
40 Trans. from Lieblein 1914, 382.
41 Trans. from Lieblein 1914, 345.
42 Rawlinson 1881, 516–17.
43 Reinecke 1902 & 1924; Montelius 1903.
44 From an address to the Egypt Exploration Fund at the 1901 AGM, cited in Drower 1985, 263–4.
45 Montelius 1899, 1.
46 Trigger 1980, 158, 170.
47 Childe 1958, 8.
48 Renfrew 1970 & 1973, Chapter 5.
49 Hollstein 1980; Pilcher et al. 1984. There are significant gaps earlier in the tree-ring sequence, in the Late Bronze Age section, while the number of tree-ring dated objects on archaeological sites falls dramatically as one goes back in time beyond the 6th century BC.
50 Müller-Karpe 1959a.
51 Sandars 1971, 10–12.
52 Harding 1984, 159.
53 Most of the evidence comes from buried hoards of metalwork containing bronzes of apparent Mycenaean type (Branigan 1972). For example, comparisons have been made between tools in the rich hoard from Surbo, southern Italy, and examples in LHIIIB hoards in Greece and Cyprus, but they are too inexact to provide useful correlations (Harding 1975). Moreover, the value of such proposed identifications is fatally flawed by the inherent difficulties of using any hoard for dating purposes – it may contain material of widely differing ages collected together at a later date, as numerous coin hoards have clearly shown. Indeed, Branigan himself (1972, 283–4) acknowledges this problem.
54 A number of Peschiera-type daggers come from Greece for which an LHIIIB-C date is assumed, but there are no good published associations (Peroni 1956). A find of great interest is the mould for making winged axes – a standard Peschiera form – found in the 'House of the Oil Merchant' at Mycenae (Stubbings 1954). Its occurrence is rather puzzling, as winged axes themselves are not found in the Aegean. The house was constructed early in LHIIIB, but the mould itself came from material dumped there after the destruction of the building – a date late in LHIIIB

for the mould is almost certain, as LHIIIC pottery was found in the layer above this (Harding 1984, 317–18). However, the mould also bears a close resemblance to the less securely dated Urnfield Culture axes from Slovakia, leaving the suspicion that it might not be an Italian product (Gimbutas 1965, 114).

55 Alexander and Hopkin 1982.
56 Harding 1984, 138.
57 Sandars 1971, 12–13, 15.
58 Harding 1980a, 126.
59 Harding 1983a, 45–9; Bouzek 1985, 19.
60 Thorpe forthcoming.
61 Kristiansen 1987.

2 *To the Pillars of Heracles*

1 Slightly later, Cumae was founded on the mainland opposite. Further south, various competing Greek cities had by 700 BC planted colonies at Sybaris, Tarentum and Croton on the arch of the foot of Italy (the Gulf of Taranto), and Rhegium and Caulonia on the toe (Graham 1982, 94–113).
2 Scullard 1967, 246.
3 Gjerstad 1965, 74.
4 Peroni 1959.
5 Peroni 1960, 496–7; Müller-Karpe 1959b.
6 Gierow 1966, 498; Hencken 1968, 436.
7 Gierow 1961, 122.
8 See Close-Brooks 1979 for a discussion of the Veii material. In the latest examination of the Rome evidence J. C. Meyer (1983) is absolutely convinced that the dispute is now settled in favour of the 'high' chronology. A confusing factor in this debate has been that Gjerstad's chronological divisions were based largely on the general shape of pottery in each phase (whether pots were short and wide or tall and thin) together with changes in technique, while Peroni preferred to take the changing forms of pottery (whether cups, jugs or bowls are used) as a basis for dividing the finds into periods. Along with the triumph of the 'high' chronology there has been a rejection of Gjerstad's clearly unsatisfactory methodology. It should be obvious that a thorough analysis would take into account both shape and form, but this realization has been slow in coming.
9 Descœdres and Kearsley 1983, 53.
10 Pallottino 1979, 206.
11 Potter 1976; Delpino 1979, 47–8.
12 Delpino 1979, 45.
13 Harding 1984, 318.
14 D. Ridgway 1988, 630.
15 Delpino 1979, 46; D. Ridgway 1988, 629–30.
16 Lukesh 1984; Smith 1987.
17 Daniel and Evans 1975, 722; Pallottino 1961.

18 Coles and Harding 1979, 425.

19 In Quagliati's work (1900) an enclosing wall was uncovered, one building fully recorded, another incompletely excavated and the presence of three others noted.

20 Coles and Harding 1979, 420.

21 Holloway 1981, 88–9.

22 Holloway (1981, 84) includes in his erosion processes the sea wearing through the soft rocks underlying the site and their subsequent collapse.

23 Säflund 1939; Taylour 1958, 81–2, 133.

24 At Thapsos scattered round huts were replaced by complexes of rect-angular rooms (perhaps warehouses) around a central courtyard, sepa-rated by paved streets. Holloway (1984 & 1985) gives up-to-date accounts of the excavations.

25 Brea 1966, 128–9.

26 Graham 1982, 94–113.

27 Isserlin and du Plat Taylor 1974, 83; Tusa 1988, 188–90.

28 In the sea off the coast of the Greek city of Selinus a statuette of the Phoenician smiting-god Reshef was dredged up (Chiappisi 1961). This is generally dated to the 13th to 12th centuries BC (e.g. Moscati 1968, 95), but it has recently been argued that the piece belongs to the 8th century BC (Falsone 1988). The other main element in the discussion has been a group of jugs with a strainer in the spout, possibly used for pouring beer, thought to copy Phoenician vessels. However, none of the Phoenician originals has ever been found in the West or even the Aegean, and the Sicilian examples are now thought to derive from Mycenaean forms (Leighton 1981).

29 Brea 1966, 130.

30 Brea 1966, 143–4.

31 Harding 1984, 270.

32 Brea 1966, 143–56 contains a good account of the general cultural succession.

33 Holloway 1984, 128.

34 Holloway 1981, 112–13. Bietti Sestieri 1979, 608 and Holloway 1985, 389 give population figures of 1000–2000.

35 Holloway 1985, 391.

36 Thucydides VI, 2.

37 Graham 1982, 105.

38 Brea and Cavalier 1956 & 1980.

39 Brea and Cavalier 1960.

40 Holloway 1981, 72–3.

41 The Ausonian I settlement contained LHIIIA, B and C pottery, while the lower levels of Ausonian II held LHIIIB and C wares. As a result Taylour (in Brea and Cavalier 1980, 817) sets the transition at c. 1230 BC.

42 Brea and Cavalier 1956; some support for this low date is given by the radiocarbon dates of 870±50 bc (R-367), 820±50 bc (R-367a) and 605±50 bc (R-181) on charcoal in Ausonian II contexts, which, when calibrated, point to a date in the 10th century BC.

43 Allen 1977, 368.

44 The oldest known Punic tomb is at Rabat, with East Greek pottery of 675–650 BC (Baldacchino and Dunbabin 1953). On Tas Silg, overlooking Marsaxlokk Bay, the Carthaginians built a temple to the goddess Astarte in the 6th century, covering a preceding native sanctuary with Borġ in-Nadur pottery (Ciasca 1988).

45 Evans 1971, 226.

46 Renfrew 1972.

47 Trump 1961.

48 At the bottom of the pit was Borġ in-Nadur phase 3 pottery together with an early Punic lamp and an Egyptian pendant and amulet, all dated to the 7th to 6th centuries BC. The excavator, Ward Perkins (1942, 34), interpreted the site as a tomb, seeing the lamp as an intrusive object left behind by a tomb-robber of Carthaginian date. However, Trump (1961, 261) has reinterpreted the pit as being either a water-cistern or a grain silo (both common features of the Borġ in-Nadur culture) and accepts the stratigraphic evidence as found.

49 Evans 1971, 107.

50 The only exception to this is the short-lived and quite rare distinctive incised pottery named after the Baħrija settlement (Evans 1971, 227–8).

51 Coles and Harding 1979, 439.

52 At Monte Prama, in a layer above a series of burials, the broken up fragments of some twenty-five over-lifesize statues of white sandstone were discovered, depicting boxers and warriors in ritual combat, along with models of Nuragic fortresses (Tronchetti 1986).

53 Acquaro 1988, 220–22; Barnett and Mendleson 1987; Sulcis, on a small island off the south coast, was also apparently founded around 725 BC, to judge by a copy of a Greek Late Geometric pot used as a burial urn in the *tophet* (Acquaro 1988, 214–17; Coldstream 1977, 241).

54 Lilliu 1952/1954.

55 Guido 1963, 20–1, 109–18; Contu in Brea and Cavalier 1980, 827–36.

56 Lilliu 1982, 12.

57 Ferrarese Ceruti *et al.* 1987.

58 Cavanagh and Laxton 1985, 415. The available uncalibrated dates for the Archaic Nuragic as a whole are:

Brunku Madagui	1820±250 bc (Gif-243)
Barumini	1470±200 bc (K-151)
Pizzinu di Posada	1399±50 bc (Lab. no. not known.)
Ortu Comidu	1360±50 bc (P-2788)
,,	1130±60 bc (P-2401)
,,	1020±50 bc (P-2402)
,,	960±250 bc (P-2399)
,,	960±220 bc (P-2400)
Albucciu, Arzachena	1220±250 bc (Gif-242)
Genna Maria	970±50 bc (P-2403)

Most of these dates are of little or no value, due to their enormous standard deviation, while the remainder (when calibrated) suggest that the Archaic Nuragic continued after 1200 BC.

59 The team certainly reject Lilliu's suggestion (1973, 300–1) that the Cypriot-influenced tripod-stand in the deposit was made in the 8th century BC. Comparisons with a Late Cypriot III tripod-stand suggest a *terminus post quem* between 1230 and 1050 BC for the hoard, while comparisons of rattles in the hoard with a miniature stool in a Villanovan grave at Vulci suggest a *terminus post quem* of 850 to 775 BC (Macnamara *et al.* 1984, 17).

60 Two boats found in the Orientalizing period (7th-century BC) 'Tomba delle tre navicelle' at Vetulonia are almost identical to the Santa Maria example; a third miniature comes from the 6th-century BC Greek sanctuary at Gravisca (Macnamara *et al.* 1984, 9).

61 Gras 1980, 526–38; Macnamara *et al.* 1984, 17.

62 F. Ridgway 1986, 93.

63 D. Ridgway 1986, 174.

64 Lo Schiavo 1985, 19 (n. 15).

65 Two bronzes, one from a *nuraghe* and another from a sacred well, are dated to *c.* 1000 BC, but this is by comparison with Phoenician examples rather than from their archaeological contexts (Barreca 1986, 131). Inscriptions from Nora and Bosa (Cross 1986, 120) may also fall in this period, but they are only tiny fragments showing a few letters, and therefore difficult to date.

66 Albright 1961, 346; Cross 1986, 120; Peckham 1972, 467.

67 Acquaro 1988, 214.

68 Taylour 1983, 143. In the Early Bronze Age the fortified villages of the Argaric Culture dominated southern Iberia. These are broadly dated by vague connections with the Wessex Culture through faience beads and by similarities between local metalwork and central European Tumulus Culture (Bronze B–C) bronzes. See Daniel and Evans 1975, 763–4.

69 Daniel and Evans 1975, 764.

70 Savory in Hawkes 1974, 87.

71 Pons Brun 1989.

72 Harrison 1988, 35. He discusses the largest deposit of Atlantic Bronzes, from a shipwreck in Huelva harbour at the southern tip of Spain – over 260 weapons and 100 smaller tools and ornaments were recovered. The cargo is dated to *c.* 850 BC by the presence of brooches found in Cypriot tombs of the time, and to 900 BC by calibrated radiocarbon dates. Many of the weapons, dated by comparison with Urnfield Europe, are, however, of types generally thought to date to *c.* 950 BC.

73 Harrison 1988, 44. The native site at Huelva shows increasing Phoenician influence – during the 8th century BC stake-built huts were replaced by stone houses and local handmade pottery gave way to wheel-turned Phoenician wares (Jurado and Tomico 1988). Similar changes are visible inland.

74 Blanco and Luzón 1969.

75 One statuette is of Reshef, the Phoenician smiting-god, often dated to the

11th century BC, and two are Egyptian figures of the 8th–7th centuries BC. See Aubet Semmler 1988, 228, and Ruiz Mata 1988 for recent summaries of the Cadiz evidence.

76 Gil 1987.
77 Albright 1950, 176.
78 Aubet Semmler 1988, 226.
79 Shefton 1982, 346.
80 Albright 1950, 176; he believed Tartessos to be a city, a notion not supported by the Bible or by classical historians, and dismissed today.
81 Ponsich 1981, 131.
82 Tusa 1988, 187.
83 Herodotus IV, 196 (trans. Grene 1987).
84 Warmington 1969, 34; Jodin 1966.
85 van Compernolle 1973.
86 Rakob 1984; Fantar 1988, 169.
87 Cintas 1970, 464–5. Another element in this discussion is a gold pendant from the Douimes cemetery at Carthage with an inscription reading 'To Astarte, to Pygmalion, Yadamilk son of Padai. Whom Pygmalion saves is saved.' The script used has been dated by some to the later 8th century BC by reference to Phoenician inscriptions from Cyprus (Cross 1986, 117). But the Douimes inscription was found with Protocorinthian vessels of 700–675 BC and it compares closely with scripts of this period as well as earlier examples.
88 Albright 1975, 524.
89 Harden 1937.
90 Culican 1959/1960, 48–54; Coldstream 1977, 240.
91 Bikai 1978a, 66.
92 Cintas 1976, 256; Benichou-Safar 1982, 321–2.
93 Moscati 1968, 115.
94 Fantar 1988, 171.
95 Miller 1971, 113.
96 Forrer 1953.

3 Beware the Greeks Bearing Gifts

1 Tylecote 1987, 33.
2 Renfrew 1986.
3 For an adequate discussion see Boardman 1980, 229–55. In most works little or no interest is taken in associating the imported East Greek wares with the local potteries and providing a better defined ceramic sequence.
4 Occasional finds moving in the opposite direction have also been noted; for example, a clay lid from Babadag Phase II is thought to resemble closely a small box of Late Protogeometric date in Kerameikos Grave 37, Athens (Stoia 1989, 46).
5 For example, at Pšeničevo in Bulgaria there was a preponderance of stamped pottery, whereas on the northern Greek island of Thasos most of the vessels have channelled decoration.
6 Kruszynski 1990.

7 Garašanin 1982, 588.
8 Čičikova 1972; Blegen *et al.* 1958, 179; Wardle 1980; Heurtley and Hutchinson 1925–6; Tončeva 1980; Garašanin 1982.
9 For example, pottery from the upper levels at Babadag resembles the wares produced in northern Rumania during the Hallstatt B period of the 10th–9th centuries BC (Morintz 1964; Zaharia 1965, 103). Others have tried to use metal types to forge connections, drawing links between the products of Yugoslavia during the 13th to 8th centuries BC (Bronze D to Hallstatt B3) and Albanian metal industries. Garašanin (1982, 591) is critical of such comparisons. An earlier attempt to produce a coherent scheme for the Balkans and Central Europe was made by Hawkes (1948).
10 Gergova 1980; Garašanin 1982, 593.
11 Harding 1984, 132.
12 Sandars 1971, 22.
13 Easton 1985.
14 The estimate of Blegen's team is 700 BC (Blegen *et al.* 1958, 249–50; Coldstream (1977, 263) dates the reoccupation of Troy to 'around 750 B.C. (Troy VIII), after lying desolate for some 350 years'.
15 D. Page 1959, 31.
16 Blegen *et al.* 1958, 10, 147, 251.
17 Blegen 1963, 172.
18 Nylander 1963; Mee 1985, 48; Bloedlow 1988.
19 It is usually argued that Knobbed Ware was brought to Troy by an invasion of *Buckelkeramik* folk (e.g. Blegen 1963, 169–71).
20 Wardle 1980, 262–3.
21 Blegen *et al.* 1958, 158.
22 Blegen *et al.* 1958, 250.
23 Hänsel 1976, 229–36; Tončeva 1980, 136.
24 Harding 1983b, 169.
25 According to the excavators, the Balkan material occurred together with imitations of LHIIIC pottery in and above a thick burnt layer (Heurtley and Hutchinson 1925–6, 10). The succeeding settlement contained later Balkan Complex and local Protogeometric pottery (Heurtley 1939, 216, 233; Desborough 1952, 179). Later on, *c.* 600 BC, the inhabitants started to import southern Greek wares (Heurtley and Hutchinson 1925–6, 30, 62).
26 The layers within which finds were recorded were extremely thick, particularly the burnt stratum, and may therefore easily have incorporated material from different periods (Wardle 1980, 262); moreover, the fact that the site was on a terrace makes it impossible to assume, as did the excavators, that material found at the same depth across the site is necessarily of the same date.
27 For the latest report on the Assiros excavations, see Wardle 1989. Phase 7 produced LHIIIB–LHIIIC pottery, while a local late LHIIIC cup dates the destruction floor of Phase 6 to *c.* 1150–1100 BC. The next three levels (5–3), which contain Iron Age pottery, appear to be stratigraphically confused.
28 Hänsel 1979. Neutron Activation Analysis (Mommsen *et al.* 1989) largely

supports the idea of a shift to local production of fine pottery in LHIIIC times, but one of their clay groups (G1) is used for fine wares from LHIIIA onwards, into the Iron Age, so some imports may have continued. Neutron Activation Analysis (NAA) is a non-destructive method of analysis used to determine the chemical composition of various substances. A specimen is bombarded with neutrons, which interact with the atomic nuclei of the elements present in the sample, forming radioactive isotopes. These decay emitting gamma rays, the energies of which allow the identification and concentration of all constituent elements.

29 Wardle 1980, 261.

30 Snodgrass 1971, 125.

31 A common type, the skyphos decorated with pendant semi-circles, is a final or even post-Protogeometric class, which may have survived in nearby Thessaly as late as the 8th century BC (Desborough 1952, 193; cf. Kearsley 1989).

32 Snodgrass 1971, 253. Preliminary reports on small-scale excavations at Nea Anchialos near Salonika show Balkan Complex finds together with Geometric pottery, suggesting a similar date-range (Sakellariou 1965).

33 Rutter 1975, 23.

34 Sandars 1983, 61.

35 Koukouli-Chrysanthaki 1981, 246, 255.

36 Condurachi 1966, 403–7.

37 A small number of radiocarbon dates are available for Assiros (Burleigh *et al.* 1982, 243–4); although the Iron Age samples are broadly in line with the conventional Greek-based chronology, 'those from earlier phases do not seem sufficiently old (by 250 yr or more). All samples appeared to be from construction timbers.' Since large timbers tend to give results which are too old (see Appendix 1) the Assiros Bronze Age dates are particularly surprising. On the other hand, the Late Bronze Age series from Kastanas is too early by some 200 years after calibration, so that Warren and Hankey (1989, 173) have 'to appeal to old construction timbers to explain the high (after calibration) level 12 Protogeometric context dates'. Clearly these scattered and woefully inconsistent dates cannot be used as a support for the conventional chronology.

4   *The 'Dark Age' Mysteries of Greece*

1 Hooker 1976, 183–90. For the Mycenaean civilization generally, see Chadwick 1976.

2 Bryce 1989.

3 Hooker 1976, 152–62; it should be noted that completely new LHIIIC sites in mainland Greece are few and situated largely on the coast. Since most of them are cemeteries they can hardly be seen as replacing the destroyed LHIIIB settlements. Oddly, the cemeteries are rich in contents.

4 Stubbings 1975, 350–8; Renfrew 1979, 490–4; Carpenter 1966; Childe 1942, 177–8. For further bibliography and discussion of the various theories see Chapter 13.

5 Kilian forthcoming; cf. Snodgrass 1987, 46.

6 Syriopoulos 1983, 126.
7 Desborough 1972, 18. His estimate of a drop in population of 90% by the end of LHIIIC would fit Syriopoulos's figures for the Submycenaean period (1983, 15).
8 Schweitzer 1971, 192.
9 Coldstream 1977, 56.
10 Kantor 1956, 169–74; Coldstream 1977, 71, 130–2.
11 de Santerre and Treheux 1947/1948.
12 Kantor 1956, 174.
13 de Santerre 1975, 255.
14 de Santerre 1975, 252–5.
15 Perrot 1895.
16 Barnett 1982, 43.
17 Mallowan 1966, 480.
18 Benson 1970, 5.
19 Benson 1970, 111, 113.
20 Lorimer 1950, 307.
21 Snodgrass 1964, 159. Greenhalgh (1973, 19–39) used much the same criteria as Snodgrass to define 8th- and 7th-century BC chariots. He felt that the chronological distance of the Mycenaean period prevented any consideration of continuity. He dismissed one fragment from an LHIII vase which may show a part of an 'Egyptian' chariot, on the grounds that its reconstruction was not safe. In general, he could not see any LHIII chariot forms repeated in Geometric art.
22 Snodgrass 1964, 160. Nonetheless, he followed the usual classification into 'Helladic' and 'Egyptian' types (1964, 163). In his view the 'Helladic' type was the most common in the Late Geometric representations. One can reasonably infer that this is the form he thought was inspired by epic poetry. In the late 8th century BC, at the end of the Geometric period, the 'Egyptian' type appeared alongside it. Snodgrass identifies this as the racing chariot used in the contests of the 7th century BC, the dominant form of the time known from models dedicated at Olympia. It was presumably inspired by Near Eastern prototypes (Crouwel 1981, 72–3).
23 Crouwel 1981, 72–4. In contradiction to Snodgrass, Crouwel felt that the 'Egyptian' type was more common during the Late Geometric, with the 'Helladic' taking over only in the 7th century BC. Both could be explained by local continuity.
24 Theocharis 1960a, 60, Fig. 73a.
25 Snodgrass 1964, 58–9.
26 Greenhalgh 1973, 64–70.
27 Higgins 1957, 32–3.
28 Snodgrass 1964, 59. The Boeotian shield is differently identified by Snodgrass and Greenhalgh. It might be that the Boeotian examples illustrated by Snodgrass (1971, 60, Pls 15a–b) are Dipylon shields in profile, as Greenhalgh (1973, 70, Fig. 43) thinks. If this is the case, it further reinforces the idea that there was considerable influence from the

Late Bronze Age. According to Greenhalgh his Boeotian type is a later derivative of the Dipylon and possibly an archaic romanticism.

29 Schweitzer 1971, 164.
30 Snodgrass 1971, 281–2.
31 Schweitzer 1971, 169.
32 H. W. and E. Catling in Popham and Sackett 1980, 93–5.
33 Snodgrass 1971, 284.
34 Snodgrass 1971, 237–9, 284, 399.
35 H. W. and E. Catling in Popham and Sackett 1980, 96.
36 Catling 1964, 215; the eleven clay models of tripod-stands from Greece listed by Catling range in date from the late 10th to the end of the 8th century BC.
37 Catling (1964, 198–9, 217) notes three finds of Late Cypriot rod tripods found in Cretan graves which he dates to c. 950 BC, although, on the basis of the associated pottery, Schweitzer (1971, 166–7) has considered somewhat lower dates. Schweitzer's dates are as follows: Vrokastro, late 9th–early 8th century BC; Knossos, 8th century BC; Fortetsa, c. 870–820 BC. Another example (see Fig. 4:5) was discovered in an 8th-century Geometric grave from Athens (Catling 1964, 194). One further find, a rod tripod amongst the 'Tiryns Treasure', seems to be effectively undatable; while Schweitzer (1971, 165) assigned it to the 9th century BC on style, Catling (1964, 195) saw no reason to date the collection as a whole later than the Bronze Age. The moulds from c. 900 BC found at Lefkandi were for casting strips decorated with linked spirals, again echoing Late Cypriot tripod design (Snodgrass 1971, 285).
38 Catling 1964, 217.
39 Schweitzer 1971, 167.
40 Catling 1984, 91.
41 Muhly 1985, 333–4.
42 Coldstream 1977, 295–302.
43 See Jeffery 1961, 17, for a criticism of the perishables theory.
44 Boardman 1980, 83.
45 Naveh 1982, 175–86. An attempt to raise the Greek alphabet to the 11th or 12th century BC was made long ago by Ullman (1934). The question of literacy during the Dark Age ultimately has some bearing on dating the Homeric epics. Albright (1950) argued from Near Eastern evidence that it is difficult to date Homer after the middle decades of the 10th century BC, in contrast to the 8th-century date generally accepted by classical archaeologists. A focal point of the 'Homeric problem' is the preservation of fragments of accurate knowledge about Mycenaean society and culture over some four centuries (Hooker 1976, 7–9). The reduction of Late Bronze Age chronology argued in this book should considerably alleviate the difficulty of accepting that Homer records genuine reflections of Mycenaean civilization.
46 McCarter 1974, 68.
47 Naveh 1982, 186.
48 Cross 1980, 17. However, it is not clear why an early Phoenician

inscription found on Crete should automatically support Naveh's case, since in his model the Greek alphabet was borrowed directly from the 'Proto-Canaanite' script before the development of the Phoenician alphabet. Sznycer (1979), the original publisher, put forward a date for the Tekke inscription around 900 BC.

49 Catling 1976/1977, 12; Cross 1986, 125–6.

50 Coldstream 1982, 271–2.

51 Desborough 1964, 31.

52 See James et al. 1987, 26–7.

53 Syriopoulos 1983, 817–19.

54 Syriopoulos 1983, 307–17.

55 This is the case for the *megaron*-shaped house at Grotta on Naxos (Kontoleon 1951, 220), the fragmentary stone walls and clay hearth at Old Corinth (Weinberg 1939, 596–9) and the workshop for the production of silver at Argos (Daux 1959, 568). The other three sites where evidence of Submycenaean architecture occurs are Asine, with remains of a house underlying a Protogeometric arch-shaped structure (Styrenius 1973, 156); Athens with a few possible wells (Anderson-Immerwahr 1971, 112, 141, 261–2); and Ayia Irini on Keos, where the sanctuary has produced Submycenaean pottery but was certainly built in the LHIIIB period (Caskey 1964, 332).

56 Drerup 1964, 180–219.

57 Snodgrass 1971, 368.

58 Coldstream 1977, 303.

59 Syriopoulos 1983, 518; Snodgrass 1971, 369; Coldstream 1977, 303.

60 Snodgrass 1987, 202–3.

61 Coldstream 1977, 312–27.

62 See Coldstream 1977, 327–32. Sites for which continuity of cult has been argued include Epidauros for the cult of Apollo Maleatas, Amyclae for Hyacinthos, Delos for Artemis, Keos for Dionysos and Samos for Hera.

63 Coldstream 1977, 317.

64 Rutter 1978.

65 Mountjoy 1988, 3–4. The most recent discovery of Submycenaean pottery stratified above LHIIIC and beneath Protogeometric has come from the settlement of Kalapodi in Phocis (Catling 1982/3, 32–4).

66 Theocharis 1960b, 49–59; 1961, 45–54; Desborough (1972, 209) tentatively identifies a single cup as Submycenaean, but the excavator Theocharis (1960b, 58) has firmly stated that the style is absent.

67 Buschor 1927; Hammond 1982, 732.

68 Snodgrass 1971, 131; Desborough 1972, 243.

69 Hammond 1982, 733.

70 Cartledge 1979, 82.

71 Coulson 1985, 63–5. Coulson (1988) sought to bridge the stylistic gap by using stray finds without certain contexts from the area.

72 Coulson in Macdonald et al. 1983, 318.

73 Coulson in Macdonald et al. 1983, 63, 319. The DA I pottery was mixed in with Late Helladic and DA II material and could be distinguished from

the latter only on the basis of differences in fabric and shape. Related small finds seem to have Submycenaean correlations.

74 Coulson in Macdonald *et al.* 1983, 319.

75 Fagerström 1988, 35.

76 Desborough in Popham and Sackett 1980, 282.

77 Desborough in Popham and Sackett 1980, 303, 312, 398 (n. 151).

78 Popham and Sackett 1980, 47.

79 Popham and Sackett 1980, 43.

80 Popham and Sackett 1980, 42; the lowest level was allocated an LPG–SG overlap date.

81 Popham and Sackett 1980, 7–8. For further discussion of Lefkandi see James *et al.* 1987, 29–30; Popham 1990; James *et al.* 1990.

82 Snodgrass 1971, 134–5.

83 Several cases of such superimposed or mixed Mycenaean/Geometric deposits are catalogued by Benson (1970, 115–23). Notable examples include Delphi, where Geometric houses were built on top of the destroyed LHIIIC settlement (Lerat 1961, 357), and Samos, where the Mycenaean levels of the Heraion are immediately overlain by substantial Geometric deposits of the 8th century BC (Boardman 1980, 30). At Pylos the Mycenaean settlement is followed by a reoccupation with 'fairly widespread activity on the site in late Geometric times' (Blegen and Rawson 1966, 294). This Geometric material was originally described by Blegen (1957, 130) as 'perhaps of the 7th century BC', but later (Blegen and Rawson 1966, 184) he ascribed it 'perhaps to the turn from the seventh to sixth century'. More recently Coldstream (1977, 160) allowed a date-range for the Late Geometric pottery of this region from 750 to 680 BC, but was not sure whether the material from Pylos was really Late Geometric or Subgeometric in character. Whatever its precise date, the Geometric ware directly overlies the latest Mycenaean pottery at Pylos, and at many points is actually mixed with it (Blegen and Rawson 1966, 175, 177–8, 181, 184, 203, 209, 291, 294, 296–8, 300–1, 303, 307). The only evidence from Pylos thought to date to the intervening period comes from a nearby *tholos* tomb which has been identified as Protogeometric (Blegen and Rawson 1973, 237–42).

84 Popham and Sackett 1980, 7.

85 Ramsay 1888, 369–71. Hogarth (1925, 503–4) considered that the similarity between the Lion Gate and the façade of the Phrygian Lion Tomb is 'close enough to approximate the two monuments chronologically', but accepting the high date for Mycenaean civilization which was by then popular, he claimed that the 'beginning of the Phrygian rock monuments must be pushed back at least as far as the eleventh century'. Yet the earliest archaeological evidence of the Phrygians can hardly predate the 9th century BC (see Chapter 6).

86 Murray 1892, 21–57, 178–9.

87 Torr 1896, 69.

88 Snodgrass 1987, 179–80.

5   *The Foundations of Geometric Chronology*

1   Iakovidis 1979; A. Mazar 1985; Hankey 1987, 50–2.

2   Snodgrass 1971, 112–13.

3   Mountjoy 1988, 26–7, Table II; cf. Hankey 1988.

4   Boardman 1974, 193–4; see also R. M. Cook 1972, 262–9; Cook 1989.

5   Michael Vickers, *in litt.*, 26/2/86.

6   Francis and Vickers 1983; but see Boardman 1984.

7   Francis and Vickers 1983, 1985, 1988; Vickers 1985b, 1987; but see Boardman 1988.

8   Diodorus Siculus XII, 3–4.

9   Starr 1970, 81.

10 Gill 1988.

11 Francis and Vickers are undoubtedly correct to question the value of much of the conventional wisdom on Archaic period dating, as R. M. Cook (1989, 170) admits. However, it is likely that a reduction in dates of the order they propose is too drastic. The support which Vickers (1984) claimed at one point from dendrochronological dates for German burial mounds has faded away after an upward adjustment of the dendrochronology, as he himself has admitted (Vickers, 1985a). However, he does not follow up the consequences of the redating, which would tend to limit the scope for any downdating of the Greek pottery types which reached Germany. Although none of the standard fixed points is quite as solid as some have thought, there is equally often little to support the alternative dates canvassed by Francis and Vickers. For example, a third possible date for the Greek remains at Meşad Hashavyahu in Palestine (see Chapter 8, n. 65) provides a better match with the archaeological and historical background to the site. Even within the confines of the conventional chronology there is room for manoeuvre, as Gill (1988) has demonstrated. Most of the historical and archaeological anomalies presented by Francis and Vickers may be resolved by adopting a chronology lying approximately halfway between the conventional placement and that which they propose.

12 Thucydides VI, 4; Herodotus VII, 156.

13 R. M. Cook 1937, 204–5.

14 Thucydides VI, 4.

15 Pindar *Olympian Ode* II, 93.

16 Miller 1970, 5.

17 For comparison Pindar also uses the term in *Pythian Ode* IV, 282, where he says of someone: 'For that man is young in the eyes of boys, but in counsel an old man with a hundred-year-old life.' The meaning is not that this individual was 100 years old exactly but that he had the wisdom of an old man – Dr S. Instone, *pers. comm.*

18 Miller (1970) sought to demonstrate that there was a mathematical logic and consistency to the dates provided by the ancient historians; but as Mosshammer (1979, 95) pointed out 'such hypotheses are at once too simplistic and too abstract'. He argues that the available information

would have been too great to be able to synthesize it into mathematical equations.

19 Coldstream 1968, 327.

20 Francis and Vickers 1985, 136–7.

21 Burn 1935, 137.

22 Coldstream 1968, 316–17, 327.

23 Coldstream 1968, 326.

24 Boardman 1980, 172. Other sites with supposedly pre-colonial pottery include Megara Hyblaea (founded 728 BC) with finds of LG I (760–735 BC); Sybaris (720 BC) with finds of LG I (760–735 BC); Mylae (716 BC) with LGI and mid-8th century BC Euboean finds (Graham 1982, 94–113).

25 Cook 1972, 262.

26 Francis and Vickers 1985, 132.

27 Coldstream 1968, 311; for the Assyrian resettlement of Hamath see *ARAB*, II, 102.

28 Fugmann 1958, 264, 269; cf. finds of Cypro-Archaic I-II pottery (750/700–475 BC) from areas G ix 118 and G xxx 22.

29 Francis and Vickers 1985, 133.

30 *ARAB* II, 27.

31 Crowfoot *et al.* 1957, 212.

32 In a letter from Kenyon dated 5/12/1967 quoted in Riis 1970, 146. However, Kenyon merely seems to have confirmed that the published report was accurate, but this (Crowfoot *et al.* 1957, 212) nowhere actually states that one sherd was found in an undisturbed Level V deposit.

33 Coldstream 1968, 309.

34 Francis and Vickers 1985, 134. Unfortunately, they incorrectly cite Riis as recording that 'all but one of the sherds . . . were found in disturbed fills . . . "derived from levelling off earlier deposits higher up the hill"'. His statement (1970, 146) actually applies to a single sherd excavated by the Harvard Expedition.

35 Coldstream 1968, 305–7.

36 Letter by Hoerth of 1/12/1965 quoted by Riis (1970, 144–6). Three other body sherds found at Megiddo were regarded by Coldstream (1968, 303) as non-Hellenic imitations, of EGII or probably of MGI date. Two sherds, one of these and a sixth piece, were taken by Riis (1970, 146–7, Fig. 47 g,h) to be parts of Protocorinthian skyphoi from about 700 BC. This made him wonder, in spite of Hoerth's opinion that 'all [the Greek sherds] are likely from the same stratum', whether the last mentioned two pieces come from Stratum III rather than from IV. In the conventional chronology the latest date allowed for Stratum IV is 733 BC.

37 Yadin in *EAEHL*, 855; see Wightman 1985 for a general discussion of the complex stratigraphy and dating of Megiddo.

38 Wightman 1985, 127. Our thanks to Dr Rupert Chapman for drawing our attention to this matter.

39 Bikai 1978b, 53, Pls. XIb, XXIIa. The key Dark Age sherds found are of Protogeometric and Middle Geometric styles, but the chronology of the contexts in which they are found is confusing. Of the nine Late Protogeometric sherds only two were found in Stratum XI, dated by Bikai

from 925 (?) to 850 BC, fitting the present LPG chronology. The others occur later, with one in Stratum X (*c.* 850), four in Stratum IX (850–800 BC), one in Stratum VIII (*c.* 800 BC) and even one in Stratum II (*c.* 725–700 BC). Middle Geometric I pieces appear in Stratum VIII and probably in Stratum IX, again agreeing with the conventional dates.

40 Katzenstein 1973.

41 It must be emphasized that Egyptologist Hermann de Meulenaere (cited in Bikai 1978b, 84) has suggested that the object should not date earlier than the 7th century BC. (NB by this stage, within the time of the 25th to 26th Dynasties, Egyptian chronology is fixed absolutely; see Chapters 9 and 10). A similar range is indicated by the Cypriot Period IV material (initially dated by Gjerstad to 700–600 BC; see Chapter 7) excavated from Stratum III at Tyre.

42 Bikai 1987, 69; in earlier publications she varies the date between 730 and 720 BC.

43 Muhly 1985, 181; Karageorghis 1969, 26. A similar anomaly is presented by the Phoenician or North Syrian bronze bowl from the Kerameikos cemetery in Athens, dated by associated MGI Greek pottery to 850–825 BC. In the Near East such bowls are commonly dated to the later 8th century BC (Markoe 1985, 153–4, 156).

44 Though the Early Geometric II skyphos sherd was discovered in Room 42 of Stratum IVb, it seems to have come from a pit associated with Stratum III (Herrera and Balensi 1986, 170). Kearsley (1989) has recently argued that this type of skyphos should be placed in Late Geometric, not Early Geometric times. Another Greek skyphos sherd, of MGII–LG date, was said to have been found under Room 42 in Stratum IVb, but it is now also considered to be from the pit cutting through from Stratum III (Herrera and Balensi 1986, 170). The Middle Geometric I Cycladic cup was apparently found in the latest level of Stratum III.

45 Balensi and Herrera 1985, 104.

46 Coldstream 1968, 303, 310; see also Cook 1972, 262.

47 Desborough 1952, 294.

48 Herrera and Balensi 1986, 171. At one stage Balensi considered a date as late as 650 BC (1985, 73, n.26), though she now envisages the 701 BC horizon of Assyrian attacks in Palestine as a reasonable lowest point (*pers. comm.*).

49 Davison 1961, 125–6.

50 Coldstream 1968, 310.

51 Desborough 1972, 343 (n. 5); cf. Hankey 1988, 36.

52 Popham 1990.

53 Iakovidis 1979, 462.

54 Some Aegean archaeologists now place a degree of faith in the relatively few radiocarbon dates which are available for Mycenaean remains. For example, Warren and Hankey (1989, 159) believe that dates from the destruction levels of LHIIIB Dendra and Mycenae confirm the conventional chronology. However, it must be noted that of these five dates, the three from Mycenae are on charcoal from timbers which could have been two centuries old at the time of the destruction (see Appendix 1).

6   *Redating the Hittite Empire*

1   For his own account, see W. Wright 1886.
2   Key biblical references include Gen. 10:15, 23:3, 26:34; Exod. 13:5; Josh. 11:3; 1 Sam. 26:6, 2 Sam. 11:3, 23:39; 1 Kgs. 9:20–1; 10:29; 11:1; 2 Kgs. 7:6; Ezek. 16:3, 45. For a discussion see Kempinski 1979.
3   Sayce 1876.
4   Of the two classical references one concerns the 'empire of the Cilicians', described by the Roman historian Solinus (*c.* 200 AD) as encompassing most of Anatolia and reaching the borders of Egypt (*De Mirab. Mundi* XLIX). The second is in Homer's *Odyssey* (XI, 521), which refers to a contingent of Ketoi warriors led by one Eurypylus son of Telephus among the allied troops defending Troy. Their names, as we now know, are acceptable hellenizations of the Hittite Urballa/Warpawalas and Telepinus, a fact which raises the intriguing possibility that the Hittites may have sent a force to prevent the capture of the Troad by the Mycenaeans.
5   Translated (by R. M. Lowery) from Puchstein 1890, 14.
6   Perrot and Chipiez (1890, 191–2) felt that the palace of Alaça Hüyük with its lions and sphinxes was 'coeval with the Ramessides'; at the same time they saw much at Boghazköy and Yazilikaya as evidence of Assyrian influence from the 9th century BC onwards.
7   Hall 1901, 115, 122–4, 273, 315–19; he was eventually forced to change his mind by Winckler's discovery of the archive at Boghazköy; see Hall 1913, 329 (n. 2).
8   For an introductory account of the history of the El-Amarna Letters, see Campbell 1960.
9   For the standard edition of the El-Amarna Letters, see Knudtzon 1907–15 and Rainey 1978; the latest English translation of most of the corpus is by Mercer 1939, while a selection of key letters relevant to Palestine can be found in *ANET*, 483–90.
10 *ANET*, 319.
11 *ANET*, 199–203.
12 Faulkner 1975, 234.
13 References to the heartland of the Hittites in Central Anatolia do not seem to appear in Assyrian records. Likewise, clear references to political or other contact with the Hittite Empire are few and of little value chronologically. There are allusions to Hittites and Hittite soldiers in the records of Shalmaneser I and Tukulti-Ninurta I (conventionally 13th century BC), but none to a Hittite state or its rulers when they might have been expected (see *ARAB* I, 116, 164). Contact between the kings of Assyria and Hatti is known from the archives at Boghazköy, but these provide only one certain synchronism, between Tudhaliya IV and a Tukulti-Ninurta (see Appendix 4). The earliest Assyrian reference to a king of the land of Hatti concerns one Ini-Teshub, almost certainly reigning at Carchemish. On the conventional chronology this reference falls *c.* 1100 BC, making him a post-Empire ruler. On the revision of Hittite and Assyrian chronologies suggested here, he would be the King Ini-Teshub

who ruled Carchemish and Syria as the deputy of Tudhaliya IV (see Chapter 12).

14 Gurney 1954, 39.
15 See for example Landsberger 1948, 15–17, 23–35; Gurney 1954, 40; Frankfort 1969, 254 (n. 5); Hawkins 1982, 372.
16 James forthcoming.
17 Abu Taleb 1976, 13, 19–21; cf. Hawkins 1982, 373.
18 Drower 1975, 138–46.
19 Woolley 1953, 167–9.
20 Madhloom 1969.
21 Albright 1956.
22 Akurgal 1946, 98–114; cf. Akurgal 1968, 95–6.
23 Akurgal 1968, 96.
24 Akurgal 1968, 96–110, 119–41.
25 Frankfort 1969, 247 (n. 47), 129.
26 Frankfort 1969, 247 (n. 47).
27 Frankfort 1969, 164, 254 (n. 7).
28 Albright 1975, 529.
29 Hawkins 1974, 67. This statement was made, of course, before his discovery that the Malatyan kings who built the Lion Gate were closely related to the Imperial Hittite rulers of Carchemish; see our p. 133.
30 Hawkins 1974, 69–73; from outside sources there is only one possible reference to a king of Carchemish (Ini-Teshub) during this period; see note 13 above and Table 6:2.
31 Woolley 1914, 96; Woolley 1952, 234–5.
32 Hogarth 1911, 371.
33 Hogarth 1924, 29.
34 Woolley 1952, 249.
35 Woolley 1952, 246.
36 Mallowan 1972, 63; see also 78–9.
37 Woolley 1952, 159, Pl. 71c. In rubble by the Long Wall of sculpture, Woolley (1952, 175) found a blue paste scarab, possibly of similar 19th Dynasty date.
38 Woolley 1952, 235, Pl. 68a. Hankey 1967, 110–11, apparently accepts the sherds as Mycenaean. However, this classification should be held in some doubt; our thanks to Mr Michimasa Doi of the Dept of Classical Archaeology, UCL, for his opinion, based on study of Woolley's photograph.
39 Woolley 1952, 250–7.
40 Güterbock 1954, 113.
41 Woolley 1914, 96.
42 Woolley 1921, 48.
43 Woolley 1952, 214 (n. 1).
44 Opificius 1965, 47.
45 Sams 1971, 286, 295.
46 Sams 1971, 295.
47 Woolley 1952, 214 (n. 1), 234–5.
48 Delaporte 1940, 38–58.

49 Bier 1976, 122.
50 Puglisi and Palmieri 1966, 82.
51 Two tests (R-214 & R-214B) on the same sample of charred wood gave uncalibrated results of 885±70 and 845±60 bc (Alessio *et al.* 1966, 405–6).
52 Orthmann 1971, 141.
53 Hawkins 1985, 65.
54 Orthmann 1971, 99–100, 141, n. 47; cf. Bier 1976, 122.
55 Puglisi and Meriggi 1964, 28–9 (trans. G. Gammon).
56 Hawkins 1988, 99.
57 Hawkins 1988, 101.
58 Hawkins 1988, 103. *PUGNUS (Latin 'fist') represents a fist-shaped hieroglyphic character which cannot yet be read.
59 Hawkins 1974, 70–2.
60 Hawkins, *pers. comm.* 1988.
61 Hawkins 1974, 71, notes Laroche's hesitation 'between the Luwian reading *Ura-Tarhundas* and the Hurrian (*Talmi-Tešub*), which would coincide with the name of the last king of Carchemish of the Hittite Empire dynasty'. In view of the Luwian character of the father's name, Hawkins prefers the former reading. Even so, the possibility cannot be discounted that such names, particularly those containing theophoric elements (Tarhundas/Teshub was the Thunder-god), were meant to be understood bilingually.
62 Graves 1960, 281–3.
63 *ARAB* II, 8, 16, 18, 42–3, 55.
64 Strabo, *The Geography* I, 3, 21.
65 Akurgal 1962, 124.
66 Özdoğan, 1987, 17; Muscarella 1988b, 177.
67 Bittel 1970, 137.
68 Bittel 1970, 137–8.
69 Bittel 1970, 142.
70 Young 1966, 276.
71 Sams 1971, 19–22.
72 Bittel 1983, 38–45; cf. Muscarella 1988b, 181–2, 187–8.
73 Sams 1971, 318.
74 Young 1971, 276.
75 Mellaart 1985, 68.
76 Mellaart 1985, 78.
77 Mellaart 1990; see James *et al.* 1990.

7   *Cyprus, Ceramics and Controversy*

1 Dikaios 1971, 514–23; cf. Catling 1975, 208; Coldstream 1985, 47–50.
2 Karageorghis 1982a, 89.
3 Negbi 1982/1983; cf. V. Cook 1988.
4 Catling 1975, 209; but cf. Catling 1986, where the language used in regard to cultural traits is toned down and more Near Eastern influence is accepted.
5 Ayia Irini, Apliki, Athienou, Enkomi, Idalion, Kition, Kouklia-

Palaepaphos, Kourion, Lapethos, Nikosia, Maa-Palaeokastro, Myrtou-Pigadhes, Pyla and Sinda (see Syriopoulos 1983, 341–7).

6 Karageorghis 1981, 112; cf. Coldstream 1985, 50–1.

7 Karageorghis 1982a, 112.

8 Stager et al. 1974, xxix.

9 Karageorghis 1982b, 518.

10 Domestic building can be seen in part of a room at Kition-Kathari (Syriopoulos 1983, 615) and the small installation at Kition-Bamboula (Yon and Caubet 1985, 27–33). During the early part of CGI there was scattered activity across the site, while repairs were made to the temples. The settlement appears to come to an end c. 1000 BC (Karageorghis and Demas 1985, 21–3, 141–63). Coldstream (1985, 52) is too optimistic when he extends the remains of the occupation at Bamboula beyond 1000 BC, as he is in believing that the problem at Kition is solved because the gap 'is filled by the CGI-II burials'. The two or three tombs in question were disturbed when discovered and their evidence is equivocal (see Karageorghis 1974, 95; Nicolaou 1976, 158–216). Such burial finds hardly fill the hiatus in occupation at Kition; occasional tombs at other sites across the island cannot make up for the lack of a continuous settlement record.

11 Stager et al. 1974, 5.

12 Menander via Josephus, *Antiquities* 8, 146; *Against Apion* 1, 119. However, we should note that the name of the people involved has been corrupted in the MS tradition and is variously given as *Eukaiois, Eukeois, Iukeois, Tituaiois* or *Tituois*. It is Albright's emendation (*Kitiois*) that is generally accepted (see B. Mazar 1964, 15; M. Stern 1976, 119–22), while the older emendation of Gutschmid (*Itykaiois*), referring to Utica in North Africa, seems now to have been abandoned – presumably due to the lack of archaeological evidence for Phoenician colonization of the West as early as the 10th century BC. Bikai's suggestion (1978a, 55) that the Hiram of Menander's episode may have been Hiram II (at the time of Tiglath-pileser III of Assyria, 745–727 BC), which would apparently solve the archaeological problem, is without foundation, since the Hiram in Menander is explicitly connected with King Solomon of Israel (mid-10th century BC). A similar episode, this time clearly involving the Kitians (*Kitieon, Kittaion, Cetuteis*), is recorded as having taken place during the reign of Elulaios in the late 7th century BC (Josephus, *Antiquities* 9, 284).

13 The complex at Kition-Kathari consists of the great temple of Astarte (over LB 'temple 1'), a smaller Phoenician sanctuary (over LB 'temple 4') and a very small *cella* with an altar (over LB 'temple 5'). At Kition-Bamboula a sanctuary is believed to be the predecessor of the Archaic temple of Heracles-Melqart (Yon 1984, 90–7). Other sanctuaries which continued to exist from an earlier period are at Ayia Irini, Ayios Iakovos and Myrtou-Pigadhes, while a sanctuary at Idalion appears at this time.

14 Gjerstad 1948, 23. CGIII houses are now known from Idalion (*pers. comm.* A. Rayes).

15 Karageorghis 1976, 96; cf. Gjerstad's convincing arguments (1979, 234–54).

16 According to Bikai (1987, 50–3), the earliest Phoenician pottery at Kition appears to date to the late 9th century BC. Coldstream (1989, 92), however, considers an earlier date on the basis of a 'very early' type of Euboean skyphos, 'unlikely to be much later than 900 B.C.' Clearly there is some conflict here between the Phoenician and Greek ceramic chronologies. (See also our Chapter 5, p. 109.)

17 Guzzo Amadasi and Karageorghis 1977, 149–60, no. D21; cf. Yon 1988; Bikai 1978a, 54.

18 Coote 1975, 49.

19 Cross 1986, 117, dates the bowl in the first half of the 8th century BC. An earlier date in line with the excavator's expectations was argued by Dupont-Sommer (1970), the original editor of the inscription.

20 Karageorghis 1982a, 63.

21 Mitford and Masson 1982, 74.

22 Chadwick 1979, 143, cf. 313.

23 Dow 1954, 112; but cf. Karageorghis and Karageorghis 1956, 355.

24 Casson 1937, 93.

25 Goody 1977.

26 Karageorghis 1982a, 120–1; cf. Karageorghis 1988.

27 Mitford and Masson 1982, 75.

28 Gjerstad 1948.

29 Karageorghis 1987, 115–19; cf. Merrillees 1977, 42.

30 Furumark 1941, 128.

31 Gjerstad 1944.

32 Furumark 1944. At this point he had to revise the structure and dates of his LHIIIC pottery. Originally he divided this period into LHIIIC1 Early, LHIIIC1 Late and LHIIIC2 (Submycenaean), ranging in date from 1230 to 1100 BC. Now he created the new phases of LHIIIC1a, LHIIIC1b, LHIIIC1c and LHIIIC2 (Submycenaean), which he dated on the basis of Cyprus to between 1230 and 1025 BC (cf. Renfrew 1985, 85). An important point of relative chronology on which Furumark continued to differ from Gjerstad concerned the so-called Proto-White-Painted Ware, which he believed to be contemporary with LHIIIC1c and Submycenaean pottery, while Gjerstad (1944, 76–7, 103) insisted that it was contemporary with Submycenaean and Early Protogeometric. This disagreement could have affected the absolute dating of Greece (e.g. Gjerstad would have begun the Protogeometric in c. 1075 BC, fifty years earlier than Furumark), but it was basically glossed over (Furumark 1944, 258). Recent work by Iacovou (1988, 1–10) seems to show that Furumark was right, though under a 'revised' absolute chronology a new relative assessment will be necessary.

33 Gjerstad 1944, 84–6.

34 See Yon 1976.

35 Karageorghis and Kahil 1967, 134; Karageorghis 1982a, 9; Gjerstad 1974, 118.

36 Birmingham 1963, 15–42; cf. Prausnitz 1972; Chapman 1972, 180–1; for an analysis see Vandenabeele 1971.

37 Birmingham 1963, 39–42. Many scarabs of the 26th Egyptian Dynasty (664–525 BC) were found on the floor of the Period 4 sanctuary at Ayia Irini, associated with Black-on-Red Ware belonging to the last part of CAIA to the first part of CAIB. This sets the middle of Cypro-Archaic I around 650 BC at the earliest, and not 100 years earlier as Birmingham's chronology would require. Working entirely with 'high' Palestinian dates, Birmingham was led to raise the Cypriot Middle Iron Age ceramic divisions quite unrealistically (cf. Coldstream 1985, 45).

38 Gjerstad 1974, 119, n. 38.

39 Albright 1943, 6, n. 2; Albright 1953, 22; Albright 1958, 3*; cf. Hanfmann 1951, 425; du Plat Taylor 1959, 89; Amiran 1969, 286.

40 Van Beek 1951, 27.

41 Van Beek 1955, 37.

42 Van Beek 1951, 27.

43 Gjerstad 1953, 26.

44 Van Beek 1951, 28.

45 In Tell Beit Mirsim B2, Beth Zur, Ashkelon and Gezer tomb 59 (Van Beek 1951, 28).

46 Yellin and Perlman in E. Stern 1978, 90.

47 Bieber in Bikai 1978b, 88–90; Matthers et al. 1983; see also Jones 1986, 532–3. However, the excavation of Tyre has shown that this ware was alien at least to the repertoire of the Lebanon and clearly an import. Bikai (in Coldstream 1988, 37) has stated that she 'has always been mystified by the suggestion that Black-on-Red is Phoenician'.

48 Stager et al. 1974, 5.

49 Furumark 1944, 258; Gjerstad 1944, 76–7, 103; Desborough 1957, 216; Coldstream 1968, 319–20; Snodgrass 1971, 117–19; Gjerstad 1977, 23–59; cf. Karageorghis 1975, 67–8; see further our n. 32, above.

50 Desborough 1957, 218.

51 Yannai 1982, 292; cf. Iacovou 1988, 10.

52 Merrillees 1977, 35.

53 E. Stern 1978, 62.

54 E. Stern 1978, 52.

55 The only Israeli archaeologist to experiment with Gjerstad's system was B. Mazar (1951, 21–5), who applied it to the stratigraphy of Tell Abu Hawam. Naturally, he found no supporters (see Van Beek 1955, 34–8), although recently Balensi has provided an even lower dating for level III of this site than Mazar's (see Chapter 5).

56 Ben-Tor and Portugali 1987, 202.

8 *Biblical Archaeology Without Egypt*

1 For a balanced introduction to biblical criticism in general, see Soggin 1989.

2 The redundancy of much literary criticism, from the perspective of modern Near Eastern scholarship, was amply demonstrated in Kitchen 1966, 112–38.

3 Bimson 1978, 115–27, 145; I. Finkelstein 1988, 297.

4 Widely differing dates have been offered by modern scholars for the Israelite Conquest, ranging (at the extremes) between 2300 and 1150 BC. The ancient Hebrews themselves believed that the Conquest took place forty years after the Exodus from Egypt, itself 480 years before the building of Solomon's Temple (1 Kgs. 6:1). As Solomon's Temple was built in the mid-10th century BC, the Exodus would have taken place *c.* 1450 BC and the Conquest *c.* 1400 BC. This would leave some 400 years for the period between the Conquest and early Monarchy, arguably consistent with the internal data in the Book of *Judges* (Bimson 1978, 87–111).

The conventional placement for the Conquest is at the end of the Late Bronze Age, *c.* 1200 BC, a date which requires a considerable telescoping of the Judges period. It also provides a poor match between the Bible and archaeology, a fact which explains why the traditional 15th-century BC dates for the Exodus and Conquest have recently been experiencing a revival in popularity (Horn 1977; Bimson 1978; Goedicke reported in Shanks 1981; Bimson and Livingston 1987; Wood 1990). Eschewing the link with the end of the LBA, Bimson discovered an almost perfect match between the biblical account and the fate which befell the MBA cities of Palestine. The end of the MBA is usually dated *c.* 1550 BC and explained in terms of an Egyptian invasion, yet recent studies have demonstrated that this theory is groundless (see Hoffmeier 1989). It is therefore no obstacle to Bimson's suggestion that the end of the MBA could be lowered to meet a Conquest date of 1400 BC. Others have experimented with an even earlier date, *c.* 2000 BC, associating the Exodus with the influx of new settlers in southern Palestine at the beginning of the MBA period (Cohen 1983; Anati 1985). While many of the links made are attractive, this placement can be sustained only by a highly implausible extension of the Judges period by some six centuries (within accepted chronology), or by models in which folk tales of much earlier settlements were integrated by the Israelites into their own origin story.

On the model presented in this chapter, the destructions at the end of the LBA would have taken place in the late 10th century BC, rather than 1225–1150 BC. This conclusion rules out once and for all a late LBA placement for the Conquest. A possible placement for the Conquest would then be the end of MBA slot suggested by Bimson. The absolute date for the end of the MBA remains, of course, *sub judice* (see Table 8:3). Wood (1990) has recently argued that the late MBA pottery found at Jericho by Kenyon actually belongs to the early LBA, lowering the destruction of its massive walls to *c.* 1400 BC (in the conventional chronology) and linking it with the biblical story. It remains to be seen how Wood's analysis affects other sites and the wider case offered by Bimson.

5 Halpern 1987; cf. Bimson 1988.

6 West 1979; cf. Wood 1990, 53–4.

7 *ANET*, 257–8.

8 For Middle Kingdom (13th Dynasty) lists of slaves with Semitic names, see *ANET*, 553–4. During the New Kingdom, 'Apiru prisoners of war

were brought in large numbers from Palestine to Egypt by Amenhotep II (18th Dynasty), while they appear as menial workers and builders in various texts from the 19th and 20th Dynasties (see Cazelles 1973, 4, 12–13; Bright 1981, 121, 139–40). The phonetic equivalence between 'Apiru (the *ḫabiru* of cuneiform documents such as the El-Amarna letters) and the biblical 'Hebrew' can hardly be doubted. It seems to be largely chronological reasons which have prevented further investigation of this obvious link, since the *ḫabiru* are described as an active political force in Palestine 150 years before the generally accepted date for the Conquest. On the model suggested here the Conquest must have taken place long before the Late Bronze/Iron Age transition. The *ḫabiru* who were so troublesome to the Egyptian authorities during the 18th Dynasty can then easily be seen as the Hebrews of the Judges to early monarchical period.

9 Malamat 1982.

10 *ANET*, 320–1; Aharoni, 1966, 307–9.

11 See, for example, Avigad 1978.

12 On the surprising absence of Hebrew royal inscriptions, see Garbini 1988, 17–18. Of the seals held to name kings, only a few examples are convincing and none is reliably stratified. For example, a seal calling its owner 'servant of Hezekiah' – very likely the king of that name – comes from the Hebron area, but not from a controlled excavation (Hestrin and Dayagi 1974). The seal of 'Shema the servant of Jeroboam' from Megiddo is thought to have been found in the ruins of the so-called 'palace' complex (Aharoni in *EAEHL*, 832), in fact within the courtyard near the gateway originally designated 'Der Palast' (Schumacher 1908, 99–100, Table XXIX; cf. Wightman 1985, 122). It is difficult to determine the precise height at which the seal was discovered, and therefore which building phase it should be associated with. Our thanks to Bob Porter for his assistance in investigating this matter.

13 Bimson 1978. Wood (1990, 49) describes Jericho as the 'parade example of the difficulties encountered in correlating archaeology and the Bible. Scholars by and large have written off the Biblical record as so much folklore and religious rhetoric.'

14 Many alternatives to the biblical account of an Israelite military invasion have been offered – from a model of slow and relatively peaceful infiltration to one of a class struggle in which the already settled peasantry of Late Bronze Age Canaan overthrew their masters; for overviews, see Gottwald 1980, 191–227, and papers by Gottwald, Herrmann, Kochavi and Mazar with discussion and responses in *BAT*, 31–95.

15 Magnusson 1977, 148, 155–6. Garbini (1988, 40–1) toyed with the idea that the achievements attributed to Solomon and his Phoenician ally King Hiram of Tyre in the 10th century BC were in fact largely concocted from the deeds of 8th-century kings – namely Azariah of Judah and Hiram II of Tyre. His case, however, is shot through with errors of fact and interpretation.

16 Kenyon 1964, 143.

17 See e.g. Tsori 1977; E. Stern 1982, 47–67, 262, n. 34.

18 E. Stern 1982, xv.

19 Albright 1946, 322.

20 See Soggin 1984, 356. Farmers were left to work the land, many refugees drifted back (Jer. 40:11–12) and the faithful still visited the site of the destroyed Solomonic Temple (Jer. 41:5). A short-lived puppet government was organized by Nebuchadrezzar (Jer. 40:1–18), while military bases in southern Palestine would have been particularly important to him in his efforts to contain the Egyptians and interfere in their dynastic struggles around 570 BC (Leahy 1988, 190–1, 194). Likewise, Egyptian armies still came and went – one can hardly imagine that Palestine was deserted.

21 Aharoni 1966, 355.

22 Tufnell 1953, 103, 48; cf. James and Kokkinos 1990.

23 Albright 1954, 142.

24 Torczyner et al. 1938, 13, 204.

25 Torczyner et al. 1938, 53, 65, 112–14, 117, 173.

26 Albright 1941, 19; D. W. Thomas 1946, 40; Diringer in Tufnell 1953, 332.

27 Albright 1938, 16.

28 Albright 1939, 19; D. W. Thomas 1958, 214–15; James and Kokkinos 1990.

29 Albright 1938, 12.

30 James and Kokkinos 1990.

31 For example, the superior of Hoshaiah, the author of the Letters, has the rare name Yaosh. This was actually found inscribed on an incense altar discovered in a cave at Lachish. The inscription was in Aramaic, and to judge from the style of both script and altar its owner lived no earlier than the mid-5th century BC (Dupont-Sommer in Tufnell 1953, 358–9; Cross 1969, 23–4; cf. E. Stern 1982, 189, 192). It is tempting to see some connection between this Yaosh and the individual to whom the ostraca were sent.

32 Albright in *ANET*, 322.

33 Bright 1981, 382, n. 18.

34 The fragmentary reference to '. . .iah' the prophet in Letter XVI could be restored as 'Shemaiah'. In Letter IV a Shemaiah is recorded as escorting someone to 'the city' (presumably Jerusalem) – Albright in *ANET*, 322. This may be another reference to the prophet Shemaiah whose role as a messenger is described by Nehemiah. However, the point, based on a conjectural restoration, must not be pushed.

35 Albright 1938, 15–16; 1939, 19–20; *ANET*, 322.

36 Precisely the same Hebrew expression is used in Letter VI to describe how the words of the princes' letters were intended to 'weaken the hands of the people'.

37 The standard mid-5th century BC dates for Ezra and Nehemiah given by the Bible are followed here. Numerous attempts have been made to challenge their sequence and placement in time, but we see no reason, on the basis of available evidence, to diverge from the traditional chronology. For the controversy see Bright 1981, 391–402; Soggin 1989, 492–7.

38 Bright 1981, 382–3.

39 James and Kokkinos 1990. Lowering the dates for Lachish II to meet those of Lachish I would also explain the 'intrusive' appearance of Persian bowls in Lachish II deposits noticed by E. Stern (1982, 97): 'At Lachish, Tufnell found several sherds of these bowls in contexts of stratum II but she rejected their chronological value.'

40 Ussishkin 1982, 25. Radiocarbon results from both long- and short-lived samples (Lachish IV, III and II) have produced a confusing scatter of results (Ussishkin 1983, 168). Indeed, it is doubtful whether radiocarbon can be of any value to the Lachish controversy; the high and low dates offered all fall within the period of the 'radiocarbon disaster' between *c.* 800 and 400 BC (see Appendix 1).

41 For a bibliography of the two schools of thought, see Ussishkin 1977, 32, and Tufnell in *EAEHL*, 753.

42 Tufnell 1953, 55, 106; Aharoni 1975, 15–16; Ussishkin 1977, 52.

43 Shea 1978; Rainey in Aharoni 1975, 49–60.

44 Paterson, 1915, Pls. 74–6; *ARAB* II, 198; Ussishkin 1977, 28–30; Ussishkin 1980a. It is often claimed that, because the city depicted by Sennacherib bears a close resemblance to Lachish III, the latter must be the settlement which he attacked. The argument does not hold water, as the plan of Lachish III is to all intents and purposes identical to that of Lachish IV, the city contemporary with Sennacherib in our model; see James and Kokkinos 1990.

45 Ussishkin 1977; B. Mazar 1986, 47; Yadin in *BAT*, 24–5; Herzog 1987, 78–9.

46 Ussishkin 1977, 51–2.

47 Ussishkin 1977, 30.

48 *ARAB* II, 153–6; for further discussion, see James and Kokkinos 1990.

49 James and Kokkinos 1990; Kitchen 1986, 383–6.

50 Aharoni 1966, 340–6.

51 Rainey 1982.

52 For references and discussion see Lance 1971, 315–17.

53 Aharoni and Aharoni 1976.

54 Kenyon 1979, 296, 298.

55 The large number of royal stamps found at Gezer west of Judah (thirty-seven – the sixth largest group from any site) poses a serious problem for the high chronology, as there is no evidence that this city was ever under Hezekiah's control. Indeed there is evidence that it remained in Assyrian hands from its conquest in 734 BC until the collapse of their empire *c.* 630 BC (see Lance 1971, 330–1; Becking 1981/1982, 78–9; Reich and Brandl 1985, 41–2). Josiah, as the unofficial heir to Assyrian authority in Palestine, expanded his control at least as far north as Megiddo, and Gezer, a major centre on the routes into Israel, is likely to have been occupied by him (see James and Kokkinos 1990).

56 Jer. 9:10; Lam. 2:2–3; Hab. 1:10.

57 For discussion and references, see Ussishkin 1976, 10–12.

58 Albright 1932.

59 Ussishkin 1976, 11.

60 Na'aman 1979, 71–3.

61 See Kenyon 1979, 289–90.

62 See e.g. Kenyon in Crowfoot *et al.* 1957, 97–8; Amiran 1969; 291; Reich and Brandl 1985, 48. There has been a tendency over the years to assign increasingly lower dates to the finds of 'Assyrian Palace Ware' in Palestine. While Kenyon felt that a date in the period 725–700 BC 'is certain', Amiran and Van Beek (in *EAEHL*, 547) opted for the second quarter of the 7th century. In 1985 Yadin (in *BAT*, 26) placed this ware between 630 and 600 BC. His dates are close to Holladay's and those preferred by the present authors; nevertheless, Yadin did not follow through the logical consequences of such a low dating.

63 Holladay 1976, 272, 282, n. 59. It should be noted, however, that the excavations at Nimrud rarely penetrated beyond the latest levels at the site, weakening the case for the absence of Assyrian Palace Ware in earlier periods. Too little, unfortunately, is known of Assyrian pottery of the Empire period; it is to be hoped that more precise datings will be obtained from the tombs of the royal necropolis at Nimrud currently being explored (see e.g. George 1990).

64 Holladay 1976, 272 (emphasis in original).

65 Over the last few years Francis and Vickers have argued for a substantial lowering of Archaic Greek chronology (see Chapter 5). At the short-period site of Meṣad Hashavyahu East Greek pottery conventionally dated to 630–600 BC was found with local wares usually assigned a 7th-century date; it was consequently placed in the reign of Josiah (late 7th century BC). However, the site also contained Persian bowls normally thought to have become fashionable during the mid-6th century; the Cypriot pottery finds also support a 6th-century date (see James *et al.* 1987, 59–60). Vickers (1985, 20) suggested that the site may have been a Persian outpost with a garrison of Greek mercenaries from *c.* 540 BC. The present authors would prefer a date in the 570s, seeing Meṣad Hashavyahu as a Neo-Babylonian border garrison – Nebuchadrezzar employed Greek mercenaries in southern Palestine, as we know from the poetry of Alcaeus (Burn 1935, 144–5).

A number of radiocarbon results also support the compression of Iron Age chronology argued here. Three samples from Tell es-Sa'idiyeh Stratum 5, conventionally dated to the 8th century BC, produced ranges of 615–410 BC (P-832), 620–410 BC (P-835) and 620–410 BC (P-1100); see Weinstein (1984, 310, 353). Unfortunately, these fall within the range of the 1st-millennium 'radiocarbon disaster' (see Appendix 1). There are, however, some interesting results from material which should, on the conventional chronology, fall before *c.* 800 BC. Weinstein (1984, 310) notes that: 'The Tell er-Rumeith dates include several anomalous determinations, all on the young side.' Stratum VII is thought to have been destroyed at the beginning of the 9th century, but charcoal from posts in the fort wall produced ranges of 785–390 BC (M-2029) and 870–560 BC (M-3030). Stratum VIII is dated to the Solomonic period (10th century), yet charcoal from posts gave a range of 825–420 BC (M-2031); see Weinstein 1984, 351–2.

66 Becking 1981/1982, 76–7.

67 Macalister's foreman found the tablet in 'a stratum contemporaneous with the early part of the Hebrew monarchy'; see Becking 1981/1982, 77, n. 9.

68 Salles 1985.

69 For examples from Lachish, 'En Gev and Dibon, see Glueck 1969, 51, n. 2; for an example from Hazor, see Amiran 1969, 291, photo 300. Our thanks to Dr John Bimson of Trinity College, Bristol, for drawing our attention to this material, as well as to the problem of Assyrian Palace Ware.

70 G. E. Wright 1959, 20.

71 Kenyon in Crowfoot *et al.* 1942, 97; Kenyon in Crowfoot *et al.* 1957, 198–9; Kenyon 1964; cf. Wightman 1985, 125–8.

72 G. E. Wright 1959, 20, 22.

73 Kenyon in Crowfoot *et al.* 1942, 94; G. E. Wright 1959, 18. Kenyon (1964, 146–7), who believed the Israelite pottery under Building Period I resulted from the activity of the builders themselves, stressed absence of any earlier settlement remains.

74 Kenyon in Crowfoot *et al.* 1942, 99; her comment applies to all the 'filling' between the enclosure wall (Building Period I) and the casemate walls (Building Period II) as well as inside the casemates. On the north side of the site she recorded an upper filling of 'definitely later character', which she ascribed to Pottery Period IV. Such later finds (see also n. 84, below) do not affect the significance of Kenyon's statement regarding the homogenous nature of the other deposits – the point is that there was no admixture of stray material from, say, the EBA settlement.

75 Kenyon in Crowfoot *et al.* 1957, 91–4.

76 G. E. Wright 1959, 22.

77 Wright 1959, 21–2 (n. 24); Kenyon in Crowfoot *et al.* 1957, 98–104; Aharoni (1982, 203) noted: 'there is no doubt that pottery from the tenth century is found at Samaria, and perhaps even eleventh, including bowls with irregular hand burnishing and other transition types from Early Israel'. Cf. Stager 1988.

78 Kenyon 1964, 147.

79 G. E. Wright 1959, 20. Kenyon in Crowfoot *et al.* 1942, 94, originally wrote: 'It would be rash to differentiate between the work of Omri and Ahab, since the former only reigned six years after his occupation of the site about 880, which would hardly be sufficient for the construction of the whole city, and the work of the two was probably continuous.'

80 *ANET*, 284.

81 Wightman 1985, 128.

82 Kenyon in Crowfoot 1957, 105.

83 G. M. Crowfoot in Crowfoot *et al.* 1957, 469–70; I. T. Kaufman 1982, 232–3.

84 While Kenyon stated that the pottery of Building Periods I and II was

exactly the same, Wightman (1985, 125) implied that some of the pottery of Period II, associated with structures which 'can be shown to have been additions to the Building Period II scheme', should be assigned a later date, conventionally in the second half of the 9th century BC. On the revised scheme this would bridge the gap between the pottery associated with the Ahabic palace and the construction of Building Period II under Jeroboam (no earlier than *c.* 790 BC).

85 Kenyon 1979, 263–4; Aharoni 1982, 242.
86 Frankfort 1969, 190; Winter 1976b, 203; Winter 1981, 123–9.
87 Yadin 1972, 193.
88 Yadin 1972, 201.
89 Dever cited in Yadin 1972, 203; see also Dever 1986, 26.
90 Ussishkin 1980b, 17; Yadin 1980, 21; Dever 1986, 26–8, 32–3.
91 Pritchard 1974, 35; cf. Kenyon·1979, 256.
92 Soggin 1984, 161–2.
93 Albright 1958; cf. Albright 1956a.
94 Frankfort 1969, 166.
95 Albright 1958, 1.
96 Jidejian 1968, 57. It should be noted, however, that Byblos was very badly excavated.
97 Bikai 1978b, 66–7.
98 Pritchard 1975, 70; cf. Anderson 1988, 407.
99 Muhly 1985, 179.
100 For the Lachish hiatus between 1150 BC and the 10th century see Ussishkin 1987, 35, 39; for the Megiddo hiatus in the late 11th-century see Aharoni 1982, 205; Wightman 1985, 126–7.
101 See I. Finkelstein 1988, 280, 316–23; London 1989, 46.
102 *ANET* 376–8; for a recent study of the 'Israel Stela', see Yurco 1986.
103 For discussion and references see I. Finkelstein 1988, 295–6.
104 I. Finkelstein 1988, 300–1; Ussishkin 1987, 39.
105 Soggin 1984, 161–2.
106 Aharoni 1982, 174; London 1989.
107 London 1989, 43.
108 Balensi in *BAT*, 94.
109 Ibrahim 1978; Balensi in *BAT*, 94.
110 Soggin 1984, 82–3.
111 Bright 1981, 232, cf. 235–6.
112 E.g. Yadin 1972, 97–8.
113 Josephus, *Antiquities* VII, 66; VIII, 76–90, 144–9; cf. *Against Apion* I, 113–15, 117–20.
114 Hiram the craftsman was the son of a Phoenician bronze-worker and an Israelite mother (1 Kgs. 7:13; 2 Chr. 1:14).
115 Ussishkin 1980b, 1, 6.
116 El Amarna Letter 115:48–53 (from the King of Byblos); for an English translation see Mercer 1939, 315–16.
117 Sandars 1985, 151–2.
118 Moorey 1988, 29.

119 Catling 1964, 222; cf. Karageorghis 1979, 208.
120 Webb and Courtois 1979, 157–8.
121 For bibliography, see Soggin 1989, 434–7.
122 Drower 1975, 160.
123 Ussishkin 1980b, 17.
124 Some of the ivories may have come from the earlier Canaanite palace of Stratum VIIB, with which the treasury was once associated. However, it clearly belongs to VIIA, which forms a transitional stratum between the Late Bronze and Iron Ages (Yadin in *EAEHL*, 847–9; Ussishkin 1980b, 4, 6–7; Dothan 1982, 70–1). A close fix for the ivories is provided by a pen-case bearing the cartouche of Ramesses III. On the chronology suggested here, Ramesses III would have been a contemporary of Solomon, and was very probably the 'Shishak' who invaded Judah *c.* 925 BC, according to the Bible (see Chapter 10). Solomon's successor in the north, Jeroboam (*c.* 930–910 BC), was a vassal of Shishak, and the pen-case and some other Egyptian material from VIIA may date to his reign. The latest ivories from the collection would then be not far removed in time from the Syrian examples of the mid-9th century, thus closing the Dark Age gap in Levantine ivory-working.
125 See Bimson 1981, 124.
126 Glueck 1969, 53.
127 Rothenberg and Lupu 1967, 54–5.
128 Glueck 1969, 51–4, n. 16, cites an unpublished article by Albright: 'the early Iron Age pottery which has been found at many of those sites [in the Arabah] is . . . definitely tenth century and thus probably Solomonic . . . Every new discovery of pottery convinces me that Nelson Glueck is right in his chronology and that Aharoni and Rothenberg are wrong.' After the discovery of the Egyptian remains, Albright (1971, 4) stated that he and Glueck had been wrong.
129 Rothenberg 1972, 128, 180.
130 Wheeler in Rothenberg 1972, 9.
131 Parr 1982, 131–3.
132 Bimson 1981, 139.
133 See Bimson 1981, 136–8.
134 Bimson 1981, 142–5; cf. the list given in Weinstein 1984, 348–50, where four of the calibrated ranges given include the 10th century BC. The dates overall suggest fairly continuous activity at the site from the 10th to 6th centuries BC, as originally claimed by Glueck.

9   *The Empty Years of Nubian History*

1 The UNESCO work is chronicled by Säve-Söderbergh 1987 and W. Y. Adams 1977.
2 For a valuable summary of all earlier work, see W. Y. Adams 1977, 71–80.
3 'Nubia' is here used throughout as a geographical term, without ethnic or linguistic connotations.
4 See Trigger 1976, Ch.7; W. Y. Adams 1977, Ch.9.

5 W. Y. Adams 1977, 240–1; Trigger 1976, 131–5.
6 Cf. W. Y. Adams 1977, 244–5, and Trigger 1976, 139–40.
7 Trigger 1976, 140.
8 Nubian history from the New Kingdom to Meroitic period is discussed in detail in Morkot 1990, where the model advocated here is argued in far greater detail.
9 W. Y. Adams 1964, 114–15; cf. Dixon 1964, 131.
10 Trigger 1976, 135.
11 W. Y. Adams 1984, 244–5.
12 The prime evidence is the stela recording the death and burial of an Apis bull (see Chapter 10) in year 20/21 of Psamtik I, giving its date of installation as year 26 of Taharqo, and its age as twenty-one years (Breasted 1906, 492; Kitchen 1986, 161–3).
13 See Kitchen 1986, 153–4; the attested year-dates are listed by Leclant 1983a, 505 (n. 9).
14 The highest certain year is 3, recorded in a text thought by some to mark Shebitqo's accession as sole ruler (Kitchen 1986, 154–9). A possible year 10, on a stela in the Metropolitan Museum of Art, New York (No. 65.45), is unpublished; cf. Leclant 1983b, 515–16 (n. 1), 518 (n. 35).
15 Kitchen 1986, 161–72.
16 The phrase 'broken reed' has been suggested to be a pun on the name 'Kush'; see W. Y. Adams 1977, 706–7 (n. 2).
17 Kitchen gives the widely accepted dates for the 25th Dynasty. A lower date for Shabaqo's invasion has been advocated by Redford (1985). The accession date of Taharqo is certain. It is universally accepted that Piye precedes Shabaqo, but there is no direct evidence to confirm this.
18 The name Piye was originally read as Piankhy. Piye is now generally accepted as the Nubian form of the name; see Kitchen 1986, 582. A convenient translation of the stela can be found in Lichtheim 1980, 66–84.
19 Gardiner 1961, 335.
20 A full discussion of the problems attending the reign of Piye, the monumental evidence and its interpretation will be found in Morkot 1990.
21 The problems of Dunham and Macadam's reconstruction are discussed at length in Morkot 1990.
22 For a detailed discussion of the Aspelta genealogy, see Morkot 1990.
23 Alara is referred to in later texts, but only by the title 'Son of Re', which is a characteristic designation of dead rulers.
24 Piye varied his titles frequently, but Shabaqo used only one set of names.
25 Published by Dunham 1950.
26 The burial of Taharqo, known to have reigned between Shebitqo and Tanwetamani, had been excavated in an earlier season's work in the cemetery at Nuri.
27 There are relatively few graves from the earliest generations. The alternative interpretation, that the cemetery is a mix of New Kingdom graves and later ones, has never been considered.
28 Kendall 1982, 21–3.
29 Kendall 1982, 22–3, no. 2, with citation of the other examples.

30 The radiocarbon tests of material from el-Kurru were carried out at the request of Dr Timothy Kendall of the Boston Museum of Fine Art. The authors are very grateful to him for his generosity in providing them with the data and permission to cite it. The interpretation is ours.

31 It might be suggested that the 20th Dynasty material was heirloom, but the nature of the pottery – clearly made for the funerary ceremonies – precludes this interpretation.

32 Rowley-Conwy 1988, 246.

33 Bonnet *et al.* (1986) advocate a low chronology for the site, but the radiocarbon dates cited place the end of the Kerma sequence around 1450 BC. Charles Bonnet (*pers. comm.*) has said that the evidence actually indicates a more substantial reduction than is apparent from the published material.

34 This following summary is argued in detail in Morkot 1990.

35 Goedicke 1972.

36 A number of monuments have been attributed to this king, and the argumentation is complex; see Morkot 1990.

37 We should like to thank Professor Ricardo A. Caminos for his information on the relief and the text, which will be published by him in Caminos forthcoming. The interpretation and dating of the text are Morkot's. The form of the name used here, Karimala, is that proposed by Caminos after his work on the text. The former reading was Katimala (Grapow 1940; Dunham and Janssen 1960, 11).

38 Caminos (forthcoming) gives a detailed commentary on all previous discussions of this text.

10   Egypt: the Centre of the Problem

1 Torr 1896.

2 Iakovidis 1979; McClellan 1979; Weinstein 1981, 17–23; A. Mazar 1985; Hankey 1987, 50–2.

3 Edwards 1982, 577–81.

4 E.g. Baer 1973; Bierbrier 1975; Kitchen 1977, 1986; Vittmann 1978; Wente 1976; Wente and Van Siclen 1976. Further studies on specific topics can be found in the bibliographies of these works and in the following notes.

5 Gardiner 1961, 53.

6 The standard edition of the fragments of Manetho's work is still Waddell 1940.

7 Gardiner 1961, vi, 46.

8 Edwards 1970, 11.

9 Edwards 1970, 12.

10 Edwards 1970, 12; Long 1974, 272–4; Ingham (1969, 39–40) recalculated the length of the Sothic cycle which ended in AD 139 as 1452–3 years.

11 Long 1974, 269–71; the name 'Menophres' used to be compared with the prenomens of Ramesses I and Seti I, founders of the 19th Dynasty, thus making the 'fixed point' of 1321 BC one of the years towards the

beginning of this Dynasty. However, as Rowton (1946) showed, Men-ophres is unlikely to be a king and is more probably the Egyptian name for the city of Memphis (*mennofir*), the sighting point from which the heliacal risings of Sirius may have been made. Cf. Wente and Van Siclen 1976, 233–4.

12 Parker 1976, 178–84.

13 Krauss 1985, 63–7, 100, 109–10; cf. Kitchen 1987, 42–3.

14 Bierbrier 1975, 109–11; Wente and Van Siclen 1976, 223–4, 250; Kitchen 1987, 39–40; Helck 1987, 26. Casperson has provided the latest detailed studies of the astronomical problems involved. In 1986 (148–50) he identified a number of inaccuracies in the calculations and tables used by Parker, and, on astronomical grounds, chose 1504 in preference to 1490 BC for the accession of Thutmose III. In 1988 Casperson dealt with the lunar data for Ramesses II and found the (low) 1279 BC date the most attractive. His otherwise valuable work is marred by the narrow chrono-logical scope of his investigations: Casperson (1986) gave scant attention even to the 1479 BC date for Thutmose III's accession currently popular among Egyptologists.

15 Ingham 1969, 39.

16 Roy 1982, 55.

17 Parker 1971, 18–19.

18 Alexander introduced the Macedonian luni-solar system into Egypt, which allowed for the occasional intercalation of a month for regulation. The old Egyptian calendar continued to operate alongside it, however, and under Ptolemy III (247–222 BC) the Macedonian calendar's links with the lunar month were broken and the two systems were synchronized. Under the same king, an assembly of priests issued the famous 'Canopus Decree' (238 BC), which prescribed the addition of one day every fourth year into the Egyptian calendar. The decree was unpopular and never really took effect. In 163 BC Ptolemy VII re-established the Macedonian calendar, an action repealed after his death in 145 BC. (See Sarton 1970, 109, 321–2; Long 1974, 271–2; Bickerman 1980, 38–41.)

19 Parker 1971, 13.

20 Our thanks to Professor J. R. Harris for drawing attention to this possibility. A fragment of Manetho (Waddell 1940, 99) records the tradition that the Hyksos King Saites of the 17th Dynasty added six days to the year, making it 365 days; while the historical veracity of this episode is negligible, the possibility of a calendrical alteration during the Hyksos period might be reflected. It has been supposed that the Egyptians did not 'correct' their year on the testimony of the Roman writer P. Nigidius Figulus, who stated that the Ptolemaic kings took an oath never to change the days or months of the calendar (see Long 1974, 263). Such an oath suggests that kings were tempted to make calendar reforms, as indeed the Ptolemies frequently did.

21 Helck 1987, 18. The Ebers Papyrus problem is more fully explained by Helck in Aström 1989, Part 3, 41; the rising of Sirius falls between two entries for the 9th of the 11th month and the 8th of the 12th. It is not

certain, however, which, if any, of these calendar dates the Sothic reference belongs to; thus Helck concludes: 'We are not allowed to use this entry for chronological calculations.'

22 Bietak in Bimson 1988, 55 (n. 4).

23 Neither the relationship between the 13th to 17th Dynasties (which seem to have overlapped considerably) nor even the total number of kings they contained are firmly established. Present studies of Second Intermediate chronology (e.g. Kitchen 1987, 44–5, 50–1) operate within the parameters allowed by the Sothic dates for the Middle and New Kingdoms.

24 Parker 1957, 39–40: 'the smaller the range in years in which a lunar date falls the greater the possibility that it may be fixed to one year. The range may be set by some other calendrical or astronomical datum such as a date for the heliacal rising of Sothis (Sirius) or for an eclipse of the sun or moon but it is more likely that purely historical considerations will set the limits. When two or more solutions for the same date are possible, historical considerations must determine which is the more possible.'

25 Berlin Museum Papyrus 10056; see Parker 1950, Excursus C.

26 Read 1970, 6, 10.

27 Parker 1970.

28 Read 1970, 4.

29 Thiele 1983, 80.

30 van der Meer 1947, 69.

31 Kitchen 1986, 298.

32 2 Chron. 11:5–10; 12:4. All the towns listed are to the south and south-west of Judah, suggesting that Egypt was the threat perceived by Rehoboam in his arrangement of the country's defences.

33 Aharoni 1966, 285; cf. Wallenfels 1983, 88.

34 Jeroboam had taken refuge at Shishak's court after his rebellion against Solomon (1 Kgs. 11:40), married an Egyptian princess named Anô (according to the Greek version of the Old Testament; Septuagint 3 Kgs. 12.24e) and returned from Egypt at Solomon's death to raise the flag of independence in Israel (1 Kgs. 12:2). While Edwards (1982, 546; cf. Gardiner 1961, 330) considers that the 'obvious' explanation of the biblical narrative would be that Shishak 'was acting as an ally of Jeroboam in order to overthrow Rehoboam', he has to reject it on the evidence of Shoshenq's town-list and assume that for some reason the Egyptians attacked their protégé as well. A more reasonable alternative is that Shoshenq listed all the cities which submitted or paid tribute to him on his campaign, including those of his vassal Jeroboam; Egyptian lists of this kind were certainly not intended to convey the idea that all the places given were destroyed or even attacked by them (Redford 1982, 117). Nevertheless, the plausible tribute theory makes the problem even worse – the omission of Jerusalem and other main Judaean cities, the submission of which was the main goal of Shishak's invasion, becomes even more conspicuous.

35 The only certain reference to a Takeloth 'I' is in the genealogy of Pasenhor (see Table 10:2). Kitchen's treatment of this king is particularly curious.

He accepts that the Pasenhor reference is the only 'unambiguous evidence of his existence', stressing that: 'Recovery of the real, and probably hitherto entirely unknown, prenomen of Takeloth I is a minor prize that awaits the spade or epigraphic eye of some future Egyptologist' (Kitchen 1986, 120, 97). Nevertheless, on the basis of some year-dates (highest 14) which do not bear the name of any king, Kitchen (1986, 121–2) grants him a reign of 'not less than 14 or (for safety) 15 years'! Elsewhere, Kitchen (1982, 220), dissatisfied with the apparent inactivity of Takeloth during these years, describes him as a 'witless nonentity who allowed all real power to slip through his fumbling fingers'! Aston (1989) attempts to find more substantial evidence for Takeloth I by dividing the monumental remains currently assigned to Takeloth II between these two monarchs. It is difficult to accept Aston's argument; all the material in question bears the same prenomen (Hedjkheperre), which he divides into two, basically on a north–south basis. Using the same methodology would result in two kings called Ramesses II and a myriad other absurdities.

36 The date once read as year 36 on a stela of Osorkon I has now been shown to be 'day 26', with the year-number lost (see Kitchen 1986, 110, nn. 127–8). This leaves the highest year-date attested for Osorkon I as 12 (Edwards 1982, 550), agreeing well enough with the 15 years given for the first Osorkon in Manetho's 22nd Dynasty. However, Kitchen (1986, 110–11) amends this figure to 35, supporting this with the occurrence of years 3 and 33 together on the linen wrappings of a mummy which also bears the name of Osorkon I. In searching for a long reign which could accommodate the Year 33 on the linen, he had to eliminate the 49-year reign of Psusennes I because it 'was too remote in time'. The model argued here, allowing a considerable overlap between the 21st and 22nd Dynasty, is not subject to this constraint. Wente (1976, 277) argued that the year 33 belongs to Shoshenq I rather than Osorkon I. He assigns a much longer reign to Shoshenq I than the 21 years normally given, and allows a 3-year co-regency with his son Osorkon in order to explain the bandage epigraphs. However, 21 is the highest attested year-date of this king (Kitchen 1986, 73).

37 Kitchen 1986, 255–6.

38 O'Connor 1983, 276.

39 O'Connor 1983, 238.

40 ANET, 294.

41 Herodotus II, 147; Diodorus Siculus I, 66, 1–2.

42 For a recent discussion of the nature of Manetho's work and its sources, see Redford 1986, esp. 203–30; cf. Aston 1989, 142, nn. 33–4.

43 Waddell 1940, 9.

44 Kitchen 1986, 405.

45 Redford 1986, 316.

46 Spencer and Spencer (1986, 199–201) argue for an Upper Egyptian, rather than a Delta, origin for the 23rd Dynasty; cf. Redford 1986, 312–16, and Aston 1989, 149, n. 67, citing a forthcoming study by Leahy.

47 Hope 1987, 45–6; cf. Aston 1989, 144.
48 Woldering 1967, 177.
49 W. S. Smith 1981, 387.
50 Bierbrier 1975, 45.
51 Bierbrier 1975, 54.
52 W. S. Smith 1981, 389–90.
53 W. S. Smith 1981, 389–90.
54 Culican 1970, 31, referring to alabaster type *d* classified in Preusser 1955, 22.
55 W. S. Smith 1981, 393.
56 Malinine *et al.* 1968; Vercoutter 1958; 1960.
57 Vercoutter 1958, 340, based on the life-spans of Apis bulls recorded on stelae from the time of Ramesses II to Ptolemy VIII.
58 e.g. Kitchen in Bierbrier 1975, x.
59 Bierbrier 1975, 45.
60 Bierbrier 1975, 54.
61 Bierbrier 1975, 2–5, 51–3.
62 For references, see Kitchen 1986, 187–94, 487 (Table 18).
63 Bierbrier 1975, 3.
64 Bierbrier 1975, 51–3.
65 See Borchardt 1935, 96–112, and Plates 2 and 2a for the Memphite genealogy given on the relief block in Berlin, apparently drawn up in the reign of Shoshenq V (the name Shoshenq is inscribed on the monument).
66 The last incumbent named is one Ankhefensekhmet, eighth in descent from the High Priest Shedsunefertem, who is securely attested in office under Shoshenq I. A partial parallel to the Berlin genealogy (in the Louvre; Malinine *et al.* 1968, 48–9) records another line descended from Shedsunefertem. His grandson Osorkon was also High Priest of Memphis, but the family was replaced in office by royal princes descended from Osorkon II in the next generation. These held office for five generations (Kitchen 1986, 192–4) until the last in the reign of Shoshenq V. The combination of this evidence gives eight generations from Shoshenq I to Shoshenq V, as in the Berlin Memphite genealogy. The known number of high priests of Memphis serving under Ramesses II is greater than that given by the genealogy, but his long reign (sixty-seven years) could have spanned four generations.
67 Kitchen 1986, 189–92.
68 A further parallel to the eight generations from Shoshenq I to Shoshenq V (see n. 66, above) is given by the Pasenhor Genealogy (see Table 10:2), which gives nine generations for the same interval.
69 Lieblein 1914. Some of his links between the dynasties were based on the assumption (in common with many early Egyptologists) that there were marriages between kings and the God's Wives of Amun. This is now known to be incorrect.
70 Černý 1946; Gardiner 1961, 319–20. For a general account of the discovery of the Royal Cache see Romer 1981, Chs 13–15.
71 Kitchen 1986, 289.

72 Gardiner 1961, 320.

73 E. Thomas 1979, 92 (n. 24) refers to a further possible 22nd Dynasty burial, of one Nesitanebtashru. Kitchen (1986, 64) considers that the bandage epigraph on this burial could pertain to Siamun, Psusennes II (21st Dynasty) or Shoshenq I (22nd Dynasty), so its attribution to the 22nd Dynasty should be treated with caution. There is the intriguing possibility that she could be the like-named mother of the HPA/'King' Harsiese who ruled in Thebes at the time of Osorkon II (Kitchen 1986, 307).

74 E. Thomas 1979, 89, 92 (n. 24).

75 Montet 1947. Dodson (1988, 224–5), in agreement with Yoyotte and Aston, argues that Tomb II must belong to King Pimay of the 22nd Dynasty.

76 Lézine in Montet 1947, 46–7.

77 Dodson 1988, 221.

78 Montet 1947, 25–6; Kitchen 1986, 317–19.

79 Montet 1947, 59–70; on Harnakht see Kitchen 1986, 323, n. 447.

80 Kitchen 1986, incorporating the results of Vittmann 1978.

81 Kitchen 1986, 201.

82 Kitchen 1986, 481–2, Table 14, cf. 595–6.

83 For the Nakhtefmut family, see Bierbrier 1975, 79–85, 89–91. The new appointee (in 725 BC according to Kitchen) was a Kushite, Kelbasken, after whom there is a gap in the record until the appointment (c. 680 BC) of Montemhat, a Theban of old and distinguished family who was married to a Kushite princess. (On the Montemhat family, see Kitchen 1986, 230–3; Bierbrier 1975, 104–8; Taylor 1987.) Kitchen is here working with a high date for the invasion of Piye, and an assumption that the Kushite removal of older families from some major Theban offices was begun by him. But it is possible that the removal of the family of Nakhtefmut (descended from Shoshenq I) was effected under Shabaqo, and that Kelbasken was immediately followed by Montemhat – thereby removing the gap in the sequence.

84 Bierbrier 1975, 107, discusses the chronological and genealogical problems of the relationships of later members of this family with the Besenmut line; cf. Bierbrier 1984.

85 Kitchen 1986, 480, Table 13B; Yoyotte 1972.

86 This is most clearly demonstrated by an inscription which records the adoption of Psamtik I's daughter Nitocris by the Kushite princesses Shepenwepet II and Amenirdis II as their eventual successor – thereby legitimizing the transfer of authority at Thebes to Psamtik I and marking the end of the Kushite Tanwetamani's reign in Egypt. See Kitchen 1986, 403–4.

87 Kitchen 1986, 356–7, 386–7, 403–5 (& n. 951).

88 Kitchen 1986, 322–3.

89 Yoyotte 1972, 39–42, 45–6; Kitchen 1986, 58–60.

90 Kitchen 1986, 56–7; Yoyotte 1972, 45–6.

91 Yoyotte 1972, 44–7.

92 Yoyotte 1972, 32–5, 48; see Kitchen 1986, 323, for Karomama G.

93 Yoyotte 1972, 48–9.

94 Weinstein 1981, 23. Two scarabs of Ramesses VIII are known from one of the tombs at Tell el-Far'ah South, (McClellan 1979, 66); the scarab from another tomb attributed by Petrie to Ramesses XI has been reascribed to Ramesses X, making three from this Pharaoh known from Palestine (Brandl 1982, 383).

95 Kitchen 1986, 280–1, attributes a campaign in Philistia to Pharaoh Siamun of the 21st Dynasty; his case is so forced that the idea may be safely ignored. It is almost inconceivable that any of the numerous Menkheperre scarabs known from Palestinian Iron Age levels belong to the 21st Dynasty HPA of that name – his authority did not even extend to the Delta. Most of these scarabs can be explained as giving the prenomen of Thutmose III, which because of its amuletic properties continued to be made into the Late Period.

96 In James et al. 1987, 58, we followed van der Meer 1947, 52, in mistakenly ascribing this stela to Stratum IVB at Megiddo; our thanks to Dr Rupert Chapman for reminding us that the find was actually unstratified; cf. Wallenfels 1983, 88.

97 Montet 1928, 54ff.; Albright 1947, 153, 157–8.

98 Albright 1947, 153, 158; Wallenfels 1983, 111.

99 Albright 1947, 160; cf. Moscati 1968, 11.

100 See Albright 1947, 154, n. 15; Wallenfels 1983, 106.

101 Albright 1947, 153–4; 1958, 5.

102 B. Mazar 1986, 231–47.

103 Wallenfels 1983, 83–4, stresses that there could have been no tomb robbery or other disturbance made through the shaftway after the interment of Ahiram. While the top half of the shaft (above an intermediate wooden floor) contained a mass of Cypriot pottery, the lower half was completely free of sherds. He therefore sees no reason to assume that the upper filling was not contemporary with the burial.

104 Wallenfels, 1983, 87–9.

105 Bennett 1975, 15; 1977, 9.

106 Milward 1975, 17.

107 Karageorghis 1969, 54. Remains of a statue of Osorkon II were found at Byblos but were unstratified and bore no Phoenician inscription.

108 Winter (1976b, 203) advised caution regarding the generally accepted link of the ivories with the Osorkon vase, stressing that only one ivory was certainly found in association with it. Ironically, she also doubts its value in dating the ivories because of the late associations of such vessels elsewhere, as at Almuñécar and Nimrud; Winter 1981, 124.

109 Preusser 1955, 22–3; Culican 1970, 29–30.

110 Kitchen 1986, 344, 352.

111 Culican 1970, 30–1.

112 Culican 1970, 32–3.

113 Gamito 1988, 46.

114 As it was discovered in the burial of the 7th/6th-century Queen Akheqa

(Dunham 1955, 130) it is certainly intrusive, but may have originally formed part of the burial equipment of Taharqo or one of his queens, which are the earliest graves in the cemetery. On the chronology of the site see Dunham 1955, 1–3.

115 Such as: the gold Bastet amulet of Pimay discovered in the West Cemetery at Meroe (Dunham 1963, 8); a silver plaque inscribed with the name of Nimlot, discovered in the Treasury at Sanam (Griffith 1922, 117, 119); and a bronze situla of Peftjauawybast from Kawa (Macadam 1949, 87).

116 Scarab of Shoshenq I from Sanam (Griffith 1923, 147); scarab of Shoshenq III (probably) from Sanam (Griffith 1923, 152); scarab of Shoshenq I from the 25th Dynasty and later cemetery at Gebel Moya (Addison 1949, 117–19).

117 Cintas 1970, 444–7.

118 Kitchen 1986, 143–4; Redford 1985.

119 Kitchen 1977, 42; 1986, 542–3.

120 Kitchen 1986, 88, 372–6.

121 E.g. Breasted 1906, 412–17.

122 The Wadi Gasus inscription is discussed in detail by Kitchen (1986, 175–9, 359–60). The dates on it have been attributed to a number of kings – the year 12 nearly always to Piye, the year 19 variously to Osorkon III, Iuput II (Kitchen) and now, most recently, to Rudamun (Aston 1989, 153). That the year 12 is not of Piye but of Shabaqo is argued by Morkot (1990). A graffito in the Wadi Hammamat (near to the Wadi Gasus) is dated to year 12 of Shabaqo and names the God's Wife of Amun Amenirdis I. In this case, year 12 of Shabaqo would be linked with year 19 of another ruler, most logically Osorkon III. Kitchen (1986, 178), on chronological grounds, regards this as impossible.

123 Amenirdis I is nowhere associated with Piye on contemporary monuments, only with Shabaqo, and there is every reason (despite the assumptions of previous writers, e.g. Kitchen 1986, 359) to assume that it was he who installed her. Equally, there is no evidence that Piye was the brother of Amenirdis I.

124 ANET, 286; see Kitchen 1986, 144, 376.

125 Peftjauawybast as High Priest of Memphis is dated by Kitchen (1986, 487, Table 18) to 790–780 BC. As the son of HPM Pediese, Peftjauawybast was the great-grandson of Crown Prince Shoshenq (son of Osorkon II) and therefore of royal blood. He may also have been a descendant of Osorkon II through the female line. The antecedents of King Peftjauawybast of Heracleopolis are completely unknown – identification with the HPM of the same name would explain his origin and claim to kingship.

126 See n. 84 and the evidence set out in Table 10:2. Kitchen (1986, 567), accepting Leahy's arguments on orthographic grounds that the King Takeloth from whom a family of viziers descended is the IIIrd rather than IInd, has lowered the dating of this group by a full century. This highlights some of the many uncertainties in placing officials accurately

during the Libyan period and the possibilities for quite drastic reappraisals.

127 Kitchen 1986, 89–90.

128 Kitchen 1986, 106–7; cf. 329–33.

129 See Baer 1973, 18–19. As this book was being prepared for publication, a new study by Aston (1989) appeared; essentially it agrees with the arguments presented here, that there must have been a considerable overlap between the reigns of Takeloth II and Shoshenq III, and that the identity of the HPA Prince Osorkon with the future Osorkon III is highly probable.

130 Cf. Kitchen 1986, 330 (n. 481); Baer 1973, 19.

131 See note 35, above.

132 See note 36, above.

133 This is not meant to imply that the 21st Dynasty began as late as the mid-22nd. This would be the case only if the usual identification of the Psusennes (prenomen Akheperre) buried at Tanis with Psusennes I, second king of Manetho's 21st Dynasty, was certain. However, the internal chronology of this Dynasty is extremely obscure and it is only the descent of the High Priests of Amun at Thebes which is reasonably certain. Their relationships with the kings reigning at Tanis, as well as the internal connections between the latter, are still a matter of conjecture (see Kitchen 1986, 473–4, Tables 7, 8). The identification of the two monumentally attested kings named Psusennes (prenomens Akheperre and Tyetkheperre) with Manetho's Psusennes 'I' and 'II' respectively has never been adequately demonstrated, and the possibility that their chronological order could be reversed must be considered. The major factor involved in the identification of Tyetkheperre as the 2nd Psusennes was the well-attested marriage of his daughter Maatkare to Osorkon I. Within the conventional dynastic sequence, this meant that Tyetkheperre must have reigned at the end of the 22nd Dynasty; by default Psusennes Akheperre was placed at the beginning.

134 Shoshenq I's campaign, which largely affected Israel, may instead be connected with the war conducted by Israel to recapture from the Aramaeans their territories north of Samaria and across the Jordan. The northern Hebrew kingdom of Israel always had friendly relations with Egypt, from its founding under Jeroboam (see Chapter 8) to the last King Hoshea, who sent messengers to Egypt to ask for help against the oncoming Assyrians (2 Kgs. 17:4). The anonymous 'saviour' sent by God to help Israel drive out the Aramaeans around 800 BC (2 Kgs. 13:5) may have been Shoshenq I.

135 Sese or Sessi (Ssysw) was a well-known abbreviation for the royal name Ramesses, most commonly applied to Ramesses II and particularly with respect to place-names either in, or en route to, Palestine (Gardiner 1920, 103; ANET, 477–8; Kitchen 1986, 374, n. 751). Though it has often been ignored by modern Egyptologists, there is no good reason to doubt Ramesses III's claim to a major campaign in Palestine; archaeological

evidence demonstrates that he had some control over the area (Weinstein 1981, 22). The campaign took place most probably in his year 12 (see Breasted 1906, 68–80), during which he brought back to Egypt considerable booty, including 'an array of elaborate metallic vessels' (Breasted 1906, 73), reminiscent of the treasures looted from Solomon's Temple by Shishak (1 Kgs. 14:26). If Ramesses III was the biblical Shishak, then the Egyptian father-in-law of Solomon (c. 950–930 BC), who sacked Gezer and gave it to him as a dowry, would have been the 19th Dynasty Pharaoh Merneptah, whose titles included 'subduer of Gezer' (Yurco 1986, 190). Further investigation of such possible synchronisms will enable us to tighten our new Egyptian chronology considerably. For example, if Ramesses III's Year 12 = 925 BC, then the beginning of the 20th Dynasty would have fallen c. 938 BC. The figure of c. 950 BC given in the text is based on very broad calculations.

136 Radiocarbon dating and Egyptian history have had a close, though not always fruitful, relationship. In its early days, the radiocarbon method was tested on 'firmly dated' Egyptian objects. It became clear that there was a consistent discrepancy, radiocarbon dates regularly producing results which were too low for the conventional dates. This led to the practice of correcting radiocarbon dates by reference to tree-ring sequences (see Appendix 1). Calibrated results are often held to produce a good match with the conventional Egyptian chronology, a view expressed by Hassan and Robinson (1987). Nevertheless, closer examination shows that the situation is less clear-cut. For the dating of Senusret III (12th Dynasty) and the Middle Kingdom in general radiocarbon has produced confusing results. Hassan and Robinson (1987, 125–6) note the wide range of results and conclude that 'we must suspend judgement . . . until better measurements are obtained'.

For the later New Kingdom they cite six main series of calibrated dates. The three dates for the reign of Ramesses II with an average of 1230±96 BC match the conventional chronology. The averages for Nebwenenef of 1277±102 BC (six results), for Bakenkhons I of 1217±134 BC (three results), for Roma-Roy of 1167±128 BC (eight results) and for Nakhtmin (or Inhernakht) of 1150±149 BC (five results) 'are also within the range of historical dates' (Hassan and Robinson 1987, 124). Nevertheless, the five dates from the tomb of Tjanefer provide an average of 976±88 BC, which is 'younger than the expected age of 1234-1135 BC' (Hassan and Robinson 1987, 125). Interestingly, the Tjanefer results have the smallest standard deviation of any of these sets. Further, all the tests were performed on reeds, halfa grass and wood, materials with a well-known tendency to produce results which are too old (see Appendix 1).

Better materials were used for a series from El-Amarna, a short-period 18th Dynasty site (Switsur in Kemp 1984). Five tests were performed on bone, skin, horn, wood and charcoal, producing an average calibrated date of 1333±50 BC (Hassan and Robinson 1987, 124). Because of their consistency and the careful selection of the samples, these dates appear to provide significant support for the conventional chronology. Nevertheless, one was performed on charcoal, another on wood, reducing the number of reliable results to three. Further, these results have to be weighed against others, such as those from the tomb of Horemheb (last ruler of the El-Amarna period), conventionally dated in the last quarter of the 14th century BC. While the result of 1410–1000 BC from chopped straw in one wall would fit the accepted dates, the date of 1255–920 BC from straw in another wall had to be explained as later 'embellishment and replastering' during the 19th Dynasty, while a result of 1260–990 BC from charcoal 'is inexplicable at present as no archaeological evidence was found for later use of this part of the tomb' (Burleigh and Matthews 1982, 161; dates from Shaw 1985, 313, who follows the Belfast calibration).

137 A notorious case of selective publishing concerns two tests performed by the British Museum on reeds (BM-642A) and dom-palm nut kernels (BM-642B) from the tomb of Tutankhamun. The results, c. 846 bc and c. 899 bc (standard deviations not available), were never formally published. Their existence came to light only when they were 'leaked' by Mr Bruce Mainwaring, co-ordinator of a radiocarbon project conducted by the University of Pennsylvania in conjunction with the British Museum (Talbott 1973/1974). Calibrated, these results would be some two centuries too young for the conventional chronology, but consistent with the revision suggested here.

11 Riddles of Mesopotamian Archaeology

1 Lloyd 1980, 97–129.
2 Mallowan 1967, 60.
3 Lloyd 1980, 146–7.
4 Lloyd 1980, 175–8.
5 For the story of Sardanapalus, see Diodorus Siculus II, 23–8; Augustine, *City of God* II, 20; for Semiramis, see Diodorus Siculus II, 4–21; Augustine, *City of God* XVIII, 2.
6 *ARAB* I, 260; S. Page 1969; see also Ch. 12, n. 28.
7 Burstein 1978.
8 See e.g. *ANET*, 317, 566–7.
9 For Ptolemy's Canon, see Burstein 1978, 38–9; Bickerman 1980, 108–9; Thiele 1983, 227–8.
10 The 'Babylonian Chronicle' as such is a series of documents, providing an episodic history from Neo-Babylonian to Seleucid times (Grayson 1975, 8–28). The text published by J. N. Strassmaier in 1887 (Grayson's Chronicle 1) was compiled in the reign of the Persian Emperor Darius I and covers the period from Nabonassar to the accession of Shamash-shum-ukin (747–668 BC); for text, translation and commentary, see Grayson 1975, 69–87.
11 Rawlinson 1873, 48. Later discoveries have extended our knowledge of the Eponym List to the year 648 BC; see Ungnad 1938, 428–9, and, conveniently, *ARAB* II, 439; Thiele 1983, 221–6.
12 Rawlinson 1873, 48.

13 Tadmor 1985, 264–5.
14 Thiele 1983, 37, 69.
15 Newton 1977, 372–6, xiii.
16 Anon. 1977, 80.
17 Whiteside 1978; Noel M. Swerdlow, Victor E. Thoren and Owen J. Gingerich as reported in Anon. 1979, 71.
18 Newton 1977, 376.
19 Sachs 1970, 20; Sachs 1974.
20 van der Meer 1947, 5.
21 See Ch. 12, n. 19; Rawlinson 1873, 50–1; King 1899a, 361–2; cf. Ch. 12, n. 17, for more recent instances of reliance on the ancient Assyrian calculations.
22 King 1899a, 368.
23 King 1899b, 448.
24 Hallo and Simpson 1971, 124.
25 Roux 1966, 251; cf. the 'dark centuries' discussed by Neumann and Parpola 1987, 162.
26 Munn-Rankin 1975, 284–94.
27 Grayson 1972, 132–47.
28 Grayson 1972, 147–53; 1976, 1–62. For Tiglath-pileser I's Mediterranean campaign, see ANET, 274–5.
29 Grayson 1976, 46, 74: 'with the decline of the Middle Assyrian Empire the number of royal inscriptions decreases. Indeed, Ashur-bel-kala is the last monarch for whom any appreciable number of texts is preserved . . . After a long period during which few royal inscriptions are known, significant numbers of texts again begin to appear starting with the reign of Ashur-dan II.'
30 Neumann and Parpola 1987, 171.
31 Wiseman 1975, 479.
32 Venit 1986, 9.
33 Reade 1975, 150.
34 A classic case concerns the famous 'White Obelisk', attributed by some Assyriologists to the reign of Assurnasirpal II (883–859 BC), but by others to Tiglath-pileser II (966–935 BC) or even Assurnasirpal I (1050–1032 BC). For bibliography and analysis of this problem, see Reade 1975, 129–50.
35 Grayson 1982, 242.
36 Wiseman 1975, 463–4.
37 von Oppenheim 1931.
38 Goetze 1931.
39 Moortgat 1955, 30–3.
40 Frankfort 1969, 175–8.
41 Albright 1956a, 152–3. He further argued (Albright 1956b, 82) that the script of the Kapara texts 'is archaic Neo-Assyrian, with forms . . . which do not appear in the Assyrian inscriptions after the revival of the late tenth century, so far as I know; the orthography is intermediate between the bad archaizing spelling of the second millennium and neo-Assyrian'. Given the general scarcity of Assyrian texts from this period, Albright's

confidence must be held in doubt – Orthmann 1971, 129, dismissed the philological and palaeographic arguments as ambiguous.

42 Hrouda 1962.

43 Orthmann 1971, 129; cf. Millard and Bordreuil 1982, 136.

44 By way of compromise, Madhloom (1970, 30, n. 1) remarked, somewhat lamely, that 'the art at Tell Halaf exhibits a confused mingling of different elements of early and late date'.

45 Kantor 1956, 174; Albright (1958, 3) noted, with barely disguised glee, this apparent dissension within the Frankfort school, which generally maintained that Syrian art of the 9th century BC represented a completely fresh start.

46 Canby 1976, 117; cf. Canby 1964.

47 Canby 1976, 117, 119.

48 Millard and Bordreuil 1982, 135–6. One ancient name of Tell Fakhariyah was Sikanu; it is sometimes thought to be the site of the missing capital of the Mitannian Empire, Wassukani.

49 Shamash-nuri's office is not named in the Eponym Canon. However, different officers of state usually held the position of eponym, according to a strict 'pecking order': Shamash-nuri's predecessor (in 867 BC) was almost certainly the governor of the adjacent province of Tushkhan, and in the 8th century BC the governor of Guzan regularly followed the governor of Tushkhan (Millard and Bordreuil 1982, 139; Millard 1983, 105).

50 Naveh 1982, 89 (n. 52).

51 Millard and Bordreuil 1982.

52 S. A. Kaufman 1986, 10.

53 S. A. Kaufman 1986, 12–13; his own rather contrived solution is that an 11th-century alphabet somehow survived for 200 years in northern Mesopotamia and that this, via an overland route across Turkey, provided the inspiration for the Greek alphabetic forms on the Ionian coast.

54 The reduction of the 11th-century BC Proto-Canaanite alphabet to the 9th century suggested here is in step with the revised dates for the Byblos inscriptions argued by Wallenfels 1983 (see Chapter 10).

55 Grayson 1975, 157–69; cf. the variant 'Chronicle P' (Grayson 1975, 170–7).

56 Brinkman 1982, 282.

57 Moorey (ed.) 1982, 223.

58 North 1957.

59 Brinkman 1982, 284.

60 Brinkman 1984.

61 R. McC. Adams 1981, 174.

62 Brinkman 1982, 284.

63 R. McC. Adams 1981, 174.

64 Brinkman 1982, 283.

65 Brinkman 1976, vii (n. 2).

66 Burstein 1978, 22.

67 See Brinkman 1984, 177.

68 The chronological framework used by the Neo-Babylonians was certainly linked to that of the Assyrian King List, as can be seen from efforts such as the so-called *Synchronistic Chronicle*, a document which lists parallel columns of Assyrian and Babylonian kings from the earliest times down to the reign of Assurbanipal (*ANET* 272–4). Such linking between the Babylonian dynasties and the linear Assyrian King List would have artificially stretched the ancient Babylonian concept of their own chronology, possibly creating a gap, or period of bleak documentation, before the reign of Nabonassar similar to that in the modern reconstructed history (see Chapter 12).

69 The earliest pottery in the Gulf region appears to have been brought by settlers from southern Mesopotamia *c.* 5000 BC; see Oates *et al.* 1977.

70 Kramer 1963, 147–9.

71 Herodotus VII, 89; Bowersock 1986.

72 Edens 1986, 196–200.

73 Kervran *et al.* 1987, 78–9, 92.

74 Edens (1986, 194) discusses the existence of a 'dark age' in the Gulf lasting from *c.* 1800/1700 to 800/700 BC. A closer look reveals that Edens's broadly defined 'second millennium "dark age"' is in fact a 1st-millennium affair.

75 Kervran *et al.* 1987, 75–9.

76 Kervran *et al.* 1987, 79–92.

77 Diakonoff 1985, 23–4.

78 See Labat 1975a, 1975b. On the invasion of Nebuchadrezzar I, *c.* 1105 BC (conventional chronology), the Elamite King Huteludush-Inshushinak fled (Brinkman 1968, 105–10). An immediate successor to Huteludush-Inshushinak is known, but only from an 8th-century BC text (Labat 1975b, 502–3). Over the next 300 years there are no other Elamite records of kings (retrospective or otherwise). Babylonian records are equally silent regarding Elam during this period, with the exception of one tangential reference which describes the little-known Babylonian ruler Mar-biti-apla-usur (984–979 BC) as being of Elamite descent (Brinkman 1968, 165, n. 1005).

79 Labat 1975b, 503.

80 Carter and Stolper 1984, 44.

81 de Miroschedji 1982, 62–3; cf. Carter and Stolper 1984, 182.

82 de Miroschedji 1978, 218–27.

83 Ghirshman 1966, 8–9, 91–2.

84 Carter and Stolper 1987, 187.

85 Carter and Stolper 1987, 184.

86 Carter and Stolper 1987, 185.

87 For a recent introduction to the problems of the Luristan bronzes, see Muscarella 1988a. Muscarella 1988c contains a useful bibliography and discussion of the excavated examples, and the dating schemes applied to them, particularly that developed by Louis vanden Berghe for the Iron Age cemetery sites covered by his extensive fieldwork. But as Muscarella (1988c, 118) notes: 'The difficulties one encounters in vanden Berghe's

sequence is not the diachronic placement of the bronzes, whether excavated or strays, into three periods, but rather the absolute dates assigned
to the periods themselves.'

88 Muscarella (1988c, 120) is cautious of the significance of the inscribed
examples, stressing that none of the fifty-six bronzes with inscriptions
was excavated in Luristan; nevertheless, he accepts that two spiked axe-
heads bearing the names of a Babylonian and an Elamite king (both
conventionally 12th century BC) are of Luristan form.

89 Schaeffer 1948, 477–95.

90 Ghirshman 1964; Kantor 1946; cf. Porada 1964.

91 Muscarella 1988a; for further discussion of the broad range of dates
possible for the bronzes, see Moorey 1971.

92 Neumann and Parpola 1987, 178–82.

93 For references, see Neumann and Parpola, 163–4.

94 Neumann and Parpola 1987, 162.

12   The Exaggeration of Antiquity

1 Josephus, *Against Apion*.

2 Herodotus II, 2–3.

3 This important theme is overlooked, for example, in the recent general
study of ancient Near Eastern historiography by Van Seters (1983).

4 Hakluyt 1907, 53–5.

5 Plato, *Timaeus*, 22–3.

6 Herodotus II, 142.

7 Burstein 1978, 21.

8 Waddell 1940, x.

9 For translation and bibliography of the standard King List, see *ANET*,
564–6; see Brinkman 1973, 314–15, on the date of the Nassouhi version.

10 Albright 1921, 86, 94 (n. 2); cf. Lewy 1970, 741. For details of such time-
spans involving Kassite kings, see Brinkman 1976, 8 (n. 5).

11 Albright 1921, 94 (n. 2).

12 Lewy 1970, 740–1; Albright 1921, 94 (n. 2).

13 Drews 1975, 48–50; cf. Van Seters 1983, 91–2.

14 Lewy 1970, 740.

15 *ARAB* I, 41 (also trans. in Grayson 1976, 85–6); *ARAB* II, 272–3.

16 To explain these discrepancies it has been suggested that Esarhaddon's
text contains scribal errors, and that the 159-year period was included by
Shalmaneser's scribe twice (counting it again within the 580 years). See
Lewy 1970, 748, 750–1; Na'aman 1984, 118–19. Nevertheless, the texts
are quite clear, and there is no objective basis for the idea of 'scribal
errors'. The possibility considered by Na'aman (1984, 119), that 'Shalmaneser's scribe consulted a kinglist different from our canonical text', is
a far more sound approach than tampering with the original data.

17 Albright 1921, 89; Rowton 1966, 254–5; Rowton 1970, 202–3; cf.
Wiseman 1975, 464–5. (See also Ch. 11, n. 21.)

18 Na'aman 1984, 116: 'We must conclude that the canonical Assyrian and

Babylonian kinglists contained all the chronological data necessary for the calculation of the time-spans of past events and that subsequent to their compilation they were the main sources for all the statements of the *Distanzangaben* [time-spans], as far as the scribes were concerned. In other words, these statements are of no value for the establishment of an exact chronological scheme or for the confirmation of a given chronological system.' Cf. Lewy 1970, 752.

19 Sennacherib, *c.* 700 BC, added an inscription to a seal of the Kassite King Shagarakti-Shuriash, once seized by Tukulti-Ninurta I. It returned to Babylonia and was recaptured by Sennacherib '600 years' later; see *ARAB* II, 158-9. Nabonidus, writing *c.* 550 BC, dated Shagarakti-Shuriash 800 years before his time (Brinkman 1976, 8, n. 5), a century more than the presently accepted chronology would allow.

20 Brinkman 1973, 310.

21 Henige 1986, 64.

22 J. J. Finkelstein 1966.

23 Hallo 1978, 5.

24 Hallo 1978, 5.

25 Hallo 1978, 6.

26 Hallo 1978, 3.

27 Hallo 1978, 3.

28 The missing rulers include the following (in chronological order with conventional dates):

(1) King Puzur-Sin, known from his one inscription to be a rival to the house of Shamshi-Adad I, *c.* 1800 BC (Grayson 1972, 29-30).

(2)(3)(4) One king-list fragment departs from the canonical tradition and replaces kings XLI to LIII (Grayson's numbering) in the post-Shamshi-Adad I period with the names of two, perhaps three, otherwise unknown kings of Assyria: Mut-Ashkur, Rem . . . and possibly Asinu (Grayson 1972, 29).

(5) Ber-nadin-ahhe, apparently a son of the 15th-century BC King Assur-nirari II, mentioned by two legal texts: 'Both the title and genealogy indicate that Ber-nadin-ahhe was a king. But he does not appear in the Assyrian King List and nothing else is known about him' (Grayson 1972, 37).

(6) Assur-danin-apli (son of Shalmaneser III), who almost certainly took the throne during the six-year rebellion he led at the end of his father's reign, 826-821 BC (Poebel 1943, 79).

(7) It has been argued that Queen Sammuramat ruled Assyria during the minority of her son Adad-nirari III (810-805 BC), though this has been hotly disputed; in any case, a queen would not have been included in the AKL even if she had been effective monarch. For arguments both for and against her regency, see Poebel 1943, 80-4; Page 1969.

29 Grayson 1972, 137.

30 Landsberger 1954, 42-4.

31 Brinkman 1973, 313.

32 Brinkman 1973, 312.

33 Wilson 1977, 89–90, discusses the variant genealogies of Assuruballit, noting that 'the genealogies in this portion of the AKL-A have been altered'.

34 Brinkman 1973, 312.

35 Brinkman 1973, 311–12.

36 Hallo 1978, 6–7.

37 Thiele 1983, 61–5.

38 Rowton 1966, 255–6; Brinkman 1976, 409–11.

39 Grayson 1972, 146; van der Meer 1947, 9–10; Poebel 1943, 61–6; Wiseman 1975, 452–3; for additional references, see *ANET*, 565 (n. 3).

40 Brinkman 1973, 313.

41 See Henige 1986, 61. For example, in Sparta two lines of kings descended from the hero Heracles shared both priestly and military duties over several centuries (Herodotus VI, 56–9). The kingdoms of Judah and Israel, which separated because of tensions within the loose tribal confederacy, often worked in practice as a dual Israelite monarchy, with periods of successful co-operation, cemented by dynastic marriages and mutual commercial ventures and foreign policy.

42 Henige 1986, 61.

43 Kramer 1963, 328–31; *ANET* 265–7.

44 Kramer 1963, 36.

45 A. L. Oppenheim in *ANET*, 265.

46 Grayson 1975, 69–87; on the Chronicle, see Ch. 11, n. 10.

47 Carter and Stolper 1984, 92 (n. 359). As an example, they cite an Akkadian legal text dated in year 15 of Hallushu, King of Elam, for whom the Chronicle allows only a reign of 5 years.

48 *ANET* 272–4.

49 Poebel 1943, 61 (n. 236).

50 Rowton 1970, 201–2.

51 Poebel 1943, 56–7.

52 Assur-nirari IV (1018–1013 BC) and Assur-rabi II (1012–972 BC) – see Grayson 1976, 70–1. The short-lived Ashared-apil-Ekur (1075–1074 BC) is also unattested by monuments (Grayson 1976, 45–6).

53 Grayson 1976, 68–70, 73–4.

54 Brinkman 1973, 312.

55 Grayson 1976, 70.

56 Brinkman 1982, 296.

57 Henige 1986, 63.

58 Brinkman 1976, 15, n. 28.

59 An alternative is that the Assuruballit of the King List and monuments is not the El-Amarna correspondent of that name, a possibility suggested by the difference in their father's names (see Appendix 4). The El-Amarna Assuruballit may be a king descended from a collateral royal line. If the scribes who drew up the King List confused the two rulers, this may explain the serious discrepancies which exist between the information given by the King List and the monuments for the ancestry of Assuruballit's predecessors (see n. 33, above).

60 Rowton 1970, 195–6.
61 See Kitchen 1987, 39–40.
62 Hanfmann 1951, 361.

13   The End of the Dark Ages?

 1 Tainter 1988.
 2 Toynbee 1939, V, 403; IV, 421–2.
 3 James forthcoming.
 4 Childe 1942, 177–8.
 5 Snodgrass 1989, 30.
 6 See Chapter 10; Mellaart 1990.
 7 Zaccagnini 1987.
 8 Renfrew 1979, 490–4.
 9 O'Connor 1983, 228–9.
10 Tainter 1988, 202–4.
11 Stiebing 1980, 16–18.
12 Carpenter 1966; Bryson *et al.* 1974.
13 Weiss 1982, 194.
14 Neumann and Parpola 1987.
15 Beug 1982, 100; Bintliff 1982, 144; Harding 1982, 9.
16 Baillie 1989.
17 Schaeffer 1948; 1968, 607–8; cf. Drower 1975, 147–8.
18 Kilian forthcoming.
19 Trigger 1976, 137.
20 Desborough 1972, 333–40.
21 Taylour 1983, 161–3.
22 Mellink 1964, 63–5.
23 Bottema and Van Zeist 1982, 321.
24 Snodgrass 1987, 188–207.
25 H. E. Wright 1972, 193–8.
26 Sordinas 1971, 2.
27 Harding 1984, 106; cf. Cline 1987, 8–12.

Bibliography

Abu Taleb, M., 1973. *Investigations in the History of North Syria* (Ph.D. diss., Univ. of Pennsylvania), Ann Arbor: Univ. Microfilms, 1976.

Acquaro, E., 1988. 'Sardinia', in Moscati (ed.), 1988, 210–25.

Adams, R. McC., 1981. *Heartland of Cities: Surveys of Ancient Settlement and Land Use on the Central Floodplain of the Euphrates*, Univ. of Chicago Press.

Adams, W. Y., 1964. 'Post-Pharaonic Nubia in the Light of Archaeology, 1', *JEA* 50, 102–20.

—— 1977. *Nubia: Corridor to Africa*, Princeton Univ. Press.

Addison, F., 1949. *Jebel Moya*, London: Wellcome Excavations in the Sudan 1–2.

Aharoni, M. & Aharoni, Y., 1976. 'The Stratification of Judahite Sites in the 8th and 7th Centuries B.C.E.', *BASOR* 224, 73–90.

Aharoni, Y., 1966. *The Land of the Bible*, London: Burns & Oates.

—— 1975. *Investigations at Lachish: the Sanctuary and the Residency*, Tel Aviv Univ.

—— 1982. *The Archaeology of the Land of Israel* (trans. A. F. Rainey), Philadelphia: Westminster Press.

Akurgal, E., 1946. *Remarques stylistiques sur les Reliefs de Malatya*, Ankara Üniv. Dil ve Tarih-Coğrafya Fakültesi Yayimlari 53.

—— 1962. *The Art of the Hittites*, London: Thames & Hudson.

—— 1968. *The Birth of Greek Art*, London: Methuen.

Albright, W. F., 1921. 'A Revision of Early Assyrian and Middle Babylonian Chronology', *Revue d'Assyriologie* 18, 83–94.

—— 1932. 'The Seal of Eliakim and the Latest Pre-exilic History of Judah, with some Observations on Ezekiel', *Journal of Biblical Literature* 51, 77–106.

—— 1938. 'The Oldest Hebrew Letters: The Lachish Ostraca', *BASOR* 70, 11–17.

—— 1939. 'A Reëxamination of the Lachish Letters', *BASOR* 73, 16–21.

—— 1941. 'The Lachish Letters After Five Years', *BASOR* 82, 18–24.

—— 1943. *Tell Beit Mirsim*, Philadelphia: Annual of the American Schools of Oriental Research 21/22.

—— 1946. *From the Stone Age to Christianity*, Baltimore: Johns Hopkins Press.

—— 1947. 'The Phoenician Inscriptions of the Tenth Century B.C. from Byblus', *Journal of the American Oriental Society* 67, 153–60.

—— 1950. 'Some Oriental Glosses on the Homeric Problem', *AJA* 54, 162–76.

—— 1953. 'Correspondence with Professor Einar Gjerstad on the

Chronology of the 'Cypriote' Pottery from Early Iron Levels in Palestine', *BASOR* 130, 22.

—— 1954. *The Archaeology of Palestine*, Harmondsworth: Penguin.

—— 1956a. 'Northeast-Mediterranean Dark Ages and the Early Iron Age Art of Syria', in S. Weinberg (ed.), *The Aegean and the Near East* (Goldman Festschrift), Locust Valley, N.Y.: J. J. Augustin, 144–64.

—— 1956b. 'The Date of the Kapara Period at Gozan (Tell Halaf)', *AnSt* 6, 75–85.

—— 1958. 'Was the Age of Solomon Without Monumental Art?', *Eretz-Israel* 5, 1–9.

—— 1961. 'The Role of the Canaanites in the History of Civilization', in G. E. Wright (ed.), *The Bible and the Ancient Near East*, Garden City, N. Y.: Doubleday, 328–62.

—— 1965. 'Some Remarks on the Archaeological Chronology of Palestine', in R. W. Ehrich (ed.), *Chronologies in Old World Archaeology*, Univ. of Chicago Press, 47–60.

—— 1971. 'Nelson Glueck in Memoriam', *BASOR* 202, 2–6.

—— 1975. 'Syria, the Philistines, and Phoenicia', in *CAH* II:2, 507–36.

Alessio, M., *et al.*, 1966. 'University of Rome Carbon-14 dates IV', *Radiocarbon* 8, 401–12.

Alexander, J. & Hopkin, S., 1982. 'The Origins and Early Development of European Fibulae', *PPS* 48, 401–16.

Allen, H. L., 1977. 'Distribution of Pottery Styles in Greece, South Italy, and Sicily and the Pantalica III Chronology', *AJA* 81, 365–8.

Amiran, R., 1969. *Ancient Pottery of the Holy Land*, Jerusalem: Masada Press.

Amyx, D. A., 1988. *Corinthian Vase-painting of the Archaic Period*, Univ. of California Press.

Anati, E., 1985. 'Has Mt. Sinai been Found?', *BAR* July/Aug., 42–57.

Anderson, W. P., 1988. *Sarepta I: The Late Bronze and Iron Age Strata of Area II, Y*, Beirut: Publ. de L'Univ. Libanaise.

Anderson–Immerwahr, S., 1971. *The Athenian Agora XIII*, Princeton, N. J.: The American School of Classical Studies at Athens.

Andronikos, M., 1969. *Vergina I*, Athens: Bibliotheke tes en Athenais Arch. Etaireias 62.

Anon., 1977. 'Claudius Ptolemy: Fraud', *Scientific American* Oct., 79–81.

Anon., 1979. 'The Acquittal of Ptolemy', *Scientific American* March, 70–1.

Aston, D. A., 1989. 'Takeloth II – a King of the "Twenty-third Dynasty"?', *JEA* 75, 139–53.

Åström, P. (ed.), 1987 & 1989. *High, Middle or Low?* Parts 1, 2 & 3, Gothenburg: Paul Åströms Förlag.

Atkinson, R. J. C., 1952. 'The Date of Stonehenge', *PPS* 18, 236–7.

—— 1956. *Stonehenge*, London: Hamish Hamilton.

—— 1969. 'The Date of Silbury Hill', *Antiquity* 43, 216.

—— 1978. *Stonehenge and Neighbouring Monuments*, London: HMSO.

Aubet Semmler, M. E., 1988. 'Spain', in Moscati (ed.) 1988, 226–42.

Avigad, N., 1978. 'Baruch the Scribe and Jerahmeel the King's Son', *IEJ* 28, 52–6.

Baer, K., 1973. 'The Libyan and Nubian Kings of Egypt: Notes on the Chronology of Dynasties XXII to XXVI', *JNES* 32, 4–25.

Baillie, M. G. L., 1982. *Tree Ring Dating and Archaeology*, London: Croom Helm.

—— 1989. 'Hekla 3: How Big Was it?', *Endeavour* 13, 78–81.

Baillie, M. G. L. & Pilcher, J. R., 1983. 'Some Observations on the High-Precision Calibration of Routine Dates", in B. S. Ottaway (ed.), *Archaeology, Dendrochronology and the Radiocarbon Calibration Curve*, Univ. of Edinburgh Dept. of Arch. Occas. Paper 9, 51–63.

Baldacchino, J. G. & Dunbabin, T. J., 1953. 'Rock tomb at Ghajn Qajjet, near Rabbat, Malta', *Papers of the British School at Rome* 21, 32–41.

Balensi, J., 1985. 'Revising Tell Abu Hawam', *BASOR* 257, 65–74.

Balensi, J. & Herrera, M. D., 1985. 'Tel Abou Hawam, 1983–1984: Rapport préliminaire', *Revue Biblique* 92, 82–128.

Balmuth, M. S., 1984. 'The Nuraghi of Sardinia: an Introduction', in M. S. Balmuth & R. J. Rowland (eds), *Studies in Sardinian Archaeology*, Ann Arbor: Univ. of Michigan Press, 23–52.

—— (ed.) 1986. *Sardinian Archaeology II*, Ann Arbor: Univ. of Michigan Press.

Barnett, R. D., 1982. *Ancient Ivories in the Middle East and Adjacent Countries*, Hebrew Univ. of Jerusalem.

Barnett, R. D. & Mendleson, C., 1987. *Tharros*, London: British Museum Publs.

Barreca, F., 1986. 'Phoenicians in Sardinia: The Bronze Figurines', in Balmuth (ed.) 1986, 131–43.

Becking, B., 1981/1982. 'The Two Neo-Assyrian Contract Documents from Gezer in their Historical Context', *Ex Oriente Lux* 27, 76–89.

Beloch, A. J., 1913. *Griechische Geschichte* I:2, Strasbourg: K. J. Trübner.

Benichou-Safar, H., 1982. *Les Tombes puniques de Carthage*, Paris: Centre National de la Recherche Scientifique.

Bennett, C-M., 1975. 'Excavations at Buseirah, Southern Jordan, 1973: Third Preliminary Report', *Levant* 7, 1–19.

—— 1977. 'Excavations at Buseirah, Southern Jordan, 1974: Fourth Preliminary Report', *Levant* 9, 1–10.

Benson, J. L., 1970. *Horse, Bird and Man*, Amherst: Massachusetts Univ. Press.

Ben-Tor, A. & Portugali, Y., 1987. *Tell Qiri* (Qedem 24), Jerusalem: The Israel Exploration Soc.

Beug, H.-J., 1982. 'Vegetation History and Climatic Changes in Central and Southern Europe', in Harding (ed.) 1982, 85–102.

Bickerman, E. J., 1980. *Chronology of the Ancient World* (rev. edn), London: Thames & Hudson.

Bier, L., 1976. 'A Second Hittite Relief from Ivriz', *JNES* 35, 115–26.

Bierbrier, M. L., 1975. *The Late New Kingdom in Egypt (c. 1300–664 B.C.): a Genealogical and Chronological Investigation*, Warminster: Aris & Phillips.

—— 1984. 'Two Confusing Coffins', *JEA* 70, 82–6.

Bietti Sestieri, A. M., 1979. 'I processi storici nella Sicilia orientale fra la tardia Età del Bronzo e gli inizi dell'Età del Ferro sulla base dei dati archeologica, in *Il Bronzo Finale in Italia*, Florence: Atti della XXI Riunione Scientifica, 599–629.

—— 1981. 'Economy and Society in Italy Between the Late Bronze Age and Early Iron Age', in G. Barker (ed.), *Archaeology and Italian Society*, Oxford: BAR Int. Ser. 102, 133–55.

Bikai, P. M., 1978a. 'The Late Phoenician Pottery Complex and Chronology', *BASOR* 229, 47–56.

—— 1978b. *The Pottery of Tyre*, Warminster: Aris & Phillips.

—— 1987. *The Phoenician Pottery of Cyprus*, Nicosia: A. G. Leventis Foundation.

Bimson, J. J., 1978. *Redating the Exodus and Conquest*, Sheffield: Journal for the Study of the Old Testament, Suppl. Ser. 5.

—— 1981. 'King Solomon's Mines? A Re-assessment of Finds in the Arabah', *Tyndale Bulletin* 32, 123–49.

—— 1988. 'A Reply to Baruch Halpern's "Radical Exodus Redating Fatally Flawed"', *BAR* July/Aug., 52–5.

Bimson, J. J. & Livingston, D., 1987. 'Redating the Exodus', *BAR* Sept./Oct., 40–53, 66–7.

Bintliff, J. L., 'Climate Change, Archaeology and Quaternary Science in the Eastern Mediterranean Region', in Harding (ed.) 1982, 143–61.

Birmingham, J., 1963. 'The Chronology of Some Early and Middle Iron Age Cypriot Sites', *AJA* 67, 15–42.

Bittel, K., 1970. *Hattusha: Capital of the Hittites*, Oxford Univ. Press.

—— 1983. 'Die archäologische Situation in Kleinasien um 1200 v. Chr. und während der nachfolgenden vier Jahrhunderte', in S. Deger-Jalkotzy (ed.), *Griechenland, die Ägäis und die Levante während der 'Dark Ages' vom 12. bis zum 9. Jh. v. Chr.*, Vienna: österreichischen Akademie der Wissenschaften, 25–65.

Blanco, A. & Luzón, J. M., 1969. 'Pre-Roman Silver Miners at Riotinto', *Antiquity* 43, 124–31.

Blegen, C. W., 1957. 'The Palace of Nestor Excavations of 1956', *AJA* 61, 129–35.

—— 1963. *Troy and the Trojans*, London: Thames and Hudson.

Blegen, C. W. & Rawson, M., 1966. *The Palace of Nestor at Pylos in Western Messenia* I, Princeton Univ. Press.

—— 1973. *The Palace of Nestor at Pylos in Western Messenia* III, Princeton Univ. Press.

Blegen, C. W., *et al.*, 1958. *Troy IV:1*, Princeton Univ. Press.

Bloedlow, E. F., 1988. 'The Trojan War and Late Helladic IIIC', *Praehistorische Zeitschrift* 63, 23–52.

Boardman, J., 1974. *Athenian Black Figure Vases*, London: Thames & Hudson.

—— 1980. *The Greeks Overseas* (2nd edn), London: Thames & Hudson.

—— 1984. '*Signae tabulae priscae artis*', *JHS* 104, 161–3.

—— 1988. 'Dates and Doubts', *Archäologischer Anzeiger*, 423–5.

Bonnet, C., *et al.*, 1986. 'Les fouilles archéologiques de Kerma (Soudan)', *Genava* 34, 1–45.

Borchardt, L., 1935. *Die Mittel zur zeitlichen Festlegung von Punkten der Ägyptischen Geschichte und ihre Anwendung*, Cairo: privately published.

Bottema, S. & Van Zeist, W., 1982. 'Vegetational History of the Eastern Mediterranean and the Near East During the Last 20,000 Years', in J. L. Bintliff & W. Van Zeist (eds), *Palaeoclimates, Palaeoenvironment and Human Communities in the Eastern Mediterranean Region in Later Prehistory*, Oxford: BAR Int. Ser. 133, 277–321.

Bouzek, J., 1985. *The Aegean, Anatolia and Europe: Cultural Interrelations in the Second Millennium B.C.*, SIMA 29.

Bowersock, G. W., 1986. 'Tylos and Tyre: Bahrain in the Graeco-Roman World', in H. Al Khalifa & M. Rice (eds), *Bahrain Through the Ages*, London: Routledge & Kegan Paul, 399–406.

Brandl, B., 1982. 'The Tel Masos Scarab: A Suggestion for a New Method of the Interpretation of Royal Scarabs', *Scripta Hierosolymitana* 28, 371–405.

Branigan, K., 1972. 'The Surbo Bronzes – Some Observations', *PPS* 38, 276–85.

Brea, L. B., 1966. *Sicily Before the Greeks* (2nd edn), London: Thames & Hudson.

Brea, L. B. & Cavalier, M., 1956. 'Civiltà preistorice delle isole eolie e del territorio di Milazzo', *Bolletino di Paletnologia Italiana* N.S., 10, 65, 7–99.

—— 1960. *Meligunis Lipára I*, Palermo: Flaccovio.

—— 1980. *Meligunis Lipára IV*, Palermo: Flaccovio.

Breasted, J. H., 1906. *Ancient Records of Egypt* IV, Univ. of Chicago Press.

—— 1916. *Ancient Times*, Boston: Ginn.

Briggs, A., 1988. *Victorian Things*, London: Batsford.

Bright, J., 1981. *A History of Israel* (3rd edn), London: SCM Press.

Brinkman, J. A., 1968. *A Political History of Post-Kassite Babylonia 1158–722 B.C.* (Analecta Orientalia 43), Rome: Pontificum Institutum.

—— 1972. 'Foreign Relations of Babylonia from 1600 to 625 B.C.: The Documentary Evidence', *AJA* 76, 271–81.

—— 1973. 'Comments on the Nassouhi Kinglist and the Assyrian Kinglist Tradition', *Orientalia* 42, 306–19.

—— 1976. *Materials and Studies for Kassite History*, Oriental Inst. of the Univ. of Chicago.

—— 1982. 'Babylonia c. 1000–748 B.C.', *CAH* III:1, 282–313.

—— 1983. 'Istanbul A. 1998, Middle Babylonian Chronology, and the Statistics of the Nippur Archives', *ZA* 73, 67–74.

—— 1984. 'Settlement Surveys and Documentary Evidence: Regional Variation and Secular Trend in Mesopotamian Demography', *JNES* 43, 169–80.

Bryce, T. R., 1989. 'Ahhiyawans and Mycenaeans – An Anatolian Viewpoint', *OJA* 8, 297–310.

Bryson, R. A., *et al.*, 1974. 'Drought and the Decline of Mycenae', *Antiquity* 48, 46–50.

Burleigh, R., *et al.*, 1982. 'British Museum Natural Radiocarbon Measurements XIV', *Radiocarbon* 24, 229–61.

Burn, A. R., 1935. 'Dates in Early Greek History', *JHS* 55, 130–46.
—— 1960. *The Lyric Age of Greece*, London: Edward Arnold.
Burstein, S. M., 1978. *The* Babyloniaca *of Berossus* (Sources and Monographs on the Ancient Near East 1:5), Malibu: Undena.
Buschor, E., 1927. 'Vom Amyklaion', *Mitteilungen des Deutschen Archäologischen Instituts: Athenische Abteilung* 52, 1–85.

Caminos, R. A., forthcoming. *The Temples of Semna and Kumma*, London: Egypt Exploration Soc.
Campbell, E. F., 1960. 'The Amarna Letters and the Amarna Period', *BA* Feb., 2–22.
Canby, J. V., 1964. Review of Hrouda 1962, *AJA* 68, 71–3.
—— 1976. 'The *STELENREIHEN* at Assur, Tell Halaf, and *MAṢṢĒBÔT*', *Iraq* 38, 113–28.
Carpenter, R., 1966. *Discontinuity in Greek Civilization*, Cambridge Univ. Press.
Carter, E. & Stolper, M. W., 1984. *Elam: Surveys of Political History and Archaeology*, Univ. of California Press.
Cartledge, P., 1979. *Sparta and Lakonia*, London: Routledge & Kegan Paul.
Caskey, J. L., 1964. 'Excavations in Keos', *Hesperia* 33, 314–35.
Casperson, L. W., 1986. 'The Lunar Dates of Thutmose III', *JNES* 45, 139–50.
—— 1988. 'The Lunar Date of Ramesses II', *JNES* 47, 181–89.
Casson, S., 1937. *Ancient Cyprus*, London: Methuen.
Catling, H. W., 1964. *Cypriot Bronzework in the Mycenaean World*, Oxford Univ. Press.
—— 1975. 'Cyprus in the Late Bronze Age', *CAH* II:2, 188–216.
—— 1976/1977. 'The Knossos Area, 1974–1976', *Archaeological Reports*, 3–23.
—— 1982/1983. 'Archaeology in Greece, 1982–83', *Archaeological Reports*, 3–62.
—— 1984. 'Workshops and Heirlooms: Prehistoric Bronze Stands in the Eastern Mediterranean', *RDAC* 69–91.
—— 1986. 'Cypriot Bronzework East or West?', in V. Karageorghis (ed.), *Cyprus Between the Orient and the Occident*, Nicosia: Zavallis Press, 91–9.
Cavanagh, W. G. & Laxton, R. R., 1985. 'Vaulting in Mycenaean Tholos Tombs and Sardinian Nuraghi', in C. Malone & S. Stoddart (eds), *Papers in Italian Archaeology IV*, Oxford: BAR Int. Ser. 245, 413–33.
Cazelles, H., 1973. 'The Hebrews', in D. J. Wiseman (ed.), *Peoples of Old Testament Times*, Oxford: Clarendon Press, 1–28.
Černý, J., 1946. 'Studies in the Chronology of the Twenty-first Dynasty', *JEA* 32, 24–30.
Chadwick, J., 1976. *The Mycenaean World*, Cambridge University Press.
—— 1979. 'The Minoan Origin of the Classical Cypriote Script', in V. Karageorghis (ed.), *Acts of the International Archaeological Symposium: 'The Relations Between Cyprus and Crete, ca. 2000–500 B.C.'*, Nicosia: Dept. of Antiquities, Cyprus, 139–43.

Chapman, S. V., 1972. 'A Catalogue of Iron Age Pottery from the Cemeteries of Khirbet Silm, Joya, Qrayé and Qasmieh of South Lebanon', *Berytus* 21, 55–194.

Chiappisi, S., 1961. *Il Melqart di Sciacca e la questione fenicia in Sicilia*, Rome: Aziende Tip. Eredi G. Bardi.

Childe, V. G., 1929. *The Danube in Prehistory*, Oxford: Clarendon Press.

—— 1942. *What Happened in History*, Harmondsworth: Penguin.

—— 1958. *The Prehistory of European Society*, Harmondsworth: Penguin.

Ciasca, A., 1988. 'Malta', in Moscati (ed.) 1988, 206–9.

Čičikova, M., 1972. 'Nouvelles données sur la culture Thrace de l'époque de Hallstatt en Bulgarie du sud', *Thracia* 1, 79–100.

Cintas, M., 1970 & 1976. *Manuel d'Archéologie punique*, Vols I & II, Paris: A. & J. Picard.

Cline, E., 1987. 'Amenhotep III and the Aegean: a Reassessment of Egypto-Aegean Relations in the 14th Century B.C.', *Orientalia* 56, 1–36.

Clinton, H. F., 1834. *Fasti Hellenici* I, Oxford Univ. Press.

Close-Brooks, J., 1979. 'Proposal for a Division into Phases', in Ridgway & Ridgway (eds) 1979, 95–107.

Clube, V. & Napier, B., 1982. *The Cosmic Serpent*, London: Faber & Faber.

Cogan, M. & Tadmor, H., 1977. 'Gyges & Ashurbanipal: A Study in Literary Transmission', *Orientalia* 46, 65–85.

Cohen, R., 1983. 'The Mysterious MBI People', *BAR* July/Aug., 16–29.

Coldstream, J. N., 1968. *Greek Geometric Pottery*, London: Methuen.

—— 1977. *Geometric Greece*, London: Methuen.

—— 1982. 'Greeks and Phoenicians in the Aegean', in H. G. Niemeyer (ed.), *Phönizier im Westen*, Madrid: Deutsches Archäologisches Institut Madrider Beiträge Band 8, 261–72.

—— 1985. 'The Geometric and Archaic Periods', in V. Karageorghis (ed.), *Archaeology in Cyprus 1960–1985*, Nicosia: A. G. Leventis Foundation, 45–59.

—— 1988. 'Early Greek Pottery in Tyre and Cyprus: Some Preliminary Comparisons', *RDAC*, 35–44.

—— 1989. 'Early Greek Visitors to Cyprus and the Eastern Mediterranean', in V. Tatton-Brown (ed.), *Cyprus and the East Mediterranean in the Iron Age*, London: British Museum Publs., 90–6.

Coles, J. M. & Harding, A. F., 1979. *The Bronze Age in Europe*, London: Methuen.

Condurachi, E. (ed.), 1966. *Histria* II, Bucharest: Editura Acadamiei Republicii Socialiste Romania.

Cook, R. M., 1937. 'The Date of the Hesiodic Shield', *Classical Quarterly* 31, 204–14.

—— 1972. *Greek Painted Pottery* (2nd edn), London: Methuen.

—— 1989. 'The Francis-Vickers Chronology', *JHS* 109, 164–70.

Cook, V., 1988. 'Cyprus and the Outside World During the Transition from the Bronze Age to the Iron Age', *Opuscula Atheniensia* 17, 13–32.

Coote, R. B., 1975. 'The Kition Bowl', *BASOR* 220, 47–50.

Coulson, W. D. E., 1985. 'The Dark Age Pottery of Sparta', *BSA* 80, 29–84.

—— 1986. *The Dark Age Pottery of Messenia*, Göteberg: Paul Åströms Forlag.

—— 1988. 'The Dark Age Pottery of Sparta, II: Vrondama', *BSA* 83, 21–4.

Crawford, M. H., 1985. *Coinage and Money under the Roman Republic*, London: Methuen.

Cross, F. M., 1969. 'Two Notes on Palestinian Inscriptions of the Persian Age', *BASOR* 193, 19–24.

—— 1980. 'Newly Found Inscriptions in Old Canaanite and Early Phoenician Script', *BASOR* 238, 1–20.

—— 1986. 'Phoenicians in the West: The Early Epigraphic Evidence', in Balmuth (ed.) 1986, 116–30.

Crouwel, J., 1981. *Chariots and Other Means of Land Transport in Bronze Age Greece*, Amsterdam: Allard Pierson Ser.

Crowfoot, J. W., *et al.*, 1942. *The Buildings at Samaria*, London: Palestine Exploration Fund.

—— 1957. *The Objects from Samaria*, London: Palestine Exploration Fund.

Culican, W., 1959/1960. 'Aspects of Phoenician Settlement in the West Mediterranean', *Abr-Nahrain* 1, 36–55.

—— 1970. 'Almuñécar, Assur and Phoenician Penetration of the Western Mediterranean', *Levant* 2, 28–36.

Cunnington, R. H., 1974. *From Antiquary to Archaeologist*, Aylesbury: Shire Books.

Curtis. J. (ed.), 1988. *Bronzeworking Centres of Western Asia c. 1000–539 B.C.*, London: Kegan Paul International.

Daniel, G., 1975. *150 Years of Archaeology*, London: Duckworth.

Daniel, G. & Evans, J. D., 1975. 'The Central Mediterranean', *CAH* II:2, 713–72.

Daux, G., 1959. 'Chronique des fouilles et découvertes archéologiques en Grèce en 1958: Argos', *BCH* 83, 754–74.

Davison, J. M., 1961. *Attic Geometric Workshops*, New Haven: Yale Univ. Press.

Degrassi, A., 1954. *Fasti Capitolini*, Turin: G. B. Paravia.

Delaporte, L., 1940. *Malatya I: La porte des lions*, Paris: Mém. de l'Inst. Français d'Arch. de Stamboul.

Delattre, P., 1890. *Les tombeaux puniques de Carthage*, Lyon: Mougin-Rusand.

Delpino, M. A. F., 1979. 'The Proto-Villanovan: A Survey', in Ridgway & Ridgway (eds) 1979, 31–51.

de Miroschedji, P., 1978. 'Stratigraphie de la période néo-élamite à Suse', *Paléorient* 4, 213–28.

—— 1982. 'Notes sur la glyptique de la fin de l'Elam', *Revue d'Assyriologie* 76, 51–63.

de Santerre, H. G., 1975. 'Notes déliennes', *BCH* 99, 247–61.

de Santerre, H. G. & Treheux, J., 1947/1948. 'Rapport sur le dépôt égéen et géometrique de l'Artémision à Délos', *BCH* 71/72, 148–254.

Desborough, V. R. d'A., 1952. *Protogeometric Pottery*, Oxford Univ. Press.
—— 1957. 'A Group of Vases from Amathus', *JHS* 77, 212–19.
—— 1964. *The Last Mycenaeans and Their Successors: An Archaeological Survey c.1200–c.1000 B.C.*, Oxford Univ. Press.
—— 1972. *The Greek Dark Ages*, London: Benn.
Descœdres, J.-P. & Kearsley, R., 1983. 'Greek Pottery at Veii: Another Look', *BSA* 78, 9–53.
Dever, W. G., 1986. 'Late Bronze Age and Solomonic Defenses at Gezer: New Evidence', *BASOR* 262, 9–34.
Diakonoff, I. M., 1985. 'Elam', in I. Gershevitch (ed.), *The Cambridge History of Iran* 2, Cambridge Univ. Press, 1–24.
Dikaios, P., 1971. *Enkomi Excavations 1948–1958 II*, Mainz am Rhein: Philipp von Zabern.
Dixon, D. M., 1964. 'The Origin of the Kingdom of Kush (Napata-Meroe)', *JEA* 50, 121–32.
Dodson, A., 1988. 'Some Notes Concerning the Royal Tomb at Tanis', *Chronique d'Égypte* 63, 221–33.
Dohl, H., 1986. 'Schliemann the Archaeologist', in W. M. Calder III & D. A. Traill (eds), *Myth, Scandal and History*, Detroit: Wayne State Univ. Press, 95–109.
Dothan, T., 1982. *The Philistines and their Material Culture*, Jerusalem: Israel Exploration Soc.
Dow, S., 1954. 'Minoan Writing', *AJA* 58, 77–129.
Drerup, H., 1964. 'Griechische Architektur zur Zeit Homers', *Archäologischer Anzeiger*, 180–219.
Drews, R., 1975. 'The Babylonian Chronicles and Berossus', *Iraq* 37, 39–55.
Drower, M. S., 1975. 'Ugarit', in *CAH* II:2, 130–60.
—— 1985. *Flinders Petrie: A Life in Archaeology*, London: Gollancz.
du Chaillu, P. B., 1889. *The Viking Age*, London: Murray.
Dunbabin, T., 1948. *The Western Greeks*, Oxford Univ. Press.
Dunham, D., 1950. *Royal Cemeteries of Kush. Vol. I: El Kurru*, Boston, Mass.: Museum of Fine Arts.
—— 1955. *Royal Cemeteries of Kush. Vol. II: Nuri*, Boston, Mass.: Museum of Fine Arts.
—— 1963. *Royal Cemeteries of Kush. Vol. V: The West and South Cemeteries at Meroe*, Boston, Mass.: Museum of Fine Arts.
—— 1970. *The Barkal Temples*, Boston, Mass.: Museum of Fine Arts.
Dunham, D. & Janssen, J. M. A., 1960. *Second Cataract Forts Vol. I: Semna Kumma*, Boston, Mass.: Museum of Fine Arts.
du Plat Taylor, J., 1959. 'The Cypriot and Syrian Pottery from Al Mina, Syria', *Iraq* 21, 62–92.
Dupont-Sommer, A., 1970. 'Une inscription phénicienne archaique récemment trouvée à Chypre (Kition)', *Mem. de l'Académie des Inscriptions et Belles-lettres* 44, 275–94.

Easton, D., 1984. '"Priam's Treasure"', *AnSt* 34, 141–69.
—— 1985. 'Has the Trojan War Been Found?', *Antiquity* 59, 188–96.

Edens, C., 1986. 'Bahrain and the Arabian Gulf During the Second Millennium B.C.: Urban Crisis and Colonialism', in H. Al Khalifa & M. Rice (eds), *Bahrain Through the Ages*, London: Routledge & Kegan Paul, 195–216.

Edwards, I. E. S., 1970. 'Absolute Dating from Egyptian Records and Comparison with Carbon-14 Dating', *Phil. Trans. Roy. Soc. Lond. A* 269, 11–18.

—— 1982. 'Egypt: From the Twenty-second to the Twenty-fourth Dynasty', *CAH* III:1, 534–81.

Evans, A., 1901/1902. 'The Palace of Knossos', *BSA* 8, 1–124.

Evans, J. D., 1971. *The Prehistoric Antiquities of the Maltese Islands: A Survey*, London: The Athlone Press.

Fagerström, K., 1988. *Greek Iron Age Architecture: Developments through Changing Times*, SIMA 81.

Falsone, G., 1988. 'Phoenicia as a Bronze Working Centre in the Iron Age', in Curtis (ed.) 1988, 227–50.

Fantar, M., 1988. 'North Africa', in Moscati (ed.) 1988, 166–85.

Faulkner, R. O., 1975. 'Egypt: From the Inception of the Nineteenth Dynasty to the Death of Ramesses III', *CAH* II:2, 217–51.

Ferrarese Ceruti, M. L., *et al.*, 1987. 'Minoici, Micenei e Ciprioti in Sardegna nella seconda metà del II millennio a. C.', in M. Balmuth (ed.), *Studies in Sardinian Archaeology III*, Oxford: BAR Int. Ser. 387, 7–37.

Finkelstein, I., 1988. *The Archaeology of the Israelite Settlement*, Jerusalem: Israel Exploration Soc.

Finkelstein, J. J., 1966. 'The Genealogy of the Hammurapi Dynasty', *Journal of Cuneiform Studies* 20, 95–118.

Fishman, B., *et al.*, 1977. 'University of Pennsylvania Radiocarbon Dates XIX', *Radiocarbon* 19, 188–228.

Forrer, E., 1953. 'Karthago wurde erst 673–663 V. Chr. Gegründet', in H. Kusch (ed.), *Festschrift Franz Dornseiff*, VEB Bibliographisches Inst. Leipzig, 85–93.

Francis, E. D. & Vickers, M., 1982. 'Kaloi, Ostraka, and the Wells of Athens', *AJA* 86, 264.

—— 1983. '*Signa priscae artis*: Eretria and Siphnos', *JHS* 103, 49–67.

—— 1985. 'Greek Geometric Pottery at Hama and its Implications for Near Eastern Chronology', *Levant* 17, 131–8.

—— 1988. 'The Agora Revisited: Athenian Chronology c. 500–450 BC', *BSA* 83, 143–67.

Frankfort, H., 1969. *The Art and Architecture of the Ancient Orient* (4th edn), Harmondsworth: Pelican.

Freud, S., 1939. *Moses and Monotheism*, London: The Hogarth Press.

Fugmann, E., 1958. *Hama: fouilles et recherches 1931–1938* II:1, Copenhagen: Nationalmuseets Skrifter.

Furumark, A., 1941. *The Chronology of Mycenaean Pottery*, Stockholm: Kungl. Vitterhets Historie och Antikvitets Akademien.

—— 1944. 'The Mycenaean IIIC Pottery and its Relation to Cypriot Fabrics', *Opuscula Archaeologica* 3, 194–265.

Gamito, T. J., 1988. *Social Complexity in Southwest Iberia 800–300 B.C.: The Case of Tartessos*, Oxford: BAR Int. Ser. 439.

Garašanin, M., 1982. 'The Early Iron Age in the Central Balkan Area, c. 1000–750 B.C.', *CAH* III:1, 582–618.

Garbini, G., 1988. *History and Ideology in Ancient Israel*, London: SCM Press.

Gardiner, A., 1920. 'The Ancient Military Road between Egypt and Palestine', *JEA* 6, 99–116.

—— 1961. *Egypt of the Pharaohs*, Oxford Univ. Press.

Gates, M.-H., 1981. *Alalakh Levels VI and V: A Chronological Reassessment* (Syro-Mesopotamian Studies 4:2), Malibu: Undena.

—— 1987. 'Alalakh and Chronology Again', in Åström (ed.) 1987, Part 2, 60–86.

Gelb, I. J., 1944. *Hurrians and Subarians*, Univ. of Chicago Press.

George, A. R., 1990. 'Royal Tombs at Nimrud', *Minerva*, 1:1, 29–31.

Gergova, D., 1980. 'Genesis and Development of the Metal Ornaments in the Thracian Lands During the Early Iron Age', *Studia Praehistorica* 3, 97–112.

Ghirshman, R., 1964. 'Invasions des Nomades', in M. Mellink (ed.), *Dark Ages and Nomads, c. 1000 B.C.*, Istanbul: Studies in Iranian and Anatolian Archaeology, 3–8.

—— 1966. *Tchoga Zanbil (Dur Untash)* I, Paris: Mém. de la Mission arch. en Iran 39.

Gierow, P. G., 1961. 'Notes on the Iron Age Chronology of Latium', *Opuscula Romana* 3, 103–122.

—— 1966. *The Iron Age Culture of Latium Rome*, Lund: Skrifter utgivne av Svenska Inst. i Rom 24.

Gil, J., 1987. 'Tartsis y Tarteso', *Veleia* 2/3, 421–32.

Gill, D. W. J., 1988. 'The Temple of Aphaia on Aegina: The Date of the Reconstruction', *BSA* 83, 169–77.

Gillespie, R., 1984. *Radiocarbon User's Handbook*, Oxford Univ. Committee for Arch. Monograph 3.

Gillespie, R. & Polach, H. A., 1979. 'The Suitability of Marine Shells for Radiocarbon Dating of Australian Prehistory', in R. Berger & H. Suess (eds), *Radiocarbon Dating*, Berkeley: Univ. of California Press, 404–21.

Gimbutas, M., 1965. *Bronze Age Cultures in Central and Eastern Europe*, The Hague: Mouton.

Gjerstad, E., 1944. 'The Initial Date of the Cypriote Iron Age', *Opuscula Archaeologica* 3, 73–106.

—— 1948. *The Swedish Cyprus Expedition IV:2*, Stockholm: Swedish Cyprus Expedition.

—— 1953. 'Correspondence with W. F. Albright on the Chronology of "Cypriote" Pottery from Early Iron Levels in Palestine', *BASOR* 130, 22–6.

—— 1962. *Legends and Facts of Early Roman History*, Lund: CWK Gleerup.

—— 1965. 'Discussions Concerning Early Rome: 2', *Opuscula Romana* 5, 1–74.

—— 1974. 'The Stratification at Al Mina (Syria) and its Chronological Evidence', *Acta Archaeologica* 45, 107–23.

—— 1977. 'Pottery from Various Parts of Cyprus' in E. Gjerstad (ed.), *Greek Geometric and Archaic Pottery Found in Cyprus*, Stockholm: Skrifter utgivne av Svenska Inst. i Ath, 4°, 26, 23–59.

—— 1979. 'The Phoenician Colonization and Expansion in Cyprus', *RDAC*, 230–54.

Glueck, N., 1969. 'Some Ezion-geber: Elath Iron II Pottery', *Eretz-Israel* 9, 51–9.

Goedicke, H., 1972. Review of Dunham 1970, *AJA* 76, 89.

Goetze, A., 1931. Review of von Oppenheim 1931, *Zeitschrift für Assyriologie* 41, 243–55.

Goody, J. R., 1977. 'Mémoire et apprentissage dans les sociétés avec et sans écriture: la transmission du Bagre', *L'Homme* 17, 29–52.

Gottwald, N. K., 1980. *The Tribes of Yahweh*, London: SCM Press.

Grafton, A. T., 1975. 'Joseph Scaliger and Historical Chronology: The Rise and Fall of a Discipline', *History and Theory* 14, 156–85.

Graham, A. J., 1982. 'The Colonial Expansion of Greece', *CAH* III:3, 83–162.

Grant, M., 1973. *Roman Myths*, Harmondsworth: Penguin.

Grapow, H., 1940. 'Die Inschrift der Königin Katimala am Tempel von Semna', *Zeitschrift für ägyptische Sprache und Altertumskunde* 76, 24–41.

Gras, M., 1980. 'L'Etruria villanoviana e la Sardegna settentrionale: precisazioni ed ipotesti', in *Preistoria e protostoria della Sardegna centro-settentrionale*, Florence: Atti della XXII Riunione Scientifica, 513–39.

Gräslund, B., 1987. *The Birth of Prehistoric Chronology*, Cambridge Univ. Press.

Graves, R., 1960. *The Greek Myths* 1 (rev. edn), Harmondsworth: Penguin.

Grayson, A. K., 1972 & 1976. *Assyrian Royal Inscriptions*, Vols. 1 & 2, Wiesbaden: Otto Harrassowitz.

—— 1975. *Assyrian and Babylonian Chronicles* (Texts from Cuneiform Sources V), Locust Valley, N. Y.: J. J. Augustin.

—— 1982. 'Assyria: Ashur-dan II to Ashur-nirari V (934–745 B.C.)', *CAH* III:1, 238–81.

Greenhalgh, P. A. L., 1973. *Early Greek Warfare*, Cambridge Univ. Press.

Grene, D., 1987. *Herodotus: The Histories*, Chicago Univ. Press.

Griffith, F. Ll., 1922. 'Oxford Excavations in Nubia', *AAA* 9, 67–124.

—— 1923. 'Oxford Excavations in Nubia: XVIII. The Cemetery of Sanam', *AAA* 10, 73–171.

Guido, M., 1963. *Sardinia*, London: Thames & Hudson.

Gurney, O., 1954. *The Hittites* (2nd edn), Harmondsworth: Penguin.

Güterbock, H. G., 1954. 'Carchemish', *JNES* 13, 102–14.

Guzzo Amadasi, M. G. & Karageorghis, V., 1977. *Fouilles de Kition: III. Inscriptions Phéniciennes*, Nicosia: Zavallis Press.

Hakluyt, R., 1907. *The Principal Navigations, Voyages, Traffiques &*

Discoveries of the English Nation I, London: J. M. Dent (originally published 1589).

Hall, H. R., 1901. *The Oldest Civilization of Greece*, London: David Nutt.

—— 1913. *The Ancient History of the Near East* (2nd edn), London: Methuen.

Hallo, W. W., 1978. 'Assyrian Historiography Revisited', *Eretz-Israel* 14, 1–7.

Hallo, W. W. & Simpson, W. K., 1971. *The Ancient Near East*, New York: Harcourt Brace Jovanovich.

Halpern, B., 1987. 'Radical Exodus Redating Fatally Flawed', *BAR* Nov./Dec., 56–61, 68.

Hammond, N. G. L., 1982. 'The Peloponnese', *CAH* III:1, 696–744.

Hanfmann, G. M. A., 1951. 'The Bronze Age in the Near East: A Review Article', *AJA* 55, 355–65.

Hankey, V., 1967. 'Mycenaean Pottery in the Near East: Notes on Finds Since 1951', *BSA* 62, 107–48.

—— 1987. 'The Chronology of the Aegean Late Bronze Age', in Åström (ed.) 1987, Part 2, 39–59.

—— 1988. 'Note on the Chronology of LH III C Late and Submycenaean', *Jahrbuch des Deutschen Archäologischen Instituts* 103, 33–7.

Hankey, V. & Warren, P. M., 1974. 'The Absolute Chronology of the Aegean Late Bronze Age', *Bulletin of the Institute of Classical Studies* 21, 142–53.

Hänsel, B., 1976. *Beiträge zur regionalen und chronologischen Gliederung der älteren Hallstattzeit an der unteren Donau*, Bonn: Beiträge zur Ur- und Frühgeschichtlichen Arch. des Mittelmeer-Kulturraumes 16–17.

—— 1979. 'Ergebnisse der Grabungen bei Kastanas in Zentralmakedonien 1975–1978', *Jahrbuch des Römisch-Germanischen Zentralmuseums Mainz* 26, 167–202.

Harden, D. B., 1937. 'The Pottery from the Precinct of Tanit at Salammbo, Carthage', *Iraq* 4, 59–89.

—— 1962. *The Phoenicians*, London: Thames & Hudson.

Harding, A. F., 1975. 'Mycenaean Greece and Europe: The Evidence of Bronze Tools and Implements', *PPS* 41, 183–202.

—— 1980a. 'Chronological Systems in the European Bronze Age', in V. Furmánek, 'Periodisation in the Central European Bronze Age', *Bulletin of the Institute of Archaeology* 17, 117–28.

—— 1980b. 'Radiocarbon Calibration and the Chronology of the European Bronze Age', *Archeologické Rozhledy* 32, 178–86.

—— (ed.) 1982. *Climatic Change in Later Prehistory*, Edinburgh Univ. Press.

—— 1982. 'Introduction: Climatic Change and Archaeology', in Harding (ed.) 1982, 1–10.

—— 1983a. 'The Bronze Age in Central and Eastern Europe: Advances and Prospects', *Advances in World Archaeology* 2, 1–50.

—— 1983b. 'The Regional Context of the Bulgarian Bronze Age', in N. G. Poulter (ed.), *Ancient Bulgaria* 1, Nottingham Univ. Dept. of Classics & Arch. Studies Monograph Ser. I., 164–80.

—— 1984. *The Mycenaeans and Europe*, London: Academic Press.

Harrison, R. J., 1988. *Spain at the Dawn of History*, London: Thames & Hudson.

Hassan, F. A. & Robinson, S. W., 1987, 'High-Precision Radiocarbon Chronology of Ancient Egypt, and Comparison with Nubia, Palestine and Mesopotamia', *Antiquity* 61, 119–35.

Hawkes, C. F. C., 1948. 'From Bronze Age to Iron Age: Middle Europe, Italy, and the North and West', *PPS* 14, 196–218.

Hawkes, J., 1974. *Atlas of Ancient Archaeology*, New York: McGraw Hill.

Hawkins, J. D., 1974. 'Assyrians and Hittites', *Iraq* 36, 67–83.

—— 1982. 'The Neo-Hittite States in Syria and Anatolia', *CAH* III:1, 372–441.

—— 1985. 'The Syro-Hittite States', Plates to *CAH* III, 65–92.

—— 1988. 'Kuzi-Tešub and the "Great Kings of Karkamiš"', *AnSt* 38, 99–108.

Helck, W., 1987. 'Was kann die Ägyptologie wirklich zum Problem der absoluten Chronologie in der Bronzezeit beitragen?', in Åström (ed.) 1987, Part 1, 18–26.

Hencken, H., 1968. *Tarquinia, Villanovans and Early Etruscans*, Cambridge, Mass.: American School of Prehistoric Research Bull. 23.

Henige, D., 1981. 'Generation-counting and Late New Kingdom Chronology', *JEA* 67, 182–4.

—— 1986. 'Comparative Chronology and the Near East', *BASOR* 261, 57–68.

Herrera, M. D. & Balensi, J., 1986. 'More About the Greek Geometric Pottery at Tell Abu Hawam', *Levant* 18, 169–71.

Herzog, Z., 1987. 'The Stratigraphy of Israelite Arad: A Rejoinder', *BASOR* 267, 77–9.

Hestrin, R. & Dayagi, M., 1974. 'A Seal Impression of a Servant of King Hezekiah', *IEJ* 24, 27–9.

Heurtley, W. A., 1939. *Prehistoric Macedonia*, Cambridge Univ. Press.

Heurtley, W. A. & Hutchinson, R. W., 1925/1926. 'Report on the Excavation at the Toumba and Tables of Vardaroftsa, Macedonia, 1925, 1926', *BSA* 27, 1–66.

Higgins, R., 1957. 'The Aegina Treasure Reconsidered', *Bulletin of the Institute of Classical Studies* 4, 27–41.

Hoare, R. C., 1812. *The Ancient History of Wiltshire* 1, London: Miller.

Hoernes, M., 1925. *Urgeschichte der bildenden Kunst in Europa, von dem Anfängen bis um 500 vor Christi* (3rd edn), Vienna: Anton Schrook.

Hoffmeier, J. K., 1989. 'Reconsidering Egypt's Part in the Termination of the Middle Bronze Age in Palestine', *Levant* 21, 181–93.

Hogarth, D. G., 1911. 'Hittite Problems and the Excavation of Carchemish', *Proceedings of the British Academy* 5, 361–75.

—— 1924. *Kings of the Hittites*, London: Schweich Lectures.

—— 1925. 'Lydia and Ionia', *CAH* (1st edn), 501–26.

Holladay, J. S., 1976. 'Of Sherds and Strata: Contributions Toward an Understanding of the Archaeology of the Divided Monarchy', in F. M.

Cross, *et al.* (eds), *Magnalia Dei: The Mighty Acts of God*, Garden City, N. Y.: Doubleday, 253–93.

Holloway, R. R., 1981. *Italy and the Aegean 3000–700 B.C.*, Louvain-La-Neuve: Archaeologia Transatlantica I.

—— 1984. 'Recent Research in Prehistoric Sicily', in T. Hackens *et al.* (eds), *Crossroads of the Mediterranean*, Louvain-La-Neuve: Archaeologia Transatlantica II, 261–5.

—— 1985. 'Synoicism in Bronze Age Sicily', in C. Malone & S. Stoddart (eds), *Papers in Italian Archaeology IV Part iii*, Oxford: BAR Int. Ser. 245, 389–98.

Hollstein, E., 1980. *Mitteleuropäische Eichenchronologie*, Mainz: Trierer Grabungen und Forschungen 11.

Hooker, J. T., 1976. *Mycenaean Greece*, London: Kegan Paul.

Hope, C. A., 1987. *Egyptian Pottery*, Aylesbury: Shire Books.

Horn, S. H., 1977. 'What We Don't Know About Moses and the Exodus', *BAR* June, 22–31.

Hrouda, B., 1962. *Tell Halaf IV, Die Kleinfunde aus historischer Zeit*, Berlin: Walter de Gruyter.

Huber, P. J., 1974. Review of Weir 1972, *Bibliotheca Orientalis* 31: 1/2, 86–8.

—— 1987. 'Astronomical Evidence for the Long and Against the Middle and Short Chronologies', in Åström (ed.) 1987, Part 1, 5–17.

Iacovou, M., 1988. *The Pictorial Pottery of Eleventh Century B.C. Cyprus*, SIMA 78.

Iakovidis, S., 1979. 'The Chronology of LHIIIC', *AJA* 83, 454–62.

Ibrahim, M., 1978. 'The Collared-rim Jar of the Early Iron Age', in Moorey, P. R. S. & Parr, P. (eds), *Archaeology in the Levant: Essays for K. Kenyon*, Warminster: Aris & Phillips, 116–26.

Ingham, M. F., 1969. 'The Length of the Sothic Cycle', *JEA* 55, 36–40.

Isserlin, B. S. J. & du Plat Taylor, J., 1974. *Motya* I, Leiden: E. J. Brill.

Jacobsen, T., 1939. *The Sumerian King List*, Chicago Univ. Press.

James, P. J., forthcoming. 'The Origin of the Sea Peoples Invasion'.

James, P. J., Thorpe, I. J., Kokkinos, N. & Frankish, J. A., 1987. 'Bronze to Iron Age Chronology in the Old World: Time for a Reassessment?', *SAC* 1, 1–147.

—— 1990. 'A Reply and Update', *SAC* 2.

James, P. J. & Kokkinos, N., 1990. 'Lachish, Arad and Chronology: A New Model for the Transition from Iron Age to Persian Judah in the Light of Lower Dating. Part 1', *SAC* 2.

Jeffery, L. H., 1961. *The Local Scripts of Archaic Greece*, Oxford Univ. Press.

Jidejian, N., 1968. *Byblos Through the Ages*, Beirut: Dar el-Machreq Publishers.

Jodin, A., 1966. *Mogador: Comptoir phénicien du Maroc Atlantique*, Tangier: Études et Travaux d'Arch. Marocaine II.

Jones, P. F., 1986. *Greek and Cypriot Pottery: A Review of Scientific Studies* (Fitch Lab. Occas. Paper 1), London: British School at Athens.

Jurado, J. F. & Tomico, P. R., 1988. 'Les Phéniciens à Huelva', in Sznycer (ed.) 1988, 71.

Kantor, H. J., 1946. 'Embossed Plaques with Animal Designs', *JNES* 5, 232–8.

—— 1956. 'Syro-Palestinian Ivories', *JNES* 15, 153–74.

Karageorghis, V., 1969. *Salamis in Cyprus – Homeric, Hellenistic and Roman*, London: Thames & Hudson.

—— (ed.) 1974. *Excavations at Kition: I. The Tombs*, Nicosia: Zavallis Press.

—— 1975. *Alaas: A Protogeometric Necropolis in Cyprus*, Nicosia: Zavallis Press.

—— 1976. *Kition: Mycenaean and Phoenician Discoveries in Cyprus*, London: Thames and Hudson.

—— 1978. *Archaia Kypros*, Athens: Ekdotike Ellados.

—— 1979. 'Kypriaka IV', *RDAC*, 198–213.

—— 1981. *Ancient Cyprus*, Athens: Ekdotike Ellados.

—— 1982a. *Cyprus: From the Stone Age to the Romans*, London: Thames and Hudson.

—— 1982b. 'Cyprus', *CAH* III:1, 511–33.

—— 1987. 'Western Cyprus at the Close of the Bronze Age', in D. W. Rupp (ed.), *Western Cyprus: Connections*, SIMA 77, 115–19.

—— 1988. 'The Greek Language in Cyprus: The Archaeological Background', in J. Karageorghis & O. Masson (eds), *The History of the Greek Language in Cyprus*, Nicosia: Pierides Foundation, 1–8.

Karageorghis, V. & Demas, M., 1985. *Excavations at Kition: V. The Pre-Phoenician Levels*, Nicosia: Dept. of Antiquities.

Karageorghis, V. & Kahil, L. G., 1967. 'Témoignages Eubéens à Chypre et Chypriotes à Érétrie', *Antike Kunst* 10, 133–5.

Karageorghis, V. & Karageorghis, J., 1956. 'Some Inscribed Iron-Age Vases from Cyprus', *AJA* 60, 351–9.

Kaufman, I. T., 1982. 'The Samaria Ostraca: An Early Witness to Hebrew Writing', *BA* Fall, 228–39.

Kaufman, S. A. 1986. 'The Pitfalls of Typology: On the Early History of the Alphabet', *Hebrew Union College Annual* 57, 1–14.

Kearsley, R., 1989. *The Pendant Semi-Circle Skyphos*, London: Bulletin of the Institute of Classical Studies Suppl. 44.

Kemp, B. J., 1984. *Amarna Reports I*, London: Egypt Exploration Soc.

Kempinski, A., 1979. 'Hittites in the Bible', *BAR* Sept./Oct., 21–45.

Kendall, T., 1982. *Kush: Lost Kingdom of the Nile*, Brockton, Mass.: Brockton Art Museum/Fuller Memorial Brockton.

Kenyon, K., 1964. 'Megiddo, Hazor, Samaria and Chronology', *Bulletin of the Institute of Archaeology*, 143–56.

—— 1979. *Archaeology in the Holy Land* (4th edn), London: E. Benn.

Kervran, M., *et al.*, 1987. 'The Occupational Enigma of Bahrain between the 13th and the 8th Century B.C.', *Paléorient* 13:1, 77–93.

Kilian, K., forthcoming. 'Peri tis Katarevsis ton Mykinaikon anaktoron tis Ypirotikis Elladas', in *Proceedings of Conference at Orchomenos (Boeotia) 1984*.

King, L. W., 1899a. 'Assyria', in *Encyclopaedia Biblica* I, London: Adam & Charles Black, 347–72.

—— 1899b. 'Babylonia', in *Encyclopaedia Biblica* I, London: Adam & Charles Black, 419–54.

Kitchen, K. A., 1966. *Ancient Orient and Old Testament*, London: Tyndale Press.

—— 1977. 'On the Princedoms of Late-Libyan Egypt', *Chronique d'Égypte* 52, 40–8.

—— 1982. *Pharaoh Triumphant: The Life and Times of Ramesses II, King of Egypt*, Warminster: Aris & Phillips.

—— 1986. *The Third Intermediate Period in Egypt (1100–650 B.C.)* (2nd. edn with supplement), Warminster: Aris & Phillips.

—— 1987. 'The Basics of Egyptian Chronology in Relation to the Bronze Age', in Åström (ed.) 1987, Part 1, 37–55.

Knudtzon, J. A., 1907–1915. *Die El-Amarna Tafeln*, Vols 1–3, Leipzig: Hinrichs.

Kontoleon, N. M., 1951. 'Anaskafe en Naxo', *Praktika*, 214–23.

Koukouli-Chrysanthaki, Ch., 1981. 'Late Bronze Age in Eastern Macedonia', *Thracia Praehistorica. Supplementum Pulpedeva* 3, 231–58.

Kramer, S. N., 1963. *The Sumerians*, Chicago Univ. Press.

Krauss, R., 1985. *Sothis- und Monddaten, Studien zur astronomischen und technischen Chronologie Altägyptens*, Hildesheim: Hildesheimer Ägyptologische Beiträge 20.

Kristiansen, K., 1987. 'From Stone to Bronze – An Essay on the Evolution of Social Complexity in Northern Europe 2300–1200 B.C.', in E. M. Brumfiel & T. K. Earle (eds), *Specialisation, Exchange, and Complex Societies*, Cambridge Univ. Press, 30–51.

Kruszynski, M., 1990. 'The Development of the Gava Culture and its Connections with the South – the Origins of Hornlike-Shaped Knobbed Ware in the Balkans and Troy VIIb2', *SAC* 2.

Kuniholm, P. I., 1988. 'Dendrochronology and Radiocarbon Dates for Gordion and Other Phrygian Sites', *Source: Notes in the History of Art*, VII:3/4, 6–8.

Kuniholm, P. I. & Striker, C. L., 1983. 'Dendrochronological Investigations in the Aegean and Neighboring Regions, 1977–1982', *JFA* 10, 411–20.

—— 1987. 'Dendrochronological Investigations in the Aegean and Neighboring Regions, 1983–1986', *JFA* 14, 385–98.

Labat, R. 1975a. 'Elam c. 1600–1200 B.C.', *CAH* II:2, 379–416.

—— 1975b. 'Elam and Western Persia, c. 1200–1000 B.C.', *CAH* II:2, 482–506.

Lance, H. D., 1971. 'The Royal Stamps and the Kingdom of Josiah', *Harvard Theological Review* 64, 315–32.

Landsberger, B., 1948. *Samal: Studien zur Enteckung der Ruinenstätte Karatepe* I, Ankara: Türkischen Historischen Gesellschaft.

—— 1954. 'Assyrische Königliste und "Dunkles" Zeitalter', *Journal of Cuneiform Studies* 8, 31–45; 47–73.

Leahy, M. A., 1988. 'The Earliest Dated Monument of Amasis and the End of the Reign of Apries', *JEA* 74, 183–99.

Leclant, J., 1983a. 'Schabaka', *Lexicon der Ägyptologie* V, Wiesbaden: Otto Harrassowitz, 499–513.

—— 1983b. 'Schabataka', *Lexicon der Ägyptologie* V, Wiesbaden: Otto Harrassowitz, 514–20.

Leighton, R., 1981. 'Strainer-spouted Jugs and the Problem of the Earliest Phoenician Influence in Sicily', *Journal of Mediterranean Anthropology and Archaeology* 1, 280–91.

Lepsius, R., 1864. 'Die Sethos-Tafel von Abydos', *Zeitschrift für ägyptische Sprache und Altertumskunde* Oct./Nov., 81–3.

Lerat, L., 1961. 'Fouilles de Delphes, à l'est du grand sanctuaire: 1950–1957', *BCH* 85, 316–66.

Lewy, H., 1970. 'Assyria *c.* 2600–1816 B.C.', *CAH* I:2, 729–70.

Lichtheim, M., 1980. *Ancient Egyptian Literature: A Book of Readings. Volume III: The Late Period*, Berkeley: Univ. of California Press.

Lieblein, J., 1873. *Recherches sur la chronologie égyptienne d'après les listes généalogiques*, Christiana: A. W. Brogger.

—— 1914. *Recherches sur l'Histoire et la civilization de l'ancienne Égypte*, Leipzig: J. C. Hinrich'sche.

Lilliu, G., 1952/1954. 'Il nuraghe di Barumini e la stratigraphia nuragica', *Studi Sardi* 12–13, 90–459.

—— 1973. 'Tripode bronzeo di tradizione cipriota dalla Grotta Pirosu, su Benatzu di Santadi (Cagliari)', in J. Malaquer de Motes (ed.), *Estudios dedicados al Prof. Dr. Luis Pericot*, Univ. de Barcelona Inst. de Arqueol. y Prehistoria Publs. Eventuales 23, 283–313.

—— 1982. *La civiltà nuragica*, Milan: Carlo Delfino.

Lloyd, S., 1980. *Foundations in the Dust*, London: Thames & Hudson.

London, G., 1989. 'A Comparison of Two Contemporaneous Lifestyles of the Late Second Millennium B.C.', *BASOR* 273, 37–55.

Long, R. D., 1974. 'A Re-examination of the Sothic Chronology of Egypt', *Orientalia* 43, 261–74.

Lo Porto, F. G., 1963. 'Leporano (Taranto) – La stazione protostorica di Porto Perone', *Notizie degli scavi di antichità* (8th ser.) 17, 280–380.

Lorimer, H. L., 1950. *Homer and the Monuments*, London: Macmillan.

Lo Schiavo, F., 1985. *Nuraghic Sardinia in its Mediterranean Setting: Some Recent Advances*, Univ. of Edinburgh: Occ. Paper 12.

Lukesh, S. S., 1984. 'Italy and the Apennine Culture', in T. Hackens *et al.* (eds), *Crossroads of the Mediterranean*, Louvain-La-Neuve: Archaeologia Transatlantica II, 13–54.

Macadam, M. F. L., 1949. *The Temples of Kawa I. The Inscriptions*, Oxford: Griffith Inst.

McCarter, P. K., 1974. 'The Early Diffusion of the Alphabet', *BA* Fall, 54–68.

McClellan, T. L., 1979. 'Chronology of the "Philistine" Burials at Tell el Far'ah (South)', *JFA* 6, 58–73.

Macdonald, W. A., *et al.*, 1983. *Excavations at Nichoria in Southwest Greece. Volume III: The Dark Age and Byzantine Occupation*, Minneapolis: Univ. of Minnesota Press.

Macnamara, E., *et al.*, 1984. *The Bronze Hoard from S. Maria in Paulis, Sardinia*, London: British Museum Occ. Paper No. 45.

Madhloom, T. A., 1970. *The Chronology of Neo-Assyrian Art*, Univ. of London: Athlone Press.

Magnusson, M., 1977. *BC: The Archaeology of Bible Lands*, London: Bodley Head/BBC.

Maier, F. G. & Karageorghis, V., 1984. *Paphos: History and Archaeology*, Nicosia: A. G. Leventis Foundation.

Malamat, A., 1982. 'How Inferior Israelite Forces Conquered Fortified Canaanite Cities', *BAR* Mar./Apr., 24–35.

Malinine, M., *et al.*, 1968. *Catalogue des stèles du Sérapéum de Memphis* I, Paris: Louvre.

Mallowan, M., 1966. *Nimrud and Its Remains*, London: Collins.

—— 1967. 'Nimrud', in D. W. Thomas (ed.), *Archaeology and Old Testament Study*, Oxford: Clarendon Press, 57–72.

—— 1972. 'Carchemish: Reflections on the Chronology of the Sculpture', *AnSt* 22, 63–85.

Mallowan, M. & Hermann, G., 1974. *Ivories from Nimrud (1949–1963), III: Furniture from SW7 Fort Shalmaneser*, Aberdeen: British School of Arch. in Iraq.

Manuel, F., 1963. *Isaac Newton: Historian*, Cambridge Univ. Press.

Markoe, G., 1985. *Phoenician Bronze Bowls From Cyprus and the Mediterranean*, Univ. of California Press.

Maspero, G., 1896. *The Struggle of the Nations*, London: SPCK.

Masson, O., 1961. *Les inscriptions Chypriotes syllabiques*, Paris: E. De Boccard.

Matthers, J., *et al.*, 1983. 'Black-on-Red Ware in the Levant: A Neutron Activation Analysis Study', *Journal of Archaeological Science* 10, 369–82.

Mazar, A., 1985. 'The Emergence of the Philistine Material Culture', *IEJ* 35, 95–107.

Mazar (Maisler), B., 1951. 'The Stratification of Tell Abu Hawam on the Bay of Acre', *BASOR* 124, 21–5.

—— 1964. 'The Philistines and the Rise of Israel and Tyre', *Proceedings of the Israel Academy of Sciences and Humanities* 1:7, 1–22.

—— 1986. *The Early Biblical Period* (ed. S. Ahituv & B. A. Levine), Jerusalem: Israel Exploration Soc.

Mee, C. B., 1985. 'The Mycenaeans and Troy', in L. Foxhall & J. K. Davies (eds), *The Trojan War: Its Historicity and Context*, Bristol Classical Press, 45–56.

Mellaart, J., 1979. 'Egyptian and Near Eastern Chronology: A Dilemma?', *Antiquity* 53, 6–18.

—— 1985. 'Troy VIIA in Anatolian Perspective', in L. Foxhall & J. K. Davies (eds), *The Trojan War: Its Historicity and Context*, Bristol Classical Press, 63–82.

—— 1990. 'Response to the Discussion Paper', *SAC* 2.

Mellink, M. J. (ed.), 1964. *Dark Ages and Nomads, c. 1000 B.C.*, Istanbul: Studies in Iranian and Anatolian Archaeology.

—— 1964. 'Postscript on Nomadic Art', in Mellink (ed.) 1964, 63–70.

Mercer, S. A. B., 1939. *The Tell El-Amarna Tablets*, Toronto: Macmillan.

Merrillees, R. S., 1977. 'The Absolute Chronology of the Bronze Age in Cyprus', *RDAC*, 33–50.

Meyer, E., 1904. *Aegyptische Chronologie*, Berlin: Abhandlungen der K. Preuss. Akad. der Wiss.

Meyer, J. C., 1983. *Pre-Republican Rome*, Odense: Analecta Romana Inst. Danici Suppl. XII.

Millard, A. R., 1983. 'Assyrians and Aramaeans', *Iraq* 44, 101–8.

Millard, A. R. & Bordreuil, P., 1982. 'A Statue from Syria with Assyrian and Aramaic Inscriptions, *BA* Summer, 135–41.

Miller, M., 1970. *The Sicilian Colony Dates*, Albany: State Univ. of New York Press.

—— 1971. *The Thalassocracies*, Albany: State Univ. of New York Press.

Milward, A., 1975. 'A Fragment of an Egyptian Relief Chalice from Buseirah, Jordan', *Levant* 7, 16–17.

Mitford, T. B. & Masson, O., 1982. 'The Cypriot Syllabary', *CAH* III:3, 71–82.

Mommsen, H., et al., 1989. 'Classification of Mycenaean Pottery from Kastanas by Neutron Activation Analysis', in Y. Maniatis (ed.), *Archaeometry*, Amsterdam: Elsevier, 515–23.

Montelius, O., 1885. *Dating in the Bronze Age with Special Reference to Scandinavia* (Engl. trans.), Stockholm: Royal Academy of Letters History and Antiquities, 1986.

—— 1899. *Der Orient und Europa*, Stockholm.

—— 1903. *Die älteren Kulturperioden im Orient und in Europa I. Die Methode*, Stockholm: Beckmans.

Montet, P., 1928. *Byblos et l'Égypte* I, Paris: Geuthner.

—— 1947. *La nécropole royale de Tanis I: Les constructions et le tombeau d'Osorkon II à Tanis*, Paris: Fouilles de Tanis.

Moorey, P. R. S., 1971. 'Towards a Chronology for the Luristan Bronzes', *Iran* 9, 113–29.

—— (ed.) 1982. *Ur of the Chaldees*, London: Herbert Press.

—— 1988. 'Bronzeworking Centres of Western Asia c. 1000–539 BC: Problems and Perspectives', in Curtis (ed.) 1988, 23–32.

Moortgat, A. (ed.), 1955. *Tell Halaf III: Die Bildwerke*, Berlin: De Gruyter.

Morgan, L. H., 1877. *Ancient Society: or, Researches in the Lines of Human Progress from Savagery through Barbarism to Civilisation*, London: Macmillan.

Moretti, L., 1957. *Olympionikai, I vincitori negli antichi Agoni Olimpici*, Rome: Atti della Academia Nazionale dei Lincei ser. 8, vol. 8.

Morintz, S., 1964. 'Quelques problèmes concernant la période ancienne du Hallstatt au Bas-Danube à la lumière de fouilles de Babadag', *Dacia* 8, 101–18.

Morkot, R., 1990. 'Post-Pharaonic Nubia: Reassessing the Evidence', *SAC* 2.

Moscati, S., 1968. *The World of the Phoenicians*, London: Weidenfeld & Nicolson.

—— (ed.) 1988. *The Phoenicians*, Milan: Bompiani.

—— 1988. 'Colonization of the Mediterranean', in Moscati (ed.) 1988, 46–53.

Mosshammer, A. A., 1979. *The Chronicle of Eusebius and Greek Chronographic Tradition*, New Jersey: Associated Univ. Presses.

Mountjoy, P. A., 1988. 'LHIIIC Versus Submycenaean: The Kerameikos Pompeion Cemetery Reviewed', *Jahrbuch des Deutschen Archäologischen Instituts* 103, 1–37.

Muhly, J. D., 1985. 'Phoenicia and the Phoenicians', in *BAT*, 177–91.

—— 1988. 'Concluding Remarks', in Curtis (ed.) 1988, 329–42.

Müller-Karpe, H., 1959a. *Beiträge zur Chronologie der Urnenfelderzeit nördlich und südlich der Alpen*, Berlin: Römisch Germanische Forschungen 22.

—— 1959b. *Vom Anfang Roms*, Heidelberg: Mitteilungen des Deutschen Arch. Inst. Röm Abt. 5.

Munn-Rankin, J. M., 1975. 'Assyrian Military Power 1300–1200 B.C.', *CAH* II:2, 274–306.

Munro, M., 1987. 'Timahoe West', in C. Cotter (ed.), *Excavations 1986*, Dublin: Irish Academic Publs, 22.

Murray, A. S., 1892. *Handbook of Greek Archaeology*, London: J. Murray.

Muscarella, O. W., 1988a. 'The Background to the Luristan Bronzes', in Curtis (ed.) 1988, 33–44.

—— 1988b. 'The Background to the Phrygian Bronze Industry', in Curtis (ed.) 1988, 177–92.

—— 1988c. *Bronze and Iron: Ancient Near Eastern Artefacts in the Metropolitan Museum of Art*, New York: Metropolitan Museum of Art.

Na'aman, N., 1979. 'Sennacherib's Campaign to Judah and the Date of the *LMLK* stamps', *Vetus Testamentum* 29, 61–86.

—— 1984. 'Statements of Time-spans by Babylonian and Assyrian Kings and Mesopotamian Chronology', *Iraq* 46, 115–23.

Naveh, J., 1982. *An Introduction to West Semitic Epigraphy and Palaeography*, Jerusalem: Hebrew Univ.

Negbi, O., 1982/1983. 'Evidence for Early Phoenician Communities on the Eastern Mediterranean Islands', *Levant* 14/15, 179–82.

Neumann, J. & Parpola, S., 1987. 'Climatic Change and the Eleventh-Tenth Century Eclipse of Assyria and Babylonia', *JNES* 46, 161–82.

Newton, I., 1728. *The Chronology of Ancient Kingdoms Amended*, London: J. Tonson.

Newton, R., 1978. *The Crime of Claudius Ptolemy*, Baltimore: Johns Hopkins Univ. Press.

Nicolaou, K., 1976. *The Historical Topography of Kition*, SIMA 43.

North, R., 1957. 'Status of the Warka Expedition', *Orientalia* 26, 250–1.

Nylander, C., 1963. 'The Fall of Troy', *Antiquity* 37, 6–11.

Oates, J., *et al.*, 1977. 'Seafaring Merchants of Ur', *Antiquity* 203, 221–34.

O'Connor, D., 1983. 'New Kingdom and Third Intermediate Period, 1552–664 BC', in B. G. Trigger *et al.* (eds), *Ancient Egypt: A Social History*, Cambridge Univ. Press, 183–278.

Opificius, R., 1965. 'Altphrygische Keramik von Büyükkale (Boğazköy)', *Mitteilungen der Deutschen Orient-Gesellschaft* 95, 81–9.

Olsson, I. U., 1987. 'Carbon-14 Dating and Interpretation of the Validity of Some Dates From the Bronze Age in the Aegean', in Åström (ed.) 1987, Part 2, 4–38.

Orthmann, W., 1971. *Untersuchungen zur späthethitischen Kunst* (Saarbrücker Beiträge zur Altertumskunde 8), Bonn: Rudolph Habelt.

Otten, H., 1959. 'Korrespondenz mit Tukulti-Ninurta I. aus Boğazköy, in E. Weidner, *Die Inschriften Tukulti-Ninurtas und seiner Nachfolger*, Graz: Archiv für Orientforschung 12, 64–8.

Özdoğan, M., 1987. 'Taşlicabiyir. A Late Bronze Age Burial Mound in Eastern Thrace', *Anatolica* 14, 5–25.

Page, D., 1959. 'The Historical Sack of Troy', *Antiquity* 33, 25–31.

Page, S., 1969. 'Adad-nirari III and Semiramis: the Stelae of Saba'a and Rimah', *Orientalia* 38, 457–8.

Pallottino, M., 1961. 'Problemi di protostoria italica nel mezzogiorno', in *Greci e Italici in Magna Grecia*, Naples: Atti del Primo Convegno di Studi Sulla Magna Grecia, 99–104.

—— 1979. 'The Origins of Rome: a Survey of Recent Discoveries and Discussions', in Ridgway & Ridgway (eds) 1979, 197–222.

Parker, R. A., 1950. *The Calendars of Ancient Egypt*, Chicago Univ. Press.

—— 1957. 'The Lunar Dates of Thutmose III and Ramesses II'', *JNES* 16, 39–43.

—— 1970. 'The Beginning of the Lunar Month in Ancient Egypt', *JNES* 29, 217–20.

—— 1971. 'The Calendars and Chronology', in J. R. Harris (ed.), *The Legacy of Egypt* (2nd edn), Oxford: Clarendon Press, 13–26.

—— 1976. 'The Sothic Dating of the Twelfth and Eighteenth Dynasties', in J. H. Johnson & E. F. Wente (eds), *Studies in Honor of George R. Hughes*, Chicago Oriental Inst., 177–89.

Parr, P., 1982. 'Contacts Between North West Arabia and Jordan in the Late Bronze and Iron Ages', in A. Hadidi (ed.), *Studies in the History and Archaeology of Jordan I*, Amman: Dept. of Antiquities, 127–133.

Paterson, A., 1915, *Assyrian Sculptures. Palace of Sinacherib*, The Hague: Martinus Nighoff.

Pearson, G. W. & Stuiver, M., 1986. 'High-precision Calibration of the Radiocarbon Time Scale', *Radiocarbon* 28, 839–62.

Peckham, B., 1972. 'The Nora Inscription', *Orientalia* 41, 457–68.

Peroni, R., 1956. 'Zur Gruppierung mitteleuropäischer Grieffzungendolche der späten Bronzezeit', *Badische Fundberichte* 20, 69–92.

—— 1959. 'Per una definizione dell'aspetto culturale subapenninico come fase chronologica a sè stante', *Notizie degli scavi di antichità*, (8th ser.), 9, 3–253.

—— 1960. 'Per una nuova cronologia del sepolcreto del Foro: sequenza a culturale e significato storico', in *Civiltà del ferro*, Bologna: Documenti e studi della deputazione di storia patria per le provincie di Romagna, VI, 461–99.

Perrot, G., 1895. 'Figurines d'ivoire trouvées dans une tombe du céramique a Athènes', *BCH* 19, 273–95.

Perrot, G. & Chipiez, C., 1890. *History of Art in Sardinia, Judaea, Syria and Asia Minor* (trans. I. Gonizo), London: Chapman & Hall.

Petrie, W. M. F., 1890. 'The Egyptian Bases of Greek History', *JHS* 11, 271–7.

—— 1896. *A History of Egypt* II, London: Methuen.

Piggott, S., 1938. 'The Early Bronze Age in Wessex', *PPS* 4, 52–106.

—— 1965. *Ancient Europe*, Edinburgh Univ. Press.

Pilcher, J. R., *et al.*, 1984. 'A 7272-year Tree-ring Chronology for Western Europe', *Nature* 312, 150–2.

Pitts, M. W., 1982. 'On the Road to Stonehenge: Report on the Investigations Beside the A344, 1968, 1979 and 1980', *PPS* 48, 75–132.

Poebel, A., 1942. 'The Assyrian King List from Khorsabad', *JNES* 1, 247–306 & 460–92.

—— 1943. 'The Assyrian King List from Khorsabad – Concluded', *JNES* 2, 56–90.

Pons Brun, E., 1989. 'The Beginning of the First Iron Age in Catalonia, Spain', in Sørensen & Thomas (eds), 1989, 112–36.

Ponsich, M., 1981. *Lixus: le Quartier des Temples*, Rabat: Études et Travaux d'Arch. Marocaine IX.

Popham, M. R., 1990. 'Response to the Discussion Paper', *SAC* 2.

Popham, M. R. & Sackett, L. H. (eds) 1980. *Lefkandi I: The Iron Age*, London: British School at Athens, Suppl. Vol. Eleven.

Porada, E., 1964. 'Nomads and Luristan Bronzes', in Mellink (ed.), 1964, 9–31.

Potter, T. W., 1976. *A Faliscan Town in South Etruria: Excavations at Narce 1966–71*, London: British School at Rome.

Prausnitz, M. W., 1972. 'Red-Polished and Black-on-Red Wares at Akhziv, Israel and Cyprus in the Early-Middle Iron Age', in V. Karageorghis & A. Christodoulou (eds), *Praktika tou Protou Diethnous Kyprologikou Synedriou* 1, Nicosia: Etaireia Kypriakon Spoudon, 151–6.

Preusser, C., 1955. *Die Paläste in Assur*, Berlin: Verlag Gebr. Mann.

Pritchard, J. B., 1974. *Solomon and Sheba*, London: Phaidon.

—— 1975. *Sarepta: A Preliminary Report on the Iron Age*, Philadelphia: The Univ. Museum of Pennsylvania.

—— 1978. *Recovering Sarepta, A Phoenician City*, Princeton Univ. Press.

Puchstein, O., 1890. *Pseudohethitische Kunst*, Berlin: V. Juni.

Puglisi, S. M. & Meriggi, P., 1964. *Malatya I: Rapporto preliminare dello campagne 1961 e 1962*, Rome: Orientis Antiqui Collectio III.

Puglisi, S. M. & Palmieri, A., 1966. 'Researches in Malatya District (1965–1966)', *Türk Arkeoloji Dergisi* XV:2, 81–101.

Pyle, D. M., 1989. 'Ice-core Acidity Peaks, Retarded Tree Growth and Putative Eruptions', *Archaeometry* 31, 88–91.

Quagliati, Q., 1900. 'Taranto: relazione degli scavi archeologici che sie eseguirono nel 1899 in unabitito terramaricolo, allo scoglio del tonno, presso la città', *Notizie degli scavi di antichità*, 411–64.

Rakob, F., 1984. 'Deutsche Ausgraben in Karthago die Punischen Befunde', *Mitteilungen des Deutschen Archäologischen Instituts, Roemische Abteilung* 91, 1–22.

Rainey, A. F., 1978. *El Amarna Tablets 359–379: Supplement to J. A. Knudtzon Die El-Amarna-Tafeln*, Alter Orient und Altes Testament Band 8.

—— 1982. 'Wine from the Royal Vineyards', *BASOR* 245, 57–62.

Ramsay, W. M., 1888. 'A Study of Phrygian Art', *JHS* 9, 350–82.

Randall-MacIver, D., 1924. *Villanovans and Early Etruscans*, Oxford: Clarendon Press.

Randsborg, K., 1967. 'Aegean Bronzes in a Grave in Jutland', *Acta Archaeologica* 38, 1–27.

Rawlinson, G., 1873. *The Five Great Monarchies of the Ancient Eastern World* II (3rd edn), London: Murray.

Rawlinson, D., 1881. *History of Ancient Egypt* II, London: Longmans.

Read, J. G., 1970. 'Early Eighteenth Dynasty Chronology', *JNES* 29, 1–11.

Reade, J., 1975. 'Aššurnaširpal I and the White Obelisk', *Iraq* 37, 129–50.

Redford, D. B., 1982. 'Contact Between Egypt and Jordan in the New Kingdom: Some Comments on Sources', in A. Hadidi (ed.), *Studies in the History and Archaeology of Jordan I*, Amman: Dept of Antiquities, 115–19.

—— 1985. 'Sais and the Kushite Invasion of the Eighth Century B.C.', *JARCE* 22, 5–15.

—— 1986. *Pharaonic King-lists, Annals and Day-books*, Mississauga, Ontario: Benben/Soc. for the Study of Egyptian Antiquities.

—— 1987. 'The Monotheism of the Heretic Pharaoh', *BAR* May/June, 16–32.

Reich, R. & Brandl, B., 1985. 'Gezer under Assyrian Rule', *PEQ*, 41–54.

Reinecke, P., 1902. 'Zur Chronologie der 2. Hälfte des Bronzealters in Süd und Nord deutschland', *Korrespondenzblatt der deutschen Gesellschaft für Anthropologie, Ethnologie and Urgeschichte* 33, 17–22, 27–32.

—— 1924. 'Zur Chronologischen Gliederung der süddeutschen Bronzezeit', *Germania* 8, 1924, 43–4.

Reiner, E. & Pingree, D., 1975. *The Venus Tablet of Ammiṣaduga* (Bibliotheca Mesopotamia 2:1), Malibu: Undena.

Renfrew, C., 1970. 'The Tree-ring Calibration of Radiocarbon: An Archaeological Evaluation', *PPS* 36, 280–311.

—— 1972. 'Malta and the Calibrated Radiocarbon Chronology', *Antiquity* 46, 141–4.

—— 1973. *Before Civilization*, London: Jonathan Cape.

—— 1979. 'Systems Collapse as Social Transformation: Catastrophe and Anastrophe in Early State Societies', in C. Renfrew & K. L. Cooke (eds), *Transformations: Mathematical Approaches to Culture Change*, London: Academic Press, 481–506.

—— 1985. *The Archaeology of Cult: The Sanctuary of Philakopi*, London: British School at Athens, Suppl. Vol. 18.

—— 1986. 'Varna and the Emergence of Wealth in Prehistoric Europe', in A. Appadurai (ed.), *The Social Life of Things*, Cambridge Univ. Press, 141–68.

Ridgway, D., 1979. 'Early Rome and Latium: An Archaeological Introduction', in Ridgway & Ridgway (eds) 1979, 187–96.

—— 1986. 'Sardinia and the First Western Greeks', in Balmuth (ed.) 1986, 172–85.

—— 1988. 'Italy from the Bronze Age to the Iron Age', *CAH* IV, 623–33.

Ridgway, D. & Ridgway, F. R. (eds), 1979. *Italy Before the Romans*, London: Academic Press.

Ridgway, F. R., 1986. 'Nuragic Bronzes in the British Museum', in Balmuth (ed.) 1986, 84–101.

Riis, P. J., 1970. *Sukas* I, Copenhagen: Munksgaard.

Romer, J., 1981. *Valley of the Kings*, London: Michael Joseph & Rainbird.

Rothenberg, B., 1972. *Timna, Valley of the Biblical Copper Mines*, London: Thames & Hudson.

—— 1988. *The Egyptian Mining Temple at Timna*, London: Inst. of Archaeo-Metallurgical Studies.

Rothenberg, B. & Lupu, A., 1967. 'Excavations at Timna: Preliminary Report on the Excavations at Camp No. 2 in Wadi Timna, 1964–1966', *Bull. Mus. Haaretz* 9, 53–70.

Roux, G., 1966. *Ancient Iraq*, Harmondsworth: Penguin.

Rowley-Conwy, P., 1988. 'The Camel in the Nile Valley: New Radiocarbon Accelerator (AMS) Dates for Qasr Ibrim', *JEA* 74, 245–8.

Rowton, M. B., 1946. 'Mesopotamian Chronology and the "Era of Menophres"', *Iraq* 8, 94–110.

—— 1966. 'The Material from Western Asia and the Chronology of the Nineteenth Dynasty', *JNES* 25, 240–58.

—— 1970. 'Chronology. II. Ancient Western Asia', *CAH* I:1, 193–239.

Roy, A., 1982. 'The Astronomical Basis of Egyptian Chronology', *Society for Interdisciplinary Studies Review* 6, 53–5.

Ruiz Mata, D., 1988. 'Les Phéniciens dans la baie de Cadix', in Sznycer (ed.) 1988, 82–3.

Rupp, D. M., 1986. 'The Canadian Palaipaphos (Cyprus) Survey Project: Third Preliminary Report', *Acta Archaeologica* 57, 27–45.

Rutter, J. B., 1975. 'Ceramic Evidence for Northern Intruders in Southern Greece at the Beginning of the LHIIIC Period', *AJA* 79, 17–32.

—— 1978. 'A Plea for the Abandonment of the Term "Submycenaean"', *Temple Univ. Aegean Symposium* 3, 58–65.

Sachs, A., 1970. 'Absolute Dating from Mesopotamian Records', *Phil. Trans. Roy. Soc. Lond.* A. 269, 19–22.

—— 1974. 'Babylonian Observational Astronomy', *Phil. Trans. Roy. Soc. Lond.* A 276, 43–50.

Säflund, G., 1939. 'Punta del Tonno', *Dragma M. P. Nilsson dedicatum*, Lund: Acta Inst. Romani Regni Sueciae, ser. altera I, 458–90.

Sakellariou, A., 1965. 'Nea Anchialos', *Archaiologikon Deltion* 20, 421–2.

Salles, J.-F., 1985. 'A Propos du Niveau 4 de Tell Keisan', *Levant* 17, 203–4.

Sams, G. K., 1971. *The Phrygian Painted Pottery of Early Iron Age Gordion in its Anatolian Setting* (Ph.D. diss., Univ. of Pennsylvania), Ann Arbor: Univ. Microfilms, 1978.

Samuel, A. E., 1972. *Greek and Roman Chronology*, Munich: Beck.

Sandars, N., 1971. 'From Bronze to Iron Age: A Sequel to a Sequel', in J. Boardman *et al.* (eds), *The European Community in Later Prehistory*, London: Routledge & Kegan Paul, 3–29.

—— 1983. 'North and South at the End of the Mycenaean Age: Aspects of an Old Problem', *OJA* 2, 43–68.

—— 1985. *The Sea Peoples* (rev. edn), London: Thames & Hudson.

Sandys, J. E., 1908. *A History of Classical Scholarship* II, Cambridge Univ. Press.

Sarton, G., 1970. *A History of Science* 2, New York: The Norton Library.

Säve-Söderbergh, T., 1987. *Temples and Tombs of Ancient Nubia*, London: Thames & Hudson/Paris: UNESCO.

Sayce, A., 1876. 'On the Hamathite Inscriptions', *Transactions of the Society of Biblical Archaeology* V, 22–32.

Schaeffer, C. F. A., 1948. *Stratigraphie comparée et chronologie de l'Asie occidentale (IIIe et IIe millénaire)*, Oxford Univ. Press.

—— 1968. *Ugaritica: Mission de Ras Shamra* V, Paris.

—— 1983. *Corpus des cylindres-sceaux de Ras Shamra-Ugarit et d'Enkomi-Alasia*, Paris: Editions Recherche sur les Civilisations.

Schliemann, H., 1875. *Troy and its Remains*, London: Murray.

—— 1878. *Mycenae*, London: Murray.

—— 1881. *Ilios, the City and Country of the Trojans*, London: Murray.

—— 1884. *Troja: Results of the Latest Researches and Discoveries on the Site of Homer's Troy, 1882*, London: Murray.

Schumacher, G., 1908. *Tell el-Mutesellim* I, Leipzig: Rudolph Haupt.

Schweitzer, B., 1971. *Greek Geometric Art*, London: Phaidon.

Scullard, H. H., 1967. *The Etruscan Cities and Rome*, London: Thames & Hudson.

Shanks, H., 1981. 'The Exodus and the Crossing of the Red Sea, According to Hans Goedicke', *BAR* Sept./Oct., 42–50.

Shaw, I. M. E., 1985. 'Egyptian Chronology and the Irish Oak Calibration', *JNES* 44, 295–317.

Shea, W., 1978. 'Nebuchadrezzar's Chronicle and the Date of the Destruction of Lachish III', *PEQ*, 113–15.

Shefton, B. B., 1982. 'Greeks and Greek Imports in the South of the Iberian Peninsula. The Archaeological Evidence', in H. G. Niemeyer (ed.), *Phönizier im Westen*, Madrid: Deutsches Arch. Inst. Madrider Beiträge Band 8, 337–70.

Shiloh, Y., 1979. *The Proto-Aeolic Capitol and Israelite Masonry* (Qedem 2), Jerusalem: The Hebrew University.

Singer, I., 1985. 'The Battle of Niḫriya and the End of the Hittite Empire', *Zeitschrift für Assyriologie* 75, 100–123.

Smith, S., 1940. *Alalakh and Chronology*, London: Luzac & Co.

Smith, T. M., 1987. *Mycenaean Trade and Interaction in the West Central Mediterranean 1600–1000 B.C.*, Oxford: BAR Int. Ser. 371.

Smith, W. S., 1981. *The Art and Architecture of Ancient Egypt* (rev. with additions by W. K. Simpson), Harmondsworth: Pelican.

Snodgrass, A. M., 1964. *Early Greek Armour and Weapons*, Edinburgh Univ. Press.

—— 1971. *The Dark Age of Greece*, Edinburgh Univ. Press.

—— 1982. 'Central Greece and Thessaly', *CAH* III:1, 657–95.

—— 1987. *An Archaeology of Greece*, California Univ. Press.

—— 1989. 'The Coming of the Iron Age in Greece: Europe's Earliest Bronze/Iron Transition', in Sørensen & Thomas (eds), 1989, 22–35.

Soggin, J. A., 1984. *A History of Israel*, London: SCM Press.

—— 1989. *Introduction to the Old Testament* (3rd edn), London: SCM Press.

Sordinas, A., 1971. *Old Olive Oil Mills and Presses on the Island of Corfu, Greece*, Memphis State Univ.: Anthropological Research Center Occasional Papers 9.

Sørensen, M. L. S. & Thomas, R. (eds) 1989. *The Bronze Age-Iron Age Transition in Europe*, Oxford: BAR Int. Ser. 483.

Spencer, P. A. & Spencer, A. J., 1986. 'Notes on Late Libyan Egypt', *JEA* 72, 198–201.

Stager, L. E., *et al.* (eds), 1974. *The American Expedition to Idalion, Cyprus: First Preliminary Report, Seasons of 1971 & 1972*, Philadelphia: BASOR Suppl. 18.

—— 1988. 'Shemer's Estate', *BASOR* 277/278, 93–107.

Starr, C. G., 1970. *Athenian Coinage 480–449 BC*, Oxford: Clarendon Press.

Stern, E., 1978. *Excavations at Tel Mevorakh (1973–1976)* I (Qedem 9), Hebrew Univ. of Jerusalem.

—— 1982. *Material Culture of the Land of the Bible in the Persian Period 538–332 B.C.*, Warminster: Aris & Phillips/Jerusalem: Israel Exploration Soc.

Stern, M., 1976. *Greek and Latin Authors on Jews and Judaism*, 1, Jerusalem: The Israel Academy of Sciences and Humanities.

Stiebing, W. H., 1980. 'The End of the Mycenaean Age', *BA* Winter, 7–21.

Stoia, A., 1989. 'The Beginning of Iron Metallurgy in Romania (1200–700 B.C.)', in Sørensen & Thomas (eds) 1989, 43–67.

Stubbings, F. H., 1954: 'Mycenae 1939–1952. Part VIII. A Winged Axe-mould', *BSA* 49, 297–8.

—— 1975. 'The Recession of Mycenaean Civilization', *CAH* II:2, 338–358.

Stuiver, M., *et al.*, 1986. 'Radiocarbon Age Calibration back to 13,300 Years BP and the ^{14}C Age Matching of the German Oak and US Bristlecone Pine Chronologies', *Radiocarbon* 28, 969–79.

Styrenius, C.-G., 1973. 'Asine', *Archaiologikon Deltion*, Chron. 155–6.

Syriopoulos, K. T., 1983. *Oi Metavatikoi Chronoi*, Athens: Arch. Etaireia.

Sznycer, M., 1979. 'L'inscription phénicienne de Tekke, près de Cnossus', *Kadmos* 18, 89–93.

—— (ed.) 1988. *Les Phéniciens*, Dijon: Dossiers Histoire et Arch. 132.

Tadmor, H., 1985. 'Nineveh, Calah and Israel: on Assyriology and the Origins of Biblical Archaeology', in *BAT*, 260–8.

Tainter, J. A., 1988. *The Collapse of Complex Societies*, Cambridge Univ. Press.

Talbott, S. (ed.) 1973/1974. 'ASH', *Pensée* 4:1, 5–19.

Taramelli, A., 1914. 'Il tempio nuragico ed i monumenti primitivi di S. Vittoria di Serri (Cagliari), *Monumenti Antichi* 23, 313–430.

Taylor, J. H., 1987. 'A Note on the Family of Montemhat', *JEA* 73, 229–30.

Taylour, W., 1958. *Mycenaean Pottery in Italy and Adjacent Areas*, Cambridge Univ. Press.

—— 1983. *The Mycenaeans* (2nd edn), London: Thames & Hudson.

Theocharis, D., 1960a. 'Iolkos', *Ergon*, 55–61.

—— 1960b. 'Anaskafai en Iolko', *Praktika*, 49–59.

—— 1961. 'Anaskafai en Iolko', *Praktika*, 45–54.

Thiele, E., 1983. *The Mysterious Numbers of the Hebrew Kings*, Michigan: Zondervan.

Thomas, D. W., 1946. 'The Lachish Ostraca: Professor Torczyner's Latest Views', *PEQ* 38–42.

—— 1958. *Documents from Old Testament Times*, New York: Harper & Row.

Thomas, E., 1979. 'The *ḳзy* of Queen Inhapy', *JARCE* 16, 85–92.

Thomsen, C. J., 1848. *A Guide to Northern Archaeology*, London.

Thorpe, I. J., 1990. 'The Mycenaeans and European Chronology – a Review', *SAC* 2.

—— forthcoming. 'The Wessex Culture – Content and Chronology', *SAC* 3.

Thurnam, J., 1873. 'On Ancient British Barrows, Especially Those of Wiltshire and the Adjoining Counties (Part II. Round Barrows)', *Archaeologia* 43, 285–544.

Tončeva, G., 1980. *Chronologie du Hallstatt ancien dans la Bulgarie de Nord-Est*, Sofia: Studia Thracica 5.

Torczyner, H., *et al.*, 1938. *Lachish I: The Lachish Letters*, Oxford Univ. Press.

Torr, C., 1896. *Memphis and Mycenae*, Cambridge Univ. Press.

Toynbee, A. J., 1939. *A Study of History* IV & V, Oxford Univ. Press.

Trigger, B. G., 1965. *History and Settlement in Lower Nubia*, New Haven: Yale Univ. Publs. in Anthropology.

—— 1976. *Nubia under the Pharaohs*, London: Thames & Hudson.

—— 1980. *Gordon Childe: Revolutions in Archaeology*, London: Thames & Hudson.

Tronchetti, C., 1986. 'Nuragic Statuary from Monte Prama', in Balmuth (ed.) 1986, 19–37.

Trump, D. H., 1961. 'The Later Prehistory of Malta', *PPS* 27, 253–62.

Tsori, N., 1977. 'A Contribution to the Problem of the Persian Period at Beth Shan', *PEQ*, 103–5.

Tufnell, O., 1953. *Lachish III: The Iron Age*, Oxford Univ. Press.

Tylecote, R. F., 1987. *The Early History of Metallurgy in Europe*, London: Longman.

Tusa, V., 1988. 'Sicily', in Moscati (ed.) 1988, 186–205.

Ullman, B. L., 1934. 'How Old is the Greek Alphabet?', *AJA* 38, 359–81.

Ungnad, A., 1938. 'Eponymen', in *Reallexikon der Assyriologie* 2, Berlin & Leipzig: Walter de Gruyter, 412–57.

Ussher, J., 1650. *Annales Veteris Testamenti, a prima mundi origine deducti*, London: J. Flesher.

Ussishkin, D., 1976. 'Royal Judean Storage Jars and Private Seal Impressions', *BASOR* 223, 2–13.

—— 1977. 'The Destruction of Lachish by Sennacherib and the Dating of the Royal Judean Storage Jars', *Tel Aviv* 4, 28–60.

—— 1980a. 'The "Lachish Reliefs" and the City of Lachish', *IEJ* 30, 174–95.

—— 1980b. 'Was the "Solomonic" City Gate at Megiddo Built by King Solomon?', *BASOR* 239, 1–18.

—— 1982. *The Conquest of Lachish by Sennacherib*, Tel Aviv Univ.

—— 1983. 'Excavations at Tel Lachish 1978–1983: Second Preliminary Report', *Tel Aviv* 10, 97–175.

—— 1987. 'Lachish – Key to the Israelite Conquest of Canaan?', *BAR* Jan./Feb., 18–39.

Van Beek, G., 1951. 'Cypriote Chronology and the Dating of Iron I Sites in Palestine', *BASOR* 124, 26–9.

—— 1955. 'The Date of Tell Abu Hawam, Stratum III', *BASOR* 138, 34–8.

van Compernolle, R., 1973. 'L'inscription de Salmanaser III, IM 55644, du Musée de Bagdad, la chronologie des rois de Tyr et la date de la fondation de Carthage (805/6 avant notre Ère)', *Annuaire de l'Institut de Philologie et d'Histoire Orientales et Slaves* 20, 467–79.

van der Meer, P., 1947. *The Ancient Chronology of Western Asia and Egypt*, Leiden: E. J. Brill.

Van Seters, J., 1983. *In Search of History: Historiography in the Ancient World and the Origins of Biblical History*, Yale Univ. Press.

Vandenabeele, F., 1971. 'La chronologie absolue du Chypro-Géométrique', *Dédalo* 7, 7–22.

Velikovsky, I., 1953. *Ages in Chaos*, London: Sidgwick & Jackson.

Venit, M. S., 1986. 'Toward a Definition of Middle Assyrian Style', *Akkadica* 50, 1–21.

Vercoutter, J., 1958. 'Une épitaphe royale inédite du Sérapéum', *Mitteilungen des Deutschen Instituts für ägyptische Altertumskunde in Kairo*, 16, 333–43.

—— 1960. 'The Napatan Kings and Apis Worship', *Kush* 8, 62–76.

Vermeule, E. & Karageorghis, V., 1982. *Mycenaean Pictorial Vase Painting*, Harvard Univ. Press.

Vickers, M., 1984. 'Hallstatt and Early La Tène Chronology in Central, South and East Europe', *Antiquity* 58, 208–11.

—— 1985a. 'Correction: Hallstatt D1 Site at Villingen', *Antiquity* 59, 124.

—— 1985b. 'Early Greek Coinage, a Reassessment', *Numismatic Chronicle* 145, 1–44.

—— 1987. 'Dates, Methods and Icons', in C. Bérard *et al.* (eds), *Images et Société en Grèce Ancienne* (Actes du Colloque International, Lausanne 8–11 Février 1984), Univ. de Lausanne, 19–25.

Vittmann, G., 1978. *Priester und Beamte im Theben der Spätzeit* (Beiträge zur Ägyptologie Band 1), Vienna: Inst. für Afrikanistik und Ägyptologie der Univ. Wien.

von Oppenheim, M., 1931. *Der Tell Halaf*, Leipzig: Brockhaus.

Waddell, W. G., 1940. *Manetho* (Loeb Classical Library), London: Heinemann.

Wallenfels, R., 1983. 'Redating the Byblian Inscriptions', *Journal of the Ancient Near Eastern Society* 15, 79–118.

Wardle, K. A., 1980. 'Excavations at Assiros 1975–1979', *BSA* 75, 229–68.

—— 1989. 'Excavations at Assiros Toumba 1988. A preliminary report', *BSA* 84, 447–63.

Ward-Perkins, J. B., 1942. 'Problems of Maltese Prehistory', *Antiquity* 16, 19–35.

Warmington, B. H., 1969. *Carthage*, London: Hale.

Warner, R. B., 1985. 'Observations on the Radiocarbon Dates from Rathmullen', *Ulster Journal of Archaeology* 48, 142–4.

Warren, P. & Hankey, V., 1989. *Aegean Bronze Age Chronology*, Bristol Classical Press.

Webb, J. M. & Courtois, J.-C., 1979. 'A Steatite Relief Mould from Enkomi', *RDAC*, 151–8.

Weinberg, S. S., 1939. 'Excavations at Corinth, 1938–1939', *AJA* 43, 592–600.

Weinstein, J. M., 1980. 'Palestinian Radiocarbon Dating: A Reply to Mellaart', *Antiquity* 54, 21–4.

—— 1981. 'The Egyptian Empire in Palestine: A Reassessment', *BASOR* 241, 1–28.

—— 1984. 'Radiocarbon Dating in the Southern Levant', *Radiocarbon* 26, 297–366.

Weir, J. D., 1972. *The Venus Tablets of Ammizaduga*, Istanbul: Nederlands Historisch-Arch. Inst. in het Nabije Oosten.

—— 1982. 'The Venus Tablets: A Fresh Approach', *Journal for the History of Astronomy* 13, 23–49.

—— 1986. 'Velikovsky's Evidence?' (letter), *Nature* 321, 466.

Weiss, B., 1982. 'The Decline of Late Bronze Age Civilization as a Possible Response to Climate Change', *Climate Change* 4, 173–98.

Wente, E. F., 1976. Review of K. Kitchen, *The Third Intermediate Period in Egypt* (1972), *JNES* 35, 275–8.

Wente, E. F. & Van Siclen, C. C., 1976. 'A Chronology of the New Kingdom', in J. H. Johnson & E. F. Wente (eds), *Studies in Honor of George R. Hughes*, Chicago Oriental Inst., 217–61.

West, S., 1979. 'Bible's Foundations Shaken', *New Scientist* 7th June, 798.

Wheeler, M., 1954. *Archaeology from the Earth*, Oxford: Clarendon Press.

White, A. D., 1896. *A History of the Warfare of Science with Theology in Christendom*, London: Macmillan & Co.

Whiteside, D. T., 1978. 'Ptolemy in the Dock', *Nature* 276, 151–2.

Wightman, G. J., 1985. 'Megiddo VIA-III: Associated Structures and Chronology', *Levant* 17, 117–29.

Wilson, D., 1975. *Atoms of Time Past*, London: Allen Lane.

Wilson, R. R., 1977. *Genealogy and History in the Biblical World*, Yale Univ. Press.

Winter, I., 1976a. 'Phoenician and North Syrian Ivory Carving in Historical Context: Questions of Style and Distribution', *Iraq* 38, 1–22.

—— 1976b. Review of Mallowan and Hermann 1974, *AJA* 80, 201–3.

—— 1981. 'Is There a South Syrian School of Ivory Carving?' *Iraq* 43, 101–30.

Wiseman, D. J., 1975. 'Assyria and Babylonia, c. 1200–1000 B.C.', *CAH* II:2, 443–481.

Woldering, I., 1967. *The Arts of Egypt*, London: Thames & Hudson.

Wood, B. G., 1990. 'Did the Israelites Conquer Jericho?', *BAR* Mar./Apr., 44–58.

Woolley, L., 1914. 'Hittite Burial Customs', *AAA* 6, 87–98.

—— 1921. *Carchemish II. The Town Defences*, London: British Museum.

—— 1952. *Carchemish III. The Excavations in the Inner Town*, London: British Museum.

—— 1953. *A Forgotten Kingdom*, Harmondsworth: Penguin.

Wright, G. E., 1959. 'Israelite Samaria and Iron Age Chronology', *BASOR* 155, 13–29.

Wright, H. E., 1972. 'Vegetation History' in W. A. MacDonald & G. R. Rapp (eds), *The Minnesota Messenia Expedition*, Univ. of Minnesota Press, 188–99.

Wright, W., 1886. *The Empire of the Hittites*, London: Nisbet.

Yadin, Y., 1972. *Hazor*, London: Weidenfeld & Nicolson.

—— 1980. 'A Rejoinder', *BASOR* 239, 19–23.

Yannai, A., 1982. 'Raising the Dates of Greek Protogeometric?', *AJA* 86, 292.

Yates, T., 1986. 'Studies of Non-marine Mollusks for the Selection of Shell Samples for Radiocarbon Dating', *Radiocarbon* 28, 457–63.

Yon, M., 1976. *Manuel de céramique Chypriote I: problèmes historiques, vocabulaire, méthode*, Lyon: Inst. Courby.

—— 1984. 'Fouilles Françaises à Kition-Bamboula (Chypre), 1976–1982', *Académie des Inscriptions et Belles-lettres, Comptes Rendus*, 80–99.

—— 1988. 'Kition un royaume phénicien à Chypre et sa capitale', in Sznycer (ed.) 1988, 34–7.

Yon, M. & Caubet, A., 1985. *Kition-Bamboula III*, Paris: Éditions Recherche sur les Civilizations.

Young, R. S., 1964. 'The Nomadic Impact: Gordion', in Mellink (ed.) 1964, 52–7.

—— 1966. 'The Gordion Campaign of 1965', *AJA* 70, 267–78.

Yoyotte, J., 1972. 'Les Adoratrices de la troisième période intermédiare', *Bulletin de la Societé Française d'Égyptologie* 64, 31–52.

Yurco, F. J., 1986. 'Merneptah's Canaanite Campaign', *JARCE* 23, 189–215.

Zaccagnini, C., 1987. 'Aspects of Ceremonial Exchange in the Near East During the Late Second Millennium BC', in M. Rowland, *et al.* (eds), *Centre and Periphery in the Ancient World*, Cambridge Univ. Press, 57–65.

Zaharia, E., 1965. 'Remarques sur le Hallstatt ancien de Transylvanie. Fouilles et trouvailles de Mediaş 1958', *Dacia* 9, 83–104.

Index